Sports

Sports Tourism

Participants, policy and providers

Second edition

Mike Weed and Chris Bull

Routledge
Taylor & Francis Group

LONDON AND NEW YORK

First published 2009 by Butterworth-Heinemann

Published 2015 by Routledge
2 Park Square, Milton Park, Abingdon, Oxon, OX14 4RN
711 Third Avenue, New York, NY 10017

Routledge is an imprint of the Taylor & Francis Group, an informa business

First edition 2004
Second edition 2009

British Library Cataloguing in Publication Data
A catalogue record for this book is available from the British Library

Library of Congress
A catalogue record for this book is available from the Library of Congress

ISBN: 978-0-7506-8375-3 (pbk)

Typeset by Macmillan Publishing Solutions
(www.macmillansolutions.com)

Contents

LIST OF TABLES vii
LIST OF FIGURES ix
LIST OF BOXES.. xi
ACKNOWLEDGEMENTS...xiii
PROLOGUE TO THE SECOND EDITION xv

Part 1: Context

Preface

Chapter 1   Tracing the Development of the Sport–Tourism Link 3

Chapter 2   Contemporary Concepts, Issues and Research 27

Part 2: Participants

Preface

Chapter 3   Conceptualizing the Sports Tourism Experience.....................57

Chapter 4   Sports Tourism Behaviours and the Trip Decision-Making
Process 77

Chapter 5   A Sports Tourism Participation Model 107

Part 3: Policy

Preface

Chapter 6   The Policy Context...127

Chapter 7   Prospects for Integration 145

Part 4: Providers

Preface

Chapter 8   Sports Tourism Products 167

Chapter 9   Provision Strategies 189

Part 5: Case Studies

Preface

Chapter 10 Sports Tourism as a Diversification Strategy in Malta..........209

Chapter 11 Urban Sports Tourism – The Case of Sheffield...................223

Chapter 12 Rural Sports Participation Tourism in Wales.....................237

Chapter 13 Winter Skiing in the European Alps................................257

Chapter 14 Cycling Sports Tourism 273

Epilogue – Progress in Sports Tourism?...293

References...299

Index...337

List of Tables

1.1   The economic impact of sports tourism in the UK   21
8.1   Potential features of each sports tourism product type   185
11.1 Types of mega-event   225
12.1 Trips featuring rural sports participation tourism
      products taken by residents of Great Britain in a five-year
      period (2001–2005)   240
12.2 All trips featuring rural sports participation tourism
      products taken during the five years to 2005   241
12.3 Characteristics of rural leisure activities   243
12.4 Ranked importance of factors in trip decision
      Twr-y-Felin Activity Centre   250
12.5 Activities available at Black Mountain Activities   253
13.1 The continuum of characteristics of Alpine resorts   259
13.2 The UK ski market size, by tour operators, independent
      travel and schools, 1980/81–2007/08   261
13.3 The UK ski market share, by tour operators, independent
      travel and schools, 1980/81–2007/08   262
13.4 Skiers and potential skiers by demographic subgroup, 2002   266
13.5 The diversification of winter sports tourism products   270
14.1 Types of cycling sports tourism   276
14.2 Analysis of Tour de France 2007 spectator expenditure –
      London and Kent   288

List of Figures

4.1	Examples of trip decisions and destination choices	82
4.2	Did your visit to the Athletics World Cup involve an overnight stay?	88
4.3	Was the Athletics World Cup the main reason for visiting London?	88
4.4	With whom did you travel to the Athletics World Cup?	88
4.5	Prior to your visit to the Athletics World Cup, when did you last watch an athletics event?	89
5.1	Hall's (1992a) model of adventure, health and sports tourism	109
5.2	Standeven and De Knop's (1999) 'forms of sports tourism'	110
5.3	Sports tourism demand continuum	112
5.4	Simplified sports tourism participation model	113
5.5	Revised sports tourism participation model	118
5.6	Potential variations in the shape of the revised sports tourism participation model for specific sports tourism products	120
6.1	The Rhodes model	132
6.2	Features of the policy community continuum	133
6.3	Levels in the GIR model	133
6.4	The sport–tourism policy network (GIR model)	135
6.5	A model of cross-sectoral policy development	135
7.1	Policy wheel for sport and tourism	148
7.2	Tensions in the sport and tourism policy communities	151
7.3	Sport and tourism policy communities: heartland and periphery	160
8.1	Model of sports tourism product types	186

List of Boxes

4.1   Travel patterns of elite British track athletes   99
4.2   Potential injury as a barrier to recreational sports
      tourism participation   101
8.1   Harvard Sports Management Group profile   176
8.2   Golf tourism in Scotland   183
14.1 Economic impact data and related methodology
      for the Tour de France 2005 event in Digne   287

Acknowledgements

In addition to our respective partners, Sonja and Alexandra, to whom we owe a large debt of gratitude for their support and patience over a considerable period of time, we would also like to thank various other people for their help and support in the writing of this text. First, considerable thanks must go to Dr Guy Jackson, formerly of the Institute of Sport and Leisure Policy at Loughborough University, now the National Cricket Performance Centre Manager for the English Cricket Board. Guy put his considerable 'archive' of sports tourism research and materials at our disposal for the first edition and this material has continued to inform aspects of this second edition. Similarly, the primary material from Dr Martin Reeves' sports tourism research and the guidance given by Dr Mick Green and Professor Barrie Houlihan at Loughborough University on international sports policy structures remain important in this second edition.

Lastly, we would like to express our appreciation to the various staff at Butterworth-Heinemann, formerly Fran Ford and, more recently, Ellie Blow, for their continued support for this project and the help they have provided.

Prologue to the Second Edition

In the years since the publication of the first edition of *Sports Tourism: Participants, Policy and Providers* in 2004, there has been a considerable growth in publications serving the area. In fact, 2004 was a significant year for the sports tourism bookshelf, as *Sport Tourism Development* by Tom Hinch and James Higham and *Sport Tourism: Interrelationships, Impacts and Issues* edited by Brent Ritchie and Darryl Adair were also published. This was followed in 2005 by the publication of *Sport Tourism Destinations* edited by James Higham. Furthermore, *European Sport Management Quarterly* and *Sport in Society* each published special issues focusing on the theoretical foundations of sports tourism in 2005. These special issues spawned two further publications. The first, published in 2006, *Sport Tourism: Concepts and Theories* edited by Heather Gibson, was a reprint in book format of the *Sport in Society* special issue, while the second took the five papers from the special issue of *European Sport Management Quarterly* and used them to structure a reader of thirty of the leading peer-reviewed articles published since 2000. The result, *Sport & Tourism: A Reader* was edited by Mike Weed and published in 2008. What this expansion in full texts dedicated to sports tourism demonstrates is a significant growth in both interest in and recognition of sports tourism as an area of academic study.

Alongside the above, Weed's (2006b) systematic review showed that eighty peer-reviewed journal articles relating to sports tourism had been published in the five years from 2000. As noted in Chapter 2 of this text, this is a considerable growth since Jackson and Glyptis' (1992) worldwide review at the start of the previous decade. Furthermore, this does not take into account the still growing number of conference papers and book chapters that examine issues relating to sports tourism.

Consequently, in approaching the development of a second edition of *Sports Tourism: Participants, Policy and Providers*, a wide range of empirical research and perspectives on sports tourism had affected our thinking. In particular, the expanding research base on participation – not all of which has necessarily been of the highest quality, as Weed's (2006b) meta-evaluation of the field showed – seemed to us to demonstrate that the analysis of sports tourism at the trip level was hampering aspects of the research effort. The failings of some of this research and the strengths of a smaller minority of it, indicated to us that to consider an entire trip as either sports tourism or not sports tourism was not a productive way forward. Therefore, drawing on our own evolving thinking about the interaction of activity, people and place (Bull, 2006; Bull and Lovell, 2007; Weed, 2005c, 2006b, 2008a) and influenced by Gibson's long standing work on role theory (Yiannakis and Gibson, 1992; Gibson, 1994, 1996; Gibson and Yiannakis, 2002; Gibson and Pennington-Gray, 2005), we have reshaped this text to consider sports tourism as a set of behaviours that are some among a number of other tourism and functional behaviours on any one trip. This is reflected in the widely redrafted material in Chapters 3 and 4, which underpins the presentation of a Revised Sports Tourism Participation Model in Chapter 5 that we feel offers at once both a simplified and more sophisticated understanding of sports tourism behaviours. In particular, the revised model incorporates a consideration of the role that sports tourism behaviours play in the trip decision-making process. This role is discussed in considerable detail in the preceding chapter, drawing on both the tourism literature on the trip decision-making process and our own empirical and secondary research resources on sports tourism participation.

Of course, our evolving perspectives on sports tourism behaviours have implications for our consideration of sports tourism provision in Chapters 8 and 9. In particular, this has led us to think about the way in which provision is made for sports tourism behaviours rather than sports tourism trips. As a result, what we have previously referred to as 'Tourism with Sports Content' appears to be a flawed product type. Consequently, we have used evidence from the increasing way in which destination managers, as well as major tourism providers such as Thomson/TUI and First Choice, use sports tourism to supplement their main product offering to present 'Supplementary Sports Tourism' as more useful broad product type. The development of Supplementary Sports Tourism, in which sports tourism provision is not the main business of the organization or destination, both reflects and reinforces our perspective of sports tourism as a trip behaviour rather than a trip purpose and, we feel, helps to present a more integrated and sophisticated understanding of sports tourism throughout the text.

We have also been influenced in the years since the publication of the first edition by work on the influence of nostalgia in sports tourism (e.g. Gammon, 2002, 2004; Fairley, 2003; Fairley and Gammon, 2005) and, in particular, by Ramshaw and Gammon's (2005) suggestion that the concept of heritage is a better way to understand such behaviours than nostalgia. We feel that the range of papers in their edited text, *Heritage, Sport and Tourism* (Gammon and Ramshaw, 2007) provide convincing arguments for the use of heritage to understand an aspect of sports tourism that is 'more than just nostalgia' (Ramshaw and Gammon, 2007). In a related development, work on the all consuming nature of the behaviours of committed spectating sports tourists (e.g. Parry and Malcolm, 2004; Millward, 2006; Weed, 2006e, 2007) has influenced our thinking about the active/passive distinction in sports tourism participation that many authors, including ourselves, have suggested over time (e.g. De Knop, 1987; Jackson and Glyptis, 1992; Weed and Bull, 2004). We have never felt comfortable that this distinction adequately covered the full range of sports tourism behaviours, however, neither were we comfortable with Gibson's (1998) suggestion that sports tourism be considered as travelling to participate (active), travelling to watch (passive) and travelling to venerate (nostalgia). We therefore now argue (following Weed, 2005c, 2008a) that as well as active and passive participation, there is the possibility of 'vicarious' participation in sports tourism. Such vicarious participation incorporates the 'imagined journey' that Gammon (2002) argues takes place during sports tourism behaviours influenced by nostalgia or heritage, but also reflects the passionate or 'fanatic' involved behaviours of spectating sports tourists that is anything but passive. As such, vicarious participation features in both our discussions of participants in Part 2 and in our analysis of provision in Part 4 and, in particular in an updated Model of Sports Tourism Product Types in Chapter 8.

One of us (Weed, 2005a, 2005d, 2006a, 2008a, 2008b) has also continued to study policy responses since the publication of the first edition and, in this area, little has changed. Policy-makers for sport and for tourism around the world still show considerable reluctance to work together and the Model of Cross-Sectoral Policy Development presented in Chapter 6 continues to provide a useful framework for policy analysis in this area. However, the most recent work (Weed, 2008b) presents an evolved position on the areas in which it might be expected that policy-makers for sport and tourism should reasonably collaborate. This leads us to present a simplified 'Policy Wheel for Sport and Tourism' that features the enduring elements of the Policy Area Matrix that we developed twelve years ago (Weed and Bull, 1997a). The Wheel is presented in Chapter 8, which also now comments more extensively on the circumstances in which collaborative policy for sport and tourism might be successfully developed.

A further implication of the expanding number of publications in the sports tourism area is that we feel even more strongly than we did when preparing the first edition of the text that a detailed coverage of the nature and extent of the impacts of sports tourism is superfluous to our analysis, which is intended to focus on stakeholders in sports tourism (i.e. participants, policy-makers and providers). As such, our coverage of the linkages between sport and tourism over time and the more recent evolution of the sports tourism phenomenon, now contains an extended discussion of the impacts of sports tourism in the last two decades. The consolidation of this material in Chapter 1 allows us to add a further contextual chapter on contemporary concepts, issues and research in sports tourism. Chapter 2 therefore presents perspectives on sports tourism from what we feel have been some of the highest quality contributions to the sports tourism literature since the turn of the Millennium. These perspectives are used to demonstrate that a knowledge of the behaviours of sports tourism participants is fundamental in not only understanding the generation of impacts but, more importantly for this text, in establishing effective policy responses and in developing provision strategies. As such, Chapter 2 provides the rationale for the structure of the text, which is briefly outlined below.

As was the case with the first edition, the book is organized into five parts, each of which is introduced by a brief preface. Part 1 (context) comprises Chapters 1 and 2, which examine the historical and contemporary development and impacts of sports tourism and what we feel are the highest quality perspectives from recent research. The second part of the book focuses on sports tourism participants and comprises Chapters 3, 4 and 5, which examine the nature of the sports tourism experience, the role of sports tourism in trip decision-making processes and the modelling of sports tourism participation respectively. Part 3 comprises Chapters 6 and 7 which focus on sports tourism policy, highlighting and examining the general lack of strategic liaison between policy-makers for sport and for tourism around the world. The fourth part of the book examines sports tourism providers, with Chapter 8 outlining the features of a range of sports tourism products and Chapter 9 examining provision strategies. The final part of the book comprises five case study chapters that illustrate the issues discussed in the earlier parts, four of which have been generally updated from those which appeared in the first edition. These four cases examine sports tourism as a diversification strategy, urban sports tourism, rural sports participation tourism and skiing in relation to Malta, Sheffield, Wales and the European Alps respectively. A fifth case study, newly developed for this second edition, examines cycling sports tourism. Finally, an epilogue discusses progress in sports tourism. A key theme throughout the book remains that sports tourism as an area of study produces a range of issues that cannot be analysed and addressed via a simple amalgamation of approaches previously applied to the individual sectors of sport and tourism. As such, sports tourism continues to be conceptualized as a social, economic and cultural phenomenon in which experiences arise from the unique interaction of activity, people and place.

As in the first edition, we still feel that we need to make a final introductory comment prior to the main text in relation to terminology. A detailed discussion of definitions and concepts is provided in Chapter 3, but some clarification is useful at the outset in relation to the use of the terms sports tourism, sport tourism and the sport–tourism link. The term 'sport–tourism link' refers to a broad concept that, in addition to the consumption and provision of trips involving sports tourism behaviours, also embraces liaison between the sport and tourism areas on issues such as resources and funding, policy and planning, and information and research. As such, it is a useful term to use in discussions of policy and in any discussion seeking to examine the historical and contemporary development of links between sport and tourism. The use of the terms 'sports tourism' and 'sport tourism' are more problematic and are the basis of some debate among academics in the area. Gibson (2002: p. 115), along with many others in the field (e.g. Delpy, 1998; Standeven and De Knop, 1999) argues that the term 'sport tourism' should be used because 'sport' refers to the broader social institution of sport, while 'sports' refers to a collection of activities that have come to be defined as such. Consequently, the term 'sport tourism' encompasses 'a wider analysis of sport as a social institution rather than the micro view of individual sports' (Gibson, 2002: p. 115). However, the use of the term 'sport tourism' for these reasons implies a reliance on sport as a social institution to define and delimit the area of 'sport tourism'. Given that one of the precepts of this text is that sports tourism is a unique area of study derived from the interaction of activity, people and place, a dependence on the social institution of sport to characterize the area would be somewhat incongruous. Furthermore, the concept of sport can, in many cases, be a misnomer, that implies coherence where none exists and detracts from the heterogeneous nature of sporting activities. As one of the unique aspects of sports tourism is that the interaction of people and place with the activities in question expands rather than limits heterogeneity, in this text the term 'sports tourism' is used, along with the focus on diverse and heterogeneous activities that the term implies.

Notwithstanding the above discussion, the wider social institution of sport does play a role in determining policy responses to the sport–tourism link. However, as discussed above, in relation to areas such as policy development, where the impact of cultural and social assumptions about the scope and nature of sport are important considerations, the broader term 'sport–tourism link' can be employed.

PART 1

Context

PREFACE

Many of the previously published texts on sports tourism have focused much of their attention on the nature of impacts, with significant emphasis often being placed on its economic impacts. Standeven and De Knop (1999), for example, took this approach presenting, after several introductory and context setting chapters, chapters on economic, socio-cultural, environmental and health impacts. In other cases, particular sub-sectors of sports tourism have been addressed. Hudson's (2000) book on 'Snow Business' fell into this category, as did his edited collection (Hudson, 2003a) which contained chapters by a range of authors on sport event, winter sport, marine, golf and adventure tourism.

In contrast to much else published in the field, the aim of this text is not to focus on an analysis of sports tourism impacts, but to examine the behaviours and interests of stakeholders in sports tourism, namely the actual participants, the policy-makers and the providers. However, an important context for this analysis is material related to the way in which links between sport and tourism have developed and the concepts, issues and research insights that are shaping contemporary sports tourism development.

Chapter 1 traces the development of links between sport and tourism over time. The approach in this chapter is to focus on the way in which developments in sport and in tourism have led to increasing links between sport and tourism, rather than revisiting material on the history of sport and of tourism that is covered in much greater detail in other sources. While some of this material is international in nature, the historical overview is presented from a British perspective for two related reasons. First, because a completely international history would be almost impossible given the diverse historical development of sport, tourism and sports tourism around the world and, secondly, given that any history will be derived from a particular perspective, the British perspective has been taken because it is the one with which the authors are most familiar and therefore best equipped to comment on. As such, the historical issues raised will, in some cases, be illustrative of the development of sports tourism rather than directly relevant in every country. In a change from the first edition of this text, the first chapter has been extended to the present day, and now includes a substantial final section on the nature and development of sports tourism at the turn of the Millennium and beyond, thus covering aspects of the material on contemporary impacts that has been the focus of many other texts. One note of particular interest is that, while the earlier sections of Chapter 1 focus on the links between sport and tourism, as the discussion progresses into the previous two decades, the increasing confluence of sport and tourism in people's lifestyles means that it becomes possible to discern the consumption and provision of sports tourism as a synergistic phenomenon that has become more than the simple combination of sport and tourism.

In extending the first chapter to bring the coverage of the development of sports tourism up to the present day, this second edition has essentially consolidated Chapters 1 and 2 from the first edition of the text into a single chapter. Consequently, Chapter 2 in the second edition provides an additional context that was perhaps missing from the first edition. Chapter 2 examines contemporary sports tourism issues, concepts and research, emphasizing in particular the fundamental nature of knowledge about sports tourism behaviours in informing the development of policy and provision, and in understanding impacts, thus laying the foundation for the remainder of the text which examines, in turn, sports tourism participants, policy-makers and providers. Chapter 2 also comments on a number of varying views on contemporary sports tourism from some of the leading authors in the field, and thus provides a context against which the analysis presented in the remainder of the text can be evaluated.

CHAPTER 1

Tracing the Development of the Sport–Tourism Link

EARLY EXAMPLES OF A LINK BETWEEN SPORT AND TOURISM

The earliest documented example of sports tourism is that of the Olympic Games which date from 776 BC. However, the pan-Hellenic games at Olympia were but the most prestigious of more than a hundred such festivals (Finley and Pleket, 1976). Athletic games were an essential part of Greek life and every self-respecting city had its own stadium (Davies, 1997). However, the touring element was an important part of the sport. The participants were professional sportsmen and toured in order to win prizes; as Davies (1997, p. 127) points out, 'athletes were not amateurs, being accustomed to arduous training and expecting handsome rewards'. In addition, thousands of spectators travelled to support their athletes and the prestige of their city, possibly in similar fashion to modern day football supporters travelling to support their team. The games at Olympia may have attracted as many as 40 000 people from all parts of Greece (Van Dalen and Bennett, 1971) and 'there was probably no other occasion in the ancient world when as many people were on the road (or on the sea) for the same destination at the same time' (Finley and Pleket, 1976, p. 53). Unlike provision for modern day tourists, there was little accommodation and visitors slept in tents or in the open air, although a hostel was established at Olympia in the fourth century (Baker, 1982, quoted in Standeven and De Knop, 1999). The tourism aspect of the games was further emphasized by its wider political aims. It is often advocated that both sport and tourism

3

may help to bring different peoples and cultures closer together and a key aim of the ancient games was to bring 'a strong sense of cultural unity to a politically divided country' (Davies, 1997, p. 127).

The Romans continued the travel element associated with sport, although in different forms. Athletic activity 'became more health and socially oriented' (Standeven and De Knop, 1999, p. 15) and less competitive and, as such, the related tourist activity was no longer significant. The gladiatorial combats and chariot races which replaced athletics as the principal spectator event were essentially home grown affairs, at least as far as the spectators themselves were concerned. One activity that did involve travel was the penchant for bathing, although how active this pursuit happened to be and thus how far it deserves to be considered as sport is no doubt open to debate. While bathing was also primarily a local activity (Rome had almost nine hundred baths), the ease of travel and the spread of the empire had led to a number of foreign towns such as Spa in Belgium, Baden-Baden in Germany, Tiberias in Israel and Bath in England becoming fashionable resorts for travelling Roman officials because of their bathing facilities (Standeven and De Knop, 1999).

The other influence on sports tourism which Standeven and De Knop (1999) attribute to the Romans is that of the survival of ball games. The Romans' disposition to travel enabled the ideology of games as a means of fitness to be disseminated throughout Europe and it is argued that but for this, ball play would probably have disappeared due to its association with pagan customs.

It is important to highlight these ancient antecedents because they demonstrate that sports tourism is not a totally modern phenomenon; that some of the motivations which may influence current activity could have been present several thousand years earlier. Despite these earlier examples, however, there is relatively little evidence of much sports tourism occurring between the Roman period and relatively recent times.

Standeven and De Knop (1999) discuss connections between sport and tourism in the middle ages and renaissance period but little is provided in terms of real sports tourism other than jousting tournaments and real tennis, and even these are rather limited. In the case of the former, professional knights would tour as a way of making their living and there would thus seem to be some similarities here between the knights and the athletes of ancient Greece, although the early tournaments were unregulated, warlike and 'there was no provision for spectators and few spectators were present' (Guttmann, 1992, p. 148). Eventually, between the twelfth and sixteenth centuries, the tournament was 'civilized' and transformed into both an elegant sport and spectacle but only for aristocrats and upper ranks of society. Similarly, real tennis, for which international games are recorded, became popular in the sixteenth century but was also purely the preserve of aristocrats.

As modest improvements in transportation enabled people to travel more easily from the sixteenth century onwards, there is no doubt that opportunities for sports tourism also increased. One key tourism phenomenon which has received much coverage in the literature is the European Grand Tour (see, for example, Towner, 1985, 1996; Withey, 1997) which began in the sixteenth century and lasted until the nineteenth, and involved the wealthy in society travelling to various destinations in Europe. Towner (1996, p. 96) describes the Grand Tour as 'a re-emergent form of cultural tourism which had existed in the ancient world' and thus we have yet another key link with the touring behaviour of the ancient Greeks and Romans. The essential influence, according to Towner (1996), was the development of a 'travel culture' deriving its inspiration from the cultural and intellectual movements of the renaissance and, then, later the enlightenment. And, while sport may not have been the principal motive, certainly in the early phases of the Tour, it did feature to some extent in later periods. While formal education was more important for the early Grand Tourists, social skills became more prominent in the seventeenth century and these included, among other things, such physical pursuits as riding and fencing; and one seventeenth century writer (quoted by Towner) clearly lists 'exercise' as one of the motives for the Tour. In addition, as Baker (1982, p. 61, quoted in Standeven and De Knop) has suggested, it is likely that 'young gentleman (may have been) more active than contemplative and physically adroit as well as learned'.

While it is possible to identify some examples of sport associated with this tourism phenomenon, it is the broader influences of the Grand Tour which have real significance for sports tourism. The Grand Tour provided an early model for the tourist industry in general, in terms of specific itineraries and the eventual development of a limited tourist infrastructure. While it was still primarily associated with the upper classes, this development laid the foundations for the eventual growth of mass tourism in later centuries. More specifically in relation to sports tourism, the Grand Tour also opened up the Alps as a tourist destination. The earlier 'classical Grand Tour', linked to galleries, museums and high cultural artefacts, eventually shifted to the 'romantic Grand Tour' which saw the emergence of 'scenic tourism' and a new taste for mountain scenery (Towner, 1996). This change in tastes and the development of centres in the Alpine region thus paved the way for the subsequent growth of sports activities, such as climbing and skiing, which are so prominent today.

INCREASING LINKAGES IN THE INDUSTRIAL AGE

One of the key constraints on the development of sports tourism prior to the nineteenth century was the lack of suitable transport. As indicated above, there were incremental improvements from the fifteenth century onwards involving more comfortable coaches and, in the eighteenth century, greatly improved roads, at least in Britain if not everywhere in Europe. But transport was primarily slow and costly. For example, the journey time from London to Bath in 1680, a distance of 107 miles, was around 60 hours. Vastly improved roads had cut this time to 10 hours by 1800 (McIntyre, 1981), but the time and cost still meant that only the wealthy in society could travel substantial distances. It was not until the development of the railways in the nineteenth century that a relatively cheap and efficient form of transport was afforded to the population at large, enabling sports tourism to develop beyond the small and exclusive upper class activity that had existed hitherto. As Vamplew (1988, p 11) points out, the railways 'revolutionized sport in England by widening the catchment area for spectators and by enabling participants to compete nationally'.

The railways were the product of industrialization which, along with the associated urbanization, had profound implications for sports tourism. The impact of new factory working regimes, urban living conditions and urban middle class attitudes on the nature and development of leisure in general and sport in particular are well documented (Myerscough, 1974; Cunningham, 1975; Lowerson and Myerscough, 1977; Walton and Walvin, 1983; Clark and Critcher, 1985; Bailey, 1987; Mason, 1989; Cross, 1990) and there would seem little point in reiterating much of that story. Similarly, much has been written on the gradual development of tourism from the latter part of the nineteenth century (Pimlott, 1947; Walton 1981, 2000; Ousby, 1990; Gregory, 1991; Towner, 1996; Withey, 1997; Inglis, 2000). What is important here is the influence of urban-industrialization on the specific activity of sports tourism and, in this respect, two clear trends can be discerned: the development of sports requiring the participants themselves to travel and the development of sporting activity involving travelling spectators.

In relation to participant sports tourists, two very different groups emerge at this time: those who travel to participate in competitions and those who travel in order to use particular facilities or resources which may not be available to them in their own locality. The nineteenth century was a particularly important era in the development of competitive sport as attempts were made to transform various forms from unorganized, rowdy traditional games into rationalized activities involving the establishment of rules and governing bodies. As Cross (1990, p. 147) points out:

These organizations replaced the muddle of contradictory regulations that customarily governed play in the village or school and made possible contests at the national and even international level.

Nowhere was this more evident than in the case of soccer, which took root in the new urban communities of industrialized society (Horne et al., 1999). The establishment of the Football Association (FA) in 1863 introduced a national code of rules and other key developments followed shortly afterwards, such as the refereeing of games in the 1870s. By 1871, rules appeared to be sufficiently standardized for the southern-based FA to travel to play a game against the Sheffield Football Club (Horne et al., 1999) and a Challenge Cup was inaugurated in 1872. Another fundamental development at this time was the growth of professionalism, which provoked intense debates within the sport (Mason, 1980; Tischler, 1981) Football had originally been a popular, folk activity but had been 'civilized' by the urban middle classes in the nineteenth century as part of the wider attack on popular culture and the diffusion of 'rational recreation' (Bailey, 1987; Cross, 1990). But the amateur ethos and related values, which had been part of this transformation in the public schools, was challenged by the eventual necessity to pay players. What had become briefly the sport of gentlemen soon returned to its popular roots as club teams sprang up in many of the growing urban centres. And, as increasing numbers of ordinary working men began playing for these teams, 'they often required financial support to pay for the time lost from work and for long-distance travel to matches' (Cross, 1990, p. 150). However, the extent of soccer tourism at this time was wider than this. Horne et al. (1999, p. 42) cite the example of the Blackburn Olympic side who, prior to winning the FA Cup in 1883, had 'spent a week in Blackpool for preparation and training before the semi-final against Old Carthusians'. Thus, improved transport, the widespread adoption of a national code of rules, the emergence of the professional player and the growth of intense competition and rivalry all combined to establish the beginnings of one of the most significant forms of sport tourism.

While soccer may be the best example of competitive sport involving inter-urban and inter-regional travel, it was by no means unique. Cricket was another sport which involved such travel. The basic rules of the game had been codified as early as 1787 by the Marylebone Cricket Club (MCC) but for almost another century it remained an essentially localized activity involving country house cricket and London-based matches among the aristocracy and local village contests involving the gentry, shopkeepers and craftsmen as well as the aristocracy (Horne et al., 1999). As with football, it was not until the second half of the nineteenth century that cricket tourism began to emerge, first, due to an all-England professional touring team that took cricket to virtually every part of the kingdom (Sandiford, 1994) and, secondly, and more enduringly, the establishment of county cricket which involved nine counties in 1873 and 16 by the end of the century. Both developments were aided by the railways and the growing importance of the sporting press, the latter being especially important in a number of sports for encouraging 'fan' consciousness (Cross, 1990).

In addition to inter-county competition, cricket is also associated with relatively early international touring. Standeven and De Knop (1999) cite the example of the Surrey (England) Cricket Club, attempting to visit Paris in 1789, as possibly the first touring team of any sport, even though it was prevented from reaching its destination due to the French Revolution. And, quoting Green (1982), they report that overseas touring by an English cricket team commenced with visits to North America in 1859 and Australia in 1861–62, aided by the newly established passenger steamship services. English cricketers regularly visited Australia after 1861 and, by the end of the century, teams were touring all parts of the empire (Holt, 1989).

The development of commercialized and professional sport also required a further ingredient, however, and that was the emergence of a sizable body of spectators. By the second half of the nineteenth century, some of the wealth creation of industrialization was beginning to trickle down to the working classes, as evidenced by a discernible increase in real wages which rose by 91 per cent between 1860 and 1913 (Myerscough, 1974). Probably for the first time significant numbers of working people were beginning to acquire disposable incomes which could be spent on leisure and this, along with the increased leisure time and the ease of travel brought about by the railways, provided the means for the growth of spectator sport. By the 1880s and 1890s, soccer was becoming commercialized with the establishment of limited companies and investment in stadiums which were attracting several thousand paying spectators to Saturday afternoon games. Football competition was also encouraging inter-urban rivalries and improved transport allowed a number of loyal fans to travel to support their teams. 'Railway specials to selected sports events soon joined the seaside excursions as part of working class leisure' (Vamplew, 1988, p. 11). And the ability to travel to away games involved more than simply the opportunity to support the team but also offered the attractive experience of the travel itself. As Holt (1989) points out:

> *For Northern fans, who made up the great majority of spectators at professional football before 1914, the chance to go to London for a big game was the experience of a lifetime. Thousands of men would go together on specially hired trains, singing and shouting as they spilled out along the London streets.*

The cricket tours referred to above and horse racing were other sports which attracted large crowds. The railways made a major breakthrough in the transport of horses and, together with the easier access they provided for racegoers, led to racing becoming a genuine national sport rather than one pursued only at a local or regional level (Vamplew, 1988). By the 1890s, race crowds of 10 000 to 15 000 were not unusual, with perhaps 70 000 to 80 000 at major Bank Holiday events.

The second major area of participant sports tourism to emerge at this time was that involving people travelling to utilize particular resources or facilities, with skiing, climbing and hiking being particularly important examples. As already mentioned in the previous section, later developments of the Grand Tour involved an attraction to mountain scenery in areas such as Switzerland and 'by the 1890s the new sport of Alpine skiing was finding favour among a few adventurous visitors' (Withey, 1997, p. 217). Travel was aided by tourist operators such as Thomas Cook and Henry Lunn and, by the early decades of the twentieth century, Switzerland had acquired a significant sports tourism industry.

> *In Switzerland clusters of ski resorts to the east and west of the country, many with their own rail links, had emerged by the 1920s with Davos (nearly 6000 beds) and St Moritz (6000 beds) in the east and Villars (2000 beds) and Leysin (2800 beds) forming major resort centres (Towner, 1996).*

Similarly, climbing and mountaineering were also stimulated by the changed attitudes towards mountain environments and, as with skiing, it was the Alpine districts of Switzerland which became one of the most important destinations for the sport, primarily because Switzerland possessed the highest mountains in Europe. Two Britons had unsuccessfully attempted to climb the Jungfrau in 1827 and it was also young British visitors who, between 1854 and 1872, made 31 of the 39 first ascents of the highest European Alpine peaks (Standeven and De Knop, 1999). Withey's (1997, p. 207) account of the development of mountaineering in

Switzerland highlights the links with education and the ideals of rational recreation that influenced so many sporting activities in the Victorian era:

The Britons who took up mountain climbing were primarily middle class professionals, many of them educated at Oxford and Cambridge, where sports and the competitive spirit were an essential part of their education and manliness was associated with endurance and courage. Climbing offered both sport and danger, as well as competition against the forces of nature (especially appealing for those who did not excel at team sports – with mountain climbing it was individual strength and determination that counted). The public school and university experience also encouraged these men to be joiners, so it was no surprise that a group of them banded together in 1857 to form the Alpine Club.

The Alpine Club aimed, among other things, to promote climbing as sport and, along with similar clubs which were created in several other Western European countries, played a significant role in developing this form of sports tourism. By the last quarter of the nineteenth century, tourism had become a mainstay of the Swiss economy and, by the first decade of the twentieth century, Switzerland was indeed 'the playground of Europe' (Withey, 1997). And, while many tourists to Switzerland came to enjoy the scenery, sport was nevertheless a major ingredient in the overall tourism product and was to become even more important later in the century.

Skiing and mountaineering were entirely the preserve of the wealthy upper and middle classes at this time, but so too were less adventurous sports such as hiking and cycling. Hiking depended on people's financial capability to travel to remoter rural areas and pay for suitable accommodation and the cost of bicycles was beyond the means of ordinary working people until the twentieth century. Apart from financial barriers, social class barriers were also important. Various clubs which were formed at this time to encourage and facilitate participation in a range of sports barred the working class from membership. According to Bailey (1987, p. 140), 'the barring of mechanics, artisans and labourers was…standard policy for the Amateur Rowing Association and the Bicycle Union' as well as other clubs such as the Amateur Athletics Association, the justification being that those whose work involved physical labour would enjoy unfair advantage in competition. There were some attempts to encourage a broader social mix in relation to hiking. For example, Tomlinson and Walker (1990) cite a number of organizations, such as the Co-operative Holidays Association and the Manchester YMCA Rambling Club, which organized walking holidays for those of humbler origins. Nevertheless, those who travelled to participate in these resource-based sports during the nineteenth century were almost exclusively upper and middle class.

A final key issue arising from nineteenth century industrialization which needs to be highlighted is that of colonization and the associated cultural diffusion of sport from its 'homelands' to distant parts of the world (Holt, 1989). This in itself, of course, was not sports tourism, as those involved in the playing or watching of the sport did not necessarily travel. The fact that cricket, for example, was now being played in many parts of Africa, the Antipodes and the Indian subcontinent as a result of British imperialism, it did not of itself involve people having to travel; the games were simply being played in different parts of the world by those who lived there. Nevertheless, such cultural diffusion was to have enormous significance for the future of sports tourism as it provided the basis for international competition. As has been indicated above, such competition was already underway in a modest form in the nineteenth century but it was to become a major aspect of sport in the twentieth century.

THE SPORT–TOURISM LINK IN THE TWENTIETH CENTURY

The previous section has illustrated how nineteenth century urban industrialization provided the necessary conditions for significant development of many forms of sports tourism and, while it still remained elitist and exclusive in character, essentially involving the upper and middle classes, the foundations were laid for subsequent expansion in the twentieth century which would embrace all sections of society in a great many different forms. To begin with, this growth essentially involved incremental change but, eventually, in the second half of the century and, especially in the last couple of decades, the expansion of sports tourism was extremely dramatic. Unlike in the previous sections where substantial detail about the nature of the contemporary sports tourism has been highlighted, it is not possible to provide such detail here as there is so much. What this penultimate section is intended to do is to provide a brief discussion of key factors that shaped the developments in the last few decades of the century, with such developments being reviewed in more detail in the final section of this chapter. Some key influences simply involved a continuation of developments which had already begun to influence change in the previous century – such as increasing wealth, increasing leisure time and improving transport, although they were still to have revolutionary impacts at certain times, especially during the latter part of the century. Other influences, such as those associated with attitudes and values, globalization, corporate capitalism, and the media were primarily of more recent relevance.

In relation to leisure time, while the working week only reduced gradually over the century, the increase in holiday time was far more dramatic. The century began with the movement to provide holidays with pay, which was achieved for most workers by the 1920s and regularized for everyone with the Holidays With Pay Act in 1938. The vast majority of people could now take a modest holiday, such as a week at the seaside, and thus the opportunity to travel away from home for more than a brief excursion was no longer the preserve of the wealthy classes. But even more significant were the changes in the last quarter of the century which provided most people with 4 or 5 weeks holiday. By then, leisure time and holiday entitlement were seen as essential components of everybody's lifestyle with significant implications for sports tourism. Not only did ordinary people now have the time to travel further afield to watch sport, and in the latter part of the century they began to do so in substantial numbers, they could also participate in physical activities away from their local area. At its simplest level this might merely involve playing sport on holiday on a relatively casual basis but, as holidays became an established part of normal life, such sports participation as a tourist became especially important. Alternatively, it also meant that ordinary people acquired the time to travel to participate as 'amateurs' in sports competitions or go on specific sports holidays (e.g. golf or cycling), often in addition to an 'ordinary' holiday. Furthermore, the latter part of the twentieth century also witnessed substantial sports tourism activity associated with retirement. Not only were people living longer once retired, due to increased life expectancy arising from improved health care, but also substantial numbers of people were able to take early retirement. With campaigns to encourage the 'elderly' to remain active, sports tourism has become an important pursuit for certain sections of this particular group, golfing and walking holidays being especially significant.

The twentieth century also produced a substantial increase in affluence for most people and, although the increases were relatively modest to begin with, by the late 1950s, full employment and a booming economy ensured incomes were both secure and rising and there was plenty of disposable income available for leisure. Not only did people have the time for leisure and travel, they also had the economic means to utilize it. Throughout the last four decades of the twentieth century, people's expenditure on leisure continued to rise such that, by the end of the century, households in Britain were for the first time spending more on leisure than on food, housing or transport (OPCS, 1999). Expenditure on tourism generally has involved an inexorable growth and sports tourism has been an important part of this development.

The expansion of sports tourism in the twentieth century has also been subsequently influenced by further developments in transportation. Just as the railways revolutionized travel in the nineteenth century, so the automobile and then aeroplanes produced even more dramatic changes in the twentieth. The significance of the car in the development of sport and tourism generally has attracted considerable coverage (see for example Patmore, 1983; Page, 1999; Shaw and Williams, 2002) and it has had no less an impact on sports tourism specifically. Although originally invented towards the end of the nineteenth century, it started to become a mass form of transport in the 1920s in the USA and somewhat later in Britain. Apart from its convenience and flexibility, the car also has the additional advantages of affording access to many areas which are not served by public transport as well as allowing the easy transport of luggage and equipment. As a result, it was invaluable for the development of many forms of sports tourism but especially those such as hiking, climbing, cycling and various forms of water sport which require the transportation of people and equipment to relatively remote locations. The introduction of air transport with its ability to transport people thousands of miles within a few hours has also had a huge impact on sports tourism. Although expensive to begin with, the development of cheap air travel in the 1960s linked to charter flights and package holidays revolutionized international tourism and allowed many forms of sports tourism to flourish, such as the growth of international competitive sport, involving both participants and spectators, the expansion of winter sports and the development of various forms of sports holiday, especially those linked to activities like golf, walking, tennis and water sports in attractive locations such as the Mediterranean.

The expansion of reasonably priced, good quality hotel accommodation associated with tourism growth generally has also facilitated the growth of sports tourism, but the specific demand for certain types of sports tourism has also produced some peculiar forms of accommodation which, once established, have encouraged subsequent growth. Holiday camps are sometimes cited as examples of this, especially those developed in 1930s Germany with their emphasis on health and fitness (Standeven and De Knop, 1999); and another example would be the establishment of Youth Hostels in Britain, also dating from the 1930s, which provided the opportunities for many people to ramble and cycle in the countryside. While more recently the term holiday camp has been dropped and replaced by terms such as 'centre', 'village' or 'holiday world' (Urry, 2001), a totally new type of holiday centre has been pioneered by Center Parcs with artificial environments where leisure and watersports tourism is of paramount importance. Originating in the Netherlands, several Center Parcs villages now exist in various parts of Europe and other companies such as Rank are establishing similar facilities.

In addition to these more tangible influences, a number of other factors have also played a prominent role in the development of sports tourism. A key characteristic of the twentieth century was a fundamental change in values and attitudes which, not surprisingly, given its influence on so many other things, also influenced the development of sports tourism. One important change was that of democratization. The elitism that had characterized both sport and travel gradually gave way to a process of wider involvement so that, by the end of the twentieth century, not only were the means available to enable most people to participate, but so too was the expectation. The wider involvement in sport was promoted through the schools and through various government promotional campaigns, at first primarily for extrinsic reasons linked to improving health and fitness and for reasons of moral welfare and social control and, then, eventually for people's individual well being and leisure. While some sports have retained a certain class bias (e.g. participation in golf is still dominated by the middle classes and polo by the upper classes), most sports are no longer socially exclusive.

In addition to the acceptance that sport and travel could be available to anyone, the other key value change was that sport and travel became central aspects of people's lives. While western nations may not have fully embraced the leisure society that some pundits were proclaiming in the 1970s, there is no denying the weakening of the work ethic and the increased importance placed on pleasure and hedonism by the end of the twentieth century. Furthermore, sport and tourism were important for many different reasons, very much in keeping with postmodern values. For some, sport was still pursued for the traditional motives of fitness, health, competition and achievement, but now many participated simply for fun and pleasure or indulged in sports for reasons of body image and fashion. Similarly, holidays were also to become an important part of many people's lifestyles. As Urry (2001, p. 5) has pointed out, 'it is a crucial element of modern life that travel and holidays are necessary' and, by the latter part of the 1980s, travel was estimated to be occupying 40 per cent of people's free time. And, for an increasing number of people, the lifestyle choice came to involve both sport and travel combined. This is illustrated in particular by two types of sports tourism – outdoor pursuits and international sporting events. The former is linked to a range of motives and values relating to health, fitness, image, excitement and even fashion, while the latter is associated with experience and spectacle.

The development of mega sports tourism events is a product of additional influences which have played a key role on the growth of sports tourism in the twentieth century, that of commercialization and globalization.

Commercialization was present in the previous century but its impact was relatively minor compared to what has occurred in recent times largely as a result of global developments. While much sport is still organized through voluntary clubs on an amateur basis, many sports have become increasingly commercialized, especially elite sport. This can be seen particularly in the development of international sport, which as Horne et al. (1999, p. 277) argue 'is a product of the jet, television and corporate capitalism'. Horne et al. highlight the fact that, whereas in 1950 there were 5 million TV sets world-wide with television only available in Great Britain, the USA and USSR, by 1970 there were 250 million sets in 130 countries and, since the early 1970s, television has spread rapidly to most of the developing world. Television is a major global business and sport is one of many phenomena that can be commodified and sold to an ever growing audience. Now, sport can be watched round the clock on several different channels. At first sight it might seem odd that television would influence sports tourism, as it allows people to watch sport without ever having to leave their home. However, its great significance is that it has popularized a great many sports and highlighted their benefits and spectacle to a mass audience and this, in turn, has encouraged international exchange in sport and the expansion of international sporting competitions (Whannel, 1985; Tomlinson, 1996). Not only has this led to many athletes travelling to participate in such competitions but it has also encouraged many people to travel to watch such events. At the same time that satellite television was allowing test match cricket from the Antipodes or the West Indies to be watched live in Britain, the English cricket team was attracting a growing and vociferous band of 'home grown' spectators at the actual matches. By highlighting, if not exaggerating, the excitement and drama at such events, television has persuaded many people to want to experience such spectacle at first hand (Chalip, 2006). International competitions such as the Olympic Games, Commonwealth Games, World Cup and continental cup football competitions, test matches, Wimbledon and Grand Prix motor racing meetings have become major tourist attractions in their own right, attracting not just the traditional fans and enthusiasts, but also those searching, in true post-modern fashion, for the spectacular tourist experience. Furthermore, the investment of corporate capital in the merchandising of team products and the global marketing of sportswear may also enhance the tourist experience linked to the need to dress or parade in the appropriate attire and to collect souvenirs.

While it is clear that private businesses have played a major role in the development of sports tourism, the role of government has not been entirely absent. As already outlined, sport has been encouraged by governments for a host of extrinsic reasons and tourism has similarly been supported in recent times due to its economic contribution, especially in relation to employment. However, the realization that certain forms of sport can attract tourists, especially the mega events referred to above, has led many governments in the latter part of the twentieth century to be especially proactive in seeking to host such competitions. Several cities have found their economies and environments significantly transformed as a result of such events with the stimulus of sports tourism producing far wider benefits for both tourism generally and the wider economy as the final section of this chapter will now show.

SPORTS TOURISM AT THE TURN OF THE MILLENNIUM AND BEYOND

At the end of the twentieth century it was possible to travel to a vast array of sports events, enabled by both traditional and new specialist tour and travel companies, and event sports tourism has become a major tourism product (see Chapter 8). Examples abound, but the 1992 Barcelona Olympics attracted nearly half a million visitors to the region (Truno, 1994; Collins and Jackson, 1999) and, in the ten years following the Games, annual visitor numbers doubled (Weed, 2006c). Furthermore, although the Games had significantly increased the city's number of tourist beds, average occupancy rates had still increased from 70 per cent to 85 per cent during this period (Sanahuja, 2002). In the UK, the Euro '96 European Football Championships attracted 280 000 visiting spectators and media to the UK, spending £120 m in the eight host cities and surrounding regions (Dobson et al., 1997).

However, spectating sports tourism is not limited to major events. Much spectating sports tourism involves travel to watch a family member or friend compete. The spectator following of events such as the London or New York Marathons and, indeed, many smaller mass participation events illustrate this point, as do the large numbers (mainly parents and family) who turn up to watch junior sports tournaments and events (Scott and Turco, 2007). In addition, the weekly leagues in a range of sports, although mostly football, in a range of countries around the world provide for regular domestic sports spectating day trips. However, the ever increasing popularity of football and the growth of competitions such as the European Champions League, leads to such trips becoming international in nature and, in the vast majority of cases, involving at least one overnight stay (Millward, 2006), with resulting economic benefits to the destination.

The term 'activity holiday' entered tourists' vocabularies in the latter half of the twentieth century and, in the UK, this has become a multi-billion-pound subsector of the tourism market (Mintel, 2005a). The majority of activity holidays involve sports tourism activities and this has boosted the sector and, particularly, the rural communities where much of this activity takes place. A whole new 'genre' of sports tourism activity has emerged which is identifiably different from the exclusively relaxation-oriented, sun-seeking tourism of the 1970s and early 1980s. The activity holiday consumer profile is diverse, including independent adults, parents and families, school parties, or groups of children at summer camps. Activity holiday markets in the UK are predominantly domestic, with 85 per cent of British consumers taking their activity holidays within Britain. Furthermore, many see activity holidays involving sports tourism as an extra break, taken outside the traditional holiday period.

Found more outside the UK, the German concept of Volkssports, which translates as 'people's sports' or 'life sports' was identified as a potential growth market in the 1990s (Jackson and Glyptis, 1992). Volkssports are family-oriented active recreations which originated in Germany, Austria and Switzerland in the early 1960s. The American Volkssports Association, which coordinates over 500 clubs in the USA, promotes the activities – walking, cycling, swimming and cross-country skiing – as sports in which anyone can participate with friends and family throughout his or her life. The concept is now found in over 20 countries around the world under the auspices of Der Internationale Volkssportverband (IVV) (The International Federation of Popular Sports). Agne-Traub (1989) predicted that their increasing international popularity would lead to their incorporation into business and pleasure travel and that events would be scheduled to attract day-tripping tourists. Unfortunately, there has been no further investigation of the Volkssports concept as a potential sports tourism product. However, a similar concept underpins the range of events established and calendared by local and municipal authorities to attract visitors and their spending, as well as providing a recreational, sometimes elite performance event, for the benefit of the local population, and sometimes to promote the city or area. British examples would be events such as the London (and others) Marathon, the Great North Run, the Scarborough Cricket Festival and the Worthing Bowls Festival.

It has been suggested that there is great potential for such initiatives to stimulate sporting activity in a range of areas (Jackson and Glyptis, 1992). Moreover, because many such activities lend themselves to universal participation, they can be linked to health promotion and active living programmes – something that has been largely neglected by sports development and health promotion professionals. The potential for sports tourism to play a role in the 'sports development process' was outlined in the early work by Jackson and Glyptis (1992) and, more recently, by Weed (2001a).

Both studies noted that there are a vast number of people who only pick up a racquet or a ball while on holiday. If the playful and health-related benefits of sport are stressed by those organizing sports tourism activities on holidays, then this can have a great impact on developing active and healthy lifestyles when the tourist returns home. In this way, holidays can be used to entice individuals to take up a sport; activity holidays by schools and youth groups often generate interests for life. In addition, 'performance camps' away from home are increasingly common for some of the nation's best young sportspeople. Such examples show the potential for sport within the sport–tourism relationship.

Weed and Jackson (2008) suggest that the 1990s saw a 'quiet revolution' in sports tourism supply development. This started with the provision of better hotel facilities (initially the inclusion of swimming pools in the product portfolio) and continued through the addition of health club facilities and access to tennis and golf provision, until the highest tariff/quality accommodation (outside city centres) saw hotels set alongside their own golf and multisport complexes. Sports tourism provision became an integral part of the established tourism product, with conference and business tourists in particular now having high-class, prestigious facilities made available to them as competition increases for their custom. Manchester, for example, used its Olympic bids and its hosting of the 2002 Commonwealth Games to spearhead its push for the conference market. Sports tourism facilities and opportunities are now seen as almost essential in attracting the highly lucrative conference market. However, in addition to providing for the conference market, many 'country-house'-type hotels began to cater for the luxury sports tourist. As Chapter 8 will show, it is often the range and quality of the facilities as well as the luxurious nature of the accommodation rather than the actual activities offered that define this product (Weed, 2001b). In fact, in a number of cases, this market has been provided for by the addition of five-star accommodation to long-established and renowned sports facilities. For enthusiasts who cannot afford such hotels, many smaller hotel operators have agreements with local sports providers to attract visitors for mutual benefit. Furthermore, a substantial number of farms diversified into tourism and provide sport and recreation activities for those on a tighter budget.

The 1990s saw both major travel operators (e.g. Thomson) and smaller 'independents' diversify their product offers into sports tourism holidays, particularly over recent years. Within the latter group, the number of specialists and products available in activities of all types grew significantly. Larger operators typically now offer multi-activity holidays, as well as sun/sea packages, and most of the latter include sports activity options. The UK now boasts over a hundred accredited independent tour operators (often specializing exclusively in sports tourism niches) offering sports tourism ranging from golf holidays to high mountain range trekking. Several other independent operators directly market their multi-activity facilities and packages, such as walking, biking, pony trekking, canoeing adventure holidays; or aquatic-oriented pursuits such as sailing, surfing, wind-surfing, diving, etc. These commercial operators are supplemented by education-sector centres and other commercial professional training/team-building centres. The diversity of sports/adventure tourism opportunities, as illustrated by these few examples, is substantial and still growing.

Sports tourism products, particularly in rural areas, have provided a whole range of tourism development opportunities ranging from those operated from enterprising small hotels to farm diversification projects. As such, there is a range of examples of the effective use of countryside resources for sport and recreation from all around the world. Jackson (1999) noted the environmentally friendly nature of cycling as an activity in National Parks in America, while in Crete and Thrace 'soft' forms of sports tourism, such as hiking, orienteering and cycling, have been promoted in rural areas (Vrondou, 1999; Vrondou and Kriemadis, 2006). In this Greek case, these 'soft' forms of sports tourism have been seen as having the potential to diversify tourism beyond the traditional 'mass' product for which Greece is known and to have substantial potential for the future of the Greek tourism industry. Vrondou (1999) provides an example of a characteristic of sports tourism that is found elsewhere. Here, sports tourism is seen as a sustainable form of tourism that might 'minimise negative effects and maximize social, environmental and economic benefits' (Regional Programme for Crete, 1994–99) while also having the potential to promote local cultures, as the activities result in greater access to alternative routes and localities, with distinct natural and cultural characteristics. This is something which the World Tourism Organisation (1988) recognized twenty years ago and has continued to promote since that time, commenting that sports tourism products can enrich the tourism experience by allowing greater interaction with destinations and a fuller appreciation of the social and cultural life of local communities.

There has also been evidence (see Jackson and Glyptis, 1992) that tourism can play a role, particularly in coastal or rural areas where the population may be dispersed, in supporting standards of sports facilities that would otherwise be unavailable to local residents. There was a range of examples in the final decade of the twentieth century of tourist support for the upkeep of recreational parkland and sports facilities in rural communities in France (Bayuex and Chazaud, 1997), North America (Donnelly et al., 1998), Australia (Johansson, 2000) and even Thailand (Tananone, 1991). In many cases, as well as catering for the local market, facility developers found it essential to account for the recreational needs of tourists (Grcic-Zubecevic, 2001). In fact, in order to realize financial targets, larger leisure pool developments found that they had to attract a high proportion of visitors from outside the immediate area. It was also recognized as being important to ensure that these visitors spend money both inside and outside the facility, because without this visitor support many significant leisure developments were simply not viable (Woodward, 1990). Thus, sports tourism has been essential in supporting local-level sports provision, as well as the local economy.

As the above discussion intimates, clear impacts from sports tourism development had emerged at the dawn of the twenty-first century. The economic impact was, and perhaps continues to be, the most obvious and has already been evidenced in terms of adding value to individual facilities and sometimes to whole destinations. Broadly, sports tourism is a dynamic and expanding sector of the tourism economy and, by definition, this is attractive economically. Sports tourism facilities and events are clearly capable of generating visitors from outside the local area and of attracting more and/or higher-spending visitors to existing tourist locations. There is economic benefit locally from sales of accommodation, food, beverages, gifts, admission fees, other spending at facilities, hire fees, use of transport, etc. Thus, there are clear benefits from attracting visitors, using sports tourism as a key part of the tourism product offer. Event sports tourism products may also generate sponsorship income, inward investment, media exposure, ongoing tourist appeal and secondary multiplier effects. There are potentially significant economic benefits to be accrued from the additional revenue, employment, infrastructure, etc. to local and national economies which sports tourism provides.

Twelve years ago, Jackson and Reeves (1996) suggested that an estimate that 10–15 per cent of domestic holidays in Northern Europe have a sports orientation was not unreasonable and, while evidence is sparse, consumer preferences in the last ten years seem to reinforce this view (Sport Business, 2005). However, they also called for a more specific and consistent focus on sports tourism in future tourism statistics collection. Three years later, Collins and Jackson (1999) attempted to synthesize a range of previous economic impact studies in disparate disciplines to present an overview of the economic impacts of the sport–tourism link, focusing on the UK. In doing so they commented that their work could only be considered 'indicative of the overall economic impact because of the inconsistent and invariably incompatible nature of the available data' (Collins and Jackson, 1999). Their 'conservative' estimates for the value of sports tourism in the UK at the end of the twentieth century are illustrated in Table 1.1, which suggests an overall

Table 1.1	The economic impact of sports tourism in the UK
Types of sports tourism	**Value £m**
Sports as a prime activity on domestic holidays	1640
Sports as a prime activity by overseas visitors	142
Sport as a prime activity on day trips	831
Total	2611

Source: After Collins and Jackson (1999)

value of over £2.5 bn annually at this time. A more 'bullish' recent estimate was provided by market analysts Mintel (2005b), who valued UK sports tourism at £3.4 bn annually, but they had a more 'inclusive' view of the activities involved. That the Collins and Jackson estimate from 1999 remains, a decade later, the most recent 'academic' estimate of economic impact is an indication of the difficulty and complexity of disaggregating information on economic aspects of sports tourism.

In the last 20 to 30 years it has been in the area of event sports tourism that most economic impact research has been conducted and it is therefore useful to review some of this research here. It has been suggested that the obvious direct benefits of major events (new facilities and visitor spending) are supplemented, in most cases, by a post-event tourism boost, although increasingly this assumption is being questioned (see Chapter 2). However, the marketing benefits of the resulting publicity are increasingly recognized as achievable positive benefits of staging such events (Green et al., 2003).

Although earlier Olympics made losses for the host cities (Munich and Montreal), since the commercial success of the Los Angeles Games in 1984 (which realized a surplus of £215 m) there has been considerable competition for the privilege of being the host city for the Olympic Games. Furthermore, understanding of the broad and indirect benefits to cities, regions and governments of hosting major events, even where there is an initial cost to a city, has undoubtedly increased in the last 20 years (see Preuss, 2004).

The act of winning the Olympic Games has been a catalyst for bringing forward general infrastructure investments that may have been on the drawing board for a number of years. As a result of the 1992 Games, Barcelona gained a ring-road, a new airport and the redevelopment of an area of derelict waterfront for the Olympic Village, as well as the associated spending in the wider region of 422 000 visitors and other event-related income. The worldwide publicity and infrastructure investment that the

Games increasingly bring should enable a host city to attract further general investment, future events and more tourists (Weed, 2008a). Even failed Olympic bids have attracted a large amount of public and private sector investment to provide some facilities and infrastructure. Manchester gained a world-class velodrome and several local infrastructure projects from its Olympic bid, which helped it to bid for and host the Commonwealth Games of 2002. The level of public investment has increasingly been justified along these lines, with the number of cities attaching importance to establishing an identity as a 'world-class city' in the circuits of international business, culture and tourism increasing considerably. At the city level, a major motivator for attracting sports tourism events may be the significant level of central government funding that is often attached to such projects. In fact, the group responsible for initiating Victoria's successful bid for the 1994 Commonwealth Games cited the infusion of federal funds into the city as one of the most important reasons for putting in a bid for the Games (D'Abaco, 1991). Rarely are major events viable without significant public sector investment. Invariably, there is a cost to the host authority, but significant benefits to the wider economy (see Preuss, 2004).

It has been recognized since the early 1990s that having staged a major games, it is important that cities seek to attract a string of future events. Subsequent events can be staged at a fraction of the cost of the original event as the infrastructure is already in place. However, the promotional, image and economic effects still persist. In this vein, Bramwell (1997a) discussed the use of the 1991 World Student Games in Sheffield as part of a sustainable development strategy that promoted and, as Chapter 11 shows, continues to promote economic efficiency, social equity and environmental integrity in the city of Sheffield. Although initially unpopular and generating much local and external criticism, the continued legacy of these games has been reflected in Sheffield's ongoing major sports events strategy that has attracted events such as Euro '96 and the World Masters Swimming Championships to the city with significant economic benefit (Gratton et al., 2005). However, it is not only large-scale events that can generate economic benefits for local communities, and this is a point that Dobson and Gratton (1997) made in relation to Sheffield's portfolio of events in the late 1990s.

A further feature of the hosting of major events that came to be widely recognized at the end of the twentieth century was that, in order for the major facilities built for such events to be sustainable in the long term, they needed to be adaptable for local community use. One of the legacies of the World Student Games in Sheffield was the Ponds Forge International Sports Centre, which comprises a 50 m swimming pool, a pool with full diving facilities, a leisure pool and an indoor sports centre. Bramwell (1997b) describes the provision of new sport and recreation facilities for the long-term use of Sheffield residents as a key objective for the hosting of the World Student Games, although more recent critiques have suggested that it has led to the closure of more locally convenient facilities in the suburbs. However, many facilities built for major games may not be best suited to ongoing community use, either for participation or spectating.

It is also important to include factors other than economic impacts in the cost/benefit assessment of event sports tourism (Mules and Dwyer, 2005). For example, many such events, particularly those where regeneration is a major objective, often require the demolition of at least some existing provision or housing to make way for facilities, infrastructure or development. At worst, this can result in the traumatic break-up of entire communities. A displacement of indigenous communities occurred in the development of Barcelona's waterfront for the 1992 Olympic Games and in Beijing's preparation for the 2008 Games (Weed, 2008a). While many would see such redevelopment as a positive benefit that enhances the environment and image of the city, for those communities that are displaced the experience can be traumatic, and such socioeconomic 'engineering' now receives very negative exposure, which denudes the positive impact which such developments and events are designed to secure.

Overall, however, sports tourism has come to be viewed as having primarily positive impacts in comparison to many other commercial development forms. Sports tourism has played a significant part in a number of countries in the generation of community identity and pride and in the economic and social regeneration of decaying urban areas. In addition, its economic potential has been harnessed in many rural areas to support the local economy and services. In the immediate aftermath of apartheid in South Africa, Nelson Mandela spoke of the role of the 1995 Rugby World Cup, hosted and won by South Africa, in 'nation building' after the years of internal turmoil and international isolation the country had suffered.

Both in Britain and the USA, sports tourism initiatives have been at the forefront of urban regeneration programmes (see Roche, 1994; Collins and Jackson, 1999; Stevens, 2005). In many urban areas, the use of sport within the tourism strategies of local government for regenerative purposes is also well documented (Law, 1992; Sheffield City Liaison Group, 1994; Silk and Amis, 2005). North American research by Rosentraub (2000) and Wilcox and Andrews (2003) discusses the substantial surge, since the early 1990s, in the number of new facilities – largely aimed at staging events, concerts, conventions, conferences, exhibitions and any other events requiring a facility with a capacity of around 20 000 people.

The prime objective identified in almost all of these cases has been economic development and revitalization. An earlier example of this is provided by Chapin (1996), who specifically reviewed the varying strategies of three facilities: Key Arena in Seattle, The Rose Garden in Portland and GM Palace in Vancouver. The construction of the Key Arena in Seattle was part of a plan to revitalize an ageing, but culturally highly significant, civic centre. Here, the former Seattle Coliseum arena was reconstructed and renamed the Key Arena, as an integral part of the Seattle Centre Entertainment District, resulting in a revamped city centre that retained much of its original heritage. In contrast, Portland chose to locate a new facility alongside an older, much smaller arena and relatively new convention centre in an out-of-town development that is now specifically marketed as a Sports Entertainment District. Finally, Vancouver, like Seattle, located the GM Palace within its city centre, but focused on a newly built sports arena with the aim of enhancing the city centre as a 'metropolitan core'. These cases illustrate three widely popular strategies for urban regeneration utilizing sports tourism and entertainment facilities likely to attract visitors, namely, reinvestment in existing facilities, development of new sports entertainment districts and investment in inner-city revitalization and redevelopment. However, a key factor in each of these cases, and one relevant to any town seeking to use sports tourism in urban regeneration, is that it be developed alongside other leisure, entertainment and tourism facilities (Silk and Amis, 2005).

In rural areas too, sports tourism has increasingly had a number of significant impacts. Despite the evident sensitivity of rural environments and the fact that there will be some negative impacts of sports tourism development (see Hinch and Higham, 2004), sports tourism has, for the most part, maintained a reputation as 'soft' tourism (discussed earlier in the Greek example), capable of contributing to the rural economy in a range of contexts across the world. Countryside pursuits, such as hiking, climbing, orienteering, fell-running and cycling, all increasingly contribute to the rural economy, but perhaps the latter has received the most recent attention in the literature. In the UK, the development of the National Cycle Network as a Millennium Project saw rural districts and small local businesses invest in cycle tourism as a key element in rural economic development strategies. Jackson and Morpeth (1999) noted that, at the turn of the century, the National Cycle Network was seen as having the potential to generate £150 m in tourism receipts annually across the UK and over 3000 jobs nationally, particularly focused in rural areas. The 'C2C Cycle Route' across the rural north of England, for example, was at this time estimated as already generating £1.5 m annually for the communities along its route. However, in more recent research, Lumsdon et al. (2004) warn that the majority of this economic impact is generated by day visitors (70%) and thus the impact is focused on 'hub' sites rather than evenly distributed along the route (see Chapter 16).

A cautionary note, however, should be sounded about an overreliance on the leisure economy. There is, of course, the long documented concern about the part-time, seasonal and casual nature of many of the jobs that are created (see Shaw and Williams, 2002). Such dependency on recreation and tourism can also result in a neglect of ecological and environmental concerns. For example, Weiss et al. (1998) studied reactions to ski tourism among ski tourists and ski resort residents in Austria and Belgium. They found that ski tourists and locals who were not financially dependent on tourism had a much higher ecological awareness than tourism-dependent locals. This was clearly a result of the latter group's vested economic interest in the industry and was further highlighted by the fact that differences between these groups on general environmental issues were minimal. Environmental concerns in relation to ski tourism were found to vary according to the extent of the personal sacrifice involved in addressing such issues.

CONCLUSION

As was demonstrated at the outset of this chapter, sports tourism possesses a long history and it is rather symbolic that the century which witnessed the most substantial growth and development of sports tourism was heralded by the revival of the modern Olympic Games in Athens in1896. Such symbolism can be further extended when looking at the Games today, in that they clearly reflect the importance and significance of contemporary sports tourism, involving many of the influences and characteristics discussed above. While the earlier examples of sports tourism do not constitute the principal concerns of this text, the chapter has discussed at some length the nature of sports tourism at the end of the Millennium and into the twenty-first century and some important points have emerged. It is clear that various factors which have influenced sports tourism in earlier times are still relevant today and it would also appear that whenever people have obtained the means and opportunities to participate they have tended to exploit them. The history of the development of sports tourism in the twentieth century has been largely about overcoming various constraints to enable such opportunities to be widened to involve most people rather than just a privileged few. As the discussions towards the end of the chapter have shown, sports tourism in its many different forms is now a substantial activity and significant collection of products in its own right. The remainder of this text thus seeks to examine the phenomenon through an analysis of the various participants, the policy making process and the providers, with related issues being further explored through a series of specific case studies. First, however, the next chapter continues to set the context for this analysis by considering contemporary sports tourism issues, concepts and research.

CHAPTER 2

Contemporary Concepts, Issues and Research

As the previous chapter shows, travel for the purposes of sports tourism participation has clearly taken place for thousands of years, with authors generally appearing to agree that the earliest documented example is the ancient Olympic Games dating from 776 BC (Van Dalen and Bennett, 1971; Finley and Pleket, 1976; Baker, 1982; Davies, 1997; Standeven and De Knop, 1999). However, despite this long history, and what appears to be an academic interest stretching back 35 years, the study of the relationship between sport and tourism is still in a relatively early stage of development.

One of the earliest writings on the relationship between sport and tourism appears to have been a paper entitled, 'Sport and Tourism' written by Don Anthony for the Central Council of Physical Recreation in the UK in 1966, which simply reviewed the role sport might play in holiday tourism. Some authors have argued (e.g. De Knop, 1990) that it was during the following decade, the 1970s, that academic interest in sport and tourism began to develop seriously, pointing to conference papers (e.g. Schreiber, 1976) and the odd report by tourist organizations (e.g. Baker and Gordon, 1976) to evidence this. However, it is perhaps Sue Glyptis' (1982) study of sport and tourism in five European countries that marks the start of a sustained academic spotlight being turned onto the area. In that publication, Glyptis pointed to a problem that endures in relation to sports tourism development today, namely that:

> [Despite]... a linkage between sport and tourism in the minds of participants, commercial providers and local authorities, [there remains] a lack of conscious integration – or even resistance to it,

by policy-makers, planners and public providers at national level
(Glyptis, 1982: p.63)

Nine years later, Glyptis (1991a: p.165) reached a similar but more wide-ranging conclusion:

Sport and tourism tend to be treated by academic and practitioner
alike as separate spheres of activity. Each has its own journals,
academic departments, learned societies and government agencies.
At an institutional level, integration of the two is rare. Yet in terms
of popular participation and some aspects of practice, they are
inextricably linked; and, in principle, there are sound reasons for
those links to strengthen.

Another seven years, and Heather Gibson (1998: p.45) had taken up Glyptis' concerns:

… the field suffers from a lack of integration in the realms of
policy, research and education. At policy level, there needs to be
better coordination among agencies responsible for sport and those
responsible for tourism. At a research level, more multidisciplinary
research is needed, particularly research which builds upon
existing knowledge bases in both sport and tourism. In the realm of
education, territorial contests between departments claiming tourism
expertise and those claiming sport expertise need to be overcome.

The reason for presenting these relatively lengthy quotations alongside each other is to highlight some of the enduring problems that scholarship in sports tourism has faced. In fact, the central issue, that of lack of integration, seems to have exacerbated over this sixteen-year period and, as Chapters 6 and 7 show, remains problematic today. Initial concerns highlighted policy, later concerns highlighted policy and academic structures, with the latest concerns also highlighting problems with the research base. These concerns perhaps originate from the nature of the body of publications at this time. In a review at the turn of the Millennium, Weed (1999b) noted that there appeared to be two identifiable strands of literature relating to sport and tourism. (A further third strand focusing on policy was also identified, but this was a very small proportion of the overall work in the area at the time.) The first of these, and at the time by far the largest strand, focused on advocacy, simply attempting to establish that there is a link between sport and tourism and to establish it as a legitimate field worthy of consideration by both academics and providers. Initially, such advocacy work comprised speculative reviews: e.g. 'Some thoughts on the influence of sport tourism' (De Knop, 1987),

'Sport and tourism in the modern world' (Redmond, 1988), as befits early
work in a field of study. However, somewhat frustratingly, as the comments of
Glyptis (1991a) and Gibson (1998) indicate, many authors continued in this
vein into the late 1990s. Yet there was some indication of a body of work, the
second strand identified by Weed (1999b), that was attempting to quantify the
links between sport and tourism, thus providing evidence of the volume and
value of different types of sports tourist. Much of Jackson and Reeves' work at
this time (e.g. 1996, 1998) was centred on the theme 'Evidencing the sport-
tourism relationship', and explicitly sought to move away from the speculative
forms of advocacy that seemed to pervade much work in the field.

However, despite a move away from speculative advocacy towards a
more empirical approach, there was an early indication in Gibson's (1998)
comments of a further concern that remains today, namely the lack of a
theoretical or conceptual base for research in sport and tourism. This was
further highlighted at an international conference in 2002 when a keynote
speaker in a plenary session was asked about what theoretical perspectives and concepts underpinned the study of sport and tourism. While the
speaker was able to point to one or two areas in which theory was prominent, this question highlighted a weakness in the body of knowledge relating
to sport and tourism at that time. Furthermore, the perception of much
of the audience, who were not researchers in sport and tourism, that the
area lacked theoretical rigour was undoubtedly grounded in the speculative
advocacy work that had been so pervasive in the 1980s and 1990s, a point
made in the first edition of this text in 2004:

> The large amount of unconnected small-scale sports tourism case
> studies, and the continued preoccupation with advocacy work, have
> meant that there is a perception among academics in sport, tourism
> and leisure studies that sports tourism research is not theoretically
> informed (Weed and Bull, 2004: p. 205).

Following these concerns, a special issue of *European Sport Management
Quarterly* addressing 'Sports Tourism Theory and Method', was published
in 2005 (vol.5, no.3). This special issue, featuring an extended guest editorial (Weed, 2005c) commenting on the state of research in the field, was
conceived to address the perception that research in sport and tourism was
not theoretically informed and aimed to showcase the use of theory in the
area by leading authors in the field. This is highlighted in the call for papers
for the special issue, which was written in 2004:

> … *indicative of sports tourism's status as a relatively youthful field
> of study, many papers and articles have sought simply to establish*

the link between the two areas rather than advance the theoretical approaches that might underpin its study. This has led to suggestions from some quarters that sports tourism should not be given specific attention as a distinctive field of study...

The suggestion that sports tourism was not a legitimate field of study underpinned the conference question mentioned above and was also discussed by Gammon and Kurtzman (2002: p. v) who noted that:

... those writing and researching in the area have been accused of clumsily diluting two already established disciplines in order to profit from professional precedence and thus committing the indefensible crime of academic triviality.

Yet, just as more public concerns about the study of sports tourism were starting to surface, there was a small but emerging body of work (since around 2000) responding to the call for greater theorization of the area. In introducing a volume of such work in 2005 (a special issue of *Sport in Society* on 'Sport Tourism: Concepts and Theories', vol. 8, no. 2), Gibson (2005a: p.134) suggests that researchers should be, 'linking their work to theories in the well-established parent disciplines such as sociology, social psychology, geography and anthropology' and a clear and explicit use of such theories is starting to emerge in the study of sport and tourism (e.g. Higham and Hinch, 2006; Harris, 2006). Of course, the use of theoretical perspectives from parent disciplines requires that researchers read research in such disciplines, rather than limiting their reading to their subject area. All too often, sport psychologists, for example, will read only work that appears in journals such as *Psychology of Sport and Exercise* and *Journal of Sport & Exercise Psychology*. Such an approach limits knowledge to the second-hand appreciation of the application of psychological theory to a particular subject, rather than ensuring that knowledge is grounded in the debates that are underpinning theory development in the broader discipline. The use of this example is not to single out sport psychologists, similar accusations might be made of a range of other areas of study that apply disciplines to a particular subject area (e.g. sport sociologists, tourism management scholars and, of course, those studying the relationship between sport and tourism). The need, therefore, is for researchers to return to disciplinary texts to ensure their work is theoretically and conceptually robust. The discussions of policy, for example, in Chapters 6 and 7 of this text, are fundamentally underpinned by perspectives from mainstream policy studies (e.g. Wilks and Wright, 1987; Marsh and Rhodes, 1992) rather than from texts on sport (e.g. Houlihan and White, 2002) and tourism (e.g. Hall and Jenkins, 2003) policy. This is because such texts, while undoubtedly useful in understanding the development of policy for sport and for tourism, do not seek to provide a thorough understanding of the way in which policy theories and concepts have developed and the conditions in which they should be applied to particular policy areas.

Following the publication of the special issues of *European Sport Management Quarterly* and *Sport in Society* in 2005 seeking to address concerns about the theoretical foundations of sports tourism, the *Journal of Sport Tourism (JST)* underwent some major changes. This journal, which had run online for seven years before being launched in hard copy in 2003, was owned by the Sport Tourism International Council (STIC). As befits a publication of a body such as STIC, *JST* attempted to serve a trade/professional audience as well as the academic community. However, while such a dual role was laudable, in practice it proved difficult to fulfil, with the result that the content of *JST* sometimes disappointed the academic community, and this, albeit inadvertently, perhaps contributed to some of the negative perceptions of research in sport and tourism. To address these concerns, in 2006, STIC relinquished its ownership of the journal (thus releasing it from its obligations to its trade/professional audience) and the journal was relaunched, repositioned and renamed as the *Journal of Sport & Tourism (JS&T)* with a new editorial team and new aims and scope which emphasize its new academic direction:

> … *the standard for publication in the* Journal of Sport & Tourism
> *is that manuscripts must make a clear contribution substantively,*
> *theoretically, or methodologically to the body of knowledge relating*
> *to the relationship between sport and tourism.*

Any field of academic study requires various markers to establish its legitimacy and, as the discussions above suggest, such markers have not necessarily been readily identifiable in sports tourism scholarship to date. In 1996, Gartner suggested that the study of sport and tourism would establish its own 'cadre' of researchers and Weed's (2006b) systematic review of knowledge in the field identifies a core group of authors who have contributed to the development of the field in the last decade. The existence of a quality peer-reviewed academic journal in the subfield is another marker of legitimacy and, as such, the relaunch of the *Journal of Sport & Tourism* as such a publication in 2006 is an important milestone. Furthermore, the recognition of the subfield by established journals in sport (e.g. *Journal of Sport Management*, *European Sport Management Quarterly*, *Sport in Society*) and tourism (e.g. *Journal of Vacation Marketing*, *Current Issues in Tourism*, *Tourism Review International*), each of which has published special issues on sport and tourism in recent years, is a further marker. Finally, the publication of the second edition of this text, the first book in the sports tourism field to be commissioned for a second edition, is a further indication that sports tourism is developing as a legitimate area of academic study which has established some longevity.

THE FUNDAMENTAL NATURE OF UNDERSTANDING SPORTS TOURISM BEHAVIOURS

Many texts focusing on the relationship between sport and tourism commence with a discussion of impacts. In fact, for some texts, the impacts of linking sport and tourism are the primary focus. However, the approach taken here is different for two reasons. First, because discussions of the impacts of sports tourism are wide ranging in the literature (see, for example, texts by Standeven and De Knop, 1999; Ritchie and Adair, 2004; Higham, 2005; and the original Chapter 2 in the first edition of this text), it does not seem productive to re-present them here, particularly as the aim of this text is to understand the stakeholders (participants, policy-makers and providers) in sports tourism. Secondly, the view of this text is that it is an understanding of sports tourism participation, experiences and behaviours that is fundamental to any attempts to generate impacts, to formulate policy, or to make provision for sport and tourism (Weed, 2005c). It is for this reason that the examination of stakeholders in this text commences with three chapters on the people who generate impacts and in response to whom policy and provision is made, the participants in sports tourism.

As Weber (2001) and Weed (2005c, 2006b) have noted, there is somewhat of a paradox in relation to research on sports tourism behaviours. Weed's (2006b) systematic review demonstrates that sports tourism behaviours and profiles were the most featured topic across research into a range of activities conducted in the first five years of the twenty-first century. This would seem to indicate that the field is well served in terms of developing an understanding of such behaviours. However, Weed (2005c) had earlier claimed that:

> ... policy, provision and impacts are all derived from participation, and it is to the detriment of the subject area as a whole that there is, as yet, only a very limited understanding of sports tourism participation.

Why, then, if the most featured topic in sports tourism research is that relating to behaviours and profiles, is understanding of sports tourism participation 'very limited'? The answer is provided by the meta-evaluation aspect of Weed's (2006b: p.14) analysis which examines 'the significance of research questions, the appropriateness of methodologies and methods in answering such questions, and the contribution that research makes to the body of knowledge in the area'. This meta-evaluation shows that much work on sports tourism participation is fairly basic and provides profiles of, rather than explanations for, sports tourists' behaviours. This is something that has been noted elsewhere, with Gibson (2004) being critical of the tendency for researchers to focus on the 'what' of behaviours (i.e. providing profiles and descriptions) rather than attempting to understand the 'why'. Weed's (2006b) meta-evaluation links this failing to the pervasive use of positivist quantitative approaches on the basis of convention rather than methodological appropriateness and calls for greater methodological diversity in the study of sports tourism, a call that was reiterated by Higham and Hinch (2006). This issue is particularly problematic in relation to sports tourism behaviours, where the application of positivist quantitative methods to profile and describe sports tourism behaviour has left the field with only limited understanding of 'why sport tourists do what they do' (Gibson, 2004). Downward (2005) reinforces the view that a more detailed explanation of participation is important in understanding the impacts derived from such participation and in informing policy and provision decisions. In this respect, Downward (2005) notes that '…explanations require "ontic depth", that is moving beyond the level of events towards an understanding of the processes that produce them'.

One way to achieve the 'ontic depth' that Downward (2005) calls for is to seek to achieve a greater understanding of the nature of the sports tourism experience. This is one of the key aspirations of Chapters 3, 4 and 5 in this text and has also been at the heart of Hinch and Higham's discussions of authenticity (2001, 2004, 2005). In particular, the more recent of these works (Hinch and Higham, 2005) discusses in detail the search for authenticity in sports tourism experiences and has clear implications for understanding the sports tourism experience as *related to, but more than the sum of,* sport and tourism. Hinch and Higham (2005) discuss the nature of sports tourism attractions and, in particular, events as sports tourism attractions. In doing so, they invoke the work of Nauright (1996) to reinforce their view that sports events and the reactions they engender are the 'clearest manifestations of culture and collective identities in a given society'. Consequently, the sports tourist attending such an event is not only a sports spectator, but a consumer of local culture and, as such, the primacy of either the sport or tourism element (if, indeed, it is possible or desirable to separate such elements) cannot be established. Hinch and Higham's

(2005) view of authenticity is an experiential one rather than being related to any objective judgement of what is and what is not authentic. They believe that many sports tourists are engaged in a search for meaningful experiences and seek to enter an 'authentic state of being'. This appears to provide support for the contention in this text that sports tourism experiences should be conceptualized as arising from the unique interaction of activity, people and place rather than understanding being limited by the simple conflation of definitions of tourism and of sport (see discussions in Chapter 3). In fact, Hinch and Higham (2009, forthcoming) utilize the activity, people and place conceptualization to underpin their discussions of globalization, mobility and authenticity in sports tourism in their forthcoming text.

One of the positions of this text, outlined in more detail in Chapter 3, is that the desire for sports tourism experiences is likely to be one among a number of sometimes competing and sometimes complementary motivations to undertake a particular trip. This view appears to be reinforced by Gibson's (Yiannakis and Gibson, 1992; Gibson 1994, 1996; Gibson and Yiannakis, 2002; Gibson and Pennington-Gray, 2005) application of role theory to understanding sports tourism participation, something that has been a core part of her work for some years. One of the assumptions of role theory is that people enact different roles at different times in different situations. In her most recent discussion of the application of the concept to the case of golf tourism, Gibson and Pennington-Gray (2005) suggest that at one extreme there is a 'sport lover' or 'sports junkie' role that people enact for the duration of their trip and which tends to leave little room for any other tourism activities. For other people (in varying degrees), the sports tourist role is one among a number of tourist roles that might be enacted on any one trip. The implication of this, therefore, is that the widely pervasive view in the literature that sports tourism can be categorized by 'trip purpose' (e.g. Gammon and Robinson, 1997/2003; Standeven and De Knop, 1999; Sofield, 2003; Robinson and Gammon, 2004) may be flawed and that a more complex understanding of the way in which sports tourism behaviours interact with other forms of tourism behaviours during any one trip may be needed. This is a fundamental part of the discussions in Chapter 3, which underpin Chapters 4 and 5 and is reflected through the remainder of the book.

Petrick and Backman (2002a, 2002b, 2002c) have also examined golf tourism and their work provides further perspectives on the motivations and experiences of sports tourists. Like Gibson's sustained interest in role theory, Petrick and Backman have conducted a number of studies into golf tourists, focusing on the related issues of satisfaction (2002a), perceived value (2002b) and loyalty (2002c) and how these concepts can affect motivations and trip-taking. A problem identified by Petrick and Backman (2002a) in researching satisfaction is that it is very subjective and interpreted differently by each individual participant. As such, previous research has often focused on satisfaction as a result of a comparison between expectations and outcome (Williams, 1989). However, Petrick and Backman (2002a) note that experiences are more complex than this and, in many cases, what is desired from an activity is not apparent until the participant realizes that it is not there. Consequently, more recent research on satisfaction (e.g. Spreng et al., 1996) has compared outcomes with desires (some aspects of which participants may not be conscious of in advance). Given this approach to satisfaction, Petrick and Backman's (2002a, 2002c) findings are revealing in that it is less often the golfing aspect of the experience that determines satisfaction, as this aspect was almost always satisfactory, perhaps because it was a conscious part of pre-trip desires and expectations, but aspects of the resort experience. This would suggest that these golf tourists were looking for a form of 'luxury sports tourism' in which the attendant facilities and levels of service can be as important to the experience as the activity itself (see Chapter 8 for a more extensive discussion of the features of this product type). It also suggests, like Gibson and her colleagues' work (Gibson and Yiannakis, 2002; Gibson and Pennington-Gray, 2005), that these golf tourists were enacting multiple roles during their golf tourism trips. Furthermore, it reinforces the assumption of this text that research on behaviours provides knowledge that is fundamental to the development of effective and efficient sports tourism provision strategies, in this case for luxury sports tourism products.

A similar illustration of the fundamental nature of research seeking to understand participation behaviours is provided by various studies of recreation conflict among skiers and snowboarders (Vaske et al., 2000, 2004; Thapa and Graefe, 2003). The participation research in these studies is helpful in addressing resource utilization problems relating to the suitability of snowboarders and skiers sharing a resource designed specifically for skiing. Vaske et al. (2000) note that much of this conflict is at least magnified by the clash of 'styles' or 'identities' between the two sports tourism participant groups derived from the visual difference in clothes, language and on-slope behaviour. They also suggest that 'place attachment', which has been little considered in previous work on recreation conflict, may be a factor in creating perceived conflict. Like Hinch and Higham's (2001, 2004, 2005, 2009 forthcoming) work on authenticity, Thapa and Graefe's (2003) and Vaske et al.'s (2000, 2004) studies would seem to reinforce the conceptualization proposed in this text of the sports tourism experience as arising from the interaction of activity, people and place. In this example it appears that the two activities struggle to coexist because of the way in which the activities interact with the people who participate in them (who each have very different lifestyle approaches) and the place (both in terms of identity and attachment, and in terms of the way it is utilized for the activities). As such, Vaske et al.'s (2000) study into how experiences conflict provides some illuminating insights into the nature of the experiences themselves which can be used to inform the way in which such conflicts are managed.

Costa and Chalip's (2005) ethnographic study of sports tourism participation in and around a small rural community in Portugal provides a further contrasting example of how an in-depth understanding of the nature of sports tourism participation can lead to a clearer understanding of how impacts are generated and to a more efficient policy. Costa and Chalip (2005), in contrast to the pervasive use of quantitative methods in the field demonstrated by Weed (2006b), collect detailed ethnographic data on the nature of participation in paragliding by sports tourists in a small Portuguese village to show that the popular perception that paragliding has a positive impact on the village is flawed. Costa and Chalip (2005) argue that if the village wishes to generate positive impacts then specific leveraging strategies need to be developed by local policy-makers and providers. The focus on leveraging benefits, rather than simply expecting that they will come, is something that has been a theme in Chalip's work over a number of years (Chalip, 2004, 2006; O'Brien and Chalip, 2007) and will be discussed further later in this chapter. The need to develop strategies to leverage benefits emerges here because Costa and Chalip's (2005) work is an holistic piece of research that seeks to develop policy and provision through a knowledge of impacts derived from an understanding of the behaviours that generate such impacts. As such, it is a clear demonstration of the fundamental nature of knowledge about sports tourism participation to an understanding of impacts and to policy-making and provision.

The sports tourism activity researched by Costa and Chalip (2005) (paragliding) can be categorized within a group of sports tourism activities that Weed (2006b) labels outdoor and adventurous activities. Weed's (2006b) systematic review and meta-evaluation of the sports tourism research notes that research into outdoor and adventurous activities that fell within the parameters of sports tourism research used for the systematic review was dominated by research on behaviours. Furthermore, behavioural research in this area tended to be much more clearly grounded in theory than the rest of sports tourism research into behaviours. As such, it is useful to dip into some examples of research in this area in developing a context for the discussions of sports tourism behaviours in the remainder of the text (particularly Chapters 3, 4 and 5). While the substantive topic of this work is the behaviours of outdoor and adventure sports tourists, much of the comment on the nature of behaviour is of broader relevance to understanding sports tourism behaviours in general.

One of the key debates in relation to 'adventure' has been the way in which adventure (or the perception of adventure) has been commodified and packaged for sports tourists. Varley (2006) discusses such commodification and the way in which meaning is 'played with'. He suggests that most 'adventure tourism' products are actually 'adventure flavoured' and are likely to provide only a shallow experience. Varley's (2006) analysis might be viewed through the lens of Hinch and Higham's (2005) discussions of authenticity, particularly the search for an 'authentic state of being' in sports tourism experiences, and leads to the question of when and for whom the commodification of adventure might adversely affect the sports tourism experience. Two examples are perhaps useful in attempting to address this question.

Kane and Zink (2004) examine the tension between the idea of a package tour and the concept of adventure through ethnographic research on a 14-day white-water kayaking package. The research reveals that participants on this tour were seeking 'capital' within the kayaking world which was linked to a part of the tour ('Heli-kayaking') endorsed by a well known celebrity elite kayaker. Kane and Zink (2004) note that the gaining of this capital was enabled by the packaged nature of the tour, which guaranteed 'safe success', something that is highly regarded within the kayaking world due to the nature of the activity. Conversely, however, Kane and Zink (2004) recognize that the participants were also well aware that any 'capital' among non-kayaking peers would be in relation to the adventurous elements of the trip and the packaged nature of such adventure would not be important. For the participants themselves, who were identified as having 'serious leisure careers' (Stebbins, 1999, 2002) in white-water kayaking, the packaged aspect of the tour was not significant, it was the kayaking experience that contributed to identity formation.

Beedie's (2003a) discussion of the role of mountain guides in providing adventure tourism as 'adventure education' addresses similar issues to Kane and Zink (2004). Beedie (2003a) shows that novice adventure tourists are seen as needing clear guidance in the mountain setting and this is the initial role of the mountain guide. However, Beedie (2003a) notes that such tourists often wish to make the transition to greater independence and set a course towards 'becoming a mountaineer'. Somewhat paradoxically, to gain greater independence, the rules of engagement with the mountains (which might be seen as a constraint) become more important, with mountain guides trying to ensure that such rules are internalized. As such, mountain guides seek to encourage individuals to move from being dependent tourists to becoming independent mountaineers through the internalization of the 'rules' of mountaineering and mountain engagement. However, at the same time, the increasing 'touristification' of mountains and the mountaineering experience leads to many adventure tourists leaving the mountains with what Hamilton-Smith (1993) and Varley (2006) would label as a shallower experience.

Taken together, Beedie's (2003a) and Kane and Zink's (2004) work have interesting things to contribute in relation to debates about both the commodification of experiences and the longevity of the experience. In the first respect, commodification, which is often viewed pejoratively, allows certain groups of mountain adventure tourists (Beedie, 2003a) and the white-water kayakers (Kane and Zink, 2004) to gain access to experiences that they would not otherwise have been able to enjoy. In both cases, 'safe success' can be highlighted as significant in allowing individuals to have 'developmental' experiences. In the second respect, longevity of experience is provided either by the educational aspect that would not have been possible without the 'choreography' of the guides, or the kayaking capital gained that would not have been possible without the packaged nature of the tour. The implication, therefore, for research into sports tourism behaviours more generally is that commodification, rather than resulting in a substandard experience (as implied by those such as Hamilton-Smith, 1993, and Varley, 2006, who view commodification pejoratively), can be enabling in allowing access to experiences that can be part of longer-term sports tourism careers. This suggests that the type of provision strategies discussed in Chapter 9 that seek to provide initial opportunities for sports tourism participation within safe settings in the hope that more prolonged participation might result appear to have a basis within research on participation. Thus demonstrating, once again, the fundamental nature of research into sports tourism behaviours.

However, it is perhaps unfair to dismiss the questions that Varley (2006) raises and it might be useful to return to them once again within the context of the conceptualization of sports tourism experiences as arising from activity, people and place. Kane and Zink's (2004) work notes that the significance of the commodification of the experience varies according to both the people concerned and the people with whom the experience is shared. Similarly, it is likely that more remote locations, regardless of the packaging of the trip, contribute to the perception of adventure, particularly if individuals have not visited them before. Weber (2001) conceptualizes this as psychological and social adventure. Finally, for those for whom the activity is unusual (those that Beedie, 2003a, suggests require 'adventure education' by mountain guides), the perception of adventure will be greater than for those taking part in an activity in which they have participated many times before. As such, the variations in activity, people and place can perhaps account for the way in which 'adventure' is experienced differently by different participants and, in particular, for the variations in the conditions required by different participants to enter into an 'authentic state of being' (Hinch and Higham, 2005) through sports tourism.

The idea that different sports tourists experience activities differently is a key assumption of the attempts to model sports tourism participation in Chapter 5 of this text, and also underpins Sung's (2004) classification of adventure travellers that derives its approach from consumer behaviour research (e.g. Dimanche and Havitz, 1994; Swarbrooke and Horner, 1999). Sung's (2004) work might usefully be compared with Gibson and colleagues' (Gibson and Yiannakis, 2002; Gibson and Pennington-Gray, 2005) approach to role theory. Sung (2004) uses a different disciplinary language in relation to adventure sports tourists to that which Gibson and Pennington-Gray (2005) use in relation to golf tourists, but she identifies six adventure traveller subgroups: general enthusiast, budget youngsters, soft moderates, upper high naturalists, family vacationers, and active soloists. Sung's (2004) subgroups might perhaps be described as adventure sports tourists roles based, as they are, on a profile of activity-related behaviours, and serve to highlight, once again, the variations in behaviours and motivations across participants (*people*) in similar *activities*, in different *places*.

A final note on research on sports tourism experiences is useful to illustrate the varied nature of sports tourism participation as active, vicarious or passive. This can be highlighted through a consideration of Fairley's (2003) work on 'nostalgia' as a key part of the sports tourist experience of fans or supporters. Research in sports tourism has often classified travelling sports fans as 'passive' sports tourists while Gibson (1998) has suggested that as well as active and passive sports tourism, there is a third form: nostalgia sports tourism. Gammon has discussed the nature of nostalgia in collaboration with Fairley (Fairley and Gammon, 2005), but has subsequently suggested that the concept of 'heritage' is a more appropriate way to understand nostalgia (Ramshaw and Gammon, 2005). More recently (Weed, 2005c) has argued that nostalgia sports tourism is a form of vicarious participation. Vicarious participation implies a more active engagement with the event than the traditional view of fans as 'passive' sports tourists. Regardless of which of these schema are used, it seems somewhat incongruous to view the fanatical engagement of many sports supporters as a 'passive' activity.

Fairley's (2003) work is interesting because it focuses not only on the attendance of fans at the event, but also their trip to the event. As such, in addition to the destination experience, there is a place experience of the bus journey itself, where past, present and future interact in an experience drawn from reliving the past (previous trips), enjoying the present (current trip), and anticipating the future (what will happen on the rest of the trip). This interaction is rooted in the past, which frames the participants' engagement with the present and future. Fairley's (2003) study is unique in focusing on the broader experience, rather than simply on the attendance at the event. This reinforces the call in this text to consider sports tourism as a trip behaviour that interacts with, complements and, in some cases, competes with other trip behaviours, rather than attempting to label an entire trip as either being or not being sports tourism (see Chapter 3). Furthermore, this could have important implications for understanding the behaviours of spectator sports tourists. Weed (2001c, 2002b), for example, has hinted that this could be a useful way of understanding football hooligan behaviour However, it certainly provides a clearer insight into the nature of the experience than the more pervasive narrow focus on the event itself.

It is intended that the discussions in this section give an insight into the sports tourism experience in a range of different settings. However, many of the issues are relevant beyond the immediate setting in which they have been researched. Role theory, for example, is generically relevant to understanding sports tourism experiences, while issues of identity, serious leisure and 'capital' can inform our understanding of experiences in a range of settings (see Green and Jones, 2005). It may seem somewhat strange that experiences in the event sports tourism setting have only been briefly addressed, as these are obviously significant sports tourism behaviours and products. However, much of the discussion in the following section focuses on event sports tourism and contains much that is relevant to understanding the fandom or spectating experience.

CONSIDERING THE IMPACTS OF SPORTS TOURISM

While an extended consideration of the impacts of sports tourism is deliberately absent from this text (see, for example, texts by Standeven and De Knop, 1999; Ritchie and Adair, 2004; Higham, 2005, and the original Chapter 2 in the first edition of this text for detailed coverage of impacts material), some discussion in this contextual chapter is required on current thinking and issues in relation to impacts research. In demonstrating the fundamental nature of an understanding of sports tourism behaviours in understanding impacts, a consideration of such impacts has been an implicit part of the discussions in the previous section – see, for example, the discussions of the work of Costa and Chalip (2005), O'Brien and Chalip (2007), Thapa and Graefe (2003) and Vaske et al. (2000, 2004).

However, not all research into the impacts of sports tourism is clearly grounded in an understanding of behaviours. With some notable exceptions, much previous research on the impacts of sports tourism has been a relatively simplistic 'end result' assessment, rather than an assessment of the processes that generate such impacts and this has been a particular feature of research into event impacts.

Event impact assessment has almost become an industry in its own right, with public sector research departments, consultants and academics all producing reports of the actual or potential impacts of events. While the findings of these reports are interesting for the hosts or sponsors of the event in question, they add little to our theoretical knowledge or understanding of the area. Nevertheless, many such reports have been published in academic journals with little consideration by the authors of how they contribute to the development of knowledge in the field as a whole (Weed, 2006b). Some authors would argue that the contribution such studies make is to understanding the nature and extent of the economic impacts of event sports tourism by building a larger volume of evidence. However, as a number of authors (Hudson, 2001; Kasimati, 2003; Preuss, 2005) have demonstrated, this claim is undermined by variations in study methodology (and, in some cases, poor methodological practices), by the lack of post-event evaluations and by a failure to understand the nature of the behaviours that create such economic impacts.

Preuss (2005, 2007) outlines methodological considerations in understanding economic impacts and, together with other authors such as Crompton (2006), Kasimati (2003) and Hudson (2001), has contributed to a small but growing body of literature that has been concerned to ensure that economic impact assessments are methodologically robust and theoretically meaningful. Taken together, this corpus of literature provides a very useful set of considerations and caveats for anyone reading reports of the economic impacts of event sports tourism.

Preuss (2005) discusses the economic impact of 'event-affected' people at major sports events. This includes not only visitors, but also residents whose spending and/or travel patterns might be affected. Furthermore, Pruess' (2005) analysis was adopted and adapted by Weed (2008a) to underpin his behavioural model of Olympic tourism flows. This model, which illustrates a range of movements of people in and out of event host cities, has not only a geographic dimension (i.e. movement in and out of a host city/region), but also a temporal dimension (i.e. switching of plans to coincide with or avoid the event). Preuss' (2005) analysis, therefore, demonstrates the need to understand the movements of a range of categories of 'event-affected' people if accurate economic impact assessments are to be made.

Like Weed (2008a), Kasimati (2003) focuses on the biggest of sports events, the Olympic Games, although her analysis is limited to the Summer Games. Kasimati (2003) compares thirteen studies of the actual or potential impacts of the Olympic Games since 1984 and shows that these studies vary in using different models which employ a range of different assumptions, a point which has been reiterated by a number of other authors (e.g. Hudson, 2001; Crompton, 2006; Pruess, 2007). Furthermore, all are *ex-ante* studies that seek to forecast economic impacts and the majority 'were commissioned by proponents of the Olympic process...potentially motivated to come up with a favourable result'. Kasimati (2003) concludes that, while the studies may be potentially motivated to show a positive outcome, if the assumptions and methods are transparent, then they are reliable (in that they measure what the assumptions indicate they measure). Crompton (2006) is less charitable, claiming that such studies are nothing more than 'instruments for political shenanigans'. This is because, although such studies may be (in Kasimati's terms) reliable, they are not comparable and the assumptions used are almost inevitably those that cast the impacts of the Games in the best light.

The question of the effect of research assumptions on the outcome of impact assessments is one that can be addressed and highlighted by meta-analysis, an approach that has long been used in the health sector to investigate the factors that might account for the differences in findings across different studies. In a study that has many implications for the conduct of impact assessments of event sports tourism, Hudson (2001) used meta-analysis to examine the variation in the economic impacts assigned to a range of US professional sports teams. Hudson (2001) identifies seven 'moderators' – factors that might explain differences between what should be very similar accounts of economic impact. Somewhat worryingly, however, only three of these moderators were substantive sources of difference (different sports, geographical difference, standard of stadiums), whereas the inconsistent application of multipliers, failure to differentiate between additional and displaced spending, failure to allow for time-switchers and inconsistent consideration of geographical boundaries are identified as moderators resulting from, at best, methodological variance and, at worst, poor methodological practice. Hudson's (2001) empirical exposure of these shortcomings further reinforces the comments of Crompton (2006), Kasimati (2003) and

Preuss (2005) and should be a reminder to all that the results of economic impact assessments can often not be taken at face value.

Of course, not all impacts are economic. Green et al. (2003), for example, examine the most effective way in which cities can benefit from media coverage of the events which they host. Through an analysis of the televized event coverage of the NCAA Women's Final Four Basketball Tournament, Green et al. (2003) show that city mentions or imagery are relatively rare, something that is reinforced by Chalip (2004) in his work on leveraging. However, Green et al. (2003) also note that iconographic images that have a clear association with the host city can be very effective in promoting that city, whereas coverage of cityscapes rarely carry with them any place identity and thus have limited city marketing utility. The conclusion is that if events are to be effective place marketing tools, then hosts must take steps to ensure that iconographic images with distinctive associations are incorporated into event-related materials such as event logos.

While Green et al.'s (2003) paper is clearly related to the impacts of sports events, the impacts discussed do not fall within the traditional framework of economic, social, cultural and environmental impacts. In certain situations, the effective marketing of cities may impact on all of these areas (positively or negatively) and may impact upon residents as well as visitors. As such, there may be a suggestion here that a framework that considers impacts may be a little outmoded and, as a number of authors (e.g. Green, 2001; Chalip, 2006; O'Brien and Chalip, 2007; Weed, 2008a) have argued, a more fruitful approach may be one that focuses on *leveraging* rather than impacts:

> *Unlike impact assessments, the study of leverage has a* strategic and tactical focus. *The objective is to identify strategies and tactics that can be implemented prior to and during an event in order to generate particular outcomes. Consequently, leveraging implies a much more* pro-active approach *to capitalising on opportunities, rather than impacts research which simply measures outcomes (Chalip, 2004).*

Weed (2008a) suggests that such a leveraging approach is essential in seeking to develop strategy for Olympic tourism. He adapts Chalip's (2004) general model of event leveraging to the Olympic Games and examines the potential development of strategies to leverage Olympic tourism in both the years before and after the Games, as well as in the Games period itself. Significantly, Weed (2008a) suggests that leveraging can be as important in minimizing undesirable effects as it can be in maximizing benefits.

Chalip's (2006) more recent discussions of leverage have focused on leveraging social elements. Similarly, Green (2001) focuses on social leverage in examining the relationship between event consumers (be they participants or spectators) and the subculture or identity formation connected with the event. Green (2001) discusses the role of subculture in transmitting consumption values and highlights the ways in which this can be capitalized upon (leveraged) to promote events. Focusing as it does on the way in which behaviours can be leveraged to provide positive outcomes, this paper further demonstrates the fundamental link between behavioural and impacts research. Furthermore, the leveraging of behaviours in this way is perhaps analogous with the 'packaging' or commodification of adventure discussed by Beedie (2003a), Kane and Zink (2004) and Varley (2006) and highlights the way in which the perspective of the stakeholders concerned can affect whether an approach is viewed positively (e.g. providers trying to maximize profit) or negatively (e.g. participants disappointed with a lack of authenticity).

However, the social impacts of sports tourism are clearly mostly felt by local communities, something which Fredline (2005) reviews in some detail. In particular, Fredline (2005) discusses the differences between extrinsic models, which tend to regard host communities homogeneously and focus on changes in attitudes over time, and intrinsic models, which examine the reasons for differing attitudes to sports tourism development within host communities. Following the presentation of four case studies of sports events, Fredline (2005) calls for a focus on developing holistic models that can provide an overall assessment of sports tourism development which will then contribute to decisions about the most appropriate forms of sports tourism development for particular destinations. This reinforces Weed's (2008a) point regarding the need for leveraging approaches to focus not only on maximizing benefits, but also on minimizing negativities. In this way, Chalip's (2006) suggestions for the social leveraging of events can be deployed to benefit the largest majority of people, but also to ensure that even a minority of people are not negatively affected.

As this section draws to a close, it is worth noting that not all the impacts of event sports tourism derive from large-scale events. Higham and Hinch (2002) suggest that the development of a strategy focusing on small-scale events can maximize positive and minimize negative impacts, while Wilson (2006) demonstrates that even very small-scale locally focused swimming events have the potential to generate meaningful economic benefits, with more than £80000 being generated over 8 days of competitions. However, Wilson (2006: p.57) notes that such expenditure levels are only stimulated if 'opportunities for secondary expenditure are provided' or, in other words, if the events are effectively leveraged for economic benefit.

An example of the impact of small-scale events from the USA (Gibson et al., 2003) examines the potential of college fixtures to generate benefits for local communities. Like Costa and Chalip's (2005) study of hang-gliding in a Portuguese village, Gibson et al. (2003) use a detailed examination of sports tourism behaviours to understand the nature of impacts. What is particularly interesting about Gibson et al.'s (2003) study is that the spectating sports tourists are supporters of the home team but have travelled an average of 142 miles to see the game. Furthermore, the 'tailgating' element of the event is seen as a key part of the experience, thus reinforcing the need to broaden the research focus beyond a simple study of attendance at the event, as also suggested by Fairley (2003). In terms of impacts, the fact that the sports tourism experience is more complex than simply attending the event may mean that more significant benefits are forthcoming for the local community, particularly as the fans, as supporters of the home team, often feel a place affinity with the local area.

While the discussions in this section have focused on impacts, it should be apparent that they provide a clear link between previous discussions on sports tourism behaviours and the following section on managing sports tourism. Specifically, that the assessments of impacts discussed in this section derive from understandings of behaviour (or advocate doing so) and they each have implications for policy and management. It should therefore be a relatively straightforward step for managers and policy-makers to utilize this knowledge in informing their policy and management decisions. However, as the discussions in the next section show, this has not always been the case.

MANAGING SPORTS TOURISM

It has been noted for some time in policy and management research in sport and tourism (see the early part of this chapter) that policy-makers and managers in the public sector for sport and for tourism are often reluctant to collaborate on sports tourism policy and management. However, the lack of collaboration in the public sector belies the established link between sport and tourism to which the discussions in this chapter, in the remainder of this text, and in many other publications attest. Whether such a link is seen as positive or negative in any given situation is immaterial, as the fact that the link exists means that there is a requirement for collaboration between sport and tourism bodies either to maximize benefits or to minimize negative impacts. As such, studies of the management of sports tourism have been concerned not only with the ways in which the links between and impacts of sports tourism should be managed, but also with the reluctance of policy-making agencies in the sport and the tourism sectors to collaborate in managing and providing for sports tourism. It is for this reason that the discussions in Chapters 6 and 7 of this text focus on understanding the dynamics of the lack of collaboration in policy-making for sport and tourism and the prospects for future policy integration. Such integration would greatly assist both policy-makers and managers in overcoming a range of issues in sports tourism policy and provision, such as seasonality and participation constraints and the ways in which sports tourism can be managed and policy developed to encourage positive outcomes for local communities.

It is perhaps useful to begin the discussion of managing sports tourism with Downward's (2005) comment on the nature of management research in sports tourism:

> *... one must view the application of management and the achievement or pursuit of policy objectives in the context of their being connected with, and deriving from, various specific institutional formations. These exist in a number of domains, such as the public or private sector. However, it remains that they are structured entities comprising internally related positions and governed in various degrees by rules, norms and trust in which obligations to act persist.*

Downward's (2005) view establishes policy and management as being formed within an institutional context (e.g. National Tourism Organization or National Olympic Committee), where there are established positions which govern potential responses (e.g. a commitment to sport for all or to social tourism) and individual behaviours (e.g. to act autonomously or within specific guidelines or less specific expectations), and from which some obligation to manage or develop policy exists. However, in relation to this latter point, the obligations are usually to make policy for, or to manage, sport or tourism respectively; rarely is there an obligation to respond to sports tourism issues and this is the point that is addressed in Chapters 6 and 7 in this text.

The consideration of policy is perhaps best considered in relation to what, following Weed (1999b), is referred to in this text as *the sport–tourism link*. This terminology, including the hyphen, is used as a deliberate strategy to refer to the range of issues that might legitimately be the concern of any policy collaboration between sport and tourism bodies. Such issues might include liaison on resources and funding, policy and planning, and information and research, many of which would not be perceived to be sports tourism. For example, tourism organizations might be interested in linking with a sports body to use a sports stadium for a tourist event such as a rock concert. This clearly does not involve sports tourism, but it does involve a sport–tourism link.

Weed (2001d, 2003c, 2005a) has shown over a number of years that the structure of policy communities for sport and for tourism, and the traditionally and historically separate development of the two sectors in many policy systems around the world has led to a separatist approach to policy (Weed, 2005a). Furthermore, despite the wide range of evidence establishing a clear link between sport and tourism, many policy-makers are still not fully aware of the extent of the sport–tourism link, or believe it is not relevant to their work, their organization or their job portfolio. In this respect, in addition to the need to educate further policy-makers about the link, Weed (2008b) has suggested that sport–tourism policy liaison is likely to be more sustainable at the regional level where specific aspects of the link relevant to historic, geographic, administrative, economic and structural regional contexts can be reflected in sport–tourism policy development. These and related issues are considered in detail in Chapters 6 and 7.

A more local perspective is provided by Houtbois and Durand's (2004) case study of equestrian activities in the Basse-Normandie region of France, which illustrates the ways in which the local public sector might encourage inward investment to reach a critical mass of concentrated provision activity. Like Weed (2001d, 2003c, 2005a), Houtbois and Durand (2004) found a lack of leadership and coordination in the public sectors, which they suggest is a *centrifugal* force likely to drive investment away. Acting alongside this was a lack of organizational skill among those working in some areas of the equestrian industry that led to the local public sector being more likely to fund activities that were already well organized, thus acting against the strategic development of new markets. Houtbois and Durand (2004), therefore, substantiate Weed's (2001d, 2003c, 2005a) findings that public sector policy-makers and managers in sport and in tourism experience a wide range of problems in forming partnerships to develop collaborative policy for sports tourism initiatives.

In moving from an exploration of the issues that mitigate against collaboration between sport and tourism bodies to a consideration of some of the issues that such bodies face in managing and making policy for sports tourism, Higham and Hinch (2002) explore the nature of seasonality in sport and in tourism and its implications for sports tourism development. Tourism has long faced problems of seasonality and Higham and Hinch (2002) distinguish natural factors (e.g. the weather) from institutional factors (e.g. timing of school holidays) in causing such seasonality. In sport, globalizing forces, professionalization and increased media and commercial interests are all cited as factors contributing to the changing of traditional seasons in sport and, in some cases, de-seasonalization. Through a case study of the development of Rugby Union in New Zealand, Higham and Hinch (2002) show how changing seasons in sport can help alleviate some of the problems of seasonality in tourism and in the process contribute to the development of a sports tourism product.

One of the longest established sports tourism sectors is the ski industry, which serves to provide examples to illustrate the analysis of both participation and provision throughout this text. However, given the wide range of provision for skiing sports tourism, the development and management of competitive advantage is an important issue for ski resort providers (Hudson et al., 2004). Crouch and Ritchie (1999) have developed a model of destination competitiveness which Hudson et al. (2004) apply to the Canadian ski industry. The industry in Canada is seen as having reached a stage of maturity and consolidation and, as such, establishing competitive advantage is particularly important. Strategic policy, planning and development are obviously vital in this stage of industry development and Hudson et al. (2004) found that three resorts that owned a single company with a reputation for extensive strategic planning scored most highly on the dimensions of competitiveness identified in the model. These dimensions – supporting factors and resources, core resources and attractions, destination management, destination policy planning and development, qualifying and amplifying determinants – are shown by this study to be a potentially useful benchmark, not only for winter sports destinations, but for sports tourism and, indeed, tourism destinations in general.

A further key issue for managers in the Canadian ski industry, as it is for skiing and sports tourism managers around the world, is to address the constraints that potential sports tourism participants face (Williams and Fidgeon, 2000). Once again, this issue demonstrates the inextricable link between understanding participation and developing policy and management initiatives. Somewhat unusually, Williams and Fidgeon's (2000) research focuses on non-participants and the factors that put off those who have never tried skiing from taking part. They suggest that non-skiers are either unaware of the benefits of the sport or, more significantly for managers and marketers, have emotional or perceptual biases that inhibit their desire to take part. While a number of strategies are suggested for managers and marketers to help overcome these inhibitions, Williams and Fidgeon (2000) strongly advocate further research that develops a more detailed understanding of the potential non-skier market and the factors that would encourage participation. The conceptualization of an 'intenders' group of potential sports tourism participants in the Revised Model of Spots Tourism Participation presented in Chapter 5 provides a framework for such research, not just in relation to skiing, but for sports tourism participation as a whole.

In concluding the discussions on managing sports tourism, it is useful to return to the concept of leveraging, as it is sports tourism managers who are often faced with having to leverage sports tourism for their own and their local community's benefit. Chalip and Leyns (2002) carried out four linked studies that examined the way in which local businesses in the Gold Coast attempted to leverage benefits from the Gold Coast Honda Indy motor race. They suggest that few businesses recognized the leveraging opportunities that the event presented and that those that did used fairly standard promotional and theming tactics. This lack of awareness is analogous to that which Weed (2006a) found existed among policy-makers and is replicated in relation to a range of sports tourism products in a range of locations across the world (Chalip, 2004; O'Brien and Chalip, 2007; Weed, 2008a). Although the business leaders on the Gold Coast favoured some coordination of leveraging efforts, they indicated that they would prefer such coordination to come from an existing business association rather than through government, thus suggesting a general suspicion between commercial providers and the public sector. Consequently, even in fairly recent times, leveraging approaches have largely been unrecognized and, as a result, are often underutilized. Bull and Lovell's (2007) study of local responses to the hosting of a stage of the Tour de France in Canterbury in the UK, for example, suggested that many businesses only realized how they could have capitalized on the event in its aftermath. However, the need to leverage sports tourism, for both economic (Chalip, 2004) and social (Chalip, 2006) benefit at both the organizational (Wilson, 2006) and policy level (Weed, 2008a) is likely to become a much more commonplace consideration for the management of sports tourism in both the public and commercial sectors in the coming years.

A VERY BRIEF META-REVIEW OF PERSPECTIVES ON CONTEMPORARY SPORTS TOURISM

In discussing the way in which research in sports tourism has developed, Weed (2005c) drew on an analogy used by Bernard Forscher in 1963 to highlight what he saw as a significant problem in the construction of social science knowledge. Forscher was concerned that too many studies ('bricks') were being randomly produced, thus contributing to haphazard piles of research that did little to build coherent bodies of knowledge ('edifices'). This analogy has been used by a number of authors (e.g. Weed, 2005b; Biddle,

2006) to discuss the nature and potential of research synthesis approaches in various disciplines in sport. Having examined sports tourism behaviours, impacts and management so far in this chapter, it is perhaps useful to conclude this chapter with a discussion of the ways in which authors that have attempted to synthesize or review research in sports tourism in recent years have viewed sports tourism development. In particular, this is done to investigate what perspectives other authors have on contemporary sports tourism, based on the body of knowledge available, and how these perspectives might reinforce or differ from the analysis developed throughout the rest of this text.

The tool for this analysis is a meta-review (or a review of reviews) which, in this case, is largely cursory and is included to ensure that the full range of perspectives on contemporary sports tourism are presented, rather than simply those that support the analysis developed in the remainder of this text. The six reviews (Gibson, 2001; Hinch and Higham, 2001; Weber, 2001; Weed, 2005c, 2006b; Higham and Hinch, 2006) represent the work of four different authors (or author teams) and stretch from 2001 to 2006. Collectively, they demonstrate how research in sports tourism has developed and progressed in recent years, while individually, the papers each present a different perspective on contemporary sports tourism development.

The early part of this chapter referred to a number of reviews conducted prior to 2000, with two in particular (Gibson, 1998; Weed, 1999b) providing a useful benchmark of the state of the field just prior to 2000. Also worthy of mention is an international review of the literature on sport and tourism commissioned by the Great Britain Sports Council in 1992. This review, conducted by Guy Jackson and Sue Glyptis, considered material largely related to impacts: the impact of sport in developing tourism, of tourism in developing sport and the positive and negative economic and non-economic impacts of sports tourism. Jackson and Glyptis' (1992) review was constrained by the limited number of works at that time that focused explicitly on sports tourism and therefore: 'much of importance had to be extracted from more general studies, and those dealing with the sport or tourism sectors separately' (p.14). Fortunately, this is no longer the case, although there continue to be many useful contemporary works that are *relevant* to the study of sports tourism, rather than being specifically about sports tourism.

A note on the Jackson and Glyptis (1992) report is useful here, because a comparison between this report and the papers included in this very brief meta-review highlights the way in which the field has developed. First, Weed's (2006b) systematic review of the field in the five years from 2000 returned 80 articles in refereed journals that focus on sports tourism, and this does not include the numerous books, book chapters and conference papers that were published in this period. As such, the volume of published work on sports tourism has increased since the Jackson and Glyptis (1992) review but, more importantly, the volume of work meeting the quality standards of peer-reviewed journals has increased. Secondly, the nature of the work included in Weed's (2006b) systematic review indicates a broadening of the field beyond the study of impacts, although impacts research still comprises a significant corpus of the work.

The first review considered is from 2005, in which Weed was concerned to highlight some of the problems that the study of sports tourism faced and which future research should take steps to address. In particular, Weed (2005c) outlined his preference for a 'conceptualization' of the area of sports tourism (rather than a definition) and explains how the first edition of this text developed the conceptualization of the field as being derived from 'the unique interaction of activity, people and place' (Weed and Bull, 2004: p. 7). This conceptualization has already been referred to in this chapter and the prologue and is explained in much more detail in Chapter 3. Weed (2005c) also explained how this conceptualization leads to his preference, adopted by this text, for the term 'sports tourism', rather than the more commonly used 'sport tourism', to refer to the area. Also included in Weed's (2005c) review are discussions about the need for a greater focus on explanations rather than descriptions in research in sport and tourism and for a more explicit and careful consideration of the application of the research methods from which knowledge about sport and tourism is derived.

Gibson's (1998) 'critical analysis of research' in sport and tourism has already been highlighted as a useful benchmark of the state of the field just prior to 2000. Gibson's (2001) review is an update of her earlier 'critical analysis' and provides the earliest overview of the field included in this meta-review. In this review, in contrast to Weed's (2005c) arguments noted above, Gibson presents the case for the use of the term 'sport tourism' and suggests a definition which subdivides the area into 'three distinct behavioural sets':

> *Leisure-based travel that takes individuals temporarily outside of their home communities to participate in physical activities, to watch physical activities, or to venerate attractions associated with physical activities (Gibson, 1998: p. 49).*

Gibson addressed the way in which the link between sport and tourism is considered by policy-makers, by researchers and by those responsible for curriculum development. Her conclusions, in 2001, were that the clearest need was to bring together the bodies of knowledge relating to sport and to tourism in order to develop a body of knowledge relating to sport and tourism that is conceptually grounded, thus sowing the seeds of critiques of the field that both Gibson and others have presented in more recent years (Gibson, 2004; Weed, 2005c, 2006b; Higham and Hinch, 2006).

One of the papers cited by Gibson in her 2001 review was another review published in the same year (Hinch and Higham, 2001). Gibson suggested that the framework presented by Hinch and Higham (2001) 'proffers a promising avenue for future research'. In fact, this was also highlighted by Weed (2005c):

> *There have been a number of publications that have sought to define and classify the area, but it is only really the framework presented by Hinch and Higham (2001) and my own analysis with Chris Bull (Weed and Bull, 2004) that have offered any conceptualization of the area…. [I]n the absence of any other contributions to this fundamental aspect of debate within sports tourism, these two propositions are clear points of reference for future research in the field.*

Hinch and Higham (2001) derive their framework for research in sport and tourism from the activity, spatial and temporal dimensions of the area. Sport is positioned as the activity dimension, while the temporal and spatial dimensions are derived from tourism. Nine illustrative rather than exhaustive themes are described which combine via the three dimensions to suggest 27 potential areas of investigation within sports tourism, thus providing a clear manifesto for future work.

A further review published in 2001 stands out against the others in this meta-review because it focuses on outdoor adventure tourism (Weber, 2001). However, as discussions earlier in this chapter have noted, adventure features significantly in some sports tourism experiences and analyses from the related and overlapping field of adventure (sports) tourism often have a wider application to sports tourism as a whole. Weber (2001) argues for a greater focus on adventure experiences in the study of outdoor adventure tourism. She suggests that adventure tourism has traditionally been seen as an extension of adventure recreation and, consequently, the tourism element has been overlooked. As such, there are clear corollaries here with the study of sport and tourism which has also struggled, as Gibson (2001) notes, genuinely to bring two bodies of knowledge together. In analyses of adventure tourism, Weber (2001) suggests that risk has been too narrowly conceived as physical risk, whereas psychological and social risk can be equally important in the adventure experience. In fact, she believes that adventure tourism can be conceptualized as being as much about the quest for insight and knowledge as the desire for elements of physical risk and, as such, contrasts somewhat with the perspectives of Hamilton-Smith (1993) and Varley (2006) discussed earlier in this chapter. Picking up on a further issue briefly mentioned previously, Weber (2001) also advocates a greater focus on interpretive qualitative methodologies in understanding adventure experiences (see, also, below).

In 2006, Higham and Hinch presented, five years on from their earlier review (Hinch and Higham, 2001), a further potential programme for research that advocates developing further their geographical perspectives on sports tourism that, at least in part, underpinned their earlier review. This more recent review responds to the call for a greater focus on building 'edifices of knowledge' in Weed's (2005c) review and appears to be indicative of some convergence of approaches to the future development of the field. Higham and Hinch (2006) use the concepts of space, place and environment as the theoretical foundations for their review, which attempts to suggest research questions that can contribute to the development of a body of knowledge for sports tourism. Hinch and Higham (2006) note that a geographic approach is but one of a number that might be applied to the study of sport and tourism and invite scholars from other disciplines, such as sociology and anthropology, also to contribute to discussions surrounding the development of the field.

The final review in this brief meta-review is Weed's (2006b) systematic review of peer-reviewed research. Unlike the other reviews, the research presented in this systematic review was selected for inclusion, not on the basis of personal judgement, but on clear and replicable criteria outlined in the review itself. Weed (2006b) identifies trends in the substantive issues addressed by contemporary research in sports tourism, but also highlights some limitations of the methods and epistemologies employed. Such limitations were also picked up by Higham and Hinch (2006) as they responded to Weed's (2005c) earlier comments relating to the predominance of empirical research employing quantitative research designs. In fact, Weed (2006b) shows that over 70 per cent of primary peer-reviewed research in the five years between 2000 and 2004 used a positivist research design. Both Higham and Hinch (2006) and Weed (2006b) agree that the problem here is not with positivist approaches *per se*, but with the dominance of such approaches and their use on the basis of convention rather than their appropriateness in answering research questions.

The reviews included in this brief meta-review give deliberately varying views – some of which are complementary, some of which are not – on the development of sports tourism concepts, issues and research in the past and present and potential avenues and approaches for the future. One such route for the future development of sports tourism is outlined in the remainder of this text, which seeks to provide useful and usable explanations for the behaviours, motivations and strategies of participants, policy-makers and providers in sports tourism, derived from previous and ongoing knowledge and research.

CONCLUSION

The complexities of sports tourism participation, impacts, management and research discussed in this chapter imply that sports tourism might best be considered as *related to, but more than the sum of,* sport and tourism rather than as a simple conflation of the two areas. As such, on one hand it is important to recognize the insights that can be drawn from the fields of sport and of tourism – for example, Stebbins' (1992, 2002) concept of serious leisure as discussed by Kane and Zink (2004) and Green and Jones (2005) or the issue of seasonality as discussed by Higham and Hinch (2002). However, on the other hand, it is important to recognize the specific sports tourism context and the nature of the sports tourism experience. Consequently, the view of this text, which has also been argued for by Weed (2005c) and Downward (2005), is that a conceptualization rather than a definition of sports tourism is most useful. Such a conceptualization (as already referred to at various points throughout this chapter) is of sports tourism as derived from the unique interaction of activity, people and place. This conceptualization, while drawing on the features of sport and of tourism, does not directly derive from definitions of sport and of tourism and, consequently, helps to establish sports tourism as a phenomenon in its own right with its own unique considerations and issues. Chapter 3, the first section in the following part of the book on participants, explores this conceptualization in more detail and its implication for the study of sports tourism behaviours.

An implication of the conceptualization of sports tourism as derived from the interaction of activity, people and place is that, because activities, people and places vary throughout any particular trip, sports tourism might be best understood as a trip behaviour rather than as a trip purpose. This allows for the interaction of a range of tourist and sports tourist roles during any particular trip (as suggested by Gibson and Yiannakis, 2002 and Gibson and Pennington-Gray, 2005) rather than defining a trip as being primarily about sport or primarily about tourism. Furthermore, it allows a trip to be understood in terms of the way in which a range of sports tourist behaviours (e.g. event attendance, active participation) take place alongside more general tourist behaviours (e.g. shopping, eating and drinking) and functional behaviours (e.g. ironing, cleaning) within trips that can rarely be conceptualized as having a single purpose. The impact that sports tourism behaviours, as some among a number of behaviours on a trip, have on the trip decision-making process is explored more thoroughly in Chapter 4.

PART 2

Participants

PREFACE

The purpose of the first part of this book was to provide a context against which to present a contemporary analysis of the sports tourism phenomenon. As such, it provided an overview of the development of sports tourism over time and of its nature at the start of the twenty-first century, as well as of contemporary issues, concepts and research. The remainder of the book now seeks to examine the motivations, behaviours and strategies of those who might be considered stakeholders in sports tourism, those who participate, those responsible for policy and those who make provision.

The specific focus of the three chapters in this part of the book is to examine and understand sports tourism behaviours, something that has been largely neglected in the sports tourism literature, which has tended to focus on impacts and supply-side considerations. The importance of identity and the sports tourism experience are examined, with particular emphasis on the nature of sports tourism as a social, economic and cultural phenomenon derived from the unique interaction of activity, people and place. The nature of this interaction, once developed in this part of the book, is a theme that will feature throughout the analysis of policy-makers and providers that follows in later chapters.

There have been considerable changes made to this part of the text since the first edition. Chapter 3, while still examining motivations for sports tourism participation, is now constructed to present a much more sophisticated analysis of the nature of the sports tourism experience and of the interaction of activity, people and place mentioned above. In particular, Chapter 3 argues that sports tourism should be analysed as a behaviour rather than a trip purpose and, as such, sports tourism behaviours should be thought of as some among a number of other tourism and functional behaviours on any one trip, rather than as the sole trip purpose.

Chapter 4 examines sports tourism behaviours further, examining in detail the ways in which opportunities to engage in such behaviours can influence the decision to take a trip and destination choice. In this respect, Chapter 4 shows that sports tourism participation opportunities can be a significant factor in trip decisions even though they may not necessarily be the most dominant activities during a trip. Chapter 4 also examines the role sports tourism can play in post-decision trip planning and also the potential for unplanned spontaneous sports tourism behaviours on a trip. This analysis replaces the descriptive overview of participation profiles that was presented at this stage in the first edition of the text.

As a result of the new thinking presented in Chapters 3 and 4, Chapter 5 presents a Revised Sports Tourism Participation Model from that outlined in the first edition. This revised model has been both simplified to focus on sports tourism as a trip behaviour (as discussed in Chapter 3), and extended to reflect the role of sports tourism in the trip decision process (as discussed in Chapter 4). A discussion is also presented that suggests that the shape of the model may vary for different sports tourism products and this is illustrated across several examples. As in the first edition, the model is used to underpin an understanding of the behaviours and strategies of providers in later chapters.

CHAPTER 3

Conceptualizing the Sports Tourism Experience

In the prologue to this text, some preliminary comment was offered on the use of the term 'sports tourism'. While this provided some guidance as to the focus of the book, the problems of defining 'tourism' and 'sport' in themselves, let alone 'sports tourism', meant that such discussion could only provide the briefest of understanding and the intention was always to explore the concept of sports tourism in far greater detail at a later stage. In many ways, the book as a whole is designed to provide this fuller understanding and this chapter will develop this task by looking at what makes the sports tourist unique. It will begin by conceptualizing sports tourism and will then turn to examine aspects of that conceptualization and the behavioural patterns that differentiate sports tourists from other tourists.

The concept of sports tourism is clearly problematic due to it resulting from a fusion of two separate terms, both of which are complex in their own right. Both sport and tourism defy simple definition and there is much debate about what each encompasses. Not only do official definitions vary and change through time, but the meanings that people derive from such concepts also vary. Given this complexity, it is clear that an understanding of sport and tourism as separate spheres must be provided before any conceptualization of sports tourism can be achieved.

DEFINITIONS OF SPORT

Attempts to define sport have engaged the energies of many writers, both academics and those involved in sports administration. Given the difficulties of producing a precise and universally accepted definition, some have suggested that the pursuit of defining sport is fruitless as the concept defies definition (Slusher, 1967; Houlihan, 1994; Haywood et al., 1995; Horne et al., 1999). Nevertheless, an understanding of sports tourism requires some exploration of the meaning of sport. Part of the debate revolves round what activities should be classified as sport, linked to the idea that it may be defined on the basis of pursuits satisfying key characteristics such as vigorous physical activity and/or physical skill, competition and codified rules (Haywood et al., 1995; Standeven and De Knop, 1999). Yet, while a great many activities could clearly be identified as sport on this basis, there are many other physical activities that are not organized along formal competitive lines and which do not involve rules but which many would still regard as sport, such as swimming (or at least the form in which most participants are involved), rambling and jogging. There are also many other situations where activities that can be pursued in a highly organized fashion are 'played' informally and thus the issue of 'context' may be important (Haywood et al., 1995). Here, some would make a distinction between sport and physical recreation, whereas others would see both as sport.

Part of the definitional problem relates to sport's historical development. Many contemporary highly organized sports were at one time pursued in a very informal and unregulated manner and it was the values of modern industrial society and the Victorian public schools that created many of the forms we see today. Pre-industrial sport also involved animal sports where cruelty to animals was a central characteristic, something that today would be regarded as completely at odds with the ideals of sport. Furthermore, there is a long tradition of field sports which, although not so important today, were once regarded as key sporting pursuits. As Horne et al. (1999: p. xv) point out:

> *Hunting and shooting are now seen as rather marginal sporting activities, yet in the eighteenth century they would have been at the heart of the meaning of the term, indeed the very notion of the sporting man referred to the hunting man.*

The term sport has thus been socially constructed and has acquired different meanings at different times in its historical development as well as in different societies. Standeven and De Knop (1999) compare the different conceptions of sport across various continents, comparing the much narrower definitions of sport in North America, where it is defined very much in terms of institutionalized, competitive activity, to those in Europe which are generally looser. For example, the Council of Europe (1992) defined sport as:

> ... *all forms of physical activity which, through casual or organized participation, aims at improving physical fitness and mental well-being, forming social relationships, or obtaining results in competition at all levels (in Sports Council, 1994: p. 4).*

Such a definition is wide-ranging and inclusive rather than exclusive and embraces not only 'formal' activities (e.g. team games such as football), but also non-competitive recreational activities involving some form of active physical participation, such as walking and cycling in the countryside, which have considerable tourism potential. As such, and along with many other authors in the field (e.g. Standeven and Tomlinson, 1994; Horne et al., 1999; Houlihan, 2003), it is this wide-ranging, inclusive definition that will be used here in attempting to understand the nature of sports tourism.

The discussion so far has focused on the nature of sport, but a related notion, and one that is central to understanding the nature of the sports tourist, is a definition of the sports participant. Such a definition is generally accepted to involve those who actively take part in sport. However, a full examination of the nature of the sports participant must also include those who observe it. As outlined in Chapter 1, there is a long history of people watching live sport, and many sports, such as football and cricket, attract huge crowds. Such spectators make an important contribution to these sports and many are equally motivated in their commitment to sport as the active participant (see Weed, 2003b), with much participation perhaps more accurately being described as vicarious involvement than passive observation (see discussions in Chapter 8). Furthermore, their presence has also had an important influence on the nature and development of sport itself. Those sports with significant numbers of spectators have developed to accommodate them and this has involved both the way the sport is played and the environment in which this occurs. In addition, spectators have provided much of the wealth that has enabled sport to develop. As such, not to include spectators in any consideration of sports participation would seriously reduce the scope of the analysis and, given the significant number of spectating sports tourists, would greatly underplay the nature of sports tourism.

DEFINITIONS OF TOURISM

As with sport, there exists a variety of definitions of tourism. They all emphasize movement away from home and most also stipulate that such movement is for leisure purposes, although some still include business trips. While traditionally 'travel' has been ubiquitous as a necessary descriptor, Weed (2005c) has argued that it is actually the places through which or to which travel takes place that are tourism's defining characteristic. The extent to which these debates are resolved and to which other characteristics and constraints are included is, in part, linked to different emphases (even motives) behind such definitions. For example, some would view tourism as an economic activity or industry and, according to Ryan (1991: p. 5), this might suggest tourism being defined as:

> *a study of the demand for and supply of accommodation and supportive services for those staying away from home, and the resultant patterns of expenditure, income creation and employment.*

Similarly, Hay (1989) defines tourism as:

> *...a process concerned with the redistribution of economic resources, from a home community to a host community which involves a trip for leisure purposes.*

Others highlight the psychological benefits and define tourism in terms of motivations (see Smith, 1989) while tourist organizations often suggest technical definitions which lay down minimum and maximum lengths of stay and strict 'purpose of visit categories' in an attempt to isolate tourism from other forms of travel for statistical purposes (Cooper et al., 1998).

The major distinction between most definitions is whether or not day trips are included. Whereas most earlier definitions of tourism included the requirement of one or more nights away from home (e.g. World Tourism Organisation, 1963, 1991), more recently, there has been a willingness to extend the definition to include day trips as well. The problem with including day trips, of course, is that it introduces further definitional issues of what constitutes such a trip. Does it require a minimum length of time and minimum distance travelled away from home? Some definitions have attempted to include precise prescriptions in this respect. The Scottish Tourist Board, for example, sees a leisure day trip as one involving more than three hours and focusing upon a specific activity (quoted in Standeven and Tomlinson, 1994). But, essentially, such prescriptions are arbitrary. Nevertheless, despite such problems, a number of authorities have suggested a wider, more inclusive approach. The British Tourist Authority (1981: p. 3), for example, has defined tourism in rather broader terms as:

> *the temporary short-term movement of people to destinations outside the places where they normally live and work, and their*

activities during the stay at these destinations; it includes movement for all purposes as well as day visits and excursions.

This is similar to the working definition adopted by Standeven and Tomlinson (1994) who see tourism as ranging from day trips within one's own locality to long haul package holidays to the other side of the world but, most importantly, always involving a sense of movement or visit. Here it is argued that this 'sense of movement or visit' is engendered by the different places through which or to which travel takes place, that it is places that provide the perception of movement. This perceptual definition is, like the sports definition earlier, inclusive rather than exclusive, encompassing all activities and trips that the tourist considers to be tourism.

CONCEPTUALIZING SPORTS TOURISM

There have been a number of attempts to define or categorize sports tourism, with some definitions (e.g. Standeven and De Knop, 1999: p. 12) simply serving to combine established definitions of sport and of tourism into a definition that labels sports tourism as 'sport away from home':

> *All forms of active and passive involvement in sporting activity, participated in casually or in an organized way for non-commercial or business/commercial reasons, that necessitate travel away from home and work locality.*

Authors (e.g. Gammon and Robinson, 1997/2003; Standeven and De Knop, 1999; Sofield, 2003; Robinson and Gammon, 2004) have also attempted to categorize sports tourism and in doing so make a distinction between 'sports tourists' (for whom sport is the primary purpose of the trip) and 'tourism sportists' (sic) (for whom tourism is the primary purpose). However, a key drawback of this work is that it assumes a view of sports tourism in which tourism is defined in terms of sport, or in which sport is defined in terms of tourism and, as such, establishes a subordinate role for either tourism or for sport in understanding the area.

Sofield (2003: p. 144) notes that the study of sport and tourism in the late 1990s suffered to a certain extent from Kurtzman and Zauher's characterization in 1997 that there are often two separate areas of research, with many studies taking either a sports perspective or a touristic perspective as their starting point. Such studies located sport at the centre and tourism at the periphery, or vice versa. As such, research would focus on sport as a tourism activity or attraction, or on tourism/travel as an incidental activity that was necessary to engage with sport in locations away from the home environment. Sofield (2003: p. 144) therefore argued for a focus on a 'trialectic' of sport, tourism and sports tourism, invoking Lefebvre's view (1991: p. 43) that a trialectic:

> ... does not derive simply from an additive combination of its binary antecedents but rather from a disordering, deconstruction and tentative reconstruction of their presumed totalization, producing an open alternative that is both similar and strikingly different.

This view is similar to the basis for the conceptualization of sports tourism presented in this book. However, Sofield appears to retreat back to the binarism from which he argued that the study of sports tourism should escape by utilizing Gammon and Robinson's (1997/2003) framework that suggests the division of sports tourism into 'sports tourism' (in which sport is dominant) and 'tourism sport' (in which tourism is dominant), with a further classification of these categories into 'hard' and 'soft' definitions. Sofield argues that this classification is a:

> 'quadripartite construct ... built on two sets of binary divisions, that between sports tourism and tourism sport, and between hard and soft forms of both (2003: p. 145).

As such, while the phenomenon may be referred to as sports tourism, there is still an emphasis on either sport or tourism as the dominant element. This is something that Pigeassou et al. (1998/2003) explicitly argue for, claiming that there is a need to establish an 'epistemological rupture' (p. 30) that 'divides the phenomena and prevents any confusion between sport, tourism and sports tourism' and that this is only possible through such domination/subordination, without which 'sports tourism would not exist and the activities described or observed would be confused with tourism phenomena' (p. 30). However, as has been argued elsewhere (Weed, 2005c; Downward, 2005), sports tourism is a synergistic phenomenon that is more than the simple combination of sport and tourism. As such, it requires an understanding of both sport and tourism (hence the discussion of respective definitions above), but it needs to be conceptualized in a way that is not dependent on definitions of sport and of tourism and which allows its synergistic elements to be understood. This resonates with Lefebvre's (1991) view of a trialectic in which sports tourism would not be 'an additive combination of its binary antecedents' but through deconstruction and reconstruction would produce a third phenomenon that is 'both similar and strikingly different'. One way in which this can be done, as argued by Weed (2005c: p. 233), is to examine the features of both sport and tourism and establish an understanding of sports tourism derived from those features.

Sport can be seen as involving some form of activity (e.g. kayaking, cycling, etc.), be it formal or informal, competitive or recreational, or actively, vicariously or passively participated in. Furthermore, sport also involves other people, as competitors and/or co-participants. For vicarious and passive participants, the people element is likely to be both other vicarious or passive participants (i.e. other spectators) and the active participants (i.e. competitors). Similarly, active competitors and co-participants may experience other people as active and/or vicarious or passive participants. Even activities that are sometimes participated in alone (e.g. mountaineering, running) are likely to involve other people because participants may reference their participation in terms of the subculture of the activity and thus experience a feeling of 'communitas' (Turner, 1974). Similarly, tourism involves other people, either as fellow tourists and/or as hosts. Even solitary tourism entails passing through areas that have been constructed by other people or other communities and it is rare for a tourist to complete a trip without encountering other tourists. Tourism also involves visiting places outside of the tourist's usual environment. There is, of course, a travel element, but this is either an instrumental factor in arriving at an 'unusual' place, or the travel takes place in or through 'unusual' places. Considering the interaction of these features of sport and tourism, it is possible to arrive at a conceptualization of sports tourism as 'arising from the unique interaction of activity, people and place', where the focus is on the 'interaction' of activity, people and place, thus emphasizing the synergistic nature of the phenomenon and moving it away from a dependence on either sport or tourism as the primary defining factor. Thinking about sports tourism in this way establishes the phenomenon as *related to but more than the sum of* sport and tourism, in Lefebvre's (1991) terms 'both similar and strikingly different'. As such, sports tourism is established as something that cannot be understood as simply a tourism market niche or a subset of sports management.

Conceptualizing sports tourism in this way has implications for terminology and has led to the use of the term 'sports tourism' in this book. However, deriving from definitions of sports tourism that are dependent on definitions of sport and tourism, the term 'sport tourism' (rather than 'sports tourism') has achieved common currency. This is usually on the basis that 'sport' refers to the social institution of sport, while 'sports' refers to a collection of activities that have come to be defined as such. However, given the discussions above and the conceptualization of sports tourism as derived from the unique interaction of activity, people and place, a reliance on the social institution of sport to delimit the area of sports tourism is, as noted in the prologue to this book, somewhat contradictory. Furthermore, the concept of sport can in many cases be a misnomer in that it implies coherence where none exists and detracts from the heterogeneous nature of sporting activities. As the conceptualization outlined here assumes that one of the unique aspects of sports tourism is that the interaction of people and places with the activities in question expands rather than limits heterogeneity, the term 'sports tourism' is used, along with the focus on diverse and heterogeneous activities that this implies.

SPORTS TOURISM PLACES

The pursuit of sports tourism almost inevitably requires specific resources. Such resources may involve particular environments or specific facilities, but the essential point is that they are not ubiquitous, they are found at specific locations. Of course, some resources are more widespread than others. While there are a great many routeways along which people may run or cycle, facilities for activities such as skiing or rock climbing are less widespread. However, even where resources are more readily available, the quality may be variable, with high quality resources only to be found in a few locations. Football played and observed in the local park is a very different experience to that encountered at a premier league stadium; and cycling through the scenically attractive landscapes of a national park contrasts markedly with cycling along the busy streets of towns and cities. In each case, it is the location of the activity in an unusual place that contributes to the uniqueness of the sports tourism experience and it is the purpose of this section to examine the specific characteristics of these places by focusing on two particular perspectives. One concerns the physical characteristics and spatial patterns of sports tourism places and the second involves the way in which such places are perceived and culturally appraised.

Various writers have attempted to classify physical resources associated with recreation and leisure (Clawson et al., 1960; Chubb and Chubb, 1981; Smith, 1983), although there have been few attempts to classify sports tourism resources or even sports resources (Bale, 1989), *per se*. Nevertheless, much of the general literature relating to recreation is also relevant to sports tourism and thus this might be a useful starting point. Implicit in much of the discussion is the idea of some form of 'continuum ranging from biophysical resources to man-made facilities' (Kreutzwiser, 1989: p. 22), a concept with considerable relevance for sports tourism resources as it accommodates outdoor pursuits at one end of the spectrum with those facilities, often urban based, that have been specifically designed for more local participation at the other. One of the earliest, and most frequently cited, examples of such a classification is that suggested by Clawson et al. (1960) who distinguished between recreation and opportunity on the basis of location and other characteristics such as size, major use and degree of artificial development. Under this system, areas were arranged on a continuum of recreational opportunities from user-orientated through intermediate to resource-based. User-orientated areas were those located close to users with small space demands and often artificial features; they included such resources as urban parks, swimming pools, golf courses and playgrounds where the landscape elements are less important. Resource-based areas, at the other end of the continuum, involved an emphasis on the quality of the physical resource with large land units involved and remoteness being a basic ingredient. National parks, forests and wilderness areas catering for such activities as orienteering, canoeing, skiing and rock climbing were typical of this group. Intermediate areas were located between the two extremes, both spatially and in terms of activity. Accessibility was relatively important with most sites within one or two hours drive from potential users. Facilities for camping, picnicking, hiking, swimming, hunting and fishing were included in this category. This system and its subsequent application to England and Wales (Law, 1967) both 'confirm the importance of distance and the "zones of influence" of recreational resources according to whether they had a national, regional, subregional, intermediate or local zone' (Hall and Page, 2006).

While the Clawson system has been criticized for its somewhat confusing terminology in that it involves a rather narrow interpretation of the term resources and seemingly ignores the fact that all recreation areas must be user oriented to some extent (Pigram, 1983), it still has some contemporary relevance for it can be modified to cover sports tourism and it also begins to provide some insights into when an activity becomes sports tourism. Under this system, user-oriented places would not be included within sports tourism as they are specifically local, often being used after school or work, with no significant travel involved. Conversely, the other two areas would be involved in sports tourism as the resource-based areas are associated with vacations and the intermediate areas with day outings and weekend visits. As such, the change in place from that which is local and everyday, to that which is unusual creates the all important 'sense of movement'. Unfortunately, however, not all forms of sports tourism activity can be accommodated by such a scheme.

The essential problem with the Clawson model is that it does not accommodate certain quality issues and quality is part of the cultural perspective of sports tourism places (Bull, 2005). Such quality may be related, firstly, to appraisals of the utility of places for sports tourism or, secondly, to appraisals of the desirability of the environment. In the first instance, the question of the utility of places is likely to be brought about when the resources that people feel they need are not readily available in their immediate neighbourhood (Hinch and Higham, 2004). This may be because local resources do not offer the challenge that is presented by many natural or man-made resources (Haywood et al., 1995) offered in other places. It may also be because local resources can provide for only the most basic or recreational level of activity. Local parks, for example, would provide open space for various types of recreational sport – 'jumpers for goalposts' being the epitome of this level of resource provision. However, where there is either a need or a desire for a more competitive or elite level of activity, higher quality resources may be preferred, even required and such resources are only found in certain locations (Bull, 2005; Higham and Hinch, 2006). They may be specific natural or semi-natural resources such as mountains, rivers, lakes and forests and thus located where they are as a result of physi cal geography. These resources, catering for such sports tourism activities as skiing, climbing, canoeing and orienteering, would clearly be accommodated in the Clawson model both in terms of their environmental and locational characteristics. Other high quality sports tourism resources, however, may be found in very different places, located in key urban centres. These resources are characterized by their purpose built features designed specifically for sports and their spatial distribution is conditioned by economic factors such as market thresholds (Bale, 1989), social and political considerations linked to social policy (Henry, 1993, 2001), or urban regeneration linked to tourism (Page, 1990; Law, 1992; Roche, 1992). For the people who live in such centres these places have a user-orientated location but, from the perspective of those who lack such facilities in their home town, the travel to such places creates a sense of the unusual and, as such, the way in which they are appraised is rather different. Consequently, cultural appraisals of places related to their utility for sports tourism participation are an important consideration.

The second aspect of resource quality linked to cultural issues is the way people evaluate and perceive resources generally (Higham and Hinch, 2006). It can be argued that all resources are in one way or other cultural appraisals (Short, 1991; Everden, 1992; Simmons, 1994) and nowhere is this more true than with various environments used for sports tourism (c.f. Bale, 1994). While many people can quite easily pursue activities close to home, they often choose to travel elsewhere to participate in what might be regarded as a preferred environment. This is not because the standard of the facility itself is better elsewhere but rather because of the ambience of the place: either the climate is better, the environment is less polluted or less crowded, it is more peaceful or the general landscape is more scenically attractive (Bull, 2005). An additional point is also provided by Urry (1990: p. 12) concerning the carrying out of familiar activities in unusual visual environments. He cites swimming and other activities which 'all have particular significance if they take place against a distinctive visual backcloth. The visual gaze renders extraordinary activities that otherwise would be mundane'. The example of cyclists preferring to cycle through rural rather than urban areas has already been mentioned, but another example would be British golfers who might prefer to play golf in Southern Spain or the Algarve instead of, or in addition to, using courses at home. Of course, the distinctive backdrop does not have to be rural, it could have a different cultural significance (Higham and Hinch, 2006), an example perhaps being spectating sports tourists visiting various sporting 'Meccas' such as Lords cricket ground in London or Yankee baseball stadium in New York.

Places associated with sports tourism are many and varied but, if any attempt is to be made at identifying or classifying them, it is clear that such a scheme would have to take account of quality issues as well as locational factors. As will be clear in the later sections of this text, a number of specific sports tourism places can be identified on this basis which might include, for example, ski resorts, outdoor pursuits environments, major cities (associated with mega sporting events) and sports training camps.

SPORTS TOURISM ACTIVITIES

Obviously 'activities' are a key component of sports tourism. However, for some authors (e.g. Kurtzman and Zauhar, 1997; Standeven and De Knop, 1999), a focus on activities led to classifying sports tourism in terms of lists of activities and to the classification of participants in the same way. This meant that a sports tourist sampling an activity as an incidental part of a trip was classified in the same way as a long-term and dedicated participant in that activity, whereas clearly these are very different participant types (Green and Jones, 2005). If, as is argued in this book, the focus is on the heterogeneous nature of sports tourism activities, then the classification of sports tourism by individual activities becomes unwieldy and unhelpful. However, another approach, and one that is adopted in the examination of sports tourism products in Chapter 8, is to focus on the features of sports tourism activities.

One such feature, identified by Glyptis in her 1982 categorization and utilized in much of the subsequent literature (Jackson and Glyptis, 1992; Hall 1992a; Standeven and De Knop, 1999) is the potential of sports tourism to be either active or passive. More recently, it has been argued (Weed, 2005c) that there is also a 'vicarious' element to sports tourism participation. Many sports spectators consider themselves to be much more than passive participants, although they are not actively taking part in the sport itself. Such spectators feel that they are interacting with the active participants and, as such, might be described as experiencing the sport 'vicariously' through such participants. However, as what Ramshaw and Gammon (2005) argue should be referred to as a 'heritage' (rather than 'nostalgia') aspect to sports tourism becomes more widespread (involving, for example, visits to sports attractions and museums), such 'vicarious' involvement may also be related to the 'imagined' (Gammon, 2002) journey and 'vicarious' experience that takes place.

A number of other features of sports tourism activities, recurring across five broad sports tourism products (Supplementary Sports Tourism, Sports Participation Tourism, Sports Training Tourism, Event Sports Tourism and Luxury Sports Tourism), are outlined in Chapter 8. In addition to the active, vicarious or passive nature of involvement, sports tourism activities may be single (e.g. Football World Cup) or multi-activity (e.g. Olympic Games), may or may not involve elite sport, may or may not involve some form of instruction, and involvement may be on an individual or group basis within a corporate or non-corporate environment (see Chapter 8 for details).

Examining the potential features of sports tourism activities is useful in focusing attention on the 'unit of analysis' for sports tourism. Partly derived from what this text argues is a flawed view of sports tourism as either being primarily about sport or primarily about tourism, sports tourism has often been analysed at the 'trip' level. However, in their most recent discussion of the 'sport tourism'/'tourism sport' framework outlined earlier, Robinson and Gammon (2004) discuss the complexity of motivation, primarily in relation to tourism, but also in relation to sport. They reach the conclusion that a single motive can rarely be identified as the sole reason for a particular trip and identify a 'multiple motivational position' (2004: p. 223). In reaching this conclusion, the work of Swarbrooke and Horner (1999: p. 56) is highlighted:

> *Most people's holidays represent a compromise between their multiple motivators. Either one motivation becomes dominant or a holiday is purchased which ensures all the motivators can at least be partly satisfied.*

The classification proposed by Robinson and Gammon (2004) focuses on a concept of primary and secondary motivations, with 'sport tourism' attributing primary trip motivation to either competitive ('hard' definition) or recreational ('soft' definition) sport and 'tourism sport' attributing primary motivation to other tourism activities with sport being either a secondary reinforcement to the trip ('hard' definition) or an incidental activity ('soft' definition). However, this focus on defining an entire trip as either 'sport tourism' or 'tourism sport' overlooks the complexity in trip motivation that Robinson and Gammon (2004: p. 223) themselves identify. It also assumes that the sport and the tourism elements of a trip and trip motivation can be separated (and thus invokes a binary view of sports tourism as the straightforward combination of sport and tourism). In this respect, Hinch and Higham's (2005) theorization of authenticity in sports tourism provides a useful contrast. Hinch and Higham, in discussing sports events and authenticity, cite Nauright (1996) in support of their view that:

> ... in many cases, sporting events and people's reaction to them are the clearest public manifestations of culture and collective identities in a given society.

As such, the experience of the sports tourist in such a situation is derived not only from the enjoyment of the sports event, but also from the participation in a manifestation of local culture. Invoking the conceptualization of sports tourism proposed in this book, this experience is derived from a synergistic interaction of activity, people and place, and the primacy of either the sport or the tourism element (if, indeed, such elements can be separated out) cannot be established.

This example and its focus on the way in which the activity interacts with people and place examines sports tourism motivations and experiences in relation to trip behaviours rather than at the broader level of trip-purpose. As such, sports tourism behaviours will be some among many other tourism behaviours during a trip, and to attempt to establish one such behaviour or group of behaviours as the primary purpose of a trip is to deny the complexity of the 'multiple motivational position' identified by both Robinson and Gammon (2004) and Swarbrooke and Horner (1999). Similarly, Gibson and her colleagues' application of role theory to sports tourism (Gibson and Yiannakis, 2002; Gibson and Pennington-Gray, 2005) suggests that tourists may enact various 'roles' during a trip, some of which will be sports tourism roles and others which will not, thus reinforcing the view that sports tourism is something that happens during a trip, rather than the trip as a whole being sports tourism. Consequently, it is argued in this book that sports tourism experiences should be understood as they relate to trip behaviours rather than as trip purposes.

A focus on sports tourism behaviours and experiences has been identified as being fundamental to understanding the phenomenon of sports tourism by a range of authors. Weed (2005c: p. 234) notes that:

> ... policy, provision and impacts are all derived from participation, and it is to the detriment of the subject area as a whole that there

is, as yet, only a very limited understanding of sports tourism participation.

While a systematic review of sports tourism research in the period 2000–2004 (Weed, 2006b) showed that 38 per cent of studies of sports tourism focused to some extent on behaviours, it has been suggested by several authors that such research has been largely descriptive. Gibson (2004) argues that there is a need to move 'beyond profiling sport tourists to understanding and explaining these profiles'. Similarly, Downward (2005) notes that explanations of sports tourists behaviours 'require "ontic depth", that is moving beyond the level of events towards an understanding of the processes that produce them'. As such, explanations and understandings, rather than descriptions, of behaviours are key to the development of knowledge in sports tourism. In attempting to provide a theoretical foundation for understanding such behaviours, the following section discusses people and their motivations for engaging in sports tourism activities.

PEOPLE – THE MOTIVES OF SPORTS TOURISTS

Having discussed sports tourism places and activities, the following paragraphs will concentrate more on the sports tourists themselves and examine more closely how people interact with such places and activities. What is it about those people who participate in sports tourism that makes them unique? One important question that needs to be examined in this respect is that of motivation (Gibson, 2005b). Both sport and tourism as separate activities involve a complex set of motivations and a considerable literature exists which reflects this. In his PhD thesis concerned with 'evidencing the sports tourism interrelationship', Reeves (2000) reviews the motivational literature relating to both sports participation and tourism and there is much evidence in this review that the motivations of both sports participants and tourists share a number of common traits which may offer some insights into the uniqueness of the sports tourist. According to Reeves (2000: p. 29), it is the socio-psychological rationales that dominate the sports motivation literature and it is this perspective that 'most closely mirrors that body of literature which attempts to explain reasons for individual engagement in tourism activity' (general reviews of tourism motivation literature can be found in Ryan, 2002 and Shaw and Williams, 2002).

People's motives for participating in sport are many and varied (Hagger and Chatzisarantis, 2005). Such activities may be shared (common) as well as unique to the individual and they are also dynamic in that they change over time. Such motivation embraces both psychological, social and philosophical perspectives. A significant amount of research on the motives behind sports participation involves the individual's characteristics – interests, needs, goals and personality (Weinberg and Gould, 1995) – and is also linked to similar work on the social psychology of leisure (e.g. Neulinger, 1991; Mannel and Kleiber, 1997). There are clearly motives which are more specifically identified with sport (rather than tourism) such as competitiveness, a desire to win, the testing of one's abilities and the development of skills and competencies, especially among more elite participants. However, many others might also be claimed by tourism (Shaw and Williams, 2004).

This can be seen quite clearly in the classification system of the various tourism motivators developed by McIntosh and Goeldner (1986) from a review of existing tourism motivation studies. Each of their four categories of tourist motivation – physical, interpersonal, cultural and status and prestige motivators – also has immediate relevance to sport. The physical motivators include those concerned with refreshment of body and mind, health purposes and pleasure; interpersonal ones include a desire to meet people, visit friends or relatives and to seek new and different experiences as well as the need to escape from routine experiences; cultural motivators include a desire to know more about other cultures and lifestyles; and status and prestige motivators include personal development and ego enhancement. In attempting to consider these motivations in relation to the interaction of activity, people and place, it seems quite clear that the physical motivators are related to activity and the interpersonal motivators to people. Cultural motivators can relate to aspects of all three, with views on places often being cultural appraisals, while activities and people each transmit cultural elements and symbols. Status and prestige motivators appear to be related to the more holistic interaction of these three factors. As such, the discussion that follows will examine these four motivators in turn before discussing how a consideration of arousal theory and the concept of ritual inversion might both account for the importance of place and link the areas together in understanding the unique attraction of the 'interactive experience' of sports tourism.

Several writers highlight the quest for health, fitness and general wellbeing (both psychological and physiological) as important motivations for sport (Gratton and Taylor, 1985; Long, 1990; Hagger and Chatzisarantis, 2005). In sport, these include such objectives as 'weight control, physical appearance and generally maintaining the body in a good physical state in order to maximise the life experience' (Reeves, 2000: p. 35). In tourism, the emphasis is more concerned with relaxation and recuperation, giving the 'batteries an opportunity to recharge' (Cohen, 1983; Mathieson and Wall, 1989; Hall, 2003).

Such health benefits are also inevitably linked to the idea of enjoyment, pleasure satisfaction and excitement – positive affective experiences which some, dating back to the work of Sigmund Freud, collectively refer to as the 'pleasure principle', a feeling of well-being (Reeves, 2000) which has, in some cases, been related to physiological responses to exercise and excitement (Sonstroem and Morgan, 1989; Williams, 1994; Buckworth and Dishman, 2002). These have been claimed as important motives underpinning sports participation but they are equally relevant to tourism (Robinson, 1976; Urry, 2001). In addition to the associated physical and psychological benefits they provide, some writers have also offered philosophical rationales to explain people's desire for pleasure in terms of a desire for a 'good life' (Kretchmarr, 1994; Feldman, 2004). Sport, for example, may be perceived as an important component within a particular lifestyle (Wheaton, 2004) and, furthermore, may also mirror developments in contemporary society and be used by individuals as a means of escaping from the pressures of everyday life. Both these motives are equally important elements within the tourism motivation literature. Holidays are now regarded as an essential component of modern lifestyles, with people prepared to forego other items rather than their annual holiday (Ryan, 2003). In addition, the sense of escapism is also seen as an important influence on tourism behaviour (Iso-Ahola, 1989; Snepenger et al., 2006). In fact, Urry (1990: p. 12) explicitly links the pleasure principle to escapism suggesting that tourists 'must experience particularly distinct pleasures which involve different senses or are on a different scale from those typically encountered in everyday life'.

In relation to interpersonal motives, a particular strong motive for playing sport is a sense of affiliation, involving the need to belong to a team, group, club or society in general (Hagger and Chatzisarantis, 2005). Carron and Hausenblaus (1998) utilize theories of group cohesion to identify two main reasons to explain this need: involvement for predominantly social reasons and the subsequent satisfaction and pleasure derived from that social interaction and for task reasons, i.e. enjoyment of working with other members of the team in common pursuit of the task completion. While the latter motive may not have immediate resonance with tourism, although it would be applicable to various forms of special interest tourism such as conservation holidays, the social interaction motive involving meeting new people, visiting friends and relatives and spiritual pilgrimage is clearly relevant and is identified in the literature on tourism motivation (see Williams, 2004). Several studies in fact refer to tourists as modern day pilgrims (Graburn, 1989; Urry, 2001; Kaufman, 2005) with most tourism involving people travelling in groups of one sort or other. As Reeves (2000: p. 34) points out, the social interaction motive 'has clearly identifiable links with the travelling or "touring" of sports teams, at all levels of participation' and Green and Chalip (1998) provide a useful illustration of this in their study of the Key West Women's Flag Football Tournament where their findings suggest 'that a pivotal motivation for these women's choice of travel and destination is the opportunity to come together to share revelry in the instantiation of their identity' (p. 286).

Cultural motivators related to seeing and experiencing 'otherness' (MacCannell, 1999) can perhaps be more widely seen in the tourism rather than the sport literature. Nevertheless, undoubtedly sport is a globalized cultural phenomenon which can also be a representation of the local (Houlihan, 2008). As noted in the previous section, Nauright (1996) believes that sporting events and people's reactions to them are the clearest public manifestations of culture and collective identities in particular societies. Furthermore, Bale (1989) identifies sport as being a major determinant of collective and place identity. As cultural motivators relate to the desire to experience other cultures and lifestyles, it seems that sport is increasingly being seen as a representation of such local cultures and lifestyles (Higham and Hinch, 2006) and is increasingly attracting the interest of the culturally motivated sports tourist. Moreover, the sports tourist watching or participating in local or indigenous activities is not only experiencing local sports, but is also participating in a local cultural celebration of collective and place identity (Hinch and Higham, 2005), with the resulting experience being derived from a synergistic interaction of the activity, the people and the place, with the primacy or importance of either the sport or the tourism element being redundant. As such, this is a clear manifestation of the coming together of motivations for sport and for tourism. The Olympic Games provides a useful example: the local (i.e. host's) interpretation of the global Olympic phenomenon is a key part of the cultural interaction that takes place. The presentation and interpretation of the Olympic Games is a clear manifestation of local culture, as the very different Games hosted by Sydney and Athens testify (Weed, 2008a). That such cultural heritage is utilized extensively in the iconography of television coverage of the Games further highlights the importance of this local and global interaction.

Status and prestige motives are equally important for both sport and tourist activity. Goal achievement is often regarded as a key motive for sport, especially in relation to elite performance (Harwood, 2002). As Reeves (2000: p. 35) points out, for some individuals, winning provides the primary motive for participation which he suggests might be explained by Achievement Goal Theory (Duda, 2001). Here, individuals who exhibit 'an ego-oriented outlook in life will tend to transfer this rationale to their participation in sport' and 'the goal or motive for such individuals is to maintain a favourable perception of their ability'. This is closely linked to the pursuit of rewards which may be tangible in the form of prizes, medals or trophies or intangible in the form of praise, encouragement, satisfaction and feelings of accomplishment. And, of course, all of this is related to the acquisition of status. Such motives are equally important for tourists. Several writers, borrowing from Maslow's hierarchy of needs, refer to the goal of self-fulfilment involving certain types of tourist achieving the ambition of 'collecting' places (Urry, 2001). Furthermore, there is also the related motive of wish-fulfilment with tourists seeking to achieve their dreams and fantasies (Hall and Page, 2006) and this is also related to status, another ambition of the sports person. Just as the sports person can achieve status through winning and achieving high levels of performance, so too the tourist can acquire status through conspicuous consumption in the form of ever more exotic and expensive holidays.

In each of the areas discussed above, it is clear that the motives of the sports participant and the tourist can be remarkably similar. Given the ideographic nature of motivation, it is likely that some individuals motivated to achieve, for example, social goals through sport, may not be similarly motivated to experience those goals through tourism. However, for others the convergence of these goals in the pursuit of sports tourism may result in a very powerful motivating force. It is here that the concept of optimal arousal is useful.

The view that 'leisure should be optimally arousing for it to be psychologically rewarding' (Iso-Ahola and Wissingberger, 1990: p. 2) could be as equally applicable to sport as to tourism (see Leitner and Leitner, 2004) and could be particularly important for certain types of sports tourist. While much of the literature on arousal in sport relates to the issue of performance, arousal levels can still be achieved by participation at a less competitive level if competence motives such as skill development or achievement motivations such as improved personal best performances are present (Hagger and Chatzisarantis, 2005). Furthermore, in sporting pursuits such as various outdoor and adventure activities, which are often necessarily sports tourism experiences, optimal arousal levels may be achieved by the perceived level of risk involved (Mortlock, 1984; Priest, 1992; Weber, 2001; Varley, 2006). Important in determining arousal levels in these activities may be ideas associated with 'locus of control' (Rotter, 1966; Beedie and Hudson, 2003) and the perception of the extent to which the individual is able to exert control over the level of risk that exists – too little risk and the activity ceases to be stimulating and the participation is likely to cease due to boredom, too much risk and a need to withdraw from the activity through anxiety results.

In tourism, Iso-Ahola (1980, 1982) has emphasized 'the importance of understanding intrinsic motivation within the framework of the need for optimal arousal' (Pearce, 1993: p. 129) and subsequent work by Wahlers and Etzel (1985) provided evidence that holiday preferences are influenced by 'the relative differences between optimum stimulation and actual lifestyle stimulation experiences' (p. 285). Those who have a high level of stimulation in their working lives will therefore seek to 'escape' stimulation on holiday while, by contrast, those with low levels of stimulation at work have a tendency to seek greater novelty and stimulation on holiday (Mannell and Iso-Ahola, 1987; Niininen et al., 2004). This approach, which emphasizes the differences between 'home-life' and tourism experiences, might be considered alongside Graburn's (1983) concept of 'ritual inversion'.

One of the key motivations for tourism, according to a range of authors (Graburn, 1983; Reeves, 2000; MacCannell, 2002; Wang, 2007) is a desire to experience things that would not normally be experienced in everyday work or leisure lives. Reeves (2000: p. 45) describes tourism as 'a vehicle for escapism which frequently allows the individual to consume outside the "normal" pattern of everyday life', while Graburn (1983: p. 11) notes how:

> ... tourism involves for the participants a separation from normal 'instrumental' life and the concerns of making a living, and offers entry into another kind of moral state in which mental, expressive and cultural needs come to the fore.

In addition to tourism being motivated by the desire to consume outside the normal pattern of everyday life, the concept of ritual inversion on tourist trips is described by Graburn (1983: p. 21) as a situation where 'certain meanings and rules of "ordinary behaviour" are changed, held in abeyance, or even reversed'. Consequently, the concept of ritual inversion maintains that individuals on holiday feel released to behave in ways significantly different to those in which they are expected to behave at home. While for individuals who experience a high level of stimulation and arousal in their 'home-lives', this may simply relate to the freedom to relax and to not worry about tasks and activities that must be completed, for others the search for optimal arousal and the experience of ritual inversion can be a powerful motivating force for sports tourism activities.

The arousal levels felt during sports tourism participation can be significantly enhanced by the interaction of activity, people and place. Many sports tourists may also engage in the activities undertaken while on tourist trips in their home environment and, as such, it is likely that these activities already provide some level of stimulation. However, arousal levels can be enhanced by the addition of the place experience to the activity. The desire to take part in activities in a range of interesting and unusual places is a result of a powerful combination of the various physical and status and prestige motivators described above. When such combined place/activity experiences also take place in the company of like-minded people who share similar motives, then the experience is further enhanced by the achievement of social interpersonal goals. In a reflexive manner, the achievement of optimal arousal through these means is both likely to contribute to, and be enhanced by, the experience of ritual inversion, the 'other kind of moral state in which mental, expressive and cultural needs come to the fore' (Graburn, 1983: p. 11). Therefore, as this chapter has attempted to illustrate, the unique interaction of activity, people and place is a significant factor in understanding and conceptualizing the sports tourist.

CONCLUSION

This chapter has sought to examine the nature of sports tourism with a view to identifying whether it constitutes a distinct phenomenon. Given the problems of defining sport and tourism as separate activities, it is not surprising that a simple definition of sports tourism would not be possible. Similarly, an assessment of the key components that interact to create the sports tourism experience, namely the *places* involved, the *activities* undertaken and the possible motives of the *people* who participate demonstrates considerable complexity.

The discussions in this chapter have shown that there appear to be certain types of places which can be clearly identified as sports tourism destinations and that such places facilitate the provision of various activities as sports tourism products. In addition, the section on motivation showed that sport and tourism share a number of motives in common and, while this does not provide a simple identification of a single type of sports tourism behaviour, it may indicate the possibility of modelling sports tourism behaviours and participation (see Chapter 5). Such a model might go some way to addressing the need, identified by Downward (2005), Gibson (2004) and Weed (2005c), to develop a more sophisticated understanding of sports tourism behaviours than that provided by the many descriptive accounts that litter the sports tourism literature. The approach of this text in attempting to develop such sophistication is to consider sports tourism as a behaviour rather than a trip purpose and to seek to understand the role that potential sports tourism behaviours play in the trip decision-making process. It is to this question that Chapter 4 now turns.

Sports Tourism Behaviours and the Trip Decision-Making Process

Chapter 3 suggests that a potential conceptual flaw in much of the previous sports tourism literature is that authors have considered and analysed sports tourism as a trip purpose. As such, classifications have differentiated between 'prime purpose' and 'incidental' sports tourism (Glyptis, 1982), between 'the pure sport holiday' and 'the incidental sport holiday' (De Knop, 1987) or between 'sports tourism' (primary purpose) and 'tourism sport' (secondary or incidental purpose) (Robinson and Gammon, 2004; Hennessey et al., 2008). In each of these cases sports tourism (or, more accurately, sport as a tourism motivator) is being considered in terms of the purpose of trip. Chapter 3 has already established the position of this text that sports tourism as the interaction of activity, people and place can often not be reduced to its sport and its tourism elements and, as such, the focus should be on 'sports tourism' rather than on sport in tourism. However, in this chapter, the focus is on sports tourism as a trip behaviour rather than a trip purpose. This assumes that sports tourism behaviours will be some among many other tourism behaviours during a trip (Gibson and Pennington-Grey, 2005) which are also likely to be supplemented by a range of functional (non-tourism) behaviours, such as ironing clothes or cleaning. As such, there are 'multiple motivational position(s)' (Robinson and Gammon, 2004) that exist in relation to any one trip and the motivation to engage in sports tourism behaviours will be one such position. However, there will be other motivations and, therefore, the key to understanding the significance of sports tourism behaviours is to examine the role that they play in trip decision-making processes.

THE TRIP DECISION-MAKING PROCESS

Many authors in the wider field of tourism have considered the process by which a particular trip comes to be undertaken. In recent years, some have considered particular factors, such as the 'ego' (MacCannell, 2002) or the desire to extend the 'gaze' and 'collect places' (Urry, 2001), others have focused on the relationship between being 'at home' and 'away' (Rosh-White and White, 2007) and on 'escape' and 'seeking' (Snepenger et al., 2006) while others, drawing on concepts similar to Stebbins' (1999, 2002) serious leisure approach, have considered 'travel careers' (Pearce and Lee, 2005). However, a significant body of literature exists on the way in which decisions are made to take a trip (e.g. Woodside and Lysonski, 1989; McKercher, 1998; Lawson and Thyne, 2001; Decrop and Snelders, 2005; March and Woodside, 2005; Braun-LaTour et al., 2006).

Woodside and Lysonski (1989) highlight Davidson's (1985), Mitchie's (1986) and van Raaij's (1986) proposal that the study of demographics and psychographics is not enough to develop an understanding of trip taking and add their weight to the suggestion that the key to such understanding is to focus on the trip decision-making process. In doing this, authors have considered the variables that affect trip decision-making, with some authors (e.g. Woodside and Lysonski, 1989) examining supply and demand variables such as marketing, traveller destination preference and situational variables, and others (e.g. Decrop and Snelders, 2005) examining contextual (e.g. environmental, social, cultural and geographic factors), personal, inter-personal and situational factors, alongside a range of decision-making variables. Regardless of the exact nature and type of variables examined, what is clear from the literature is that the trip decision-making process is affected by a wide range of such variables. However, a key further factor is destination awareness, which may derive from unaided recall from memory, aided recall or newly stimulated awareness (Woodside and Carr, 1988). The study of awareness has led to a longstanding and continuing body of work on the processes by which destinations are categorized or sorted into different 'sets' in the trip decision-making process (Lawson and Thyne, 2001; Decrop and Snelders, 2005), with a residual 'unaware' set containing the wide range of destinations of which, or about which, little or nothing is known. Before considering such sets in a little more detail, there are three further issues of note. The first is that trip decisions are often not made by individuals, but by what Decrop and Snelders, (2005) term a Decision-Making Unit (DMU). Such units may comprise the family, a group of friends, work colleagues or members of a club. A DMU collectively makes a decision about a trip and a certain level of compromise between individuals is inevitable as a result of this. Secondly, Moutinho (1987) demonstrates that trip decision-making processes can take place over an extended period of many months and, consequently, Decrop and Snelders (2005) note that people will often be involved in more than one trip decision-making process at any one time, perhaps in a range of different DMUs. Finally, many models of the trip decision-making process are linear (e.g. Um and Crompton, 1990; Mansfield, 1992), with the decision to take a trip being a logical first step preceding the decision about the destination for the trip. However, Decrop and Snelders (2005) suggest that for many, the decision is not linear and that the trip decision-making process can feature in day-dreaming long before a decision to take a trip is made, or that for those who routinely travel, the decision to take a trip is by-passed and the decision is entirely focused on where and when the trip should take place.

The trip decision-making process, therefore, appears to be one in which DMUs which, in the majority of cases, will comprise more than one individual, are affected by a range of personal, contextual and supply-side variables in initially allocating a range of destinations of which they are aware to a number of 'sets' from which they decide upon one destination for their trip. This process, and the variables that affect it, is dynamic, may or may not be logically linear, and is likely to be taking place alongside other trip decision-making processes involving individuals in other DMUs.

A key element in this process is clearly the allocation of destinations to 'sets' and the understanding of this is derived from consumer behaviour research on brand awareness and recognition (e.g. Howard, 1963; Howard and Sheth, 1969). Howard (1977) suggests an 'evoked' set of brands that comprises those that a consumer considers buying from among those that he or she is aware of. Spiggle and Sewall (1987) suggest that this 'evoked' set might be subdivided into an 'action' set (towards which further progress or action is taken, such as requesting a brochure) and an 'inaction' set. In terms of tourism destinations, the evoked set has often been referred to as a 'consideration set' (Woodside and Lysonski, 1989) and the inaction set as a 'hold set' (Church et al., 1985). Of course, if some destinations are being considered, then others must have been rejected. Narayana and Markin (1975) suggested that the 'reject' set can be subdivided into an 'inept' set, which has been evaluated on the basis of information from a range of sources, including advertising, recommendations, perceptions and memories, and an 'inert' set, of which the consumer is aware, but about which he or she does not know enough to make either a positive or a negative evaluation. These reject sets have been examined in relation to the trip decision-making process by Decrop and Snelders (2005), Lawson and Thyne (2001) and Woodside and Lysonski (1989).

In summary, therefore, tourism destinations may be subdivided into those that DMUs place in a consideration set (Woodside and Lysonski, 1989) or a reject set, with the reject set including an inept set of those that have been actively rejected (Lawson and Thyne, 2001) and an inert set of those for which it has not been possible to make an evaluation (Narayana and Markin, 1975). Of those in the consideration set, some will progress to an action set (Spiggle and Seall, 1987) about which further information is sought, while the rest will remain in a hold set (Church et al., 1985). Finally, one of the destinations in the action set will be chosen as the destination for the trip.

In understanding sports tourism participation, the key question is how does the desire to engage in sports tourism behaviours on a trip impact upon the trip decision-making process? More specifically, as a decision-making variable, how do motivations towards sports tourism behaviours impact upon the allocation of destinations to the consideration and then the action set and, finally, as the chosen destination for the trip. Furthermore, what is the respective influence of sports tourism behaviours in relation to other tourism behaviours that might influence the trip decision-making process?

Of course, it may be that sports tourism motivations have no impact upon the decision to make a trip to a particular destination, even though sports tourism behaviour may feature to a greater or lesser extent in the trip. Reflecting Decrop and Snelders' (2005) suggestion that the trip decision-making process is not linear, the process does not end when the decision to make a trip has been taken and the necessary purchases to make the trip have been made. Many trips are planned in detail after the main elements of the purchase (travel, accommodation, etc.) have been made and motivations to engage in sports tourism behaviours can feature prominently in this post-decision, pre-trip planning phase (Weed, 2008a). Whether these behaviours regularly take place on a range of trips for particular travellers (such as a golf tourist making arrangements to play golf during a trip once the destination has been decided), or whether they are one-off arrangements (such as a family of English tourists arranging to watch the New York Yankees play baseball once they know they are going to New York), they can still become important parts of the trip, even though they are not part of the decision about the trip destination.

In addition to sports tourism featuring in the trip decision and in post-decision trip planning, it may also occur as an unplanned spontaneous behaviour during a trip (Robinson and Gammon, 2004). Such behaviours may take place, *inter alia*, opportunistically, as alternative plans for bad weather, or as the result of being made aware of the availability of particular activities during a trip. However, the defining feature of such sports tourism behaviours is that they are spontaneous and have not affected either the decision about the destination or featured in pre-trip planning.

The above context relating to the trip decision-making process would appear to provide a useful framework within which to consider how motivations to engage in sports tourism behaviours affect trip decisions, planning and behaviours. As such, the remainder of this chapter will consider sports tourism behaviours at three levels: as a variable in the trip decision and destination choice, as part of post-decision trip planning, and as a spontaneous behaviour during a trip.

SPORTS TOURISM AS A VARIABLE IN THE TRIP DECISION AND DESTINATION CHOICE

As noted in the earlier discussions, there are two potential key trip decisions. The first is *whether* to take a trip (Um and Crompton, 1990; Mansfield, 1994 and the second is *where* to go on a trip. However, as has been pointed out, one or other, or indeed both, of these decisions may be pre-determined (Decrop and Snelders, 2005). In considering the role of sports tourism in the trip decision-making process, it is useful to consider two questions that a decision-making unit (DMU) might consider: (a) *shall we go on a trip that involves sports tourism participation*; and, (b) *where shall we go on a trip that involves sports tourism participation?* For each of these questions, a decision may or may not be made. For example, an avid golf tourist would not consider the question of whether to take a golf tourism trip, only of where to go. Conversely, an avid football fan would not choose where to go to watch the Football World Cup (as the destination is pre-determined), only whether or not to take the trip. A family considering a holiday may consider both whether to take a beach holiday that allows for sports tourism participation and where to take such a trip, while an elite athlete often has little or no choice in both whether or where to travel for training and competition. These and other examples are illustrated in Figure 4.1 and discussed in greater detail below.

Trip Decision Where Both the Taking of the Trip and the Destination are Chosen

Perhaps seemingly paradoxically, it is likely that of those trips where sports tourism affects trip decisions, those where most choice is exercised are those where the sports tourism element is likely to be of lesser importance and participation is likely to be lower as sports tourism is one among a

		Choice to take a trip involving sports tourism participation	
		Chosen	Pre-determined
Destination for a trip involving sports tourism participation	Chosen	*Holiday camp & beach tourism* *Horse-racing events* *Golf & ski tourism*	*Athletics events* *Football & cricket fixtures & tours* *Mass participation events*
	Pre-determined	*Outdoor, adventurous & 'alternative' sports tourism* *Golf & ski tourism*	*Elite athlete training & competition* *Outdoor, adventurous & 'alternative' sports tourism* *Football & cricket fixtures & tours*

FIGURE 4.1 *Examples of trip decisions and destination choices*

range of behaviours on a trip. One example of this is the traditional beach or holiday camp tourist.

The holiday camp is perhaps a peculiarly British phenomenon, but it is useful to consider it alongside traditional 'mass' beach tourism for two reasons. First, the holiday camp concept evolved from demand for traditional British seaside tourism, with the original camps being situated in popular resorts such as Skegness and Bognor Regis (Holloway and Taylor, 2006). Secondly, for a time, the 'mass' tourism market among the working classes in Britain was the market for holiday camps, which provided accommodation, meals, entertainment and activities for an all-inclusive price (Page, 2003). As such, there are many similarities between mass beach tourism and the British holiday camp market.

Both mass beach tourism and the British holiday camp market represent trips where the DMU is likely to be either the family (Oh, 2008), with choices being made based on the desires of the parents and the parents' perception of what their children want, or young friendship groups where decisions are often made by consensus (Decrop, 2006). In each case, the decision is likely to be about whether the trip should include opportunities for sports tourism behaviours and the destination for the trip, with often the wish for opportunities for participation being more important than the destination.

For many, the availability of sports tourism opportunities, particularly watersports on beach holidays and, particularly, activities for children on holiday camp tourism, can be an important factor in destination choice. As such, the desire to take a trip involving some sports tourism is more important than the decision about where to go, although both are likely to have been the subject of discussion in the DMU. Reeves' (2000) study of sport at Butlins (a British holiday camp) illustrates this, with 73 per cent of respondents being on holiday with their children. Many respondents were repeat visitors (85 per cent had been to Butlins in the previous 3 years) and, for 69 per cent, the availability of sports tourism opportunities had played a part to some extent in the choice of Butlins as their holiday destination, with some specific comments including:

> When we were thinking about a holiday this year, we knew that Butlins holiday camps had loads of sports, particularly for the kids, so we actually spent most of our time discussing which camp to come to.

> We weren't really bothered about the sports and recreation facilities for ourselves, but we have two young children and they get bored very easily, so this was an easy choice to keep them out of trouble and in one place.

> To be frank, the wife booked it and the kids were really happy about it. They looked at the brochures and were excited about the swimming pool and the go-karting.

These comments reflect an almost simultaneous consideration of whether to take a particular type of trip and of where to choose as a destination, and reinforce Woodside and Lysonski's (1989) and Oh's (2008) comments that DMUs often simplify considerably the decision-making process and actually include very few destinations in their consideration and action sets based on a limited number of variables.

However, despite sports tourism appearing to be one such variable for these travellers, an indication of the relative lack of importance of sports tourism opportunities for those taking these types of trip is that actual participation tends to be much lower than intention. Tokarski (1993), in a relatively dated study of sports participation on beach holidays in Corfu, compared the sports participation of British and German tourists and discovered that, excluding walking and swimming, only 30 per cent of Britons and 20 per cent of Germans took part in any sport at all on such holidays.

Evidence at the turn of the twenty-first century from the UK (Keynote, 2001; Mintel, 2002c) suggests that sports facilities (particularly those in hotels), while playing an important role in the marketing mix, are actually utilized by surprisingly few guests. The Butlins studies (McKoy, 1991; Reeves, 2000) further substantiate these findings, with the comments of tourists including:

> I must admit, I had all these great ideas of taking advantage of the facilities both indoors and outdoors, and in ten days all I've managed is a couple of games of snooker with a guy I met on the first day.

> It all looked great in the brochure, and ... [the sport] ... was one of the reasons we chose Butlins, but I've got to admit I've found it hard to motivate myself to actually do anything, particularly after a night in the bar.

This highlights the 'multiple motivational position' (Robinson and Gammon, 2004) noted earlier and that sports tourism is often one among many behaviours that make up a trip (Gibson and Yiannakis, 2002; Gibson and Pennington-Gray, 2005). In fact, for some, sports tourism participation is something to be avoided, although participation does sometimes take place to please partners or other family members, as noted by some tourists in the Butlins studies (McKoy, 1991; Reeves, 2000):

> I do more than I probably realize, to be honest I prefer to relax. But I'm always having to play with the kids or I'm in the pool with them, but none of that is my own time and not really organized. It just happens when you have to look after the young ones.

> Having the sports going on adds to the atmosphere of the place, but it's not really my idea of what to do on holiday, although my wife has got me playing badminton a couple of times.

Again, this reinforces the point that, although part of the trip decision, both importance and levels of sports tourism participation can be quite low. This is also the case in a further contrasting example where choice is exercised over both the taking of the trip and the destination, that of horse-racing spectators. In the previous edition of this text (Weed and Bull, 2004), travellers interested in the 'associated experience' of some sports tourism products were discussed. This referred to those sports tourists who were motivated by some aspect of the experience other than the activity itself, and horse-racing spectators were suggested as one example of such sports tourists.

Kim and Petrick (2004) have suggested that spectating at horse racing can be an important and high-spending sports tourism activity. In a detailed anthropological study in the UK, Fox (1999) examined all members of 'The Racing Tribe', including jockeys, trainers, owners and bookmakers as well as spectators. However, it is possible to utilize her data to comment on the participation profiles of 'race-goers'. Fox identified two distinct groups of horse-racing spectators, which she named 'socials' and 'enthusiasts'. As might be expected, the socials were spectators who knew little about horse racing and who were in attendance for the associated social experience. However, some of the enthusiasts might also be similarly described because, although they have some knowledge of and interest in horse racing, other aspects of the experience were more important to them than the horse racing itself.

Fox (1999) estimated that 'socials' could comprise between 30 and 70 per cent of the horse-racing crowd, depending on the weather, the day of the week (Sunday being most popular) and the importance of the event in the social calendar. Fox recognized that the structure of the sport lent itself to such 'associated experience' participants. The following, somewhat lengthy, quotation notes this point and also gives a useful flavour of the social aspect of horse-racing spectating:

> I had to recognize that racing is qualitatively different from any other spectator sport, in that all of the actual sport takes place in just a few minutes of the afternoon, interspersed with half hour periods in which there is no 'action' at all. This promotes a much higher than usual degree of social interaction among spectators. At almost any other spectator event, socializing means missing the action; at the races, social contact is an integral part of the action. This factor is instrumental in transforming an amorphous crowd into a distinctive and complex society. Out of the half-hour gaps between races an entire culture has developed, with its own language, religion, traditions, customs, rituals and etiquette (Fox, 1999: p. 13).

Notwithstanding the above, the 'associated experience' horse-racing spectator is by no means an homogeneous group. A number of distinct 'types' were identified (Fox, 1999). For three of these – 'pair-bonders', 'family day-outers' and 'lads' and girls' day-outers' – the races simply provide an unusual day out spent with partners, family or friendship groups. As such, the trip decision has involved a consideration of whether to take a trip involving, in this case, horse racing, and also (given the wide availability of horse-racing venues) where to go.

Fox (1999) also identified as types within the 'socials' group, the 'suits' (those corporate race-goers occupying the hospitality boxes who are either trying to forge business relationships, or for whom a trip to the races is part of an incentive package paid for by their company) and the 'be-seens' (who are concerned with conspicuous consumption, and are most evident at the 'big occasions' such as Royal Ascot).

The features that link these various groups are their lack of interest in, or knowledge about, horse racing, their 'interpersonal' or 'status and prestige' motives for attendance (see Chapter 3) and the experience of some level of 'ritual inversion' (Graburn, 1983) in their behaviours when they become part of what Fox (1999: p. 21) describes as a 'liminal world' segregated from everyday life (Chalip, 2006). However, their almost complete ignorance about the sports tourism activity that has provided, at least nominally, the reason for their trip, means that, like those at holiday camps and on traditional beach holidays, the sports tourism is actually relatively unimportant. This is despite the fact that it has featured in both their decision to take the trip and its destination.

A final example relating to this type of trip decision is perhaps useful to illustrate trips where sports tourism behaviours might be more important and participation might be higher: that relating to trips on which people learn to play or participate in a particular activity, of which golf and skiing are perhaps the two most obvious examples. While, as discussed later, many golf and skiing sports tourists are long-term committed participants (Hudson, 2000; Readman, 2003), for others, a trip involving these sports tourism behaviours offers an excellent opportunity to learn the activity, perhaps with a view to developing a longer term interest (Mintel, 2002b). For such sports tourists, an important reason for the trip is the need for the resources to take part (Bull, 2005). While this obviously refers to the physical resource of the golf course or the slopes, it also includes the 'expertise' resource of an instructor. The concept of 'novelty' may also play a significant part (Petrick, 2002), as the novelty of a trip involving new or unusual behaviours can be a significant element in the trip decision-making process (Grabler and Zins, 2002).

Obviously, for those choosing to take a trip including activity instruction as a sport tourism behaviour, choice has been exercised over the two aspects of the trip decision. First, the DMU, which for 'first-timers' could equally be family or friendship groups, has decided that they would like to take a trip that involves learning this particular activity. Secondly, a decision has been taken about the destination to which they would wish to travel. It is likely that, in respect of the first question, a trip involving extensive instruction has been evaluated against trips involving other types of behaviours and so the consideration set may well have included trips that did not involve learning a sports tourism activity. However, the decision to take such a trip will have been a key part of the filtering process from the consideration to the action set, which will have been constrained by the availability of both the physical and the instructional resources described above (Hinch and Higham, 2004; Bull, 2005). Consequently, once the decision to take a trip of this nature has been taken, the sports tourism activity, unlike those in the other examples in relation to this type of trip decision, becomes a very important factor in destination choice.

Trip Decisions Where the Destination is Pre-Determined, but the Taking of the Trip is Chosen

In this and the remaining two types of trip decision, sports tourism is important enough to the DMU for it to constrain some aspect of the trip decision. The examples here relate to those trips where the time and place specific nature of the sports tourism activity dictates the destination to which a trip is taken (Hinch and Higham, 2004) and the only remaining decision is whether or not to travel. In the majority of cases, it is travel to watch or participate in sports events that comprises trip decisions of this nature.

With the exception of studies of their economic contribution (e.g. Gratton et al., 2000; Shibli and Gratton, 2001), research on spectators has largely focused on deviant behaviour (see later discussions on football spectators). While there has been some work conducted on various elements of spectator behaviour and identity by Daniel Wann and his colleagues in the USA (see Wann et al., 2001), it is generally fair to say there is little known about the behaviour patterns and motivations of non-violent spectators. This is particularly the case when such spectatorship is not related to some specific long-term commitment to a particular team (such spectators are discussed in the next section). Consequently, the discussions here focus largely on two studies of athletics spectators in the UK in the 1990s (Train, 1995; Reeves, 2000). While this might appear to result in a limited and somewhat specific discussion, the issues raised are likely to be illustrative of behaviours of similar types of spectators in other contexts.

The studies in question were of the Europa Cup athletics event, held in Birmingham in 1994 and the Athletics World Cup, held at Crystal Palace (London) in 1994. The results from these two surveys were very similar and, as such, the studies verify and validate each other. The attendance profile of the vast majority of spectators did not include an overnight stay (Figure 4.2) and, as such, most were only attending one day of the two-day event. Nevertheless, in all but the smallest minority of cases, sport was the prime purpose of the trip (Figure 4.3).

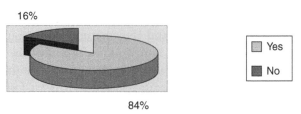

16%

84%

FIGURE 4.2 *Did your visit to the Athletics World Cup involve an overnight stay?*

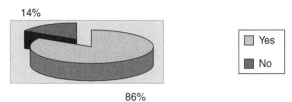

14%

86%

FIGURE 4.3 *Was the Athletics World Cup the main reason for visiting London?*

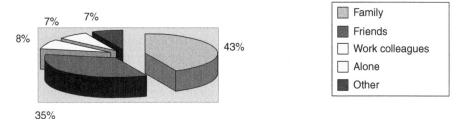

7% 7%

8%

43%

35%

FIGURE 4.4 *With whom did you travel to the Athletics World Cup?*

The largest number of spectators were attending with family members, while a significant number attended with friendship groups (Figure 4.4), and the vast majority were not regular attenders at sports events (Figure 4.5). A significant minority (25 per cent) were regular athletics participants themselves, while a further minority (19 per cent) had attended because a family member had wanted to come. For many of the spectators, the novel experience was an important motivation for attending, as they had not travelled to spectate at an athletics event before. This is illustrated by the 60 per cent of respondents who stated that they were spectating in London for the first time.

What observations, then, can be made about the features of these athletics spectators that might be generalizable to similar types of spectators in other contexts? First, there was a significant group, mostly families with children, that attended because the event provided a unique or novel day

FIGURE 4.5 *Prior to your visit to the Athletics World Cup, when did you last watch an athletics event?*

out, an acknowledged tourism trip motivation (Pearce and Lee, 2005). It is likely that this type of spectator will be common at many large 'one-off' events, such as the Olympic, Pan-American and Commonwealth Games, but also at smaller scale events such as those described here. Furthermore, such 'curiosity' spectators are also a feature at many league matches in sports such as ice hockey and baseball (subject, of course, to the availability of tickets). Similarly, there was a significant minority for whom interest in the event was derived from their own participation and it is likely that 'championship' events in a whole range of less popular sports will attract this type of spectator. Finally, the type of spectator that has attended because a family member wanted to attend is likely to feature in crowds for the vast majority of sports events.

Here, the destination of the trip has not been part of the decision. As such, the filtering of destinations into reject, consideration and action sets has not taken place, the only decision has been whether to take a trip to watch a particular event or fixture, thus reflecting Decrop's (2006) and Oh's (2008) comments on the non-linearity and simplification of the decision-making process. The decision variables have been twofold: (a) interest in the sports tourism activity (i.e. the event or fixture) and, (b) awareness and convenient availability of the opportunity. For those for whom the novelty or curiosity value is high, the convenience factor is likely to be of greater importance, while for those who have a wider interest and engagement in the activity, this will be less significant. However, the nature of this type of spectating sports tourist is that their participation is unlikely to be regular and, as such, ease of opportunity is a key factor in determining behaviour.

In contrast to the irregular or opportunistic spectating sports tourist described above, there are a great number of spectating sports tourists who are committed fans that have supported 'their' team around the world. In particular, the sports of cricket and football generate such committed sports tourists as fans. As noted earlier, much of the work on football supporters has focused on violent or deviant fans (Dunning et al., 1988; Kerr, 1994; Armstrong, 1998), with one study focusing specifically on the way in which football hooligans might be conceptualized as undesirable sports tourists

(Weed, 2002b). However, there has been some work that has examined the behaviours of non-violent fans (e.g. Jones, 2000; Giulianotti, 2002; Millward, 2006). Taken together, what these studies highlight as a common element among both violent and non-violent fans is the level of commitment that exists among those who regularly travel to watch 'their' team play and, as such, violence aside, many of their behaviours and motivations are remarkably similar. The same might be said of the 'Barmy Army' group of England cricket fans who spend vast amounts of time and money travelling the globe to watch what has often been a less than successful team (Parry and Malcolm, 2004). While there have been those among cricket's 'traditional' support who do not approve of their vocal 'carnivalesque' behaviour (Weed, 2002a), what is not in doubt is their commitment to following the team and, consequently, it would seem reasonable to consider them alongside committed football fans.

As the nature of football and cricket fixtures, tours and tournaments is such that their time and place are dictated to the potential traveller, once again there is no decision to be made about the destination for a trip, it is simply whether to take the trip or not (Millward, 2006). However, as for many committed football and cricket fans, an identity as a sports fan is a central element in their lifestyle (Jones, 2000; Wann et al., 2001), the motivation to reinforce such identities through sports tourism behaviours is much stronger than that of the athletics spectators described previously, for whom the convenience of the trip is a key factor. For committed fans there is a distinct subculture that surrounds their sports spectating and this has been noted by Marsh et al. (1978), Jones (2000), Millward (2006) and Weed (2002b). The desire to be with like-minded people, an 'in-group' (Jones, 2000) towards which an elevated positive attitude exists, and within which a 'career' as a sports spectator develops (Marsh et al., 1978; Stebbins, 2002), provides a powerful mix of 'interpersonal' and 'status and prestige' (related to spectator 'career development') motives for this type of sports spectating. Furthermore, the importance for these fans of the wider experience associated with spectating sports tourism (c.f. Fairley, 2003) means that the place experience is a broad one, with memories of particular matches being related not only to the experience of the stadium, but also of the place in which the fans stayed and socialized (Bale, 2003; Millward, 2006). Consequently, the interaction of activity, people and place contributes significantly to the sports tourism experience.

Not surprisingly, the profile of these sports fans is largely male, although cricket fans are less exclusively so (Parry and Malcolm, 2004), with travelling companions being friendship rather than family groups, although the DMU can often be simply the individual, who will make the decision about whether or not to join the group trip. The subcultural nature of the groups means that newcomers need to demonstrate their commitment before being fully accepted (hence the concept of 'career development'), although the cricket fans studied (Weed, 2002a; Parry and Malcolm, 2004) appeared to be generally more welcoming and inclusive of newcomers than the football groups, as the following extract from the Barmy Army website illustrates:

> *The Barmy Army is a style of support started by a large group of dedicated cricket fans that follow England's team around the world giving highly vocal and visual support. Its core aim is 'To make watching cricket more fun and much more popular'. It is free to join because there isn't any membership scheme, the groups that you see on television evolve spontaneously because what we are is a style of support and the group will be made up of whoever wants to join in with the fun on the day (Barmy Army website – quoted in Weed, 2002a).*

Given the need to demonstrate and maintain commitment within and to the subculture, an individual would not take the decision to miss an important fixture or event lightly (Parry and Malcolm, 2004), as this could affect their position within the group. Consequently, there is likely to be considerable peer pressure on the individual as the DMU to take the trip. As such, for the most committed fans it is only likely to be the most constraining barriers, such as lack of finance, or family or work commitments that would cause a trip to be missed (Millward, 2006). For these reasons, trips are often made on a budget and thus accommodation is usually in cheap hotels or youth hostels. However, the sheer volume or length of trips taken means that over the course of a year spend per person is relatively high. Due to the commitment levels required to retain a 'status' position in the subculture, many people will eventually move on from the type of committed participation profile described here (Weed, 2002b). This may be due to growing family or work commitments, lack of time and money, or simply moving on through the life course (c.f. Gibson, 2005c). It is unlikely that spectating sports tourism participation will cease, but the nature of the participation as an all-consuming, committed, subcultural experience will change. This 'post-career' stage is likely to involve fewer away trips or may involve family groups with children being taken to matches. In such cases, the broader social experience of the trips will obviously change.

A similar subcultural element can be found in those whose sports tourism engagement is through participation in, rather than spectating at, events. At this stage, this does not refer to elite athletes (see discussions of those who have no choice in either trip-taking or destination), but to those sports tourists taking part in 'mass-participation' events (Shipway and Jones, 2008). Such events might vary from some major events, such as the New York marathon, which may be the highlight of the sporting year for some participants, to more regularized events, such as local 10K races or half marathons, that stimulate relatively brief day-trip sports tourism (McGehee et al., 2003). In fact, it might be argued that many of the latter events should not be considered sports tourism at all. However, as for the purposes of this book a definition of tourism is being used that relates to travel for activities that are 'out-of the ordinary' and that are perceived to fall outside the rhythm of everyday life, it is reasonable to consider such smaller events that are likely to involve other family members, either as spectators or as participants, as being, in the majority of cases, trips involving sports tourism behaviours.

In many cases, mass participation events involve trips with family groups, who often attend as spectators supporting their partners, parents or, in some cases, children. This type of sports tourism is often a day-trip, or involves only one overnight stay. While spend per person may be fairly low, the size of some events – the London Marathon now 'limits' entrants to 46 500 (London Marathon Ltd, 2008) – means that the cumulative economic impact of this type of sports tourist can be significant.

For many of these participants, like the committed cricket and football fans discussed earlier, sport may be a significant part of their lifestyle – considerable time is known to be spent by non-elite athletes training for and competing in such events (Smith, 1998). However, sports tourism may not be perceived to be equally as important. Such participants are interested in the activity and the interaction with other participants but, with the exception of major events such as the big city marathons (Shipway and Jones, 2008), the place experience may not be so important. As such, the tourism element of such trips may be functional and, given the lack of engagement with place, may be more accurately described as travel rather than tourism. This is perhaps not surprising for a group who have not chosen the destination to which they have travelled, only whether or not to travel to take part in a particular event. It may be that the shorter day-trip duration of such trips also contributes to the lack of engagement with place and this is something that contrasts with the desire for a broader place experience of many committed cricket and football fans on longer trips (Millward, 2006).

Nonetheless, the concept of subculture is important in relation to this group. However, in many cases, the interaction with the subculture is likely to be through conspicuous consumption of the symbols associated with it, such as magazines and a particular type of dress (Smith, 1998; Shipway and Jones, 2008). At events, interaction with other participants is on the level of 'familiar strangers' (Nixon, 1986 – detailed in Nixon and Frey, 1995), where people may know who others are and may have raced against and spoken to them many times, but will know very little else about any other aspect of their lives. There are, however, some patterns of participation that involve a different type of subcultural interaction. Here, the stay away from home is longer than the short day-trip or overnight stay, often being around four or five nights, with the event either being a tournament or gala spread over a number of days, or a one-day event with a programme of associated activities over a number of days (Dobson et al., 1997; Ryan and Trauer, 2005; Gillett and Kelly, 2007). The participation pattern in such cases is often with friendship groups, with the event being seen as an opportunity to meet up with old friends to 'celebrate' their involvement in the subculture (Green, 2001). Green and Chalip (1998) describe a women's flag football tournament in these terms, with other examples being events such as the World and European Masters Swimming Championships, which occur in alternate years and provide an annual opportunity (for Europeans at least) to meet up with old friends in new and interesting places. Here, as with the football and cricket fans, the subcultural element is likely to mean that individuals would miss such a trip in the face of only the most considerable constraints or barriers.

Trip Decisions Where the Taking of the Trip is Pre-Determined, but the Destination is Chosen

As in the previous section, in this type of trip decision, sports tourism is important enough to the decision-making process to constrain an aspect of the decision. However, here the commitment to the sports tourism activity is such that there is no question of whether a trip involving that activity should be taken, only of where the destination will be. Almost invariably, the sports tourism behaviours that feature in this type of trip decision involve active participation, although aspects of the 'associated experience' can also be important. Like the previous type of decision, as might be expected as sports tourism behaviours become more important within the trip, subcultural elements can be important (Shipway and Jones, 2008).

Many outdoor, adventure and 'alternative' sports tourism activities have an overt subcultural nature (Wheaton, 2004), often deriving from the interaction of the activity with the people and places involved. However, another interesting element is that the nature of many of these sports tourism activities is such that participants cannot take part in them at home (Hinch and Higham, 2004). This is because, as discussed in Chapter 3, they are usually dependent on natural resources that cannot be found in the home area (Bull, 2005). Thus, the activity can only be pursued as a sports tourism behaviour. It is for this reason that the decision about whether to take a trip is not in question, only where to go. This also reinforces the importance of considering the phenomenon of sports tourism as a synergistic one, rather than considering it as the simple combination of sport and tourism, because in these examples the activity cannot take place without the place and, as such, the sport and the tourism elements cannot be separated.

There is increasing literature surrounding surfing, windsurfing and snowboarding discussing the subcultural nature of these activities (Wheaton, 2004). Furthermore, there is some evidence that suggests that many participants take part in more than one of these activities (National Ski Areas Association, 2000 – quoted in Hudson, 2003b), perhaps because the subcultural flavour is similar. These activities have been variously characterized as encompassing a 'culture of commitment' (Wheaton, 1998), a 'subculture' (Wheaton, 2000, Butts, 2001), a 'distinct cultural community' (Johnson and Edwards, 1994), and a 'fraternity' (Weed, 2000) or 'scene' (Farmer, 1992). Within such subcultures, the place experience is clearly valued, with many surfers describing the 'serenity of the ocean' and the importance of the condition of the ocean and the environment (Butts, 2001). However, the very nature of subcultures as providing the 'structure of an alternative value system' (Longhurst, 1995) which is constructed by members of the subculture means that, clearly, interpersonal motivators are important and the interaction of not only the activity and the place, but also the people is important. As such, what might be termed 'alternative' sports tourists perhaps most obviously exemplify the nature of the sports tourism experience as being derived from the unique interaction of activity, people and place.

However, it is not just 'alternative' activities that can lay claim to the subcultural label. While some authors have argued that the term subculture relates to a group with norms and values that are in opposition to the 'dominant' culture (see discussions in Crosset and Beal, 1997), others have argued that subcultures do not have to be in opposition to dominant culture, they are simply characterized by their own, unique value system and norms of expected behaviour (Albert, 1991; Donnelly, 1993). As such, many groups of participants might be considered as subcultures. Mountaineers have certainly been described in this way by Johnson and Edwards (1994), while Beedie's (2003b) discussion of a range of adventure sports tourists can be viewed through a subcultural lens. This view is perhaps further strengthened by studies that have examined 'career trajectories' among such sports tourists (e.g. Bartram, 2001). Drawing on Stebbin's (1992, 2002) work on serious leisure, it is possible to examine the ways in which participants in such activities develop and become accepted into the wider 'fraternity' of participants as their knowledge, experience and ability increases (Smith and Weed, 2007). Consequently, in a similar manner to 'alternative' sports tourists, the experience of outdoor adventure sports tourists is also derived from the interaction of activity, people and place.

Notwithstanding the availability of 'synthetic' or man-made facilities for some of these activities (e.g. indoor climbing walls), the dependence on natural resources means that the interaction of activity and place plays a big part in the experience of this group of sports tourists. Furthermore, facilities such as indoor climbing walls have been shunned by many 'purist' mountaineers as an aberration and not part of the activity as they see it (Morgan, 1998). Consequently, both participants in traditional outdoor activity sports tourism, such as kayaking, sailing, mountaineering, potholing and hiking, and those involved in the 'alternative' sports tourism activities described above, all require specific natural resources, access to which will usually involve travel.

A defining characteristic of this group, therefore, and one which differentiates them from many other sports tourists, is that they do not take part in the activity at home. As a consequence, trips involving sports tourism behaviours are often very regular and such participants will take any opportunity to get away to pursue their chosen activity. Quantitative evidence from Reeves' (2000) study of activity tourism participants at Twr-y-Felin in Wales suggests that this is the case, with a very significant 85 per cent of visitors on the centre's mailing list indicating that they take these types of activity holidays between monthly and four times per year. For many, collecting places as referred to in Chapter 3 (Urry, 1990, 2001), can be an important characteristic of their behaviour and, in some cases, potential or planned visits to 'mythical' places – such as Oahu's North Shore in Hawaii for surfers – can become a defining moment in the 'careers' of such sports tourists (Green and Jones, 2005). This relates to the status and prestige motivators described in Chapter 3, with the addition of a diverse range of sports tourism places being a significant element of status within some sports tourists groups, particularly 'alternative' groups given their subcultural flavour.

In terms of the influence of sports tourism behaviours on the trip decision-making process, clearly the activity is pre-defined and the question becomes one of which places and with which people the activity will take place. As such, these factors will play a significant role in filtering destinations into reject, consideration and action sets. Again, the process is unlikely to be neat or linear (Oh, 2008), as the subcultural nature of the activity means that recommendations for places to visit through word of mouth (including the Internet) are important, with discussions about where to go on the next trip often taking place among groups of participants during a trip (Green and Jones, 2005). Similarly, the 'mythical' places described above will feature in every participant's consideration set, although it may take a particular stimulus to move such a place into the action set of likely destinations to visit in the immediate future. As such, people feature both in terms of being a consideration in choosing a destination (will there be other like-minded people there?), but also in providing recommendations about places. This means that the DMU for such decisions, which in most cases is likely to be friendship group (or, in a smaller number of cases, club) based, is likely to be influenced by recommendations from (and the mythology of) the wider subculture. This may wield such an influence that the boundaries of the DMU might best be considered 'fuzzy', with the subculture itself perhaps actually being conceptualized as part of the DMU.

A final note is required on the pursuit of some activities, climbing perhaps being an obvious example, in a solitary environment. In this case, the solitary nature of the activity in relation to the often imposing nature of the place, can be important. However, even in such a solitary environment, participants symbolically demonstrate their membership of a subculture – both to themselves and to others – by their adherence to the norms and values of that subculture in the way the activity is carried out (Williams and Donnelly, 1985). Consequently, and particularly in relation to the participant's 'identity' as a particular type of sports tourist (Green and Jones, 2005), the symbolic presence of the subculture through adherence to its norms and values, means that people are still an important part of the sports tourism interaction, even when participation takes place alone.

A different type of more conservative culture surrounds two other activities for which the decision about whether or not to take a trip is rarely made, namely: golf and skiing. Earlier in the chapter, trips involving instruction in golf and skiing were discussed; however, here the focus is on the more regular golf and skiing sports tourist (Hudson, 2003b; Readman, 2003). As described elsewhere in this book, golf and ski tourists, despite the very different nature of the activities, are very similar in many ways in terms of their behaviours and motivations. Some golf and ski tourists, for whom the 'nineteenth hole' and the 'après ski' experience may be more important than the activity itself, exhibit some of the 'associated experience' motivations that were discussed earlier in relation to horse-racing spectators. However, if the market for school skiing trips is left to one side, many adult golf and ski tourists can be committed sports tourists that exhibit very similar characteristics.

As discussed in Chapter 3, for many sports tourists resource quality is an important issue (Hinch and Higham, 2004). While resources to participate in these activities may exist in the home area (perhaps a dry-ski slope or a municipal golf course or driving range), the desire for a higher quality resource, along with associated facilities in terms of relatively luxurious accommodation (Weed, 2001a), has been shown to be a central motivator for these sports tourists (Bull, 2005). As ever, the company of like-minded people is a further enhancement to the experience (Green, 2001), highlighting again the importance of the interaction of activity, people and place.

The concept of 'novelty' (Petrick and Backman, 2002a) was discussed in relation to the novice golf or skiing sports tourist described earlier in the chapter. However, novelty can also be an important motivating factor for more experienced participants, where the novelty is that of taking part in a new destination, of 'collecting places' (Urry, 2001). In this case, like the outdoor, adventure and 'alternative' sports tourists described above, golf or skiing is likely to be a defining part of the participants lifestyle (Green and Jones, 2005) and the ability to 'boast' an impressive list of golfing or skiing destinations visited can be an important status and prestige motivator. A further indicator of importance is that, given the often luxurious nature of the attendant accommodation and facilities, spend per trip is usually high (Weed, 2001a; Mintel, 2002b, 2003a). Such attendant facilities often include the opportunity to try other activities and, notwithstanding a primary interest in skiing or golf, such trips often include incidental participation in other sports tourism activities and the opportunity for such participation may well be an important factor in the trip decision-making process.

Of course, for many, the 'associated experience' of the 'après ski' experience and the 'nineteenth hole' is an important part of the culture of golfing and of skiing sports tourism behaviours, perhaps more important than the golfing or skiing itself. Hudson (2000: p. 164) believes that resorts need to concentrate more on the après ski experience, noting that the trend is toward skiers spending less and less time on the slopes, the average now being three hours per day. Williams and Dossa (1990) estimated that between 20 and 30 per cent of visitors to ski centres in Canada did not ski at all, with Cockerell (1994) noting that the estimate for non-skiing French ski resort visitors is around 40 per cent. Hudson (2000, 2003b) suggests that there is now a trend towards the development of 'mountain theme parks' rather than ski resorts, offering a whole range of activities, some of which (e.g. swimming, tennis and indoor golf) have no association whatsoever with traditional snowsports. In fact, in Zermatt, one of Switzerland's top ski resorts, where one in eight visitors in the mid-1990s was a non-skier (Wickers, 1994), visitors can even take language courses, thus complicating the trip decision for those interested in the associated experience rather than the skiing itself. Aspects of conspicuous consumption associated with ski resorts cannot be ignored (McGibbon, 2007), and 'social and prestige' motivators will interact with the more obvious 'physical' and 'interpersonal' motivators among many ski resort visitors.

A similar trend is to be found among many golf tourists, aided by the increasing development of golf tourist venues as country house hotels offering a range of activities associated with sport and health. The 'nineteenth hole' may be a particularly attractive part of the golfing trip experience for the business traveller that is not too keen on the activity itself, but for whom attendance on such trips makes an important contribution to developing business relationships. Of course, the lifestyle image associated with golfing holidays may be part of the attraction for many interested in the 'associated experience'. The image of a luxurious country house hotel, bathed in sunshine, with a view over a picturesque golf course can provide powerful 'status and prestige' motivations for many participants (Gottdiener, 2000), but also provides an easy way to 'buy into' a particularly desirable lifestyle, even if only for a few days in the year.

Lifestyle and subculture are a key part of the trip decision-making process for DMUs considering a trip involving any of the sports tourism behaviours described under this type of trip decision (Green and Jones, 2005). Clearly, the interaction of the activity, people and place plays a central role in deciding on the destination for outdoor, adventure and 'alternative' sports tourists, and also for committed golf and ski sports tourists (Bull, 2005), although it may be that the people and the place take on a greater importance for those who are motivated by behaviours associated with the activities rather than the activities themselves (c.f. Gottdiener, 2000; McGibbon, 2007). However, undoubtedly, motivations relating to status and prestige, be it within the subculture or in society at large, play a considerable role in the destination choice for all of the behaviours considered in this section.

Trip Decisions Where Both the Taking of the Trip and the Destination are Pre-Determined

While many people might argue that the *rasion d'être* of tourism is that it is a discretionary activity, and therefore it should involve an element of choice (Dwyer and Forsyth, 2006), there are a number of trips involving sports tourism behaviours in which no choice is exercised over either the taking of the trip or the destination. Several of these examples overlap with those already discussed; however, the clearest illustration of this type of trip decision is the travel patterns of elite athletes.

Elite athletes are an atypical group, but they are undoubtedly some of the most prolific sports tourists. Their trips are both domestic and international and can be for either training or competition. Studies of elite British track athletes have shown that the number of days travelled per year can be significant and ranges from 69 days a year for a junior international to 146 days for an established senior athlete (Box 4.1).

Box 4.1 Travel patterns of elite British track athletes

Two illustrative examples of annual travel volumes for training and competition:

Andrew Young (20) GB & Scotland Junior International, 800 m		Mark Richardson (23) GB & England Senior International, 400 m	
Days per year travelled for…		*Days per year travelled for…*	
Training in the UK	16	Training in the UK	40
Competition in the UK	29	Competition in the UK	20
Training overseas	14	Training overseas	38
Competition overseas	10	Competition overseas	48
TOTAL	69 days	TOTAL	146 days

Illustrative comments on training and competition overseas:

'This year I went to Lanzarote for a week at the end of February. I then went to Jamaica for a week in March. I have also been to Portugal, America and Spain to train'.

(Mark Richardson, 23, GB & England Senior International, 400 m)

'I went to Portugal for one week, I have been to Gainsville, Florida for two weeks, I was also in France earlier this year for four or five days, to catch up on a bit of pre-season warm weather training'.

(Lesley Owusu, 17, GB & England Junior International, 200 m)

'I have been to Portugal for two weeks, I have been to New Zealand for a month, I have been to America for a week and I have been to Spain for a week on numerous occasions'.

(Paul Hibbert, 30, England Senior International, 400 m hurdles)

'I've been to Uruguay, Holland, California, Tenerife, Spain, South Africa and most other European countries'.

(Jackie Agyepong, 26, GB & England Senior International, 100 m hurdles)

Sources: Reeves (2000); Jackson and Reeves (1998)

The group is, however, atypical on a number of levels. First, while for the vast majority of sports tourists the unique interaction of activity, people and place is central to the sports tourism experience, for elite athletes the place experience is often unimportant except in the sense that it provides quality facilities, expertise or a warm climate. For most elite athletes, whether supported by commercial sponsors or government funding, their sports participation, and thus their sports tourism behaviour, is essentially their job. As such, elite athletes might be considered as business tourists, for whom travelling expenses are paid and for whom both the taking of a trip and the destination are chosen by others, be this a venue for a training camp or location of a competition. Consequently, in the majority of cases, travel is incidental to the motivation of elite athletes. It is a necessary part of their participation over which they have no control or choice. In fact, the research among British track athletes in the late 1990s (Jackson and Reeves, 1998; Reeves, 2000) showed that many athletes considered the travel element an inconvenience. The unique aspect of the sports tourism behaviours of elite athletes is that they play no part in the DMU that decides their trip. In fact, the DMU is broad and comprises the international sporting organizations (such as the International Olympic Committee) who decide the venues for competitions and the national sports organizations and coaches that decide on the team's competition schedule and the overseas training schedules.

While, as noted in Chapter 3, most other sports tourists will undertake a range of tourist behaviours in terms of shopping, sightseeing, eating out, etc., in many cases, elite athletes do not exhibit such behaviours. Time not spent training or competing is spent resting for the next training session or event. Some sightseeing may take place but, as dietary considerations are often essential, eating out is not possible. Furthermore, recreational participation in other sports tourism activities, while often welcome as a diversion from training, can be problematic due to the fear of injury (Box 4.2).

Clearly, the motivation for this group is advancement and achievement in elite sport and, as such, the 'status and prestige' motivations discussed in Chapter 3 will be the primary motivators, with the place element of the sports tourism experience being less important. However, there may be exceptions to this. In some team sports, such as rugby and football, the social element of the trip may be more important (Hinch and Higham, 2004). Interpersonal motivations, such as being part of a team of people who are the best in their country at their sport, may be an important part of the experience. Similarly, both anecdotal (e.g. *The Times*, 2003) and academic (e.g. Bale, 2003) sources have described how some places can be an inspiration to top quality performances in sport, heightening the experience of 'optimal arousal' (Iso-Ahola and Wissingberger, 1990) discussed in

---

Box 4.2 Potential injury as a barrier to recreational sports tourism participation

Illustrative comments of elite British track athletes on fear of injury:

'We go swimming. Quite often we use it as a session. We play a bit of basketball, but I tend not to play too many other sports because your muscles are not used to it and there is a greater chance of sustaining an injury'.

(Mark Richardson, 23, GB & England Senior International, 400 m)

'I tend not to play other sports as I'm usually too tired after my athletics training. There is also the risk of injury. I do a bit of swimming, but really when I am away I believe that I'm specifically there to train. I try not to do too many active things so that I can conserve my energy and put it into my training. I cannot risk getting injured'.

(Angela Davies, 28, GB and England Senior International, 1500 m)

'A couple of years ago when I was in Lanzarote, I went in early December so you are not too close to competition time. So that time I got involved in surfing, cycling and played tennis. When I went in March time just before competition, I would not do anything for fear of injury. I did swim recreationally, but nothing dangerous'.

(Sonya Bowyer, 23, GB & England Intermediate International, 100 m)

'I do fancy skiing holidays, but the risk of injuries is so high that I would be worried about breaking a leg and missing a season'.

(Spencer Newport, 29, England Senior International, 3000 m steeplechase)

Sources: Jackson and Reeves (1998); Reeves (2000)

Chapter 3. The backdrop of the Barcelona skyline during the diving competition at the 1992 Olympics must surely fall into this category (Weed, 2008a), as would competing at 'sporting Meccas' such as Yankee stadium in New York or Lords cricket ground in London.

Some of the sports tourists described under previous types of trip decision might argue that, in fact, they have no choice over their trip taking and destination. For example, many committed football and cricket fans might argue that, for the most significant competitions (e.g. the Football World Cup or The Ashes in cricket), not taking the trip is simply not an option and, therefore, they have no choice over the taking of the trip or the destination (Millward, 2006). Similarly, some business people for whom sports tourism behaviours are an important part of developing business relationships or entertaining clients would say that the choice over their trips is exercised by their company or their clients.

One interesting element, however, of the outdoor, adventure and 'alternative' sports tourists' behaviours that comes about as a result of the lack of resources for their activities in their home environment, is that some favourite destinations may become perceived as their 'home' places, even though they may be many miles from where they live and work. Such 'home' places may be a beach, a particular river or lake, or a favourite activity centre. Quantitative evidence from Reeves' (2000) study of activity tourism participants at Twr-y-Felin in Wales suggests that a significant minority see the area as a 'home' place, with 30 per cent of visitors having visited previously within the last 6 months and a further 15 per cent within the last month. Furthermore, 44 per cent stated their intention to 'definitely return' to the centre. As these participants' only participation in these activities is through sports tourism participation, there may be some trips that become so regular that there is no question of either whether to take the trip or where to go (this is also noted by Decrop and Snelders, 2005, in relation to some aspects of generic tourism). However, unlike the other examples described in this category, the decisions are not being made by a DMU of which they are not part, rather there is no need for a DMU as the trips have become a regular part of their lives (Hall and Muller, 2004).

What an examination of the various types of trip decision shows is that there is considerable variance in the importance attached to the opportunity to engage in sports tourism behaviours in the decision to take a trip and the destination choice. Furthermore, the more important the sports tourism behaviours and the higher the levels of participation, the less choice is exercised. While this may appear somewhat paradoxical, it is simply a reflection that sports tourism behaviours can be perceived to be important and widespread enough for travellers to tolerate restriction in the choices they exercise over whether to, and where to, take a trip involving sports tourism participation.

SPORTS TOURISM AS A VARIABLE IN POST-DECISION TRIP PLANNING

As the previous discussions have shown, there are many examples in which the opportunity to engage in sports tourism participation features in the decision to take a trip and/or in destination choice. Of course, for all of these examples, sports tourism will also feature in the planning that takes place once a trip has been booked. However, there are also those trips in which sports tourism has not featured in the decision to take a trip or the destination choice, but where it does feature in pre-trip planning and this is the focus of this section. In some cases, such plans will be realized during the trip, in others they will not (Oh, 2008). Some plans will be firm and definite and may involve elements of pre-payment, while others will involve a general intention to engage in sports tourism behaviours. Finally, some plans will be what might be termed 'opportunity' plans, with travellers ensuring they are sufficiently prepared to take advantage of participation opportunities that may arise during a trip, but without making any specific arrangements for participation. These three types of plans (firm, general intention and opportunity) are each discussed in turn in the following paragraphs.

Firm Pre-Trip Planning for Sports Tourism Participation

The defining element of the way in which sports tourism features in this type of pre-trip planning is that the plans lead to some sort of action in the pre-trip period. Such actions will mean that there is a certain level of commitment (Oh, 2008) to engage in the sports tourism behaviours that have been planned. Examples of this type of planning can be found in Event Sports Tourism, Sports Participation Tourism and Supplementary Sports Tourism. Perhaps the most obvious of this type of planning is the pre-purchase of tickets for an event, which may be a one-off event such as the European and World Cup Athletics events discussed in the previous section, or a visit to a regular fixture, such as a US Major League Baseball or a UK Premiership Football Match. The pre-purchase of tickets may serve two purposes: the first may be to ensure that attendance is possible, as tickets may sell out closer to the event; the second may be to establish the visit to the event in the minds of all members of the trip DMU as a fixed part of the trip. While such plans have been made after the decision to take a trip and the destination choice has been made, this does not mean the planned behaviours do not become an important part of the trip. In fact, as discussed elsewhere in this text, often 'must-see' activities (such as a visit to an event or fixture at the destination) can be focal points in many trips, even if they have not played a role in destination or trip choice. Other firm plans may not involve pre-payment. However pre-booking, for example, a tee-time for a round of golf at a course at the destination, indicates a firm commitment to participate (Readman, 2003). Similarly, making arrangements to meet others to engage in a particular activity also elevates plans to a firm or committed level. An example from sports participation tourism may be agreeing to meet friends to hire cycles for a day, an emotional commitment that it may be difficult to break.

Plans as General Intentions

Unlike the way in which sports tourism features in the firm plans outlined above, this type of planning is psychological and emotional (c.f. Hagger et al., 2002) rather than involving any firm actions or arrangements towards participation. It may well involve investigating the facilities and opportunities that are available for sports tourism participation during a forthcoming trip, but does not involve making bookings or setting timetables. As such, it may be that this level of planning takes place at the individual level rather than within the DMU. These types of general intentions have been shown to lead to a relatively low level of take-up (Reeves, 2000) and it is partly for this reason that an 'intenders' group is included in the Revised Sports Tourism Participation Model in Chapter 5. In fact, it may be that participation planned in this way is not realized because individuals do not engage the DMU in such plans and consequently, there has been no agreement to participate (Oh, 2008). As bookings are not made for these planned behaviours, the sports tourism product type involved is usually Supplementary Sports Tourism (such as the availability of watersports on beach holidays) that are widely available at destinations as 'turn-up-and-play' activities. As actual engagement in sports tourism behaviours planned as general intentions tends to be lower than that for other behaviours, it would appear that they are less important within the overall context of the trip. However, as the previous section has noted, some behaviours that play a role in the decision to take a trip and destination choice can sometimes not be realized. As such, the importance of such plans should not be dismissed as they can play an important role in vicarious engagement through pre-trip day-dreaming (Decrop, 2006), even though they may not actually take place.

Opportunity Planning

While firm planning involves some sort of commitment to engage in sports tourism behaviours and general intentions involve psychological and emotional planning for behaviours that are intended to take place, opportunity planning takes place without any necessary intention to participate. The plans are preparations that are made to allow participation to take place should the opportunity arise and they may either be made on an individual basis or within the DMU. Keen golfers, for example, may take their golf clubs on a trip without necessarily making any plans to participate, but wishing to be equipped to do so should the time and opportunity to play golf present itself (Hennessey et al., 2008). Similarly, hotel guests may take sports and swimming equipment on a trip to allow participation to be possible, but without definitely intending to do so. Such planning involves taking some action towards participation (by making preparations to make participation possible), but not making any psychological or emotional commitment to participate. This may be because there are many other tourism behaviours planned for a trip and sports tourism behaviours may be 'crowded out' in terms of time. This crowding out may either be agreed between the DMU or may involve compromise on the part of one or more individuals (Decrop and Snelders, 2005). Again, this may appear to indicate a lack of importance being attached to sports tourism behaviours, however, the 'crowding out' of such behaviours may be the result of commitments to take part in family activities on a leisure trip, or to attend meetings on a business trip. As such, the sports tourism behaviours may be important (hence the planning to allow for them if possible), but not necessarily possible. Similarly, it may be that destination factors may constrain behaviours (Bull, 2005) – there may simply not be, for example, a golf course conveniently available at the destination.

Sports tourism behaviours can feature to varying extents in post-decision pre-trip planning and this shows that not all decisions about trips are made before a destination choice and booking is made (Decrop, 2006; Oh, 2008). Sports tourism behaviours can become a significant part of trips even at this stage in the process. Equally, they may just be considered a relatively insignificant supplement to a trip for which many other behaviours are planned (Gibson and Yiannakis, 2002). Of course, not all decisions about trip behaviours are made pre-trip and it is to sports tourism behaviours that take place spontaneously while on a trip that the final section of this chapter now turns.

SPORTS TOURISM AS A SPONTANEOUS TRIP BEHAVIOUR

The types of sports tourism behaviours that take place spontaneously during a trip are potentially infinite and, almost by definition, they tend to be less important to participants as they have not featured in the plans for the trip. Similarly, such behaviours require that opportunities are available at the destination without the need to pre-plan or pre-book (Standeven and De Knop, 1999; Higham, 2005); essentially, that tickets for events are available on the day of the event or that activities can be participated in on a 'turn-up-and-play' basis (Weed and Jackson, 2008). While the 'supply' requirements for this type of participation are similar to those required for those planned as general intentions discussed in the previous section, the 'demand' features are very different, because the participant has not thought about such participation before arriving at the destination. Consequently, the product type is likely (although not certain) to be Supplementary Sports Tourism and the opportunities offered are likely to be either those that potential participants were not aware of before the trip

(Weed, 2008a), or those that may be taken up as alternatives to pre-planned activities that may no longer be available due to capacity being reached or inclement weather.

Although spontaneous sports tourism behaviours are largely less important within the trip, they do not necessarily remain so for future trips. As Chapter 9 explains, often providers make provision for people to take part in 'taster sessions' for a range of activities. Such activities are intended to 'capture spontaneous behaviour', with the hope that such behaviours will become part of pre-trip planning or even play a part in the destination choice for future trips. Consequently, while spontaneous sports tourism behaviours can begin as an unimportant part of the trip, they can progress to being an important trip behaviour for future trips (Green and Jones, 2005).

CONCLUSION

The discussions in this chapter have served to provide specific illustrations of the role that sports tourism can play in the trip decision-making process. In particular, the focus has been on the way in which the desire to engage in sports tourism behaviours during a trip can affect the decision about the taking of trips and the destination choice and that the more important sports tourism behaviours are and the higher levels of participation are likely to be, the more likely they become to constrain elements of such choices. That individual choices are constrained can also be a function of the existence of decision-making units (DMUs) that collectively make choices about trips and within which individual compromise is often required (Decrop and Snelders, 2005). In some extreme circumstances (e.g. elite athletes), decisions about trip taking and destinations may be made by a DMU of which the participant is not a part. This chapter reinforces the conclusion of Chapter 3 that sports tourism behaviours are diverse and heterogeneous. However, the variations on dimensions such as importance, participation levels and the trip decision-making process suggest the potential to model such behaviours and it is to the development of such a model that Chapter 5 now turns.

A Sports Tourism Participation Model

Chapter 3, the first chapter in this participants section, opened with a discussion of possible definitions of sport, of tourism and of sports tourism and found the establishment of such definitions to be problematic. This is because, as Houlihan (1994: p. 4) states:

the more one attempts to capture the essence of meaning of a human activity, the more one becomes aware of the ambiguities and the compromises necessary to arrive at a plausible definition.

Furthermore, as demonstrated by the range of examples of the influence of sports tourism in the trip decision-making process in Chapter 4, both sports tourism and the sports tourist are heterogeneous concepts and therefore no single definition is adequate. Consequently, much of the discussion in Chapter 3 focused on conceptualizing the sports tourist, attempting to go beyond a simple definition and move towards a deeper understanding of the nature and motivations of the sports tourist, which was subsequently used to examine the role of sports tourism behaviours in the trip decision-making process in Chapter 4.

The previous two chapters have demonstrated that, although sports tourists are a heterogeneous group, there may be similarities in motivations and trip decisions that allow a number of typical sports tourist behaviours to be conceived and, consequently, allow a model of participation behaviours to be constructed. This chapter presents such a model, derived from the discussions in the previous two chapters and, in particular, from the discussions of trip decisions in Chapter 4. The 'Revised Sports Tourism Participation Model' (revised from that presented in the first edition of this text, Weed and Bull, 2004) is dynamic and is not only useful in developing an understanding of the behaviours of sports tourists but also, following the discussions in Chapter 2, of how impacts are generated and how providers might operate to develop a successful sports tourism product.

PREVIOUS MODELS OF SPORTS TOURISM

There have been a number of attempts at developing a typology of sports tourism or of sports tourists. Perhaps the first attempt was that proposed by Glyptis (1982) following her investigation of the relationship between sport and tourism in five European countries. She suggested five 'demand types', namely: sports training, 'up-market' sports holidays, activity holidays, sports opportunities on general holidays, and sports spectating. While these categories were proposed as demand types, they essentially amount to a supply side categorization of sports holidays. However, the Glyptis categorization has been taken up by a number of other authors with, for example, Weed and Bull (1997a) utilizing it to demarcate sports holidays within their Policy Area Matrix for Sport and Tourism (see Chapter 7 for an updated version of this model). Two key concepts that Glyptis' early work highlights are that sports tourism may be either active or passive (i.e. include involvement in activities themselves or as a spectator) and that sports may be the primary purpose of the trip or be 'incidental' to holidays that have other prime purposes. In the case of the latter division, as Chapters 3 and 4 have noted, other authors have also divided sports tourism into whether sport or tourism is the primary purpose of the trip (e.g. De Knop, 1987; Robinson and Gammon, 2004). However, these chapters argued for the need to move towards a synergistic view of sports tourism that is not reliant on the primacy of either the sport or the tourism element which, in many cases, cannot be separated out. This text argues that considering sports tourism as one among a number of touristic and instrumental behaviours on a trip can help move the analysis of sports tourism participation beyond the rather simplistic primary/secondary purpose duality.

The active/passive distinction is also one that has been utilized subsequently by other authors, although Chapter 3 argued that 'vicarious' participation should also be considered. Hall (1992a), for example, in his conceptual framework for adventure, health and sports tourism, plots the level of activity against the level of competitiveness to derive a nine-category matrix (Figure 5.1). The use of competitiveness as a dimension is a useful one and Hall's model is helpful in that it illustrates the range of activities from those in the top left hand corner that are recreationally based to those in the bottom right hand corner that fall clearly into the competitive sport category.

Less Active ——————————— More Active			
Non-competitive	**Health Tourism** (e.g. spa tourism, health travel)	**Health Tourism** (e.g. fitness retreats)	**Adventure Travel** (e.g. whitewater rafting, SCUBA diving, hiking)
	Adventure Travel (e.g. yacht chartering)	**Tourism Activities** … which contain elements of health, sport and adventure (e.g. cycling, sea-kayaking)	**Adventure Travel** (e.g. climbing)
Competitive	**Sport Tourism** (e.g. spectating)	**Sport Tourism** (e.g. lawn bowls)	**Sport Tourism** (e.g. ocean racing)

FIGURE 5.1 *Hall's (1992a) model of adventure, health and sports tourism*

In plotting out 'forms' of sports tourism, Standeven and De Knop (1999) also use the active/passive distinction, alongside a number of other subdivisions. 'Tourism relevant to sport' is split into holiday and non-holiday trips, each of which is subdivided into active and passive trips before further subdivisions are made (Figure 5.2). A useful concept introduced in this categorization is the distinction made under passive sport between the casual observer and the connoisseur. While in some senses this may appear to be analogous to the primary/incidental distinction made by Glyptis (1982), it also implies that the level of importance attached to sports tourism is a key factor. This is a slightly different distinction, therefore, to the trip purpose division proposed by Glyptis and, while it is not accorded any great significance within this categorization, it is something that has not been raised in other models. Strangely, however, Standeven and De Knop do not make a similar distinction for active sports tourism.

Later in their book, Standeven and De Knop (1999) propose a 'conceptual classification of sport tourism' which they describe as a 'theoretical framework to support the concept of sport tourism as a cultural experience on two dimensions: sport and tourism' (p. 49). In this model, the sport experience (based on Haywood's, 1994, classification of sport as environmental or inter-personal challenge) is plotted against the touristic experience (based on Burton's, 1995, description of tourism environments as natural or manmade). While this may seem a useful conflagration of two established models, the further subdivisions made make the model overcomplicated.

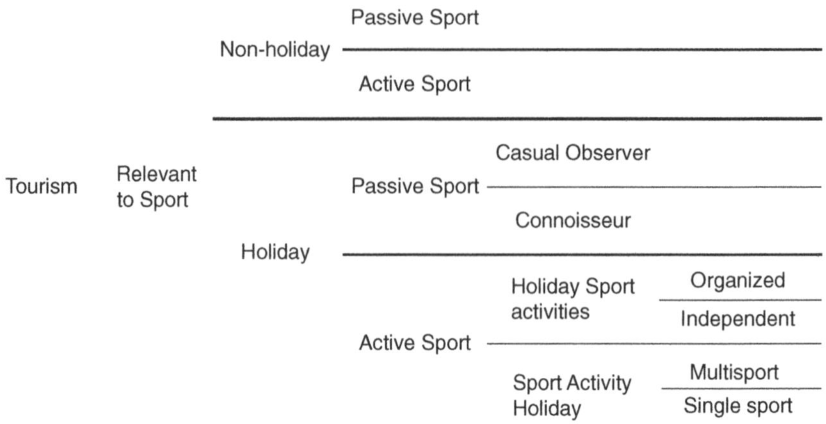

FIGURE 5.2 *Standeven and De Knop's (1999) 'forms of sport tourism'*

Furthermore, it retreats to the perspective of sports tourism as being the simple addition of sport and tourism rather than a 'trialectic' concept (Lefebvre, 1991) in which sports tourism would not be 'an additive combination of its binary antecedents' but through deconstruction and reconstruction would produce a third phenomenon that is 'both similar and strikingly different'. The trialectic concept leads (see discussions in Chapter 3) to the development of a conceptualization of sports tourism as arising from the unique interaction of activity, people and place, where the focus is on the 'interaction' of activity, people and place, thus emphasizing the synergistic nature of the sports tourism as *related to but more than the sum of* sport and tourism and moving it away from a dependence on either sport or tourism as the primary defining factor.

In addition, plotting sport against tourism results in a model, like those already described above, that is activity based. While this may be useful in illustrating the range of sports tourism types, it is of little use in analysing or examining the sports tourist or, in fact, the sports tourism phenomenon (Green and Jones, 2005). In fact, it provides little information beyond that which would be provided by an extensive list of sports tourism activities.

DEVELOPING A SPORTS TOURISM PARTICIPATION MODEL

In developing a model that might be used as an analytical tool, both to appreciate the complex nature of the sports tourist and to develop a greater understanding of the sport tourism phenomenon, a focus is required, as has been the case in the previous two chapters, on sports tourism behaviours. Previous work, some of which has been described in the previous two chapters, has contributed to the development of a 'Sports Tourism Demand Continuum', early versions of which were described by Reeves (2000) and Collins and Jackson (2001), before it was presented in its final iteration by Jackson and Weed (2003) and later critiqued by Weed and Jackson (2008). As well as focusing on the nature of the sports tourist, rather than sports tourism activities, this model is derived from empirical research. The model takes its basic concept from the English Sports Council's 'Sports Development Continuum' that plots the movement of sports participants from the introductory Foundation level, through Participation and Performance, to the elite Excellence level. The Sports Tourism Demand Continuum, similarly, begins with Incidental sports participation on general holidays and moves through various levels of commitment – Sporadic, Occasional, Regular and Committed – ending with the Driven sports tourist involved in year-round travel for elite competition and training (Figure 5.3).

This model, however, still has a number of implicit weaknesses. First, there is an implication that in moving along the continuum from Incidental to Driven participation there is an increase in sports ability. This is particularly highlighted by the conceptualization of the Driven group profile as 'elite groups or individuals'. This also calls into question the applicability of the model to 'passive' sports tourists or spectators. In every other sense it appears that the continuum would apply to spectators, but the implication that levels of ability increase with movement along the continuum is difficult to reconcile with the concept of sports spectating. How would one's ability as a sports spectator be defined? The dual concept of sports tourists as both active participants and passive spectators (and now, as suggested in Chapter 3, also as vicarious participants) has been one that authors have struggled with in developing models of sports tourism, as there are often significant differences in behaviour patterns and motivations between active, vicarious and passive sports tourism behaviours. In fact, this might be said of sports tourism as a whole because the range of activities often included as sports tourism makes it a heterogeneous rather than a homogeneous phenomenon. This heterogeneity is what makes activity-based models problematic, as it becomes increasingly difficult to include the full range of issues within a model that is simple enough to be useful.

Perhaps the most significant weakness in the Sports Tourism Demand Continuum is the assumption that for participants towards the Incidental end of the scale, sport is insignificant and, consequently, sports tourism is unimportant. While this may be the case for a significant number of people

Summary characteristics	Incidental	Sporadic	Occasional	Regular	Committed	Driven
Decision-making factors	Impromptu	Unimportant	Can be determining factor	Important	Very important	Essential
Participation factors	Fun or duty to others	If convenient	Welcome addition to tourism experience	Significant part of experience	Central to experience	Often sole reason for travel
Non-participation factors	Prefer relaxation non-activity	Easily constrained or put off. Not essential to life profile	Many commitment preferences	Money or time constraints	Only unforeseen or significant constraints	Injury, illness or fear of illness
Typical group profile	Family groups	Family and friendship groups	Often friendship or business groups	Group or individuals	Invariably groups of like-minded people	Elite groups or individuals with support
Lifestyle	Sport is insignificant	Sport is non-essential. Like but not a priority	Sport is not essential but significant	Sport is important	Sport is a defining part of life	Sport is professionally significant
Sports expenditure	Minimal	Minimal except sporadic interest	High on occasions	Considerable	Extremely high and consistent	Extremely significant. Funding support from others

FIGURE 5.3 *Sports tourism demand continuum (Jackson and Weed, 2003 – derived from Jackson and Reeves, 1996; Reeves, 2000)*

towards this end of the continuum, it fails to recognize the importance of trips involving sports tourism to individuals' perceived self-identity (Green and Jones, 2005), the result being that, even where levels of participation are low, the importance placed on that participation can be significant. In seeking to address this weakness, this chapter proposes a 'Revised Sports Tourism Participation Model' which has been developed from the model proposed in the first edition of this text (Weed and Bull, 2004). This model continues to utilize the concept of a continuum of sports tourism participation but, unlike the model presented in 2004, it does not incorporate the various 'participant types' outlined in the demand continuum. The first step in the revision, the 'Simplified Sports Tourism Participation Model', continues to plot sports tourism participation against the importance placed on sports tourism behaviours and is illustrated in Figure 5.4 as the first step towards a more extended revision of the model.

The Simplified Sports Tourism Participation Model (Figure 5.4) plots sports tourism participation against the importance placed on sports tourism behaviours. Levels of participation increase along the horizontal axis, while the vertical scale indicates the amount of importance attached to sports tourism behaviours by individuals. The model illustrates that towards the left of the scale the level of importance attached to sports tourism behaviours may vary from a relatively high level, to little importance, or even negative importance. At the right of the scale, however, both importance and participation are high. This creates a 'triangle' of participation, the size of which corresponds to the *number* of sports tourists at each particular level.

Reeves (2000), utilizing empirical data from his study of sports participation at Butlins Holiday Worlds in the UK, describes reluctant participation that accounts for the existence of participants who attach a negative importance to sports tourism. For such people it is actually important *not* to engage in sports tourism behaviours on holiday. Such participation is usually a result of a sense of duty to others, particularly family members such as children or partners. Participation takes place although there may

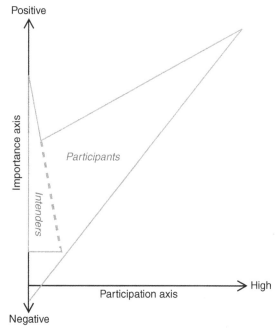

FIGURE 5.4 *Simplified sports tourism participation model*

be an antipathy towards it. At the other end of the importance axis at the left of the scale is participation that individuals feel is important to their sense of self or identity (Green and Jones, 2005) even though actual levels of participation may be low. Such sports tourism participation is important as it affects the identity that participants wish to portray to their peers on return from the trip. The importance of 'returning' as a significant part of the tourism experience is described by MacCannell (1996: p. 4) who explains that 'returning home is an essential part of being a tourist – one goes only to return'. MacCannell (2002) believes that tourists are people who leave home in the expectation that they will have some kind of experience of 'otherness' that will set them apart from their peers on their return. Here, the experience of otherness is the sports tourism behaviour(s) while on holiday, with the importance being attached to the perceived kudos that the telling and re-telling of the experience, often based on relatively low levels of participation, gives the participant on returning home (MacCannell, 2002). An example of this level of importance may be of someone who takes a beach holiday and spends most of the time soaking up the sun on the beach. However, this person may be goaded by his or her family into participating in a 30-minute water-skiing session. This may be the sum total of this individual's sports tourism behaviours on this holiday, but the impression that may be conveyed to his or her peers on return, through exaggerated re-telling of the experience, would be of a holiday full of sports tourism participation – an impression that may accord the individual a certain level of esteem among his or her peers. A perceived identity is constructed that means that the sports tourism behaviours during his or her trip have a relatively high importance despite the very low level of actual participation. Of course, in this example, the level of importance is a result of extrinsic factors – the identity which is portrayed to others. For other participants on the left and towards the middle of the scale, engagement in sports tourism behaviours may be important for more intrinsic factors. Trips involving sports tourism participation may be an opportunity to take part in lapsed activities for which the time or opportunity for participation does not exist at home. Here, significant importance may be attached to such participation because sports tourism participation, no matter how low, may be the only link that such individuals have with past sports participation and, consequently, with a continued conception of themselves as a 'sportsperson'. This is something that may be of major importance to someone who has previously been a very active participant in sports or, indeed, in sports tourism, but for whom other responsibilities now restrict participation. In both these examples, the contribution that sports tourism behaviours can make to individuals' perceived self-identity means that sports tourism can be important to individuals for whom actual levels of participation are low.

As levels of participation and broad levels of importance increase with a move from left to right in the model, the quality of the sports tourism experience becomes more important as sports tourism behaviours become a significant factor in tourism destination choices (see Chapter 4). As discussed in Chapter 3, the nature of the place can contribute considerably to the quality of such experiences (Bull, 2005). This may be through the standard of facilities available at the destination, but also as a result of the general environment, the place ambience, the scenic attractiveness and the presence of other like-minded people. Furthermore, Urry (2001) notes the specific motivation of some regular sports tourists to 'collect places'. This may be the development of a 'collection' of as wide a range of places as possible, a factor among many of the 'active event sports tourists' to Malta described in Chapter 10 and by Shipway and Jones (2004), many of whom had competed at non-elite level in running events around the world, often combining such participation with a subsequent family holiday. Alternatively, such 'place collection' may relate to particularly significant or 'mythical' sports tourism places. An example of this, as noted in Chapter 4, might be visits by surfers to beaches in Hawaii that are regarded as surfing 'Meccas'.

The significance of the unique interaction of activity, people and place would appear to increase with movement towards the right of the participation triangle. However, for some at the far right of the scale, the place experience may be less important than technical requirements related to the quality of facilities. Such participants are the elite athletes described in Chapter 4 and by Jackson and Reeves (1998) and Reeves (2000). For these participants, factors related to place environment – with the exception of climate which is, of course, important for 'warm-weather training' – are relatively insignificant. This, along with their elite sports ability, sets such participants apart from other sports tourists. However, with the exception of the elite athlete, high levels of sports ability and performance are not a pre-requisite for even the most committed of sports tourists. Surfers are a good example of such committed sports tourists who are not necessarily concerned with elite performance and for whom the experiential aspects of the activity are clearly of great importance (see Wheaton, 2004 and discussions of surfing narratives in Smith and Weed, 2007). This is highlighted by Butts (2001) who notes that many of the surfers in his study described the 'serenity of the ocean' and the importance of the condition of the ocean and the environment to the surfing experience.

Also at the far right of the model are spectating sports tourists for whom both participation and importance are high and for whom spectating is a defining part of their self-identity. An example from this end of the scale might be the 'Barmy Army' group of England cricket fans who, since their emergence in the mid-1990s, have demonstrated a very high level of commitment to following a less than successful England cricket team around the globe (Parry and Malcolm, 2004). Football fans are also a good example of the committed spectator and much of the work on football hooliganism (see Dunning et al., 1988; Carnibella et al., 1996; Weed, 2001c) certainly suggests that many are committed participants for whom their identity as a hooligan is of central importance. That is not to suggest that football supporting is not important to non-violent football fans (Millward, 2006) – in fact, the level of commitment shown by some fans has been compared to religion (Bale, 2003) – but is merely an indication of the area in which the majority of research on sports fans has been concentrated.

The example of football fans is a useful one to continue with in examining sports spectators at the left of the triangle where participation is low. Here, there will be a vast number of people for whom identity as a football fan is of great importance, but for whom participation in live football spectating as a sports tourism experience is minimal. Similarly, there will be those who have spectated at football, but for whom it is not an important part of their identity. In fact, as with participants in active sports tourism, it is likely that for some, such participation has a negative importance as it has taken place out of a sense of duty to others such as partners or children (Reeves, 2000).

A discussion of spectating sports tourists provides a useful avenue through which to introduce another concept into the model – that of the 'Intender'. Intenders were described in relation to arts audiences by Hill et al. (1995: p. 43) as 'those who think the arts are a "good thing" and like the idea of attending, but never seem to get around to it'. Such a concept would also seem to be useful in relation to sports tourism and perhaps spectators provide the most useful illustration. The growth in televised coverage of sport has created a vast number of spectators who are highly committed and for whom watching sport is important, but who rarely travel to a live event (Weed, 2006d). Many such spectators often express a desire to go to a live event, but like Hill et al.'s (1995) arts intenders, 'never seem to get around to it'. Of course, some intenders will attend the odd match and so the boundary with participation is fluid. However, this group is largely made up of those for whom watching sport is important, but for whom attending a live event never becomes more than a whimsical intention.

The Intenders categorization is, of course, equally significant in relation to active sports tourism. In the same research in which he identified sports tourism behaviours that take place as a duty to others, Reeves (2000) also describes those who go on holiday with the intention of taking up some of the sports tourism opportunities available, but never actually get round to it. The promotion of the range of sports tourism opportunities available in hotel and resort brochures can create the intention to engage in sports tourism behaviours but, in many cases, such intention is not converted into actual participation. Even where such sports tourism opportunities may play a part in resort or hotel choice (see discussions of the trip decision-making process in Chapter 4) and the intention may be described to peers pre-trip (in the same way as low levels of participation may be exaggerated post-trip as discussed earlier) as a way of boosting perceived identity, there is no guarantee that such intention will be converted into actual participation (Keynote, 2001: Mintel, 2002c).

THE SPORTS TOURISM PARTICIPATION MODEL AND THE TRIP DECISION-MAKING PROCESS

Having outlined the basics of the model, it is now possible to incorporate the role of sports tourism in the trip decision-making process as discussed in Chapter 4. The three levels (sports tourism as a deciding or contributing factor in the decision to take a trip and the choice of destination, sports tourism as a factor in trip planning that takes place after the trip decision and destination choice has been made and sports tourism as a spontaneous trip behaviour) are illustrated as part of a Revised Sports Tourism Participation Model as shown in Figure 5.5.

The diagram shows that, as might be intuitively expected, sports tourism behaviours are a factor in the trip decision in the top half of the model where importance is high (area A), they are a factor in post-decision trip-planning in the upper part of the lower half of the model where importance is moderate (area B) and are a spontaneous trip behaviour at the bottom of the model where importance is low (area C). Sports tourism intentions (as indicated by the Intenders classification) can also influence trip decisions and planning, even though this may not be carried through to actual sports tourism behaviours, although as indicated by the dotted line between intenders and participants, this boundary can be fluid. Finally, the small area indicating participants for whom a negative importance is attached to sports tourism behaviours (i.e. those to whom it is important *not* to engage in sports tourism behaviours, but who do so to please others such as family and friends) is likely to include those whose behaviours have featured at every level of the trip decision-making process.

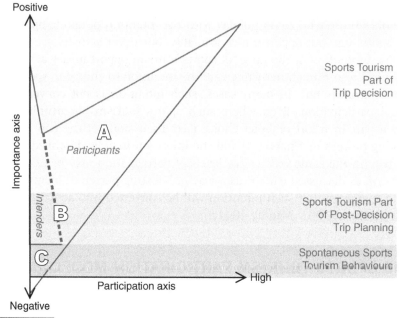

FIGURE 5.5 *Revised sports tourism participation model*

Of course, as noted in Chapter 4, sports tourism will play a part in trip planning in the majority of cases where it has been a factor in the trip decision, but area B refers to those participants for whom sports tourism behaviours were not considered in the trip decision, but for whom they do play a part in trip planning. The model indicates that the majority of sports tourism behaviours take place on trips where they have played a part in the trip decision (area A), with fewer behaviours taking place as a result of trip planning (area B) and fewer still as spontaneous behaviours (area C). This suggests that at even the most incidental level of sports tourism participation, such as swimming in a hotel pool, such participation is likely to have been considered pre-trip (areas A and B).

Chapter 4 noted that day-dreaming can be a part of the trip decision-making process even before a decision to take a trip is made (Decrop and Snelders, 2005). Indeed, day-dreaming may provide significant experiences even if a trip is never made (i.e. when the trip decision-making process results in a decision not to take a trip). It is this type of 'vicarious' participation through imagining what it would be like to take a trip involving sports tourism that accounts for the (relatively small) group of participants in the Intenders triangle in area A for whom participation is low but importance is very high. Of those discussed in Chapter 4, this might include those committed spectators (e.g. committed cricket and football fans) for whom the spectating sports tourism trip is very important (Millward, 2006), but for whom it is not possible to make the trip.

Another factor discussed in Chapter 4 was the degree of choice exercised in the trip decision-making process, both over whether to take a trip involving sports tourism behaviours and over the destination for a trip involving sports tourism behaviours. The discussions noted that the level of choice exercised may vary and that this may be linked to both the importance placed on sports tourism behaviours within the trip and the levels of participation. If this is considered within the context of the Revised Sports Tourism Participation Model, it is likely that at the bottom left corner of area A (where importance is moderate and participation is low), choice is exercised over both the decision to take a trip and the destination for a trip, while at the top right corner of area A (where both importance and participation are high), it is likely that there will be little or no choice over either the taking of a trip or of the destination. For the remaining participants in area A that fall in the centre of the area (where importance is moderate to high and participation is moderate), choice is likely to be exercised over either the taking of the trip or the destination. Examples of the choices and behaviours of sports tourists in area A are provided in Chapter 4.

THE REVISED SPORTS TOURISM PARTICIPATION MODEL FOR DIFFERENT SPORTS TOURISM PRODUCTS

The 'Revised Sports Tourism Participation Model' presented in Figure 5.5 is intended to be a generic representation of participation in sports tourism. However, in concluding this chapter it is perhaps worth considering the extent to which the shape of the model might vary according to the sports tourism product on offer. Chapter 3 suggested five broad sports tourism products that are discussed in much more detail in Chapter 8. These products – Supplementary Sports Tourism, Sports Participation Tourism, Sports Training Tourism, Event Sports Tourism and Luxury Sports Tourism – provide for the sports tourism behaviours discussed in Chapter 4 and it is perhaps useful to examine examples within each of three of these broad product types to illustrate the way in which the shape of the 'Revised Sports Tourism Participation Model' may vary.

Figure 5.6 shows four potential model shapes for particular sports tourism products, one each within Sports Participation Tourism and Sports Training Tourism, and two examples within Event Sports Tourism. The shape at the top left illustrates what the Sports Tourism Participation Model

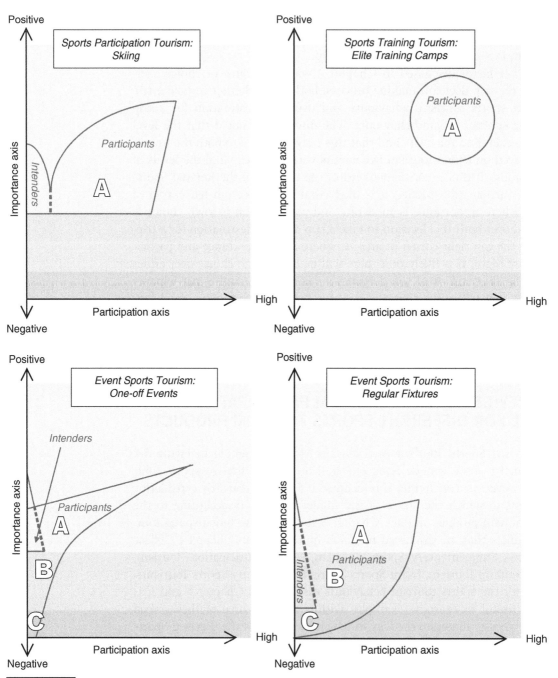

FIGURE 5.6 *Potential variations in the shape of the revised sports tourism participation model for specific sports tourism products*

might look like for skiing sports tourism within the Sports Participation Tourism product type. As skiing sports tourism behaviours almost universally require forethought and the booking of a trip to ski destinations, there are no spontaneous skiing behaviours or skiing behaviours that have been planned after the decision to make a trip and the destination choice have been made. As such, only area A (sports tourism as part of the trip decision) from the generic model is included. However, the shape allows for a great deal of variance in participation in skiing sports tourism behaviours, with some participants skiing every day and others skiing only occasionally. Some intenders may travel intending to take part in skiing sports tourism, but on arrival engage only with the après ski experience, while other intenders will engage only vicariously and will not take the trip.

The shape at the top right of Figure 5.6 illustrates elite training camps within the Sports Training Tourism product type. The shape here is straightforward, with elite sports training tourism behaviours featuring significantly in the decision to travel and the destination choice, but with the elite athletes themselves having little or no say in either decision. Importance and participation is high and there is no intenders group.

The two shapes at the bottom of Figure 5.6 illustrate two different types of Event Sports Tourism products. The shape on the left illustrates how the Sports Tourism Participation Model might look for spectating sports tourists to a one-off event such as the Athletics World Cup discussed in Chapter 4. The majority of these behaviours are likely to have featured in the decision to take the trip (area A), albeit perhaps only a day-trip, to watch the event. Some travellers may realize the event is taking place after they have booked their trip to the destination (area B) and so may include spectating sports tourism behaviours in their pre-trip planning. However, it is likely that there will be relatively few spontaneous spectating sports tourists (area C), as one-off events can often be sold out in advance. The likely need to pre-book tickets means that the intenders group is only likely to comprise those who consider travelling, but eventually do not make the trip.

The other Event Sports Tourism shape (on the bottom right of Figure 5.6) illustrates the likely shape for a regular sports fixture, such as US Major League Baseball or UK Premiership Football Matches. Here, assuming that tickets are available at the venue on the day of the match, the number of spontaneous spectating sports tourist behaviours are likely to be high (area C), as are those that have featured in pre-trip planning (area B), with a significant number of intenders travelling with the intention to attend the fixture, but not actually doing so once at the destination. As spectating sports tourism at such a fixture is likely to be only one among a number of other equally or more important tourist behaviours, the numbers for whom such behaviours feature in the decision to take the trip and the destination choice is likely to be lower than for other sports tourism products. However, numbers in both areas B and C are likely to feature 'must see' spectating sports tourism behaviours among those who see, for example, a trip to see the New York Yankees play baseball as an essential part of a trip to New York.

CONCLUSION: THE UTILITY OF THE REVISED MODEL

The 'Revised Sports Tourism Participation Model' described in this chapter allows for the profiling of a range of sports tourism behaviours across the sports tourism product range. As such, it can be of practical use to both policy-makers and providers in sports tourism, as it provides a fairly comprehensive illustration of the wide range of sports tourism behaviours and their respective roles and importance in the trip decision-making process.

Providers, for example, are likely to be interested in the 'Intenders' group and the extent to which they will be able to develop strategies to convert such intention into participation, thus boosting their customer base. Policy-makers may also be interested in the Intenders group and the development of strategies that might stimulate sports tourism participation that can contribute to healthy lifestyles. At another level, policy-makers might be interested in the development of a 'sports tourism' identity for a particular area as part of a regeneration or diversification strategy. Such development and promotion is likely to be aimed at both intenders and spontaneous sports tourism participants, but also at the genuinely 'multi-lingual' sports tourist who may be a committed participant across a range of sports tourism products. At the top right of the model, where both importance and participation are high, some providers, such as Club La Santa in Lanzarote, have developed a reputation of providing quality facilities for the elite athlete on warm weather training, but also for sports tourists who want to take part in sports training tourism at a non-elite level while also sampling the fairly wide range of sports tourism activities on offer.

The conceptualization of sports tourism as being the result of the unique interaction of activity, people and place is a theme that has run throughout these participation chapters. Chapter 3 examined how this interaction might motivate sports tourism behaviour, while Chapter 4 discussed the interaction in relation to the role of sports tourism in the trip decision-making process. In modelling sports tourism participation, this chapter has sought to illustrate how a range of sports tourism behaviours might interact with activities, people and places. In the remainder of the book, and particularly in the study of providers, both the model described here and the underpinning idea of the interaction of activity, people and place, will be important concepts in examining, analysing and understanding the behaviour and strategy of those involved in sports tourism provision.

PART 3

Policy

PREFACE

The first chapter of this book demonstrated that there has been a significant expansion in the development of sports tourism over time and that, in recent years, sports tourism has been shown to provide a range of important positive impacts. This suggests that, for policy-makers, there is a significant range of mutually beneficial advantages to be gained from a link between the sport and tourism sectors. However, as the two chapters that comprise this policy section will show, agencies responsible for policy for sport and for tourism around the world have shown a distinct reluctance to work together. Consequently, while in an ideal world these chapters would focus on the most effective ways in which sport–tourism policy might be developed to cater for the unique interaction of activity, people and place outlined so far in this book, the focus is necessarily on the paucity of meaningful policy partnerships that cater for the sport–tourism link. As such, the clear links that are made between related issues in other areas of this book are not as prevalent in this section. This is because the discussions here draw on perspectives from policy studies to focus on how the lack of liaison between sport and tourism agencies might be explained and understood, rather than on how sport–tourism policy should be developed in the light of knowledge about the behaviours and motivations of participants and providers.

There are some examples of sports tourism activity by policy-makers around the world and a number of these are referred to in the following chapters. However, as Weed and Bull's (1997a) review of regional policy in England showed, many policy initiatives related to sports tourism are implemented unilaterally by agencies from the sport or the tourism sector. Consequently, Weed and Bull (1997a: p. 146) concluded that:

> *... while there exists an increasing level of sport–tourism activity, this has not been matched by an increase in liaison amongst the agencies responsible for sport and tourism policy... It may be that these bodies are generally reticent to collaborate with any agency outside their area of interest ... as they may feel their interests would be threatened.*

Furthermore, more recent work (Weed, 2006a) on the perceptions of policy-makers across the UK suggests that little has changed in the decade since this research. While these comments are based on UK research, similar situations have been shown to exist in other countries around the world and, as such, it is the role of the following two chapters to explore the full extent of this reticence to collaborate and its effect on sport–tourism policy development.

Chapter 6 utilizes the concept of the policy community and the related ideas of policy universe and policy network, to establish a theoretical framework for the study of sport–tourism policy. This framework has been shown to endure over time (Weed, 2005a, 2006a) and, as such, its relevance has been reinforced since the publication of the first edition of this text.

Chapter 7 considers those areas in which policy-makers for sport and tourism might be expected to collaborate and, in doing so, utilizes Weed's (2008b) more recent perspectives to restructure the Policy Area Matrix for Sport and Tourism (Weed and Bull, 1997a) presented in the first edition into a 'Policy Wheel for Sport and Tourism' which shows that the core concepts of the Policy Matrix have endured, although the contemporary issues the sectors face have evolved. The consideration of the potential for the future development of collaborative sport–tourism policy remains in Chapter 7, but the chapter concludes with an updated discussion on the successful development of policy for sport and tourism.

The Policy Context

An examination of policy responses to the sport–tourism link suffers from a 'double dearth' in terms of supporting literature. While the previous chapters of this book have provided an overview of sports tourism and analysed in detail the motivations and profiles of sports tourists, in comparison to other areas of study, the area of sports tourism, while growing, is not particularly well served by a significant coherent body of literature (Weed, 2006b), particularly when compared with the related areas of leisure, sport and tourism. Similarly, although leisure studies is now a relatively established field of academic analysis, there is still surprisingly little literature relating to the dynamics of the leisure policy process. With the exception of work such as that by Henry (2001) on the politics of leisure policy, which focuses more on ideological concerns than the dynamics of the policy process, examples of the limited work in this area are those by Houlihan and colleagues (Houlihan and White, 2002; Green and Houlihan, 2005; Houlihan and Green, 2007) on sport, and Hall and Jenkins (2003) and Kerr (2003) on tourism. Furthermore, while the work of these authors is useful in informing an examination of sport–tourism policy, they do not extend their analysis beyond sport and tourism respectively, nor do they look in any detail at cross-sectoral liaison.

Across the globe, there are few examples where agencies responsible for sport and tourism have developed links or worked together. Furthermore, in the very few areas where links have emerged, they have done so in a very piecemeal and ad-hoc manner. This is evidenced by perhaps one of the highest profile areas of the sport–tourism link, major events. In many countries, the potential of major events to attract visitors to an area is recognized, however, the partnerships that emerge are often short term or uncoordinated and, in some cases, virtually non-existent. In the UK, for example, the national sports agency, UK Sport, has a Major Events Group, which works to attract events to the country. Similarly, Visit Britain has a Sports Tourism Department to promote sport in Britain to overseas visitors. However, to date, there are very few significant examples of any partnerships between these agencies in this area and certainly no longer-term strategic collaborations (Weed, 2006a). Yet there are some examples of how such long-term policies for the promotion of sport event based tourism can be developed, one of which is illustrated by the case study of Sheffield in Chapter 11.

Notwithstanding any reluctance among sport and tourism agencies to work together, developing policy to support the diverse nature of sports tourism, evidenced by the discussions of participants in the previous three chapters, is no simple task. The heterogeneous nature of sports tourism, based on the interaction of activity, people and place, makes the task of policy development in this area a complicated one. That the development of such policy takes place against a general backdrop of indifference from many of the policy agencies that might reasonably be expected to be involved only serves to make the task more complicated. A number of factors can be initially identified that contribute to such indifference. In many countries around the world, the agencies and structures that exist for developing sport and tourism respectively have been established and have developed entirely separately. This separate development is often compounded by a significantly different 'culture' or 'ethos' in the two sectors. There is often a tradition of public sector support, subsidy and/or intervention in the sports sector (the exception, perhaps, being the USA, where the United States Olympic Committee, although granted a role via legislation, receives no public sector funding), while the tourist sector is largely seen as a private sector concern and agencies are often limited to a marketing or business support role. These factors are further complicated by the different levels at which responsibility for policy development lies. Organizations may exist at national, regional and/or local level and in countries such as the USA or Australia, which have federal systems of government, the significant role of state governments also needs to be considered. The respective responsibilities of these agencies can mean that, in some instances, liaison would need to take place not only across sectors, but also between levels. In England, for example, the lack of a tourism organization for England often means that regional bodies such as the Regional Development Agencies or Regional Tourist Boards are the more appropriate bodies for the nationally focused Sport England to liaise with. The relative scarcity of such liaison is a testament to the range of problems that exist.

However, before the detail of policy liaison is addressed, a framework within which sport–tourism policy might be analysed is required. This book draws on literature on policy communities, both general and in relation to sport–tourism policy, to provide such an analytical framework. The chapter initially discusses the origin of the policy community concept, before outlining a descriptive Model of Cross-Sectoral Policy Development. It then draws on empirical work, largely based in the UK (although also highlighting examples from other countries), to examine how sport and tourism policy communities might be structured before discussing how such structures affect the emergence of sport–tourism policy networks. This analysis provides the context against which the potential for integration of sport and tourism policy is assessed in Chapter 7.

THE ORIGINS OF THE POLICY COMMUNITY CONCEPT

The theory of the policy community stems from several different areas of research, many of which are longstanding concepts which have, nevertheless, survived considerable academic scrutiny. Organizational sociologists comment on the concern of organizations with the requirements of organizational maintenance and enhancement (Wilson, 1973) and their occupancy of 'policy space' (Downs, 1967) which Jordan and Richardson (1987) likened to the concept of 'territory'. Group theorists see public policy as the product of the interaction of clusters of interest groups identified with particular policy areas which reflect the balance of influence at that time, but which also exhibit a degree of stability over time (Richardson and Jordan, 1979).

Combining these two areas of research, it is possible to view policy-making as taking place inside a sectorized arena where the policy process tends to fragment into relatively autonomous sectors. It is in conceptualizing these sectors that the idea of the policy community has emerged.

The concept of the policy community is a descendent, albeit a distant one, of the general pluralist theory of the state. Political pluralism developed as a rejection of absolute, unified and uncontrolled state power as exemplified by the absolutist monarchies of Western Europe in the eighteenth century (Skinner, 1978). The rationale for institutionalized pluralism – the separation of powers and federalism – was set out during the writing of the American Constitution by James Madison, in 'Federalist Paper No 10' (1787). Madison argued that a number of institutional checks and balances were required to prevent the abuse of power. First, that the powers of the executive (the President), the legislature (Congress) and the judiciary are vertically separated and, secondly, that sovereignty is horizontally divided through federalism and the provision of vetoes. In addition, Madison suggests the cultivation of an extended republic of heterogeneous social groups and territorial areas in order that political factions are numerous and diverse. Dahl (1956) argues that social pluralism – non-institutionalized checks and balances on authority such as the extended republic suggested above – is as important as institutionalized pluralism. It is this idea of social pluralism that contributes to the policy community model.

However, while pluralist ideas provide a context for the development of policy community models, other strands of research, such as the American sub-government literature, have had a more recent and more direct influence. Unlike pluralism, sub-government theory is applicable at the level of the particular policy process rather than the general level. Freeman (1955) is identified by Jordan (1990) as an important figure in the development of the sub-government literature. He emphasizes the need for the study of policy-making to be disaggregated to subsystems in which bureaucrats, Congressmen and interest groups interact. Freeman (1955: p. 11) describes such a subsystem as:

> ...the pattern of interactions of participants or actors involved in making decisions in a special area of public policy...although there are obviously other types of sub-systems, the type which concerns us here is found in an immediate setting formed by an executive bureau and congressional committees, with special interest groups immediately attached.

Sub-governments are viewed as being concerned in the main with routine areas of policy. However, the sum of these 'routine' policies represents a significant influence on public policy as a whole (Marsh, 1983). Furthermore, sub-governments will attempt to deal with as many items of policy as it is possible to reach agreement on. Failure to reach agreement will result in the drawing together of a wider audience which may impinge on the activities of the sub-government. The deliberations of such a wider audience may result in basic policy realignments that may reduce the power of, or work against the interests of members of the sub-government (Ripley and Franklin, 1980). Therefore, there is a strong incentive for sub-governments to compromise and reach agreements.

Although the influence of the sub-government literature on the concept of the policy community is indisputable, Rhodes (1986) emphasizes that this literature owes a lot to non-American sources, particularly European work on inter-organizational theory and work by Heclo and Wildavsky (1974) on decision-making in the British Treasury. Regardless of its origin, the policy community/network literature is related to the American sub-government work in that it focuses on the integration of interest groups into the policy-making process. There are a number of reasons why governments involve interest groups in policy-making, three perhaps being particularly influential. First, most groups have political connections with the media and thus, if they are not involved, have the potential to make 'noise and nuisance' (Jordan and Richardson, 1987). As a result, it is better for governments to pre-empt such 'noise and nuisance' through co-option. Secondly, in some cases, governments lack experience in particular policy areas and it is therefore sensible to draw on the knowledge of interest groups. Finally, it is now accepted that implementation is an important factor in the policy-making process and thus cooperation at the implementation stage is essential.

MODELS OF THE POLICY COMMUNITY

The most interesting developments in the policy community literature took place when, in the early 1980s, the Economic and Social Research Council in the UK funded two initiatives utilizing the concepts of policy community and policy networks: the inter-governmental relations (IGR) initiative focused on central–local government relations, while the second initiative focused on government–industry relations (GIR). Between them these initiatives generated thirty research projects with a number of important theoretical developments (IGR, see Goldsmith and Rhodes, 1986; GIR, see Wilks, 1989). However, these initiatives developed in distinctive ways and, while the GIR initiative was designed to build on the IGR studies, the GIR study produced a recognizably different model.

Of the IGR studies used the Rhodes model (Rhodes, 1981) while the GIR studies developed a different model (Wilks and Wright, 1987). One of the major problems in comparing these two models is the different definitions used for the concepts of policy community and policy network, something which is a source of considerable confusion in subsequent literature with a number of authors confusing the models and definitions used.

Rhodes initially uses Benson's (1982: p. 148) definition of a policy network as a:

> *...cluster or complex of organizations connected to each other by resource dependencies and distinguished from other clusters or complexes by breaks in the structure of resource dependencies.*

However, he subsequently elaborates on this, identifying five types of networks along a continuum from highly integrated policy communities to loosely integrated issue networks. The term 'policy network' is used as the generic term encompassing all types (Figure 6.1).

Type of Network	Characteristics of Network
Policy Community	Stability, highly restricted membership, vertical interdependence, limited horizontal articulation.
Professional Network	Stability, highly restricted membership, vertical interdependence, limited horizontal articulation, serves interests of profession.
Inter-governmental Network	Limited membership, limited vertical interdependence, extensive horizontal articulation.
Producer Network	Fluctuating membership, limited vertical interdependence, serves interests of producer.
Issue Network	Unstable, large number of members, limited vertical interdependence

FIGURE 6.1 *The Rhodes model (Rhodes, 1981)*

A problem with the Rhodes model, later recognized by Rhodes himself (Rhodes and Marsh, 1992) is that while it is easy to see the policy community and issue network as opposite ends of a continuum, it is difficult to see the other three models as progressive points on that continuum. It was partly in order to address this problem that Marsh and Rhodes (1992) revised and updated the Rhodes model. The updated model continues to conceptualize the policy network as existing on a continuum, with at one end the tightly formed policy community and at the other the loosely structured issue network. However, the new model does not, as previously, include other types through the continuum, but describes five dimensions along which communities may vary, these being membership, interdependence, insulation, resource distribution and members interests. The first four of these will change incrementally along the continuum, while members' interests may be governmental, economic or professional at any point on the continuum (Figure 6.2).

Both the updated and original versions of the Rhodes model emphasize structural relationships between institutions at the sectoral level. However, it might be argued that a significant shortfall of these models is their failure to include any analysis of relationships at the disaggregated, subsectoral level.

The GIR model, outlined by Wilks and Wright (1987), stresses the disaggregated nature of policy networks, using the term 'policy community' to describe interaction at the aggregate or sectoral level. A policy community is seen as having three characteristics: differentiation, specialized organizations and policy-making institutions, and interaction (Grant et al., 1989).

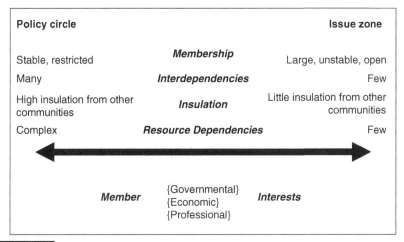

FIGURE 6.2 *Features of the policy community continuum (Weed, 2001d – adapted from Marsh and Rhodes, 1992)*

	Policy Level	Policy Actors
Policy area	Education, health, leisure, etc.	Policy Universe
Policy sector	Sport, tourism, arts, etc.	Policy Community
Policy subsector	Sports tourism, countryside sports, elite sport, etc.	Policy Network

FIGURE 6.3 *Levels in the GIR model (adapted from Wilks and Wright, 1987)*

Beyond this level, subsectoral policy networks can be identified. Grant et al. (1989: p. 74) conclude that the policy community is:

> ... *a useful conceptual tool for ordering the material ... [but] ... any analysis which ignored the subsectoral level would be incomplete.*

The GIR model thus uses the term 'policy community' as a generic at the aggregated, sectoral level in the same way the Rhodes model uses the term 'policy network'. However, 'policy network' in the GIR model is reserved for the disaggregated, subsectoral level. In addition, the term 'policy universe' is used to refer to the general policy area within which activity takes place (Figure 6.3).

The groupings of these policy actors can be defined (based on Wright, 1988: p. 606) as:

> *Policy Universe* ... the large population of actors and potential actors who share a common interest in a policy area (e.g. leisure) and may contribute to the policy process on a regular basis.

Policy Community ... those actors who share an interest in a particular policy sector (e.g. sport or tourism) and who interact with one another in order to balance and optimize their mutual relationships.

Policy Network ... a linking process, the outcome of those exchanges within a policy community or between a number of policy communities.

Wilks and Wright (1987) argue that a major advantage of the GIR distinction between community and network is that it allows for the possibility that members of a policy network may be derived from different policy communities. This is of major significance here where the specific focus is on the cross-sectoral policy liaison required in sport–tourism policy development. A simple Venn diagram (Figure 6.4) illustrates the location of sport and tourism policy communities within a leisure policy universe, where the area of overlap is where a sport–tourism policy network should emerge.

There is, however, a third dimension to this diagram, because the membership of a particular network need not come exclusively from within the policy universe (Wright, 1988). Thus it is conceivable that an interest in the sport–tourism policy network may come from, for example, the economic development or foreign affairs policy communities.

It would appear that the GIR model provides the most useful framework for analysing sport–tourism relations as it focuses on relations at the sub-sectoral level. However, the updated Rhodes model (see Figure 6.2) would also seem capable of offering useful insights. This is particularly the case in this examination of cross-sectoral liaison where the nature of communities at the sectoral level influence the formation of cross-sectoral networks at the subsectoral level. In fact, Dowding (1995), in his critique of the Rhodes model, identifies its failure to address the subsectoral or microlevel as a significant omission. Therefore, in addressing this criticism, and given the cross-sectoral nature of sport–tourism policy, the most productive way to proceed is to combine the two models. In doing so, the three policy levels of the GIR model are maintained – policy universe, policy community (sectoral level) and policy network (subsectoral level) – but the continuum outlined in the updated Rhodes model is included at the sectoral level, thus allowing for an analysis of the influence on the subsectoral level of the structure and organization at the sectoral level. Combining the models in this way creates problems with terminology, with the terms community and network meaning different things in each model. As the overall framework is provided by the GIR model, the conceptions of 'policy communities' as occurring at the sectoral level and 'policy networks' as referring to the subsectoral level are maintained. To avoid confusion, the updated Rhodes policy community continuum (although the updated Rhodes model still uses the term 'policy network' as a generic term at the sectoral level) will be characterized as having a tightly structured policy circle (Rhodes' policy community) at one end and a loosely structured issue zone (Rhodes' issue network) at the other. The combined Model of Cross-Sectoral Policy Development is illustrated in Figure 6.5.

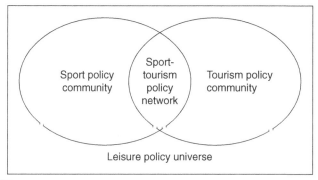

FIGURE 6.4 *The sport–tourism policy network (GIR model)*

Policy Universe	

Policy Community	
Policy Circle	Issue Zone
Stable, restricted membership	Unstable, open membership
Many interdependencies	Few interdependencies
Highly insulated from other policy sectors	Little insulation from other policy sectors
Complex patterns of resource dependencies	Few resource dependencies
Governmental, economic or professional member interests	

Policy Network	

FIGURE 6.5 *A model of cross-sectoral policy development*

This model can now be used to examine and compare the respective structures of sport and tourism policy communities. The following discussion is based on empirical research conducted by the authors in the UK, but it refers to structures and problems in other countries by way of further illustrative examples. The focus of the analysis is on the extent to which the structures of sport and tourism policy communities might affect the emergence of a sport–tourism policy network.

THE STRUCTURE OF POLICY COMMUNITIES FOR SPORT AND TOURISM

Policy community membership varies from being fairly stable and restricted to being relatively unstable and open to a wide range of groups. Smith (1993) claims that a tightly formed policy circle will usually involve one government agency or section within that agency which Rhodes (1986) believes will usually give a lead to the community. However, leadership in both sport and tourism policy communities is often not clear cut. In the UK, the lead government department would be expected to be the Department for Culture, Media and Sport; however, historically policy issues for sport and tourism have been devolved to partially autonomous, 'arms-length' government agencies, namely Sport England and UK Sport/Sport England and Visit Britain respectively. However, the Department for Culture, Media and Sport (DCMS) also has a Tourism Advisory Forum, made up of prominent figures from the tourism industry, to advise it on tourism matters, which is the exact role the national tourist organization structure was set up to fulfil in 1969. The existence of the Tourism Forum, therefore, is a clear indication by the DCMS of the marginalization of Visit Britain to a marketing rather than a strategic role. The Department also increasingly restricted the autonomy of the national sports agencies, with Sport England now spending much of its time focusing on distributing Lottery Sports Fund grants in accordance with principles established at government department level. The DCMS now exerts a much greater level of control over Sport England direction and, consequently, the organization has become an agent rather than an instigator of national sports policy. In both sport and tourism policy communities, this situation creates tensions between governments, which ultimately control the purse strings, and national agencies where, in theory, expertise is invested.

In other countries around the world, the situation is often less complex because tensions are not created by any formal 'arms-length' principle. Consequently, while tensions may exist between government departments and national agencies, these tensions are often resolved by the power or resource superiority of the government, or the status of national agencies as a branch of the government. In France, for example, there is no national agency for sport and sports policy is developed directly by the Ministry of Youth and Fitness. In respect of tourism, the Loi Mouly (a new law for tourism administration passed in 1992) made provision for regional contributions to tourism policy, albeit under strict central control by the federal government who, as might be expected given France's formal economic planning system (Jeffries, 2001), maintain tight control over the registering and classification of resorts and the subsectors of accommodation and catering. In Canada, both Sport Canada and the Canadian Tourism Commission (CTC) are branches of the federal government, which obviously prevents any tensions between government and national agency. The Australian system is perhaps most similar to that of the UK, with the Australian Sports Commission (ASC) and the Australian Tourism Commission (ATC) reporting to separate departments of the federal government. However, a significant difference exists in that both the ASC and the ATC accept that they are subject to direction over policy by the government and, thus, while tensions may emerge, there is little question as to where the power of veto lies. The one major country where government control over both sport and tourism is slight is the USA. The general ideological commitment in many areas of life in the USA to the supremacy of the free-market means that the majority of sport and of tourism provision is dictated by market forces. This obviously leaves little room for government agencies and, in line with such thinking, the country's National Tourism Organization, the United States Travel and Tourism Association (USTTA), was abolished in 1996, leaving the operation of the industry to the private sector. Similarly, the United States Olympic Committee (USOC), although having a legislatory base, receives no government funding but funds its activities through the significant share of monies it receives from the International Olympic Committee's television contracts.

Laumann and Knoke (1987) believe that policy communities have primary and secondary communities. The primary core contains the key actors who set the rules of the game and determine membership and the main policy direction of the community, while the secondary community contains the groups that, although abiding by the rules of the game, do not have the resources or influence to greatly affect policy. It would appear that this distinction of a primary and secondary community is useful in examining the differences between structures of sport and tourism policy sectors. In the UK, although neither community could be said generally to have stable restricted membership, as is the case in a policy circle, the nature of the primary and secondary communities does vary. The sports policy community has a fairly stable primary community which includes the Department for Culture, Media and Sport, Sport England and the other national Sports Councils and UK Sport. The secondary community, the membership of which is fairly open, contains a wide range of interest groups, sports organizations and clubs, and local authorities. It might be argued that local authorities, or at least their representative organizations, form part of the primary community, although evidence suggests (Weed, 2005a) that they have little input into the development of national policy. Similar situations can be found in other countries. In Australia, for example, a fairly tight group of organizations exists around the Australian Sports Commission (ASC), although the primary focus of Australian sports policy tends to be elite sport (Green, 2002). The Australian government, the ASC, the Australian Institute of Sport (AIS) and, to a certain extent, the Australian Olympic Committee (AOC) constitute a fairly closed primary community for elite sport in Australia. The position of the AOC in this primary group has been boosted by the recent hosting of the Olympics in Sydney. Although Australia has a federal system of government, sport, particularly elite sport, is seen as something that is too important to be managed by the states, who are expected to follow the lead given by the federal government and the ASC (Houlihan, 2002).

The situation in tourism policy communities is often different and it may not be possible to define clearly primary and secondary communities. This is often due to the nature of tourism as a primarily commercial concern. In Britain, as in many other countries, there is a government sponsored tourism agency, but the change from the developmental and strategic role of its predecessors to the marketing role fulfilled by Visit Britain, means that there is no key group of organizations to comprise a primary core. This tends to be the case in many other countries around the world – for example, as mentioned above, the USA abolished their government-funded national tourism organization in 1996, and now the commercial sector, under the auspices of the entirely privately funded Travel Industry Association of America, conducts any overseas marketing that takes place (Jeffries, 2001). In some countries, such as France, there is a greater public sector involvement due to a tradition of providing for *social tourism* (subsidized development for the benefit of low income groups). However, this does not mean that there is an identifiable group of agencies that comprises a primary core across the full range of issues (which in tourism sectors around the world are particularly diverse) and, consequently, tourism policy communities tend to lack the division between primary and secondary communities. This leads to the conclusion that tourism policy communities tend to show more of the characteristics of an issue zone, where membership is unstable and groups join or leave the community according to the issues being discussed. This often contrasts with sports policy communities which, while having fairly open secondary communities, appear to have primary communities of which membership is fairly stable and restricted and, thus, at least in comparison to the tourism sector, show some of the characteristics of a policy circle.

These differences in the basic structures of the communities clearly cause problems for sport–tourism liaison. In the UK, the lack of an identifiable lead agency for development and strategy in the tourism policy community means that there is no organization with which sports agencies can liaise on strategic matters. Arguably, in the past, the Regional Tourist Boards have fulfilled this lead role at sub-national level, although now it is the more broadly focused Regional Development Agencies to whom the majority of funding is directed. Furthermore, the regional nature of both of these organizations means that they cannot provide a lead for the tourism policy community at national level. This situation has resulted in some liaison taking place at regional level (Weed and Bull, 1997a), but a dearth of initiatives nationally (Weed, 2006a). In countries with federal systems of government, such as France, Canada, the USA and Australia, it might be expected that there would be a greater focus on this regional level. In Australia, as discussed above, while the states are expected to follow the lead of the federal government in relation to elite sport, they do have a freer reign in relation to recreational participation. Furthermore, in many states there are specific government departments and statutory agencies with a tourism promotion remit. This may mean that, as in the UK, the regional level is likely to be where most productive sport–tourism partnerships are established. The exception is in relation to what has become known as 'leveraging' major events (Chalip, 2004), which refers to a range of strategies employed to maximize the economic effects of events such as the Sydney Olympic Games (Morse, 2001; O'Brien, 2006). Here, a national lead has been taken by the federal government. In the USA, given the independence of the USOC and the entirely commercial operation of the TIAA and the variation in the ideological commitment to state involvement among the 50 states, it is not surprising that it is difficult to provide any sort of general characterization of structures for sport and for tourism. However, while at national and state level this may be the case, it should be noted that over one hundred 'sports commissions' have been established, often under a Convention and Visitor Bureau umbrella, in cities and regions across the USA (Standeven and De Knop, 1999). The range of studies of the use of sport in 'city marketing' in the USA (Silk and Amis, 2005) further highlight that the city level is perhaps the most important for sport–tourism partnerships in this country. In Canada, the states and municipalities are often quite fierce about their independence. It might be argued that this has affected Canadian sports policy over the last thirty years. During this time, there has generally been an overt or underlying emphasis on 'National Unity' in sports policy at the federal level (Green, 2002) and, as such, particularly in relation to elite sport, the federal government and Sport Canada have taken a controlling lead role, based on historical precedence, legislation and funding. There has been a fairly overt split in responsibility for sports policy in Canada, with the states/municipalities being asked to take responsibility for recreational sport, while the federal government takes responsibility for elite sport. However, the more militant states, such as Quebec, have developed their own elite programmes, based on developing state identity. In relation to tourism, the Canadian Tourism Commission has been promoting 'product clubs' that are based on tourism niches rather than particular regions or destinations. It would appear, therefore, that the adoption of 'product clubs' based on sports tourist niches would be a significant opportunity for the promotion of state identity and serves to make the regional state level an important level for sport–tourism liaison in Canada.

One of the major issues facing both sport and tourism policy communities in many countries is the extent to which they can insulate themselves from other policy areas. Houlihan (1991) highlighted the inability of the sports policy community in the UK to insulate itself from other more powerful policy areas. An example of this is the response to the problem of football hooliganism in the 1980s, where the sports policy community was overridden by the law and order policy community in defining responses to that problem. Another example would be the inner city policy area, which, in the UK and in many other countries, often impinges on the work of sports policy communities. While the 'city marketing' emphasis was identified above as being important in the USA, there may still be a worry about the extent to which initiatives are for the benefit of sport or for marketing purposes. Of course, the market oriented ideology of many US states means that often no distinction is made between the two (Kavaratzis, 2004).

The changing priorities of the inner cities also impinge considerably on the work of tourism policy communities. In the UK, often the funds that are offered to Regional Tourist Boards by the government on a competitive bidding basis are for urban regeneration purposes through the Single Regeneration Budget or are earmarked via the Regional Development Agencies. In this way, government is able to direct the Regional Tourist Boards' activities towards their regeneration priorities by offering them funds with conditions attached that direct the focus of initiatives towards the economic and social regeneration of communities. Of course, regeneration is not always focused on urban areas. The programme for the regeneration of the Languedoc Roussillon region of France focused on an area of coast running 180 kilometres from the south of Montpellier to the Spanish border. This programme, initiated in 1963, had the personal and powerful backing of the then French President, General de Gaulle. While this initiative was largely successful in developing a tourism product, it was undoubtedly driven by the need to restructure the regional economy and provide employment opportunities for an area where income was significantly lower than the national average (Jeffries, 2001). The French emphasis on social tourism was also incorporated into this development, as it also aimed to provide subsidized recreational outlets for the French population (Ferras et al., 1979). The conclusion to be drawn in the instances of both sport and tourism policy communities is that they cannot insulate themselves from other, more powerful and politically important, policy communities and thus, in this respect, they both display the characteristics of an issue zone. Perhaps the reason for this is that, in all but the smallest minority of cases, political ideologies for both sport and tourism are often linked to other policy areas rather than seeing the provision of sport and tourism as an end in itself. The extent to which this occurs can perhaps be best illustrated by a consideration of the effect the European Union (EU) has had on tourism. Jeffries (2001) points out that a superficial examination would suggest that the Union's involvement has been virtually negligible if the focus is on the work of the Tourism Directorate within Directorate Generale for Enterprise (DGE). The part played by the DGE is slight because the EU has no formal competence in tourism. However, the EU has considerable powers to decide policies and allocate funding to shape development in areas which are also bound to shape tourism. The European Commission's paper 'Tourism and the European Union' (1995) lists over twenty such areas, which include regional and social development, competition policy, transport policy, environmental protection, economic and monetary union (single currency) and employment and social policy. Thus, tourism policy at European level is clearly and overtly derived from other policy areas. Furthermore, the situation for sport is little different (Henry and Matthews, 1998; Parrish, 2003)and this European example reflects, although perhaps to a more extreme degree, the situation in many countries throughout the world. Deriving policies from other policy areas clearly makes long-term strategic planning difficult because political objectives for sport and tourism are liable to change in the short to medium term. This obviously does not assist in the creation of links between the sport and tourism agencies as each is dealing with more specific aims and objectives laid down by the political thinking of the time.

The level of interdependency in a policy community is often linked to resources. Resources come in a range of forms, most obvious are financial resources, but also important are knowledge, information, legitimacy and the goodwill of other groups (Smith, 1993). A policy circle has many interdependencies and the relationships between groups are often exchange relationships. In the more loosely constituted issue zone, the relationship changes from being one of exchange to one of transmission or consultation. Tourist agencies, as discussed above, may often have to forgo their independently established strategic plans in order to tap into funds offered by governments on a competitive bidding basis – control over direction is exchanged for financial resources. To a certain extent, this has also occurred in the sports policy community in the UK, where Sport England has sacrificed much of its independence (although not necessarily willingly) in exchange for a central role in the distribution of Lottery funds. There does, however, appear to be more significant interdependencies in sports policy communities than is the case with the tourism sector.

Although a complex pattern of resource dependencies often exists in tourism policy communities between commercial sector organizations and between the commercial sector and semi-public sector bodies, governments tend to retain a privileged position due to their greater economic resources (Rhodes, 1988). This means that governments are often able to wield considerable influence in the areas they consider to be important. However, the open and unrestricted nature of tourism communities' membership means that, with the exception of that with government, there are no major resource relationships upon which such communities are dependent. The relationships are complex, but they are small and the loss of any one of them would not greatly affect the operation of the community as a whole.

In contrast, sports policy communities do tend to have a range of resource relationships upon which the community is dependent. In the primary community, the resource relationship between government and national agencies is important because such national agencies could not survive without government grant aid. In the UK, this relationship helps ensure that Sport England accepts the lead of the Department for Culture, Media and Sport over general policy direction. However, the government in general does not wish to involve itself with the detail of all aspects of sports policy and thus Sports England's expertise is required to convert general policy direction into implementable specifics. It is this exchange relationship that ensures these agencies comprise the primary core of the sports policy community. Their relationship with the secondary community is as a result of the dependence of much of that secondary community on Sports England grant aid and Lottery Sports Fund money. The actors in the secondary community do not have anything to exchange for these resources and, as a result, have to accept the general policy directions and terms and conditions under which they are offered. The primary cores of the sports policy communities in the Canadian and Australian cases described earlier are similar to the UK situation, with the distinction between primary and secondary communities being largely, although not exclusively, based on the resource dependence of much of the secondary community on the primary actors. In addition, in the USA, the USOC, apart from its legislative base in the 1978 Amateur Sports Act, is able to wield a powerful influence over the rest of the sports policy community due to its significant resource base derived from the large proportion of the television rights money it receives from the International Olympic Committee.

In summarizing the nature and features of sport and tourism policy communities it is possible to characterize tourism policy communities as showing many of the characteristics of an issue zone. Often membership is unstable and open with no clear leadership and few major interdependencies. Furthermore, there is often virtually no insulation from other policy sectors and member interests are mainly economic, although governments often retain a privileged position as a result of their resource position. By contrast, while sports policy communities are often not strong enough to be labelled so (Houlihan, 1997), they do show some of the characteristics of a policy circle, certainly in relation to the tourism community (Weed, 2005a). The membership of the primary core tends to be stable and restricted, although the secondary community is fairly open; there are a number of major interdependencies, both in terms of finance and expertise, that dictate the structure of, and relationships in sports communities; and member interests, particularly in the primary community, are mainly governmental, supplemented by professional connections. The one factor that prevents sports policy communities being characterized as a policy circle is their historical lack of insulation from other, more powerful, policy areas such as education and thus, at times, their inability to define their own agenda, something that Laffin (1986) sees as a significantly important variable.

However, while neither the sport nor tourism communities are able to exclude more powerful policy sectors from impinging on their respective work, they are able to define their agenda within the leisure policy universe. In fact, within the leisure area, the communities are able to establish a greater degree of insulation as neither tourism nor sport sectors are seen as more politically important than each other. It is perhaps the case that, due to their greater correspondence with the features of a policy circle, sport policy communities are more able to exclude tourism interests than tourism communities are able to exclude sport. This may have a significant effect on the extent to which such communities can generate a sport–tourism policy network, particularly as they are often more concerned with defining their own agenda within the leisure policy universe rather than seeking connections.

CONCLUSION

The discussions above would seem to indicate that the structures of both sport and of tourism policy communities have the potential to cause problems for liaison between sports and tourism agencies and may affect the development of sport–tourism policy networks. Problems such as these lead Houlihan (1991: p. 161) to state:

> ...while every policy sector will generate a policy community this is no guarantee that a policy network will emerge to deal with particular issues. Some communities may lack the necessary value consensus or strength of mutual interests to provide the basis for the formation of a network.

Research in the UK (Weed, 2006a) suggests that sport and tourism agencies and communities act independently, due to a lack of value consensus or perceived mutual interest across the two policy communities, and thus, at least at national level, no sport–tourism policy network emerges.

It is perhaps useful to return at this point to the conceptualization of sports tourism as a unique interaction of activity, people and place, and to consider how this might dovetail with the work of policy agencies for sport and for tourism. A useful way of approaching this might be to consider the work of sports policy-makers as focusing on the interaction of activity and people, while policy-makers in the tourism industry focus on the interaction of people and place. Clearly, when sports agencies consider, for example, policy for supporting voluntary sports clubs, there is little overlap with tourism policy. However, in relation to sports tourism, the activities of these agencies should overlap because they are considering policy for the same people – sports tourists. While these ideas might provide a useful framework for considering the areas of policy on which sports and tourism agencies should liaise, the reality is that an understanding of policy for sports tourism is necessarily concerned with identifying how policy-makers for sport and for tourism can be encouraged to work together in the first place.

The discussions in this chapter have set out the context and suggested a theoretical framework against which the potential for development of collaborative sport–tourism policy might be explored. The next chapter develops the policy discussion further, highlighting in particular the importance of specific regional contexts, histories, geographies, administrations and perceptions, alongside the commitment and background of key individuals, as key factors determining the extent to which sustainable sport–tourism policy networks might emerge.

CHAPTER 7

Prospects for Integration

The previous chapter has set out the policy context within which the sport and tourism sectors operate, outlining in the process the usefulness of ideas associated with policy communities and developing a Model of Cross-Sectoral Policy Development as a theoretical framework with which to understand this context. Examining sport–tourism policy utilizing the policy community concept is useful because the model developed is a fluid one, which can be adapted in order to be a useful explanatory tool in a range of countries where the nature of the policy process differs. The model allows, for example, for dominant member interests to be professional, governmental or economic (i.e. commercial), thus the model is useful in describing both the sports policy community in the USA, where commercial interests dominate, and in Canada, where governmental interests are more prominent. Such flexibility allows disparate policy processes to be understood in a consistent way and, consequently, provides a very useful backdrop for the discussions in this chapter which seek to develop further an understanding of the sport–tourism policy process and to focus particularly on the prospects for greater integration between sport and tourism policy communities throughout the world

This chapter examines the potential for sport–tourism policy networks to develop in a range of countries around the world. However, initially it is useful to review those areas in which it might reasonably be expected that mutual benefits would accrue to members of sport and of tourism policy communities in working together in a sport–tourism policy network. A 'Policy Wheel' is presented which illustrates such areas and the issues associated with them. Following this, a number of tensions within and across policy communities, which might affect the potential for sport–tourism policy networks to develop, are discussed. Finally, the ways in which sport–tourism policy networks might operate are discussed.

AREAS FOR POLICY INTEGRATION

Standeven and De Knop (1999: p. 294) in their introductory text, describe their belief that:

> ... the international trend toward market-led economies has brought about a growing emphasis on a market-oriented entrepreneurial approach to sport tourism....[Furthermore] we identify an inexorable global shift toward efficiency and income maximization and away from public involvement.

While undoubtedly the trend toward market-led economies is internationally identifiable, the claim that there is an 'inexorable' shift away from public involvement is doubtful for two reasons. First, there are very few examples around the world of public policy partnerships in relation to the sport–tourism link, therefore it is hardly possible that there can be a move away from public involvement. Furthermore, there are distinctly different trends in the sport and tourism policy communities. While there are exceptions in some countries, generally, there seems to be an increase in government interest in sport and a move away from government involvement in tourism, which in itself creates tensions for policy development. Secondly, there are undoubtedly strategic and developmental issues, leading to a range of mutual benefits that can only be addressed by some form of public sector policy partnerships. Perhaps the best illustration of this is the range of issues identified by Weed and Bull (1997a) in their Policy Area Matrix for Sport and Tourism.

Previous attempts have been made to identify the different areas of sport–tourism linkage that require attention or guidance by policymakers. Glyptis (1991a), for example, identified 'potential roles that governments may choose to adopt in relation to sport and tourism'. She sought to *suggest* roles that governments could *choose* to adopt, depending on the administrative arrangements in their particular country. However, while this gave a broad overview of the issues, it did not identify detailed areas for policy attention.

In 1997(a), Weed and Bull conducted a review of regional policies for sport and tourism in England. A framework was required for this review and so a Policy Area Matrix for Sport and Tourism was compiled. The

Matrix outlined six broad areas for policy attention: Sports Holidays (taken from Glyptis, 1982), Facility Issues, Environmental Countryside and Water Issues, Resources and Funding, Policy and Planning, and Information and Promotion. These areas were further subdivided into 21 subgroups across which 16 issues and considerations affecting policy development were identified. In the ten years since Weed and Bull (1997a) developed the policy area matrix, the issues and considerations affecting policy development have changed, while the conceptualization of what was termed 'Sports Holidays' has evolved into a classification of 'Sports Tourism Products' (see discussions in Chapter 8). However, the six broad areas for policy attention and the 21 subgroups have been shown, with some minor adaptations, to retain a contemporary relevance (Weed, 2006a, 2008a). In recognizing that some elements of the policy matrix appear to endure over time, while others are more changeable, Weed (2008b) suggested that a simplified Policy Wheel for Sport and Tourism that reflects the more permanent aspects of Weed and Bull's (1997a) policy matrix should be used (Figure 7.1).

Many links can be identified across the groups (inner circle) and subgroups (outer circle) in the Policy Wheel. For example 'marina development' under 'Rural, Environmental and Water Issues' is linked to 'Event Sports Tourism' under 'Sports Tourism Products' due to the potential of many marina areas to stage large events (an example would be the World Powerboat Championships held at Hartlepool Marina in the North East of England in 1994).

The Policy Wheel aims to summarize those areas in which it might reasonably be assumed that agencies responsible for developing policy for sport and tourism might collaborate and there are examples from around the world of such collaboration. Such examples might usefully be considered in the context of the nature of sports tourism as being derived from the interaction of activity, people and place, with many policy initiatives focusing on the place element. Perhaps the most obvious examples are in relation to Event Sports Tourism within Sports Tourism Products. While the focus is usually on maximizing the economic contribution of such events, a further consideration relates to the post-event use of major arenas and specialist facilities constructed for such events. The athletics stadiums used for the Atlanta Olympics (1996) and the Manchester Commonwealth Games (2002) incorporated temporary stands which allowed for the adaptation of the facilities for the long-term use of the Atlanta Braves baseball team and Manchester City football club respectively. In each of these cases, the experience of place generated by and associated with athletics is different to that required for both baseball and football. Consequently, modifications to these stadiums were made to ensure their long-term use, where a different group

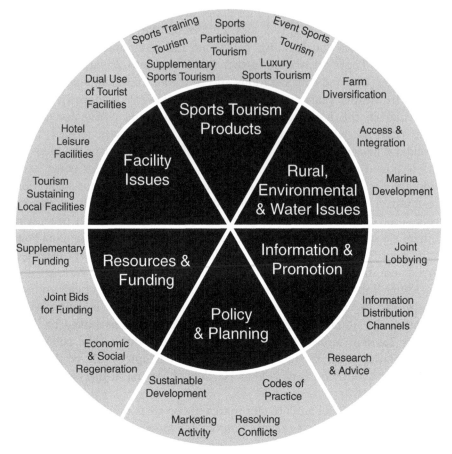

FIGURE 7.1 *Policy wheel for sport and tourism*

of people would expect a different place experience in watching a different type of activity. An example from the Facility Issues segment of the Wheel is provided by the City of Sheffield, which was keen to ensure that the facilities constructed for the 1991 World Student Games were suitable for dual use for both spectator events and general casual community sport. Here, the requirement was for a place that would be capable of adaptation to produce different place experiences for different people participating in or watching a range of different activities. Consequently, the Ponds Forge swimming pool continues to be one of the most flexible facilities in the world and is continuously adaptable for use by Sheffield local residents and as part of the city's ongoing sports events strategy.

One of the areas that has received little attention in the literature under the Rural, Environmental and Water Issues segment of the Wheel is that of farm diversification into tourism. Sports tourism can comprise a significant element of this with Busby and Rendle (2000) listing horse-riding, fishing, shooting and boating as part of this product. Farm tourism has become particularly important in some economically depressed areas of Europe, with the European Union offering funds to develop this type of recreational sports tourism product. Here, the experience of the place is changed, not by wholesale physical changes, but by its interaction with a new group of people participating in new activities.

Securing and using Resources and Funding to promote and develop sports tourism is a key segment of the Wheel where collaboration between sport and tourism interests could develop much further than is presently the case. While the channelling of resources into projects that use high profile sport to regenerate communities has been a feature of city marketing in the USA for some time, there are also some less high profile examples of the use of resources for sports tourism as part of the marketing of rural areas. For example, the Adirondack North Country Region of New York State has developed a regional marketing plan based on cycle tourism with the aim of supporting the rural economy and sustaining local tourism services. In such cases, the emphasis is on attracting new people to an area through the packaging and promotion of a range of new and existing activities. The aim is that new people and activities will serve to revitalize the place and consequently improve both the sports tourism experience and the lives of local residents. Related to such initiatives are areas of Policy and Planning such as the development of codes of practice. In Wales, where outdoor pursuits in rural areas are an important sports tourism product, the Wales Tourist Board established an Activity Holidays Advisory Committee to supplement the work of the British Activity Holidays Association, through which it liaises with the Sports Council for Wales to develop and maintain codes of practice to ensure the safety of activity holidays. The final segment of the Wheel relates to Information and Promotion, and Gunn (1990) describes a collaborative initiative in South Africa relating to research and advice. The South African Tourism Agency and the Recreational Planning Agency collaborated on a joint research programme to identify tourism strengths in relation to sports and recreation facilities and resources. These examples highlight the ways in which the sports tourism experience might be enhanced by collaborative accreditation and research initiatives that ensure that people use the most appropriate places in the most effective and safest ways for the most appropriate activities.

Of course, the collaborations described above do not necessarily indicate the existence of sustained strategic sport–tourism policy development.

In fact, although the research on which the original Policy Area Matrix was based (Weed and Bull, 1997a) revealed an increasing amount of sports tourism activity among policy agencies in England, such activity was not matched by any significant liaison between them. The vast majority of sports tourism activities that the agencies were involved in were promoted unilaterally, with no involvement of agencies in the other sector. Genuine examples of multilateral sport–tourism initiatives were few and far between and there were very few signs that a sport–tourism policy network might emerge. Furthermore, more recent work (Weed, 2006a) on the perceptions of policy-makers across the UK suggests that little has changed in almost ten years.

However, there are some examples around the world of piecemeal liaison between sport and tourism policy communities, but there are few places where sustained strategic collaboration leading to the emergence of a sport–tourism policy network takes place. The reasons for the lack of any longer-term strategic liaison are perhaps explained by examining the various tensions that exist within and between sport and tourism policy communities.

A note is perhaps useful at this point on the nature of policy research in the sports tourism field. It might be expected that the study of sport–tourism policy should relate to the ways in which, as described above, policy-makers might respond to various issues associated with the interaction of activity, people and place that make the sports tourism experience unique. However, as touched upon at the end of Chapter 6, until sports agencies and tourism agencies around the world begin to work consistently and strategically together in supporting sports tourism, the focus will necessarily be on the factors that inhibit liaison and the ways in which such factors might be addressed and overcome.

TENSIONS IN THE SPORT–TOURISM POLICY PROCESS

The previous chapter, in developing and utilizing a Model of Cross-Sectoral Policy Development, outlined the way in which the sport–tourism policy process is structured and operates. Now that the areas in which sport and tourism policy communities might be expected to collaborate have been established, it is useful to outline some of the tensions within sport–tourism policy processes that might affect long-term integration. Such tensions might be within or between national government and the respective national agencies, or between national, regional and local tiers of administration, or between any combination of these organizations. However, they all have the potential to affect relationships within and between sport and tourism policy communities and are summarized in Figure 7.2.

Income Generation	.V.	Strategic Direction
Resources	*.v.*	*Knowledge*
Top-Down Policy	.V.	Bottom-Up policy
National	*.v.*	*Regional*
Imposed initiatives	*.v.*	*Ownership of initiatives*
Change	*.v.*	*evolution*
Organization	.V.	Individuals
Professionalization	*.v.*	*Adhocracy*
Framework	*.v.*	*Flexibility*
Internal Focus	.V.	External Focus
Organizational survival	*.v.*	*Future development*
Project Based Liaison	.V.	Ongoing Liaison
Initiatives	*.v.*	*Advocacy*

FIGURE 7.2 *Tensions in the sport and tourism policy communities*

Figure 7.2 lists five main tensions (derived from research in the UK by Weed, 2003c) within sport and tourism policy communities. Also listed are a number of subsidiary tensions related to each of the five main tensions. Of course, these tensions are by no means mutually exclusive, in fact they are inextricably interlinked and are important because their causes are the factors that can affect the development of sport–tourism policy networks.

The way in which non-statutory agencies such as the Regional Tourist Boards (RTBs) in England and the Regional Tourism Organizations in New Zealand (which are similar in structure to the English RTBs) can sustain a central role in policy communities is through the development of a strategic function, however, there is often pressure to focus on income generation. Such tension between income generation and strategic direction is the first major tension highlighted in Figure 7.2. Agencies can often virtually be forced into bidding for funds for projects of minor relevance to their strategic priorities because they need to generate income, the result being that strategic developments are increasingly secondary to the generation of funds. This change is highlighted by Hall (2000), who believes that strategy is becoming increasingly secondary to more commercial interests in national tourism agencies '...in countries as geographically dispersed as Australia, Austria, Canada, New Zealand and the UK' (p. 152). This means, therefore, that unless central funding mechanisms are promoting sport–tourism relationships (which has been the case in only a very few examples), this tension is likely to work against sport–tourism links because agencies will not have the strategic capacity to develop such links. The subsidiary tension also works in this way because governments often use their control of national agency funding to dictate policy direction. The tension here is between the specialist knowledge that resides with national agencies and the resource control exercised by governments (Gouldner, 1954). Even where agencies are part of the federal government, as is the case in Canada, there is still the potential for tension between those with specialist knowledge and those who control the purse strings. However, there are two ways in which governments could alleviate some of the problems associated with this tension. Governments could take a more holistic view of the leisure sector and, as suggested above, allocate funding to projects that might encourage the development of relationships between sport and tourism agencies. For example, funding opportunities offered by governments could include sport–tourism partnership criteria. Alternatively, if governments were to respect the independence of national agencies for sport and for tourism then it may be likely that they would move towards greater collaboration as they identify their own strategic priorities. That it is difficult to find any examples of this around the world is a testament to the continued interference of governments in national agency activities rather than an indication of the potential for collaboration to develop in such circumstances.

The second tension highlighted in Figure 7.2 is between top-down and bottom-up policy development. Obviously this is related to the previous tension as, in many countries, there is clearly a significant element of top-down influence from government. The previous chapter describes how often both sport and tourism policy communities are unable to insulate themselves from the imposition of initiatives or priorities from other, often more important or influential, policy areas (Houlihan, 1991). For example, many funding opportunities offered by governments for tourism focus on economic and social regeneration. In addition, research has shown (Weed, 2006a) the importance of staff and organizations feeling they have ownership of initiatives. In this respect, initiatives or directions suggested or developed internally by organizations were shown to have a much greater chance of success than those imposed externally. Analogous to these ideas is the differentiation that can be made between evolution and change. Evolution can be seen as a development of the organization that usually would be internally instigated, whereas change is often seen as disruptive and as being externally imposed. Consequently, it is often the case that externally imposed change causes organizational instability and can lead to an internal focus on organizational maintenance. This was certainly the case with the drawn out restructure of the Sports Councils in the UK, the objectives of which changed considerably over a seven-year period in the 1990s (Weed, 1999a). Similar problems occurred in Canada, with Green (2002: p. 10) pointing out that:

> ... because of the emphasis put on elite sport development by the federal government, the period dating from the early 1990s and into the 21st century can be characterized as one of confusion, turmoil and introspection for the Canadian sports community.

The consequences of these tensions are twofold. First, that while governments continue to take a segregational view of leisure, imposed or top-down initiatives are unlikely to assist in developing sport–tourism partnerships. Secondly, even if governments were to attempt to impose sport tourism initiatives on sport and tourism policy communities, it is unlikely that they would meet with much success. Strategic sport–tourism relationships and, consequently, a sustainable sport–tourism policy network, are only likely to emerge if organizations are encouraged to draw up their own agenda for liaison of which they feel they have ownership.

A central tension, not only in the sport–tourism policy process, but in the policy process more generally, is the tension between the organization and the individual (Dalton, 1959; Crozier, 1964). The extent to which this tension manifests itself will depend on the structure and culture of the organization (Morgan, 1986, 1997). In fact, given the nature of much of the work in sport and tourism agencies throughout the world, which often allows staff some autonomy, the tension between individual and organization can be magnified because staff have the opportunity to divert from organizational goals and priorities. Research in the UK has shown that the sports agencies there tend to work with a 'professionalized' structure that allows employees autonomy within a framework, while the tourist agencies, particularly at regional level, work to a more 'adhocratic' structure that gives employees greater flexibility (Weed, 2002c). Because, in many cases, relationships between sport and tourism bodies are new and therefore outside of the parameters of many organizations' structures, flexibility is a key element in developing such relationships. In fact, where sport–tourism relationships have developed in the UK, key staff have been given the flexibility to pursue such relationships. However, this UK research also highlights that it is possible for key individuals within organizations to work outside the framework laid down by their organization if they have the seniority and inclination to do so (Weed, 2006b). Nevertheless, examples also exist of situations where staff have attempted to work outside the framework laid down by their organization which has resulted in tensions that have caused the staff members concerned to leave the organization.

Tensions between internal and external foci of organizations have already been touched upon above. In many cases, such tensions are explicitly related to the tension between income generation and strategic direction. The emerging commercial culture that Standeven and De Knop (1999) claim exists within sports tourism certainly exists throughout most of the world in tourism policy communities. Such a culture can lead to a more internal focus on organizational maintenance and 'fire-fighting', dealing with the day-to-day survival of the organization rather than focusing externally on future development. In some cases, such as the Thames and Chilterns Regional Tourist Board in England, and the United States Travel and Tourism Administration, the fight for organizational survival has been lost and this can do little to reassure other such agencies that this will not happen to them. As already noted, non-statutory agencies must continue to operate strategically if they are to sustain a central position in policy communities and a requirement in doing so is an external focus and a concern for future development.

At the sectoral level, the tension between an internal and external focus exists in both sport and tourism policy communities. Discussions have already taken place on the inability of both policy communities to insulate themselves from other policy areas (Houlihan, 1991) and this may lead communities to focus on establishing a clearly identifiable policy heartland (Jordan and Richardson, 1987), rather than on working on areas in their policy periphery – which is where the majority of sport–tourism issues lie. Added to this is perhaps an ideology in some quarters of many sport and tourism policy communities that sport–tourism issues are not a legitimate concern of either the sport or tourism policy communities, or of their organization, or in their geographical area. The sum of these factors is an internal focus for both sport and tourism communities, whereas what is required for successful sport–tourism liaison is an external focus and a culture of developing partnerships outside immediate policy heartlands.

The final tension highlighted in Figure 7.2 is that between project based and ongoing liaison. Notwithstanding the discussion in the previous paragraph, there is usually a general acknowledgement within sport and tourism policy communities that some liaison between them is desirable (although in many cases both organizations and individuals believe the responsibility for developing such liaison does not lie with them). However, opinions often vary as to whether ongoing strategic liaison is required or whether liaison should take place in an ad hoc manner as and when projects arise. Quite patently, those who favour a more commercial culture within their organization are likely to believe that liaison should take place in an adhocratic, project-based way, while those who believe the focus should be strategic would prefer to see ongoing liaison. It would appear that a focus on advocacy and developing an agreed agenda for responding to projects proposed by other organizations might be the best way forward. Such an approach represents a compromise between the project-based and ongoing approaches and has been successful in some areas. A useful example of this approach is provided by France, where partnerships have been established as a result of a general understanding and acceptance of the relationship between sport and tourism at national government level. One example of such a partnership would be the programme for the regeneration of the Languedoc Roussillon region discussed in the previous chapter, while another would be the Interministerial group established to administer land planning on the Aquitane coast, which included a number of sports-tourism projects.

Having identified tensions within the sport–tourism policy process, it is important to focus on those factors which are the root causes of such tensions. Weed (1999a, 2003c) has attempted to do this, suggesting six factors that might affect relationships within and between sport and tourism policy communities, namely: ideology, definitions, government policy, regional contexts, organizational structure/culture, and individuals.

First, ideology causes tensions at all levels of the policy process. At one level, ideology can be identified as important in the policy context, contributing to the environment within which policy is made. However, it is also clear that tensions between income generation and strategy, change and evolution, organization and individuals, and organizational survival and future development are caused in some instances by conflicting ideological stances. Such ideologies may be the result of political beliefs, professional frameworks, or they may be more personal ideologies that are not necessarily professional or political.

Linked to ideology in some respects is the influence wielded by individual and organizational definitions and conceptions of sport, tourism and sports tourism. Government definitions of sport and tourism are often imposed on national agencies, causing conflicts related to the tension between resources and knowledge. Definitions and conceptions can also cause tensions between organization and individual and between internal and external foci. A more narrow definition of either sport or tourism leads to a more sharply defined policy heartland and less willingness to work in an organization's or community's periphery (see later discussion) and this is one area which varies considerably around the world. In Australia and Canada, for example, the focus of the national sports agencies is on elite sport, which consequently narrows the focus for collaboration with tourism agencies at national level largely to issues related to major events. However, this is not the case at regional/state level, where examples of sport–tourism collaboration are more common, because the sports agencies have a wider focus which encompasses recreational sport.

Perhaps one of the most significant influences is 'regional contexts'. In this respect, historic, geographic, administrative, economic, structural and a whole range of other factors that vary between regions can cause tensions in different ways in different regions. For example, the extent of the tension between project-based and ongoing liaison is affected by regional contexts such as geographical resources for sports tourism, historical liaison (or non-liaison) between regional bodies and the strength and structure of the regional economy. To a certain extent, individuals may be seen as regional contexts as they can cause specific tensions in their region. However, the influence of individuals is also prevalent at national level and within government and therefore still merits separate consideration. While 'regional contexts' may appear a slightly eclectic label, it is nevertheless a useful one in helping to understand the variations between regional approaches to the sport–tourism link.

Government policy is perhaps the most straightforward cause of tensions within the sport–tourism policy process. As earlier discussions show, government policy, in a range of forms and both intentionally and non-intentionally, causes tensions between income generation and strategy and between top-down and bottom-up policy development in a number of ways. Organizational structure and organizational culture clearly contribute to many of the tensions identified in Figure 7.2 and it might be expected that they should be considered separately, as originally proposed by Weed and Bull (1998). However, subsequent work (Weed, 1999a, 2002c, 2003c) has shown that it is almost impossible to separate out their influence in practice. In fact, it appears that, in many cases, culture and structure evolved together and are inextricably interlinked. Consequently, it is perhaps more useful to combine these factors and consider them as one.

Individuals have already been mentioned briefly in the discussion of regional contexts. However, initial work on this influence on sport–tourism policy (Weed and Bull, 1998) referred to 'key staff' rather than 'individuals'. It is perhaps more useful to use the term 'individuals' as this would also allow for the influence of, for example, significant political figures. In this respect, John Major, as British Prime Minister, has had a significant influence on sport–tourism relationships because the sports policy statement, 'Sport: Raising the Game' (Department of National Heritage, 1995), that contained proposals for the English Sports Council to withdraw from the promotion of recreational activities in order to focus more on competitive sport, is widely seen as bearing the personal stamp of the Prime Minister (Collins, 1995). Consequently, John Major was responsible for a number of tensions related to top-down policy development and organizational change and instability. However, it should perhaps be pointed out that individuals are not always aware of the wider implications and repercussions of their actions. It is unlikely that John Major gave any thought to the effect his proposals would have on sport–tourism relationships and, as such, the consequences for sport–tourism links were unintended.

These causes of tension within the sport–tourism policy process can now be viewed within the Model of Cross-Sectoral Policy Development outlined in the previous chapter. This model allowed for an analysis of the way in which the structure of policy communities at the sectoral level might affect the development of policy networks at the subsectoral level. As such, the structure of the communities themselves might be causes of some tensions within the policy process. Generally, sports policy communities were identified as having a closed primary core but a more open secondary community, while tourism policy communities were altogether more open. Although in relation to tourism policy communities sports policy communities tend to show more of the features of a policy circle, both communities are often unable to insulate themselves from other, more politically important policy areas. Consequently, tensions surrounding the imposition of initiatives and the ability to define strategic direction may be related to the structure of the two policy communities. Specifically, that both policy communities are susceptible to the imposition of initiatives from other, non-leisure, communities.

Locating the causes of the tensions discussed here within the Model of Cross-Sectoral Policy Development results in a general model where a leisure policy universe will contain a sports policy community with a tightly defined primary core, but a more open secondary community and a generally open tourism policy community. Six influences can be identified as affecting relationships between these communities and, as per the above discussion, these are:

- Ideologies
- Definitions
- Regional contexts
- Government policy

- Organizational culture and structure
- Individuals.

The next stage of the analysis is to assess the extent to which the influences discussed above affect the abilities of sport and tourism policy communities around the world to generate sustainable sport–tourism policy networks. This assessment also includes an evaluation of the prospects for more strategic integration between sport and tourism through a discussion of the potential operation of sport–tourism policy networks.

THE POTENTIAL OPERATION OF SPORT–TOURISM POLICY NETWORKS

This final section of this chapter attempts to link the previous discussion of factors affecting the development of sport–tourism policy networks with an evaluation of the potential for the development of long-term strategic sport–tourism collaboration through a consideration of those issues pertinent to sport–tourism that concern the effective operation of policy networks. Wright (1988: pp. 609–10) identifies a number of 'rules of the game' that act as an 'unwritten constitution', guiding the behaviour of actors within policy networks. The first of these rules is mutuality. Members of a network accept and expect that mutual advantages and benefits will result from their participation in the network. It is therefore necessary that both sports and tourist agencies believe that there is a positive link between sport and tourism and that they both stand to benefit from it. Earlier chapters and, indeed, the very existence of this book, are testament to the wide range of benefits to be gained from linking sport and tourism. However, it often appears to be the case that sport and tourist agencies and their employees are not aware of the full extent of these benefits and thus they believe that mutuality does not exist within a sport–tourism policy network. This is not to say that such agencies and employees dismiss that any link between sport and tourism exists, rather that a belief exists that the benefits of such a link are minimal, or exist in only one or two areas, most often perceived to be related to major events. This is the case at national level in Australia (as highlighted earlier) and increasingly in the UK, where the establishment of a Major Events Group within UK Sport and a Sports Tourism Department within Visit Britain has focused work on this area. The awarding of the 2012 Olympic and Paralympic Games to London has also further exacerbated the more narrow focus on events within sport–tourism policy-making (Weed, 2008a). While there remains little ongoing strategic liaison (as opposed to ad hoc collaborations) across the sports tourism product range between the UK agencies, the London 2012 Games appears to have administered an 'exogenous shock' to the policy system. As a result of this shock, there is some emergent evidence of increasing collaboration on Olympic tourism issues (Weed, 2008a). However, whether such collaborations will continue post-2012 remains to be seen. Certainly, the failure to ratify the draft national sports tourism strategy in Australia once the Sydney 2000 Games had passed suggests that they may not. It is fair to say, therefore, that, in many countries around the world, often liaison is considered either to be required only on an ad hoc basis or in relation to specific events (as with the UK and Australian examples), or to yield so few benefits that it would be unproductive. It still appears, therefore, that one of the most significant factors in the future development of sustainable sport–tourism policy networks is the education of policy-makers about the full range of mutual benefits that could be gained from greater integration. However, a broadening of focus is also needed among the academic community in its discussion of sports tourism. There are many areas of the sport–tourism link that receive very little attention from both academics and policy makers (see discussions in Chapter 2).

A second rule relates to consultation, both the willingness of an agency to consult within the network and the expectation by agencies that they will be consulted. In the case of sport–tourism, where the policy network draws its membership from two different policy communities, it may be that some issues are seen by the sports policy community as falling exclusively within their 'territory', while the tourism policy community will feel that certain issues fall exclusively within their territory. This obviously creates problems for consultation within the policy network. However, Jordan and Richardson's (1987: p. 55) discussion of the extent of organizations' territory is helpful in addressing this issue:

> ... each organization has a notion of its own 'territory', rather as an animal or bird in the wild has its own territory, and it will resist invasion of this territory by other agencies. There is not a precise definition of exactly where the territory ends. For example, there is territory which is at the periphery of the bureau influence and where it has some, but not great influence and there is territory which is quite 'alien' to the bureau and where it has no influence. On the other hand, it has its heartland which is quite alien to any other bureau and which it will defend with great vigour and determination.

It is perhaps useful to modify Figure 6.4 in Chapter 6 to show the areas of policy heartland and policy periphery of the sport and tourism policy

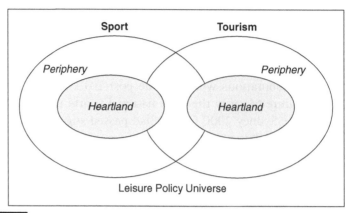

FIGURE 7.3 *Sport and tourism policy communities: heartland and periphery*

communities. Figure 7.3 shows that much of the policy deliberations of a sport tourism policy network will fall within the policy periphery of both the sport and tourism policy communities. In these cases, there should be no problem with consultation. However, in order to deal with those areas falling within one or other communities' policy heartland, it is necessary to consider the issue of leadership. Neither a sports agency nor a tourist agency could provide a permanent lead to a sport–tourism policy network as they would be invading the other's policy space and, consequently, some sort of joint or floating leadership initiative would be necessary. It is certainly the case that, in order for a sport–tourism policy network to consider the full range of issues, one of the sports agencies must be allowed to lead the network on issues falling within their policy heartland while one of the tourist agencies must lead on predominantly tourism issues. Major conflict is avoided because the policy heartlands of the two communities do not overlap and thus a flexible, floating network leadership allows the full range of issues pertaining to sport–tourism to be addressed. Of course, the perceived and actual policy heartlands of the agencies concerned will vary between countries according to the roles such agencies have been assigned. The difference, for example, between the tourism policy heartland in the UK, where social tourism is not a key policy issue and in France, where social tourism is a major concern, will be marked and, while this may lead to greater mutual ground with sports organizations, it may also create greater conflict. Similarly, problems can also occur if the sports and tourism communities have differing perceptions of their individual policy heartlands and the issues which they feel they own exclusively. Paradoxically, a further problem for the development of a sport–tourism policy network occurs where almost all sports tourism issues fall in the periphery of both agencies. This might be considered to be the case in the USA where the Travel

Industry Association of America focuses on overseas marketing, while the United States Olympic Committee largely concerns itself with the administration and organization of representative sport at all levels. Situations such as this can result in the neglect of sports tourism as a policy area because each community perceives that it is on the margins of their work and, as discussed above, mutuality is not considered to exist. Clearly, the extent of mutuality will vary around the world according to the definitions of, and policy traditions in sport, tourism and sports tourism.

The third 'rule' identified by Wright (1988) emphasizes informality within the network. In a sport–tourism policy network it would be expected that the officers of sports and tourism agencies would feel able to communicate with each other on an informal basis. Evidence from the UK (Weed, 2006a) suggests that informal contacts can be vital to the development of a sport–tourism policy network. In one example from the English regions (Weed and Bull, 1998), the departure of one member of staff led to the cessation of informal contacts and the failure of an emergent sports tourism initiative to move beyond an initial joint policy statement. Other examples describe the contribution of informal networks, often sustained outside of the work context, to the success of initiatives. While these examples are from UK research, the observations are clearly applicable to other countries.

In many cases, informality can be assisted by a fourth rule: that policy issues are discussed in a commonly accepted language. However, this may be problematic in a sport–tourism policy network, where the actors in the network may come from distinctly different backgrounds and cultures which use different modes of communication and specific technical languages. On a more basic level, as suggested above, there may be different perceptions of definitions of sport, tourism and sports tourism which, if communication is already minimal, can lead to a lack of liaison through misunderstanding or misconception. Of course, this is an area where differences will occur around the world. In Australia, where the work of the sports bodies is almost entirely focused on elite sport, and a relatively tight primary core of organizations exists supporting this goal, room for discussions in a commonly accepted language with the tourism sector may be limited. However, in France, where both sport and tourism are considered to, at least in part, contain elements of social-welfarist policy, discussions in a commonly accepted language are likely to be easier.

The final network rule relates to the recourse to higher authority, be that the courts or the state, or the opening up of an issue to wider debate involving those outside the immediate policy network. It is generally accepted that, as far as possible, policy networks will resolve issues within the network. This is generally because the opening up of an issue to wider debate outside the policy network will result in other organizations impinging on the network's 'territory'. Consequently, as far as is possible, policy networks attempt to resolve issues within the network. It is unclear how this rule might work within a sport–tourism policy network as there are relatively few examples of long-term or strategic sport–tourism policy partnerships. However, it may be the case that were an issue to become contentious, the sport and tourism agencies would retreat to their policy heartlands and take up fairly entrenched positions. This may result in the issue going unresolved, or in it being left either to the sport or the tourism agencies to resolve unilaterally or, if the issue is important enough, in decisions being made without either sport or tourism policy communities being consulted. In short, rather than recourse to higher authority, the inability of a sport–tourism policy network to resolve problematic issues is likely to lead to the withdrawal of one or more agencies from the network.

SUCCESSFULLY DEVELOPING POLICY FOR SPORT AND TOURISM

The nature and extent of the influences outlined in the previous section will determine whether any meaningful or sustainable sport–tourism policy network emerges. Some evidence (Weed, 1999a) suggests that while sport–tourism policy networks are unlikely to emerge at national levels, there is much greater potential for their development at the regional/state level. This is largely due to the influence that can be attributed to regional contexts and individuals. These influences allow for a considerable variation between regions/states, thus causing problems for national level liaison, but they can also be strong influences on the development of regional/state level liaison. Regional sport–tourism policy networks are more likely to be grounded in the particular needs of the region/state and are more likely to be amenable to the influence of individuals who believe that mutual benefits are derived from a link between sport and tourism (Weed, 2006a). However, a major factor in the success of such networks is the extent to which they have the ability to determine their own agenda according to the resources, people and attitudes that exist in their region. In this respect, perhaps the most effective antecedent of greater sport–tourism links may be the raising of awareness of the benefits of such links among key policy-makers and organizations that are then allowed to work up their own agenda for collaboration.

The above would appear to suggest that size and complexity may be a factor in the successful development of sport–tourism policy networks. Some evidence suggests that smaller countries (such as Malta, as discussed in Chapter 10, and Trinidad) can develop national level policy partnerships that may have some chance of success (Weed, 2008b). It would appear that this is because the policy systems (i.e. the range of diverse policy universes and policy communities) are less complex and because the potential sports tourism product mix is less heterogeneous. As such, the national policy systems in such countries are similar to those at regional/state level in larger countries where, as suggested above, there appears to be greater potential for successful partnership and policy development. Certainly for countries of the size of Trinidad (which might legitimately be compared with the size and complexity of the city-level example of Sheffield in Chapter 11), national level sport–tourism policy structures may be a realistic aspiration.

As the explanation for the greater potential of delivering successful national-level policy partnerships in smaller countries appears to be related to the more limited sports tourism product range that such countries provide, it may be that for medium-sized countries national single product sports tourism strategies may have a chance of succeeding. An example of this is the relatively successful development of a national strategy for golf tourism in Scotland VisitScotland (2000). However, beyond such single product initiatives, a national sport–tourism policy structure that attempts to deliver across the sports tourism product range is unlikely to be successful, even in medium-sized countries. Finally, in large complex systems with historically entrenched structures and interests, such as those discussed throughout this chapter, a national sport–tourism policy network (even with a narrowed product range/brief) is unlikely to deliver successful policy outcomes and, as such, the emphasis should be on regional/state policy development.

There does, however, appear to be one potential exception to this final point. Recent research on Olympic Tourism (Weed, 2008a) suggests that the successful operation of a sport–tourism policy network can be stimulated by an 'exogenous shock' to the policy-making system. The prospect of generating a wide range of benefits linked to sports tourism from the hosting of an Olympic Games, the genuine belief that such benefits can be realized and the much higher political profile of both the sport and the tourism sectors in the run up to an Olympic Games appear to lead to a perception of 'mutuality' and the stimulation of policy partnerships and liaisons that would not otherwise emerge (Weed, 2008a). Whether there are any other such 'exogenous shocks' that can have a similar effect remains to be seen.

CONCLUSION

The discussions in this and the previous chapter have served to highlight the relatively undeveloped nature of sport–tourism policy partnerships around the world. Few countries have any long-term strategic sport–tourism policy collaborations at national level and, given the significant influence of regional contexts and individuals discussed above, it is perhaps unrealistic to expect such collaborations to develop. However, it would appear that the potential for collaboration is greater at regional or state level (or at national level in smaller countries of 'city-size'), where partnerships can focus more clearly on the particular needs of the region or state and where individuals who believe that mutual benefits are derived from the sport–tourism link may wield greater influence. Similarly, in medium-sized countries, partnerships based on the development of single products (such as golf or skiing sports tourism) may also be successful.

These policy chapters have necessarily focused on the reasons for the limited liaison that exists between sport and tourism agencies around the world. However, some brief final comment is perhaps useful on the links between policy and both participants and providers. The conceptualization of sports tourism as an interaction of activity, people and place may, again, be useful in this regard. Tourism policy tends to focus largely on the development of place, while much sports policy focuses on the activity element (although also on the development of appropriate facilities and places in which activities can take place). The link between these two areas is a common need to consider people and it is here that the discussions in Chapters 3, 4 and 5 can feed into policy development, highlighting particularly those areas where sports people and tourists are one and the same. Consequently, policy-makers might be encouraged to consider how policy for activities and places might be developed to maximize the benefits for both the tourist and the sports participant and, more specifically, for the sports tourist.

The relationship between policy and providers is a complex one because, particularly at destination level, policy-makers can effectively also be providers. The most obvious examples of this are in relation to events, where cities, states/regions and, in the case of the largest events, nations, become both policy-makers and providers. In other areas, policy-makers can assist in promoting confidence in providers, through various safety and accreditation schemes, particularly for outdoor adventure and activity tourism. Policy-makers may also play a role in policing developments ensuring, through planning regulations, strategies, legislation and advice, that sports tourism provision is both appropriate to the area and is coordinated with other related developments to ensure an efficient overall pattern of provision. The relationships between providers and policy-makers and the occasional blurring of the roles of the latter with the former, will become clearer as providers are discussed in the next two chapters.

PART 4

Providers

PREFACE

The previous policy section has highlighted the various problems associated with developing sports tourism policy partnerships. However, sport and tourism have long been linked in the minds of commercial providers, from large multinational tour operators, such as Thomson's, to small independent single-site outdoor activity providers. Public sector providers which, as the previous section highlighted, are also often policy-makers, have been less quick to link provision for sport and tourism, although in some cases (e.g. event sports tourism) and in some locations (e.g. urban areas), the public sector has been more involved (see Sheffield case study in Chapter 11). In fact, it is perhaps in the area of event sports tourism which, as Gammon and Kurtzman (2002) note, is mistakenly viewed by some as the only significant area of sports tourism, that the most extensive provision partnerships exist. Furthermore, much that has been written about sports tourism provision has, as with much other work in the field, focused on impacts, and even then the subject of this work has largely been events or outdoor pursuits. Consequently, a significant proportion of this part of the book is taken up with establishing the full extent of provision for sports tourism.

This part of the book commences with Chapter 8, which examines the supply side of sports tourism, developing in the process a categorization of five broad sports tourism product types. As with material elsewhere in the book, this categorization has evolved since the first edition to reflect contemporary developments in sports tourism provision, but also as a result of the view of sports tourism as a trip behaviour rather than a trip purpose discussed in Chapter 3. The chapter uses the revised categorization to examine the nature and extent of sports tourism provision and the range of sports tourism providers. As the categorization has evolved, so too have the potential features of sports tourism product types derived from the discussions in the chapter and, thus, an updated Model of Sports Tourism Types is presented in the conclusion to Chapter 8. In particular, a new development is that this model features the possibility of provision for vicarious consumption of some sports tourism products, thus incorporating more clearly those sports tourism products that feature aspects of nostalgia or heritage.

Chapter 9 is both the second providers chapter and the final substantive chapter before the case studies in Part 5. It draws together material from the participants and policy sections, in conjunction with the updated Model of Sports Tourism Types developed in Chapter 8, to examine a number of provision strategies that might be employed by sports tourism providers. Consequently, this chapter provides not only an overview of provision, but is also useful in demonstrating the inherent links between issues associated with sports tourism participants, policy and providers. As such, it illustrates the impact on provision strategies of the new thinking on participation, policy and provision presented throughout this second edition.

CHAPTER 8

Sports Tourism Products

It may seem a little strange, eight chapters into this book, only now to be considering sports tourism products. In fact, some authors would argue that it has been providers, particularly commercial providers, that have led the growth in sports tourism. However, while this might very well be the case, and acknowledging that the relationship between participants, policy-makers and providers is cyclical, the need for providers to understand the motivations and behaviour of participants and the problems of developing a coherent policy for sports tourism (see Chapter 2) means that providers are most profitably considered after participants and policy-makers have been examined.

As the title suggests, it is the role of this chapter to consider the range of sports tourism products and the nature of the organizations that provide them. In doing so it is also useful to consider the aims and objectives of such providers, which might range from creating an image for an area to simply running a profitable business. The ways in which providers attempt to fulfil their aims and objectives is the subject of the next chapter, which considers provision strategies.

The tradition within leisure and sports studies is to consider providers under the categories of commercial, public and voluntary sector provision and it is worthwhile considering the extent to which such a structure would be useful here. Clearly, much sports tourism provision is by the commercial sector, ranging from large scale conglomerates such as Thomson's Holidays, through sports holiday village providers such as Club Med or Center Parcs, to very small-scale independent companies that provide a specific activity or set of activities at one particular destination. The public sector is involved in provision through financial support for sports events at national level, promotion of destinations at regional level and sports facility provision at local level. Other aspects of public provision might include supporting or providing 'social tourism' and contributing to the attraction or maintenance of sports franchises. While it might be argued that much of this provision is not primarily aimed at sports tourists, it does make a significant contribution to sports tourism provision. Such provision also shows that policy-makers can often also be providers.

It might be expected that the voluntary sector would contribute little to sports tourism provision. Yet, if this sector is conceptualized as a broader 'not-for-profit' sector, then it does make a contribution. A number of membership organizations, such as motoring organizations, cycle touring and camping clubs, and youth hostel associations, make up a significant minority of sports tourism provision.

It is, however, doubtful whether examining sports tourism providers under commercial, public and not-for-profit categories would allow for a particularly sophisticated analysis given that the vast majority of provision occurs by the commercial sector. The nature of providers as commercial, public or not-for-profit is clearly important in understanding motivations and objectives, but it does not allow for the required level of detail in analysing the full range of providers. In addition, some providers, such as outdoor activity education centres, do not fall easily within such a categorization.

Another option in examining providers might be to consider provision that is made to cater for the different sports tourism behaviours detailed in the 'Revised Sports Tourism Participation Model' developed in Chapter 5. Clearly, provision made for spontaneous sports tourism behaviours is very different to that needed to cater for sports tourism behaviours that have played a significant and important part in the trip decision-making process. However, examining providers in this way would define provision in terms of participation behaviours, which would not be particularly useful in understanding the nature, aims and objectives of providers. Furthermore, the ways in which providers cater for different types of sports tourism behaviours is more relevant to the examination of provision strategies in Chapter 9, which utilizes the 'Revised Sports Tourism Participation Model' to help illustrate and understand such strategies.

It appears, therefore, that neither 'types of provider' nor 'sports tourism behaviours' provide a fruitful categorization for analysing sports tourism providers. However, an analysis based on 'sports tourism products' would seem to be possible. In Chapter 5, a number of previous models of sports tourism activities were briefly reviewed. Standeven and De Knop (1999) suggested a categorization (see Chapter 5, Figure 5.2) based on a number of polarized dimensions, namely: holiday/business, active/passive, casual/connoisseur, incidental/prime purpose, multi-/single sport and organized/independent.

While some of these dimensions are useful in understanding sports tourism types, the categorization is of little use in analysing provision as the number of dimensions results in a proliferation of categories that would make any analysis too fragmented. Hall's (1992a) model of adventure, health and sports tourism (see Chapter 5, Figure 5.1) would also not be appropriate to use as it does not illustrate the full range of provision as it is based on only two dimensions. However, the five 'demand types', suggested by Glyptis' (1982), may provide a useful framework for analysis if they are reviewed and updated according to the contemporary nature of sports tourism.

In one of the pioneering works in the field, Glyptis (1982) investigated the links between sport and tourism in five European countries and made some comparisons with Britain. She identified five 'demand types' – namely: general holidays with sports opportunities, activity holidays, sports training, spectator events and 'up-market' sports holidays – which, although proposed as relating to demand, essentially amount to a supply side categorization of sports holidays. As such, these categories, with modification, can be useful in examining the range of provision and the types of providers for sports tourism. The first generic modification is that contemporary analyses tend to refer to tourism rather than holidays, in part to allow for the inclusion of day-visits, which the vast majority of tourism definitions now include. As such, the word 'holidays' is simply replaced with 'tourism' where necessary in the categories. In terms of Glyptis' (1982) individual categories, the 'activity holidays' category, while perhaps not initially intended to do so, has come to imply outdoor adventure or countryside pursuits such as rock climbing, pot-holing or hiking or trekking. It is useful to rename this category as 'Sports Participation Tourism' to encompass the full range of sports tourism activities that might take place. The 'spectator events' category is a useful one because it allows for the 'passive' aspect of sports tourism. However, some other of Glyptis' (1982) categories, such as general holidays with sports opportunities, may also include passive sports tourism. In addition, it is useful to allow for active involvement in events, particularly mass participation events such as the big city marathons (Shipway and Jones, 2008). Consequently, this category is more usefully labelled as 'Event Sports Tourism'. The 'up-market sports holidays' category has been identified (Weed, 2001a) as being characterized not by the nature of the sports tourism activities offered, but by the luxurious nature of the accommodation and attendant facilities provided. As such, it is perhaps useful to label this category as 'Luxury Sports Tourism' more accurately to reflect this. Finally, Glyptis' (1982) saw the 'general holidays with sports opportunities' category as allowing for what she labelled 'incidental' sports tourism participation. However, as the focus here is on providers and broad sports tourism product types, this category can be re-labelled as 'Supplementary Sports Tourism' to cover those sports tourism products that are not the main product offered by providers, but a supplement to, or one small part of, their main product. As a result, the updated sports tourism types are:

- Supplementary Sports Tourism
- Sports Participation Tourism
- Sports Training Tourism
- Event Sports Tourism
- Luxury Sports Tourism.

The remainder of this chapter will now discuss the range of provision and types of providers for each of these broad sports tourism products, highlighting links between them, particularly in relation to providers that make multiple provision of sports tourism products. The chapter will conclude with a model, derived from the analysis, illustrating the features of the broad sports tourism product types.

SUPPLEMENTARY SPORTS TOURISM

This is the broadest of the sports tourism product types, including not only the widest range of activities, but also the widest range of providers (Weed and Jackson, 2008). As earlier chapters have indicated, trips may include spontaneous sports tourism behaviours or relatively low levels of planned sports tourism participation and these are often provided as a supplement to a provider's main product. However, providers can vary considerably, from large scale multinational operators, such as Thomson's, to small leisure or sports centres that would not consider themselves to be part of the tourism industry, but that might be seen by local destination managers as providing an important sports tourism supplement to the main tourism product of the area. As such, providers in this category are drawn from the commercial sector in terms of individual businesses and corporations, but also from the public sector, particularly in considering provision at the destination level rather than at the level of the individual organization (see discussions in Chapter 9). There is also a limited number of examples from the 'not-for-profit' sector (Jackson and Glyptis, 1992; Hinch and Higham, 2004). The defining characteristic of this category is that the provision of sports tourism opportunities is not the main business of the provider or the destination. However, given that provision may be considered at a destination or at an organizational level, this category may overlap with Event

Sports Tourism (where sports tourism provision may be the business of the organization, although not of the destination) and Luxury Sports Tourism (where the provision of an 'associated experience' with the sports tourism activity may be important).

In exploring this category, it is perhaps useful to begin with the simplest form of sports tourism mentioned above, where sports tourism is not an organized part of the holiday, where sports tourism facilities or opportunities do not play any part in the choice of destination and which would often take place spontaneously rather than being pre-planned. Examples of such activities may be a trip to the local swimming pool, perhaps due to other activities being limited due to bad weather, or a trip to watch an ice hockey match as an alternative evening activity. As such, providers may be local public sector municipal provision (as in the case of the swimming trip) or a National Hockey League commercial franchise, neither of whom would consider sports tourism provision to be their main business. In each case, the participation has not been pre-planned, nor has it been part of the organized element of the holiday. Some research suggests (see Judd, 2002) that city breaks may often be most conducive to this type of spontaneous supplementary sports tourism, as such breaks often involve a significant element of 'wandering around' the city and tourists may be attracted to events, activities or facilities that they had previously no knowledge of. The recent growth in 'sports museums' may be an example of this. Visits to attractions such as 'Halls of Fame' or 'Stadium Tours', as with many museums, can often be a spontaneous activity (Snyder, 1991; Gammon, 2004). Again, the providers may be commercial, public or, in some cases 'not-for-profit' in the form of trusts or charities.

Of course, as described in Chapter 4, the activities described above may also be a planned part of a tourism trip. Once sports tourism becomes such a planned part of the trip, it is possible to examine the range of activities by reference to the importance of sports tourism in the trip decision-making process. In such cases, sports tourism can be the deciding factor between a number of different tourism destinations, in effect, it is a 'Unique Selling Proposition' for providers. As an example, a family may wish to take a beach holiday and, as described in Chapter 4, may have narrowed the choices down to an 'action set' (about which they actively seek further information) of three or four choices (Decrop and Snelders, 2005). In many cases, if sports tourism behaviours are perceived as important to the family, then the opportunities for activities such as water-skiing, scuba diving and other such activities may be the deciding factor between destinations once the decision to take a trip involving sports tourism behaviours has been taken. This is why the major tour operators' holiday brochures contain such a large number of photographs of sports tourism activities and references to sports tourism opportunities. Furthermore, while some statistics suggest (Keynote, 2001) that the actual take-up of such opportunities may be low (hence the existence of the 'Intenders' group in the 'Revised Sports Tourism Participation Model' in Chapter 5), that does not detract from their importance in the decision-making process and, therefore, from the importance of supplementary sports tourism provision to tour providers. Many hotels around the world use their supplementary sports tourism facilities as a major factor in their marketing strategies, whether they are on the hotel's site, or provided by a local health club. In a number of cases in the UK, hotel chains have taken over or made strategic alliances with commercial health club providers to run facilities on their sites (Keynote, 2002).

The studies of sport at Butlins (McKoy, 1991; Reeves, 2000) described in Chapter 4, highlight how a British 'holiday camp' chain has attempted to use sports tourism provision to 're-vamp' and 'refresh' its product. Evidence from the tourists suggested that this had worked to a certain extent, as many said that the opportunity to engage in sports tourism behaviours had at least played a part in their destination choice. In many cases, it was the sports tourism opportunities that existed for the children that were seen as important. Some families thought it was a useful way of keeping the kids occupied, while others were impressed by the opportunities for children to have some instruction. In fact, where instruction was available, a small but significant minority of adults took the opportunity to be introduced to new activities, something that has the potential to be a significant part of future sports tourism provision (Weed, 2008a). The provider here, similar to those discussed in the previous paragraph, is a commercial chain using sports tourism as a supplement to sell its products and, while the Managing Director knew that it wasn't sports tourism alone that was bringing people to Butlins, he did feel that it was part of the mix of factors that affected choice and also that it was a factor in generating repeat visits:

> To be honest, sport in general isn't at the top of our marketing agenda, but it's clearly part of the mix for families with children. I'm sure that the popularity of sport among the kids is one of the reasons that Butlins has a fairly loyal core market of returners (from empirical data collected by Reeves, 2000 – not quoted).

In other cases (again, as discussed in Chapter 4), sports tourism can be a part of trip planning once the destination choice has been made. In such cases there may be sports tourism behaviours that are considered 'must see' or 'must do' activities when visiting a particular area. For example, for many non-American tourists visiting the USA, a trip to an American football or baseball game may often be regarded as such. As part of broader research on sports spectator motivations and behaviours in 2002 (see Weed, 2003b), a number of focus groups and interviews were conducted with sports spectators, the following is an excerpt from one such focus group:

Interviewer: *...so what about sports spectating outside Europe? Has anyone travelled across the world to watch sport?*

Respondent: *Well, not specifically to watch, but I went to New York this year – my girlfriend and I went to visit a friend of hers who lives out there now. As soon as I knew we were going I wanted to see the (New York) Yankees play, I've never seen a baseball match, and don't really follow it, but it's something that you've got to do if you visit the States isn't it.*

Interviewer: *What about your girlfriend, did she want to go to the game too?*

Respondent: *Yeah, that's the strange thing. She doesn't really follow sport at all over here, but as soon as I suggested it she was dead keen – she said going to a baseball match in New York was the same as visiting Buckingham Palace for American tourists in London. She didn't seem to think it was sports spectating in the same way as watching football is here, she'd never come to football with me in England.*

There are three interesting things in this example. First, this example of sports tourism falls into the 'Visiting Friends and Relatives' (VFR) sector which, similar to the city breaks described above, are often particularly conducive to supplementary sports tourism. Secondly, the visit to the baseball game became a part of the holiday plans from the first moment the destination choice was made as a 'must see/do' part of any visit to that city, but it was not a decision factor itself. Finally, the game was seen as more than a sports event, particularly by the respondent's girlfriend, who saw it as a representation of the country's culture, thus highlighting the inextricable interconnection of sport and tourism. While this is only isolated qualitative evidence, taken from a study that had other aims, it does give an indication of the types of factors that can be important in this type of sports tourism. It seems reasonable to assume that the VFR sector is important, that supplementary sports tourism provision can be an important part of pre-destination planning and that, in some cases, sports tourism can have an important role in providing cultural representations of the destination (Hinch and Higham, 2005).

The above discussions and examples can only be illustrative of this sports tourism product type. While supplementary sports tourism is defined by the fact that sports tourism provision is not the main business of the provider, it is virtually impossible to define or characterize provision in this area. This is because the range of potential sports tourism activities that are provided by either organizations or destinations as supplements to their main product are almost infinite. Many of the providers, such as municipal sports facility providers or professional sports teams, would not see themselves as part of the sports tourism sector, or even of the tourism industry. These are, perhaps, incidental providers and, along with the large-scale commercial tour operators, hotel chains, sports museums and small-scale destination sports providers, make up the eclectic mix of provision in this category.

SPORTS PARTICIPATION TOURISM

While the previous category is the broadest in terms of both range of activity and types of provider, the Sports Participation Tourism category (where active or, in fewer cases, vicarious sports tourism opportunities are the main product offering) is perhaps the most obvious – essentially it refers to 'sports holidays', which is what most people would think of when they come across the term sports tourism. As with the previous category, there are some overlaps with other sports tourism types, particularly luxury sports tourism. Overlaps with other categories are best dealt with by exclusion. In this respect, active participation in event sports tourism, except at the most basic level, is excluded from this category, as is any extended form of instruction or training. This category, therefore, encompasses the remainder of multi-activity or single-activity sports participation tourism and, with only a few exceptions, providers in this section tend to be drawn from the commercial sector.

Perhaps the least obvious products within this broad product type are those catering for vicarious participation in activities that have elsewhere been referred to as nostalgia sports tourism (see brief discussion of this in Chapter 3). Gammon (2002: p. 65) describes two journeys that take place during nostalgia sports tourism, 'the journey made to the attraction or event and the imagined journey that takes place once there', hence the vicarious nature of the participation. He includes visits to sports museums, such as the Wimbledon Tennis Museum, visits to sports halls of fame, such as the National Baseball Hall of Fame, and participation in 'sports fantasy camps', where sports tourists are coached by former sports heroes or take part in sport in famous venues. The visiting of sports halls of fame or sports venues may, for some, be similar to pilgrimage and involve a certain amount of wish-fulfilment or 'place collecting' (Urry, 2001).

Consequently, providers are wide ranging and some products (such as the provision of a Club Museum at the Manchester United Football Ground) might legitimately be included in the supplementary sports tourism category. However, other products are significant operations, with the National Baseball Hall of Fame in Cooperstown, New York being a significant player in the local community's economy (Fyfe, 2008).

For the examination of sports participation tourism that does not involve a vicarious element, a fairly obvious framework is to consider multi-activity and single-activity trips. One single-activity product, skiing sports tourism, has been the subject of entire texts in its own right (e.g. Hudson, 2000). Here, as with many aspects of supplementary sports tourism, the major tour operators are the main providers, although they are obviously dependent on local destinations for much of their product. Probably almost as significant as skiing is golf, although providers are more likely to be independent courses and hotels, albeit often linked by producing or subscribing to golf holiday brochures to allow people to choose their own 'golf tour' if they wish (Weed and Jackson, 2008). Strangely for activities that are so different, there are two significant similarities between sports tourism trips to take part in these activities. First, there is often demand for some form of instruction, although where instruction is a significant factor in destination choice or trip planning such trips would fall into the sports training tourism category. Secondly, aspects of the trips other than the skiing or the golf itself can be important, and the 'après ski' and 'country club' experiences respectively often mean that these sports tourism products fall into the luxury sports tourism category (Weed, 2001a), a significant consideration for providers wishing to maximize profits.

At the more recreational end of the sports tourism spectrum are opportunities where the sports tourism itself may be the method of transport for the trip, such as sailing, hiking and cycling. In the latter two cases, the 'not-for-profit' sector is an important provider, with various hostel organizations such as the YMCA, which at the end of the twentieth century existed in 122 countries around the world (World Alliance of YMCAs, 1998), being important. In the UK, the Cyclists' Touring Club, formed in 1878, provides advice and support for touring cyclists (Bull et al., 2003) and other similar organizations, such as the Cascade Bicycle Club in Seattle, exist throughout the world, mostly linked to the International Bicycle Fund which acts as an international campaigning and umbrella organization for cycle transport and touring. Camp sites, usually very small independent commercial operations that subscribe to national 'guides' for promotional purposes, are also often a significant part of a cycling or hiking sports tourism trip.

Sailing as a sports tourism product can be divided into two distinct categories: that where the boat itself is the transport and accommodation for the trip; and that where the sailing takes place in the same place (e.g. at a lake venue) and the accommodation is provided nearby (Jennings, 2003). Sailing providers include commercial boat hire companies and marina developers, specialist commercial sailing holiday operators (that own a lake, equipment and accommodation) or networks of sailing clubs from the 'not-for-profit' sector that organize exchange visits. In fact, across a range of sports, exchange visits, often organized independently between sports clubs and sports tours, usually organized through commercial operators, are a further element of single-activity sports participation tourism. The most obvious examples are perhaps rugby and football tours, by professional, semi-professional, amateur and youth teams, often organized by commercial companies such as Travel International Sports, Harvard Sports Management Group and International Sports Tours (Box 8.1). However, in almost any sport such tours or exchange visits are commonplace.

Bridging the division between single and multi-activity sports participation tourism are outdoor adventure providers. In some cases, people will go on pot-holing or rock climbing trips and accommodation may be, like

---

Box 8.1 Harvard Sports Management Group profile

Harvard Sports Management Group, Inc. was founded in 1991 by a group of corporate executives with the initial aim of providing sports tour experiences for their own children. Since then, the company's mission has been expanded to provide sports tours for all ages throughout the USA. Now the company offers 'sports tour experiences' for the first timer or the seasoned international traveller, the young player, or a young-at-heart adventurer, the youth league or the NCAA team.

As an example, youth football sports tour packages will typically include all aspects of tournament participation including: accommodations, meal plans, entry fees and transfers. The company will suggest possible tournaments and advise on the expected standard of other teams to ensure a competitive experience. In addition to arranging tournament details, the company also offers pre-tournament activities including:

- The hire of a professional coach from the English FA, Dutch KNVB or Italian Serie A
- A tailored schedule of friendly games in the run up to the tournament
- Tickets to see a 'professional' league match
- A 'behind the scenes' tour of a professional club.

Harvard Sports Management offers similar tours for a range of other sports, such as hockey, basketball and volleyball, as well as training camps and also 'familiarization' trips for coaches.

the cycling or hiking trips described above, provided by hostels or camp sites. Similarly, some outdoor activity providers cater for single activity sports tourism. However, the vast majority of such sites provide for the multi-activity outdoor adventurous sports tourism trip, including canoe-ing, climbing, kayaking, pot-holing and a range of other outdoor adventur-ous activities. Examples of such centres would be the Twr-y-Felin Activity Centre in Pembrokeshire (discussed elsewhere in this text) and the National Mountain Centre at Plas-y-Brenin, both located in Wales, a popular venue for outdoor and adventurous sports participation tourism (see Chapter 12). Often such sites are independent commercial operators that generate much of their income through repeat business (Reeves, 2000; Weed, 2001a). Many operators also target children, providing either educational visits for schools or summer camps. PGL Activity Holidays, for example, was ini-tially established in the UK and, while it provides for independent sports tourists, its core market is school trips. The company now operates in Europe and offers skiing trips and environmental based study trips in addi-tion to its traditional adventure trips. In the USA, Camp America has long experience of providing summer activities for children, through both 'day camps' and 'on-camp' stays including both 'sporting and athletic' and 'cre-ative and recreational' activities.

Increasingly, the corporate market is becoming important, as centres that provide educational courses for schools are branching out into man-agement training, using outdoor sports tourism activities such as ori-enteering as team building exercises because skills are thought to be transferable (Burke and Collins, 2002). While some of these companies, such as Ultimate Outdoor Adventures in British Columbia, offer corporate training alongside traditional adventure sports tourism trips and children's camps, others, such as Corporate Outdoor Training, based in Melbourne, Australia, concentrate on management training, offering activity pro-grammes variously designed for 'team development', 'team building' and 'leadership development'.

Multi-activity provision is also made by many hotels, although often a single product, such as golf, is the primary activity on offer. Often such pro-viders are 'country house hotels' catering to the luxury market and, as such, they will be discussed under luxury sports tourism. The number of com-mercial companies, mostly operating multiple sites, specializing in multi-activity sports participation tourism is increasing. The forerunner of this type of trip was Club Med, which now attracts over 2 million 'clients' per year (Club Med, 2007), however, other providers have emerged, particularly in Europe, that provide a 'sub-tropical pool' as the centre piece of their facil-ities. Operators such as Center Parcs also provide for relaxing participation in activities such as tennis and snooker, alongside a range of restaurants and other facilities, usually set within a forest location. Perhaps the final type of 'multi-activity' provider is the 'health spa' concept, where the emphasis may either be on activity focused on weight loss or on a more relaxing 'revitalization' visit. Providers here tend to be individual independent hotels, or small chains, however, the growth of this market (Mintel, 2003b) means that some bigger players, such as the French Accor Group, have become involved (Weed, 2003e).

While this sports tourism product type is relatively wide ranging, it is possible to identify some provider profiles involved in this market. Provision is largely by commercial companies, the only exception being the 'not-for-profit' provision of accommodation and support by hostel organizations and cycle touring clubs. Within commercial provision for this category, it is only the multinational tour operators catering for the skiing market and the multi-activity provider Club Med that can be labelled as large-scale providers. Most other provision is by independent single-site operators or small chains. There are perhaps two characteristics common to many of these independent sites. First, they often join together to produce, or subscribe to, guides or brochures both to market themselves and to help tourists to organize their own trip itinerary. The second characteristic, across a range of provision as diverse as adventure activity providers and health spas, is their reliance on and ability to generate repeat business (see Chapter 9).

SPORTS TRAINING TOURISM

The Sports Training Tourism product type is much narrower than the previous two sports tourism product types discussed above. It comprises, quite simply, sports tourism trips where the prime purpose is instruction or training. This might range from a weekend instruction course for beginners on how to sail a dinghy, to an elite training camp at altitude for a national athletics squad (Weed, 2001a). Provision can be by both the commercial and public sector, with public sector provision often being that for elite athletes.

It is possible to identify three areas within this broad product type: 'learn to' courses, advanced instruction, and elite training. In the first area, the purpose is to learn the necessary skills to take part independently in a particular activity. Sailing has already been mentioned as a good example and, within the UK, the Royal Yachting Association (RYA) accredits residential courses at facilities throughout the country. Southwater Watersports, for example, offers water-sports tourism involving residential instruction in a range of activities for individuals, couples, families and groups of adults or children. In addition to learning an activity, coach education and training can also be included. Many courses to train coaches are residential and, as such, should be considered as part of this 'learn to' category (Pigeassou, 2002). The similarity between coach education and 'learn to' courses is that in both cases some National Governing Body standard or certificate is often the end product of the course.

While any conceivable activity could be included in the 'learn to' category, another good example is golf, and here it is not just the technical skills needed to play golf that are important, but the cultural skills such as course etiquette (Bull and Weed, 1999). In this case, provision is usually by golfing hotels with a residential professional (Readman, 2003; Butler, 2005). In addition, the same sites would provide, also through a residential professional, advanced instruction in golf and, as with golf sports participation tourism, such holidays often are towards the luxury end of the market.

In the commercial sector, the same providers often cater for both advanced instruction and elite training. Club La Santa in Lanzarote is a good example of such a facility, with a range of activities on offer at top class facilities. In Reeves' (2000) study of elite British track and field athletes, Club La Santa was a regular training venue. However, a smaller related study also described a trip to the facility by a small amateur squash club for 'advanced instruction'. The members of the club all contributed towards the cost of taking their own coach with them and they emphasized that, while the purpose of the trip was squash coaching, all ability levels could join in and benefit from the trip. Similar facilities to Club la Santa exist around the world (e.g. La Manga in Southern Spain), while other popular sports training tourism venues are focused on destinations rather than a specific site (e.g. Hilton Head Island in South Carolina and San Diego in California) that have a concentration of top-class facilities and a favourable climate. In both cases, a significant proportion of business comes from repeat visits, particularly from elite athletes.

Sports training tourism destinations may be in exotic locations, they may be linked to event venues or they may be located where expertise exists. In the latter case, Loughborough University can be considered a sports tourism venue, regularly hosting training camps in a range of sports for both national and international teams. The sports training facilities have been subsidized by the UK National Lottery's Sport Fund for the specific development of elite sport (Green and Houlihan, 2005). Other sites in the UK have been similarly subsidized with some, such as the National Water Sports Centre at Holme Pierrepont, which has a 2000 m rowing lake and slalom canoe course that can and have been used for international competition, being linked to event venues. However other centres, such as the picturesque Bisham Abbey, which often hosts England hockey and football team training and is home to the Lawn Tennis Association and English Hockey Association, are purely training venues. In such publicly subsidized facilities, the needs of elite training take precedence over any other use. Of course, the extent of publicly subsidized elite sports training tourism provision in any given country will depend on the attitude of that country's government to the use of public funds for sports development purposes (Green, 2002).

The types of providers involved in catering to the sports training tourism market are relatively simple to identify. 'Learn to' providers are largely small-scale independent commercial operations, but courses often work towards achieving ability levels or certification linked to national sports governing body standards in both participation and coach education. Commercial sector providers exist throughout the world for advanced instruction and elite training and the same sites will usually cater to both markets. Similar to 'learn to' provision, which some of these sites may also provide, these providers are also often single-site operations. In some cases, elite training facilities may be subsidized by the public sector and, in these instances, it is unlikely that such sites would be available to any great extent to the advanced instruction market.

EVENT SPORTS TOURISM

As with sports training tourism above, this sports tourism product type is relatively easy to define. It refers to the provision of Event Sports Tourism opportunities, both for participants and spectators. Provision may be by the commercial or public sector, or by a partnership of the two and, in most cases, sports organizations are involved, so there can be voluntary sector involvement. Event sports tourism provision can range in size from mega-events such as the Olympics and Football World Cup, to the smallest of local events, such as a 5-kilometre fun run. Regardless of size or importance, all events will attract both participants and spectators (Weed and Jackson, 2008).

Much has been written about the political and economic impacts of mega-events (e.g. Burbank et al., 2001; Hall, 2001; Gratton et al., 2005) and it would not be productive to repeat this material here – a brief discussion and reference to other sources can be found in Chapters 1 and 2. Needless to say, in order to stage an event of the magnitude of the Olympics, Football World Cup or Commonwealth Games, partnership between the public, commercial and voluntary sector is required (Weed, 2008a). For such major events, a country or city is nominally the provider as the named host, however, this is far from the full story. Certainly, government support is essentially to winning the right to stage such events, but even the most centralized of governments would not attempt to stage a wholly publicly funded mega-event. The last example of this would have been the Moscow Olympics of 1980 but, at that time, both world politics and the USSR's political system were very different to the present day. The commercial sector's involvement is likely to include, *inter alia*, sponsorship, management expertise, facility provision and equipment supply (Getz, 2008). In addition, the voluntary sports sector, through sports governing bodies, will be needed to oversee the technical side of the sports competition. However, while the provision of such mega-events involves a complex set of partnerships among sectors, it is unlikely that the initial impetus to stage or bid for the event will come from the commercial sector, it will usually come from the city, country or, in some cases for individual sports, the national governing body for that sport.

Mid-size events, such as national championships or international championships in less high-profile sports such as judo, will generally gravitate to areas where suitable facilities exist or to areas that have organizations that are prepared to host such events (Getz, 2005). In many cases, mid-size events will be hosted in the run up to, and the aftermath of, mega-events. The Sheffield case study in Chapter 11 highlights the way in which the facilities developed for the World Student Games in 1991 are still an important part of that city's event-based tourism strategy (Gratton et al., 2005). Similar to the mega-events described above, provision of mid-size events is often through a partnership of the three sectors, although public sector support may be less important. Most events depend to some extent on commercial sponsors and almost all events involve some form of involvement from sports organizations that will usually supply officials. Even the smallest of local fun runs will usually have some level of commercial sponsorship, will involve the public sector, if only in terms of permission to hold the event, and will be organized largely by volunteers.

The events discussed above are mostly led by the voluntary or public sector, however, there are some events that are commercially owned. Examples would include some of the big city marathons, Major League Baseball and Formula One Motor Racing. Here, commercial companies own the patent to the event name and, while the public sector may be involved in terms of street closures or stadium subsidy, the events are organized along commercial lines for profit rather than any 'public benefit' (Getz, 2003).

While events attract commercial sponsors who get involved for the advertising and marketing benefits, it is important to highlight a further involvement of the commercial sector in relation to corporate hospitality. Such involvement may be through entertaining clients or providing incentive rewards for employees (Brown, 2007). Corporate hospitality will obviously be most prevalent at more high profile sports and at high profile events but, to some extent, corporate hospitality can exist and can be important to providers at many lower profile events (Lambton, 2001).

Provision for event sports tourism in the overwhelming majority of cases will take place through a partnership of the public, commercial and voluntary sectors. The lead sector may vary, depending on the event, but it is unlikely to be the commercial sector unless it is an event for which that sector owns the trademarks and rights and thus can be exploited as it sees fit for commercial gain. Much that has previously been written on events has focused on their impacts and such impacts are important to providers because, in most cases, they provide the motivation or impetus for provision.

LUXURY SPORTS TOURISM

Unlike any of the previous product types, luxury sports tourism is not defined by reference to the nature of the sports tourism activity involved in the trip. Rather it is the quality of the facilities and the luxurious nature of the accommodation and attendant facilities and services that define this type of sports tourism (Weed, 2001a). Consequently, it overlaps with all the other product types, as it simply caters for the luxury end of the market in each case. As such, it may seem a strange category to include, however, the nature of the clientele attracted, the tourism experience provided and the aims and objectives of the providers themselves, mean that it is a useful and legitimate category. The nature of provision in this market is exclusively commercial.

As described earlier, golf and the country house hotel are high profile examples of this type of sports tourism. In many cases, the luxury market is exploited by the addition of five star accommadation to long-established and renowned facilities (Readman, 2003; Butler, 2005). Golf provision in Scotland is a very useful example of this type of exploitation of historical facilities (Box 8.2).

In addition to golf, some aspects of skiing provision might legitimately be labelled luxury sports tourism (Mintel, 2002b; Hudson, 2003b). In many cases, this is as much a function of the exclusivity of the resort as the nature of the facilities, although five star provision is still the defining element of this sports tourism type. The type of recreational sailing involving luxury motor yachts that might be a questionable inclusion as *sports*

Box 8.2 Golf tourism in Scotland

While clearly not all Scotland's golf tourism provision might be labelled 'up-market', the existence of commercial organizations such as *Connoisseurs Scotland*, which seeks to cater for 'discerning travellers who expect the highest standards wherever they go', indicates that there is significant provision in this area. Such provision includes: the Turnberry Hotel, which has staged the British Open Golf Championship; the St Andrews Old Course Hotel, which hosts the home of golf – the Royal and Ancient Club; and Gleneagles, offering the Kings and Queens courses and a further course designed by Jack Nicklaus. Golf tourism in Scotland has benefited from partnerships between sportsscotland and the Scottish Tourist Board which have, in partnership and independently, promoted Scotland as a golfing destination. The Scottish Tourist Board provides, in partnership with Golf Monthly magazine, an annual guide to 'the Home of Golf', including where to play and stay, course listings and suggested itineraries for a golfing tour of the country, while sportsscotland maintains a published information digest on current provision and further opportunities to develop golf in Scotland. While neither of these initiatives is specifically aimed at promoting 'up-market' tourism, its impact on the Scottish economy means that such provision is promoted and encouraged. In highlighting the range of activities available at such country house destinations, it is useful to consider Gleneagles. In addition to the three golf courses, Gleneagles provides for horse riding, shooting, falconry, fishing and, a recent addition, off-road driving. The opportunity to 'enjoy virtually all Gleneagles has to offer for a single daily rate' is priced such that a couple taking up this opportunity would not have much change from £1000.

tourism would also fall into this category (Jennings, 2003). Similar to the ski market, the luxury nature of motor yachting is defined by the exclusivity of the resorts visited, such as Monaco and San Tropez, where a marina berth would be prohibitively expensive for many aspirant tourists.

Luxury sports tourism can include the top end of the corporate hospitality market. The nature of the hospitality provided at many of high-profile events, such as the Monaco Grand Prix, would certainly put such provision into the luxury category. Similarly, incentive packages for high achieving executives can quite often include a sports tourism break at the type of country house hotel described in Box 8.2. Of course, some elements of elite training might be also be described as luxury sports tourism, particularly for those at the very top of their profession travelling with national teams.

The nature of luxury sports tourism provision is exclusivity, or at least the perception of exclusivity. Such perceptions can be created by both the standards of facilities and the reputation of the resort. The need for exclusivity means that provision tends to be by independent operators – if the provider were part of a chain this would detract from the perception of exclusivity. In addition, provision is entirely commercial and potential profits in this sector can be quite large (Lilley and De Franco, 1999). Such large returns mean there is no need or desire for public sector investment or provision in this area.

CONCLUSION – FEATURES OF SPORTS TOURISM PRODUCT TYPES

The discussion above has described five types of sports tourism and examined an illustrative range of providers associated with those types. As a conclusion to this analysis, it is useful to identify, both from the discussion and the broader literature, key features of sports tourism provision and to examine which features might be associated with each of the five sports tourism types.

First, and perhaps most obviously, sports tourism may involve multi-activity or single-activity participation. This is one of the dimensions identified by Standeven and De Knop (1999) in their categorization of sports tourism and, as the discussions in this chapter show, all of the five broad sports tourism products identified may involve either single-activity or multi-activity participation. Further features of sports tourism, identified by Glyptis in her 1982 categorization and utilized in much of the subsequent literature (Jackson and Glyptis, 1992; Hall 1992a; Standeven and De Knop, 1999) are its potential to be either active or passive. While each of the sports tourism types discussed here may be active, passive participation can only take place in the supplementary sports tourism (e.g. incidental spectating), event sports tourism (as a spectator) and luxury sports tourism (e.g. as a corporate hospitality guest) product types. More recently, it has been argued (Weed, 2005c) that there is also a 'vicarious' element to sports tourism participation. Many sports spectators consider themselves to be much more than passive participants, although they are not actively taking part in the sport itself. Such spectators feel that they are interacting with the active participants and, as such, might be described as experiencing the sport 'vicariously' through such participants. This might be true of spectators in the case of event sports tourism, luxury sports tourism and supplementary sports tourism as noted above. However, as visits to sports attractions and museums become more widespread, such 'vicarious' involvement may also be a part of sports participation tourism, where the participation is the 'imagined' (Gammon, 2002) journey and 'vicarious' experience that takes place.

The five features identified so far exist on dimensions where the features are mutually exclusive: multi-/single activity and active/passive/vicarious activities. Consequently, features are associated with sports tourism product types insofar as each product type *may* potentially display that feature, rather than the feature being a defining part of a particular sports tourism product. The remaining features identified do not exist to the exclusion of other features, but they are still associated with sports tourism product types as potential features.

The discussions of sports training tourism outlined how this sports tourism product type is not only about elite training, but might also incorporate elements of 'advanced instruction'. However, instruction is also a potential feature of supplementary sports tourism (e.g. water skiing instruction on beach holidays), sports participation tourism (e.g. advice about technique on cycling touring holidays) and luxury sports tourism (e.g. advice from a resident professional on golfing holidays). In each of these three cases 'instruction' has not been a key factor in the decision to take the trip or the destination choice as that would define the activities as sports training. Consequently, instruction might feature as part of four of the five sports tourism product types. Sports training tourism is also readily associated with elite sport although, as with instruction, this is not the only sports tourism product type that might potentially involve elite sport. Elite sport may feature in both event sports tourism (e.g. Olympic Games) and luxury sports tourism (e.g. national squad 'get togethers' at luxurious facilities). Finally, involvement in sports tourism as part of a corporate group can

Table 8.1 Potential features of each sports tourism product type

	Multi-activity	Single-acitvity	Active	Passive	Instruction	Elite	Corporate
Supplementary sports tourism	•	•	•	•	•		
Sports participation tourism	•	•	•		•		•
Sports training tourism	•	•	•		•	•	
Event sports tourism	•	•	•	•		•	•
Luxury sports tourism	•	•	•	•	•	•	•

be a feature of sports participation tourism (e.g. outdoor activity management training), event sports tourism (e.g. corporate hospitality) and luxury sports tourism (e.g. a weekend in a country house hotel as a performance reward). A summary of the potential features of each broad sports tourism product type is provided in Table 8.1, while Figure 8.1 presents a model of sports tourism product types which illustrates these associations.

Each of the features described has recurred in relation to at least three of the sports tourism types and three of them – multi-activity, single-activity and active participation – may be a feature of every sports tourism type. It is perhaps useful to take one of the sports tourism types as an example to illustrate the potential features identified in the model. The model shows that event sports tourism may be either multi-activity (e.g. Olympic Games) or single-activity (e.g. Football World Cup), may be active (e.g. as a

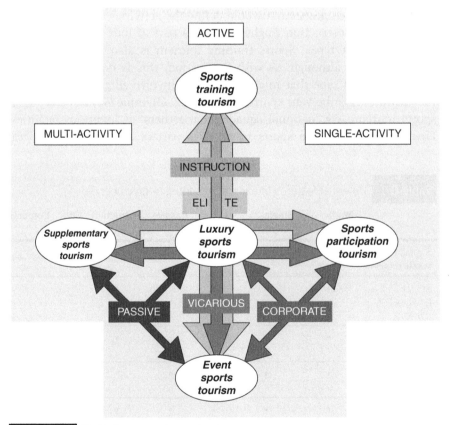

FIGURE 8.1 Model of sports tourism product types

participant in the Chicago Marathon), passive (e.g. as a neutral spectator at a New York Yankees Baseball Game) or vicarious (e.g. as an emotionally involved spectator at an Ashes cricket test match), may involve the elite (e.g. international championships) and may involve participation as part of a corporate group (e.g. the corporate hospitality boxes at Royal Ascot Horse Racing Events).

Developing a model such as this is useful in the context of studying sports tourism provision because an understanding of the nature and potential features of each broad sports tourism product type can assist in examining the range of strategies used by sports tourism providers. As such, this model is used, in conjunction with the Revised Sports Tourism Participation Model developed in Chapter 5, as the context for the analysis of provision strategies in Chapter 9.

Provision Strategies

Throughout this book it has been maintained that the unique phenomenon of sports tourism arises from the interaction of activity, people and place. The participation chapters, particularly Chapter 3, discussed how activities, people and places contribute to the experiences of sports tourists. Such experiences and their role in the trip decision-making process discussed in Chapter 4 led to the development of a Revised Sports Tourism Participation Model in Chapter 5 (see Figure 5.5). As noted in the previous chapter, this participation model is a useful tool in examining the provision strategies of sports tourism providers as it assists in segmenting the sports tourism market and identifying the role of sports tourism in the holiday decision-making process.

However, the Revised Sports Tourism Participation Model, while illustrating the range of sports tourist participants, does not allow for a similar illustration of provision. For such an illustration, it is useful to turn to the Model of Sports Tourism Product Types, developed from the discussions in the previous chapter (see Figure 8.1). The use of these two models allows a discussion of provision strategies that can examine the ways in which providers match sports tourism behaviours with sports tourism products. In some places this may mean varying one or all of the activity, the people or the place, in others, it may mean creating new sports tourists through, for example, converting intenders into actual participants.

A key consideration for the examination of provision strategies is the unit of analysis. Sports tourism providers come in all shapes and sizes, from an independent cycle hire firm that provides cycles and suggested routes for day hire, to large tour operating conglomerates, such as Thomson's and First Choice, for whom sport is an important part of much of their product and who operate on an international basis. Obviously, the strategies of these firms will vary considerably as a result of their size. In some places, for example the Thrace region of Greece (Vrondou, 1999; Weed and Jackson, 2008), an area, city or region may be attempting to promote itself as a sports tourism destination. In these situations, it is likely that there will be some public sector involvement from local or regional government. Again, the unit of analysis is important, because the focus could either be on the destination as a whole, incorporating a range of both commercial and public sector organizations, or on the strategies of an individual provider. Strategies at the 'destination' level, while not unrelated to those of individual providers, are likely to take on a different form, particularly in relation to marketing and promotion (Weed, 2003d). A further consideration is the nature of provision as on-going, or as a one-off occurrence like the Olympic Games. Much research exists (Collins, 1991; Bramwell, 1998a, 1998b; Getz, 2003; Weed, 2008a) detailing the importance of capitalizing on major events in attracting pre-event tourists and continuing to attract tourists after the event. However, these strategies for provision are very different to those employed by providers, such as Club Med, that offer an 'on-going' product.

The previous paragraph notes that, particularly at 'destination' level, some providers may be from the public sector and this is perhaps particularly the case in cities such as Manchester and Sheffield (see case study in Chapter 11), where the public sector has had some role in relation to policy and planning, facility provision, marketing and promotion, or research. However, in many cases, the role of the public sector relates to the support or facilitation of provision by others and, as such, it is important to recognize the relationship of provision strategies to the role of policy-makers. The Policy Wheel, discussed in Chapter 7 (see Figure 7.1), highlights the range of potential activities and issues for sports tourism policy-makers although, as the discussions in Chapters 6 and 7 show, collaboration on these issues is often not as developed as it might be. Nevertheless, the discussions in this chapter will, where appropriate, highlight the role of policy-makers in supporting provision.

The discussions in this chapter are organized around a range of provision strategies that are illustrative rather than exhaustive and relate to the issues raised in the Revised Sports Tourism Participation Model and the Model of Sports Tourism Product Types. These strategies are:

- converting intenders
- generating repeat visits

- expanding participation profiles
- cooperative marketing
- capturing spontaneous behaviours
- creating competitive advantage
- exploiting intenders.

The extent to which varying the activity, the people or the place can be an effective way of expanding provision is discussed and the relationship of provision to policy is highlighted. A key factor in the following discussions, developing further the perspectives in Chapters 4 and 5, is the role of sports tourism in the trip decision-making process.

CONVERTING INTENDERS

The concept of 'intenders' was drawn from work on arts audiences by Hill et al. (1995). In Chapter 5, the concept was outlined as relating to those who are positively inclined towards sports tourism and the idea of a tourist trip involving sports tourism behaviours, but who never quite 'get round to it'. However, there is an important division in the intenders category and this relates to the role of sports tourism behaviours in the trip decision-making process. As Chapters 3 and 4 noted, sports tourism is often a factor, albeit one among many others, in destination choice. Here, people may have undertaken a trip with the intention of engaging in some sports tourism behaviours while away but, in the event, not actually done so (as evidenced by, *inter alia*, Tokarski, 1993; Reeves, 2000; Keynote, 2001). In such cases, the differentiation between intenders and participants is not apparent until the trip is undertaken. Issues relating to this category of intenders are discussed later under the 'Exploiting Intenders' heading.

For many sports tourism products, the differentiation between intenders and participants is apparent pre-trip, simply because participants will book a trip involving sports tourism behaviours while intenders will not. Often, because there is a positive attitude towards the idea of sports tourism participation on a trip, intenders will appear on providers' mailing lists because they are likely to have sent off for brochures or registered an interest in sports tourism. Converting such intention into actual participation is clearly one potentially productive strategy for providers.

The potential sports tourism product that intenders are considering will obviously affect the way such strategies are followed. For providers in the 'Sports Participation Tourism' category, it may be that special discounts for 'first-time' sports tourists are offered, or 'taster' days or weekends with other newcomers where all equipment, instruction and accommodation is provided on site. A useful example of such provision is provided by the National Mountain Centre at Plas-y-Brenin in Wales. Alongside provision for more experienced and advanced sports tourists, introductory two-day courses are offered in rock climbing, mountaineering, kayaking and canoeing. These courses include on-site accommodation, all necessary equipment and training and supervision by qualified instructors. Specially tailored versions of these 'taster' courses are run to cater specifically for families and, as discussed in the next section, further 'intermediate' or 'technique development' courses are offered to encourage repeat visits.

In these cases, the strategy is similar to that followed by those tourism companies that offered the first overseas package holidays to tourists that had never travelled abroad before. The strategy is to make booking the trip as easy as possible and, as everything is provided through one contact, the customer will feel comfortable and at ease with trying a new activity (Holloway and Taylor, 2006). Such feelings of comfort and safety are further enhanced by the involvement of policy-makers who draw up 'safety codes' and 'accredit' providers, particularly for the types of outdoor and adventurous activity sports tourism described in the above example.

Simple targeted marketing is one way in which intenders are converted. The discussions in Chapter 5 highlighted the importance of identity (Green and Jones, 2005) to understanding sports tourism participation. These discussions also noted that it is possible for intenders to be highly identified with an activity, without actually participating in it. One such example is spectating. For many intenders, watching sport on television is an important part of their lives, although they may never have actually attended a live event (Weed, 2003a). The targeting of such people by event providers is one key way in which intenders may be converted. This may be through advertising the event on television during another televised event, through targeted mail-outs to those subscribing to satellite or cable channels or, in cases where intending spectators are also active participants in the sport in question, by targeting clubs. Athletics provides a useful example of two of these strategies. In Britain, the ticket office for forthcoming athletics events is often advertised during televised athletics events broadcast on the BBC. This is almost unique, as the BBC (British Broadcasting Corporation) is a publicly funded broadcaster that carries no commercial advertising. Addresses of athletics clubs are also often passed on to event promoters by UK Athletics, the sport's national governing body, who are then targeted to receive ticket offers for forthcoming events.

Of course, the targeting of clubs is also a strategy for both event sports tourism and sports training tourism providers to generate new custom. For many sports participants, the idea of combining active sports tourism participation in an event (such as the New York marathon) with a holiday may be attractive, as may the prospect of a trip involving sports training tourism with friends and training partners. There are a number of companies who specialize in offering trips to events and to training venues and, while much of their advertising is done through sports-specific magazines such as *Runners World*, *Adventure Kayak* and *Triathlete*, they also target sports clubs with special offers for group bookings. The 'Volcano Triathlon Training Camp' at Club La Santa in Lanzarote, for example, has been specifically targeted at triathlon club secretaries and can incorporate participation in the Volcano Triathlon, which in 2007 was in its twenty-third year.

The market for corporate hospitality is also about converting intenders, but here the intenders are companies requiring a unique venue to entertain clients and, increasingly, to reward and entertain their own employees in what has been termed 'participative hospitality' (Lambton, 2001). A key element in converting such companies to hospitality participants is the extent to which they can be convinced that the venue and event in question is congruent with their corporate image and target audience. A successful hospitality operation at an event sports tourism venue can provide a significant income – research from the Corporate Hospitality and Event Association showed that the UK hospitality market was worth £650 million in 2000. However, Lambton (2001) believes that there is no question of hospitality making or breaking an event financially, rather it 'is there to reflect the event's inherent qualities' (p. 56) and is a key part of brand building. As such, the decision as to which type of corporate 'intenders' an event or venue seeks to attract is important and should be aimed at generating a truly mutually beneficial and complementary relationship between event organizer and hospitality client.

In a similar way that sports participation tourism providers may offer 'taster' weekends for 'first-timers', luxury sports tourism providers may attempt to capitalize on their corporate conference or incentive market to encourage guests to return on another occasion with friends or families. Many country house hotels, such as Pawleys Plantation Country Club in Myrtle Beach, South Carolina, have both extensive conference and sports and leisure facilities. Complementary access to sports and leisure facilities for conference guests is one way in which such providers attempt to covert such participants who may fall into the intenders category into participants with their families.

Strategies aimed at converting intenders for whom sports tourism plays a significant role in the trip decision, tend to relate to individual providers, or groups of providers packaged together by the specialist sports tour operating firms described above. In many cases, strategies at the destination level, while sometimes relating to the conversion of intenders, largely fall within the other categories discussed below.

GENERATING REPEAT VISITS

The generation of repeat visits is a provision strategy that is inextricably interlinked with the conversion of intenders. The offers and incentives used to attract first-time sports tourists described above are made because it is hoped that having got a taste of sports tourism participation, guests will return for another, longer, higher-priced stay. Here, sports tourists are being offered a sports tourism experience that they know and that, in many cases, they cannot get at home. As discussed in Chapter 4, sports participation tourism based around such activities as mountaineering and kayaking often cannot be accessed in the home environment, due either to lack of resources, lack of equipment, lack of like-minded people or lack of place experience. While a lack of resources and equipment can prevent the activity from taking place, a lack of like-minded people and imposing or extraordinary places can detract from the experience that is a key part of sports tourism (Weed, 2002d). Activity centres such as Plas-y-Brenin, described above, and Twr-y-Felin in South Wales, provide not only the necessary equipment and resources for the activity, but also the people and the places necessary for the experience. Consequently, as described in Chapter 4, much of their trade comes from repeat visits. The study of Twr-y-Felin (Reeves, 2000) showed that 45 per cent of visitors had previously visited the centre within the last six months, while 44 per cent indicated their intention to 'definitely return'.

The role sports tourism can play in generating both visits and repeat visits for family groups should not be underestimated. For many families, the availability of activities that will keep the children occupied can be a central factor in destination choice. The study of Butlins Holiday Worlds in the UK (Reeves, 2000) provided evidence of this, with 73 per cent of respondants being on holiday with their children and 85 per cent having previously visited Butlins in the last three years. The opportunity for sports tourism participation had played some part in determining holiday choice for 69 per cent of these holidaymakers, with the following comment from a focus group being representative of many others in emphasizing the importance of sport in providing activities for children:

We weren't really bothered about the sports and recreation facilities for ourselves, but we have two young children and they get bored very easily, so this was an easy choice to keep them out of trouble and in one place.

Similarly, the availability of sports tourism opportunities on beach holidays has been shown to be a factor in generating repeat business (Jackson and Weed, 2008), although the repeat business in such cases is more likely to be to another destination owned by the same tour operator. This is because holidaymakers come to recognize certain brands as providing a certain type of product (Morgan and Pritchard, 2000), in this case good provision to engage in sports tourism behaviours.

At the top right of the Revised Sports Tourism Participation Model, the subcategory of elite athletes is a lucrative market for providers. Evidence of the importance of repeat visits in this sector is given by the fact that certain destinations have almost cornered the market in this area (examples being La Manga in Southern Spain, Club La Santa in Lanzarote and San Diego in California), although some of the bigger players such as Disney are now moving into provision in this area. However, the nature of the product can be very different to that of other sports tourism types. The elements of the place that are important are less related to experience and more related to quality of facilities and support and climate (Jackson and Reeves, 1998). Consequently, some elite sports training tourism venues, such as Club La Santa in Lanzarote, also provide for sports participation tourism and trips involving non-elite training and instruction. However, other venues, such as Bisham Abbey and Loughborough University, both in the UK, where the emphasis is on facilities and sports science support and the trips are usually more intense training days or weekends, only provide for the elite element of sports training tourism (Weed, 2008a). As such, their ability to attract repeat visits has been based on the quality of service they are able to offer to elite athletes. In fact, in recent years, in recognition of the quality service such venues provide, their development has been publicly funded as a result of government policy initiatives related to the development of elite sport and the provision of a network of facilities and services comprising an English Institute of Sport (Shakespear, 2002).

In relation to event sports tourism, there has been some research on customer loyalty, particularly in relation to football (King et al., 2002), focusing on the utility of relationship marketing, which Clowes and Tapp (1998) suggested may be a more appropriate approach than a price or promotion response to the need to fill seats. A specific study of stakeholders at Nottingham Forest Football Club in the UK (Hearne, 2003) suggests that the relationship approach has worked in developing a good rapport with supporters groups. However, despite these specific examples, there must be some doubt as to the extent to which this approach is as useful in other areas where there is not such an emotional attachment to the teams and clubs in question.

Some event sports tourism products are used as a way to introduce tourists to a particular area and to generate repeat visits, either to other sports tourism events and activities or to other tourist related aspects of the destination. One of Manchester's policy goals in hosting the Commonwealth Games was to introduce visitors to Manchester as a broader urban tourism destination and to showcase other elements of Manchester's tourism product, some of which comprise sports tourism products (Regan, 1999). Lancashire's County Cricket Ground, which is also a venue for Test Match Cricket, and Manchester United's Old Trafford Stadium, which contains a museum and visitor centre, were both prominently promoted in Commonwealth Games material, as was the city's range of cultural attractions, theatres and bars. In addition to introducing visitors to the broader tourism product on offer, strategies such as this may also play a role in expanding the participation profile of sports tourists.

EXPANDING PARTICIPATION PROFILES

One of the strengths of the Revised Sports Tourism Participation Model is that it is both a generic model illustrating sports tourism participation as a whole (see Figure 5.5 in Chapter 5), and can also be used to illustrate the different 'shapes' of participation for different sports tourism products (see Figure 5.6 in Chapter 5). Similarly, individuals may appear at one point in the model for one sports tourism product (e.g. an individual may be a committed football spectator at the top right of the participation triangle), but at another point for another product (e.g. as a spontaneous participant in water-sports tourism at the bottom left of the model). While the generation of repeat visits discussed above often relies on providing an experience of activity, people and place that cannot be attained in the home area, repeat visits can also be generated by strategies that attempt to expand the sports tourist's participation profile, thus offering a similar place experience, but through a different activity for which the sports tourism experience will inevitably be different.

A useful example of this type of strategy comes, initially, from the elite end of the sports training tourism market. During warm weather training trips, athletes often have long periods of rests between training sessions and, within the constraints of avoiding injury, other sports tourism activities often provide a useful diversion, both physically and mentally. Evidence from Reeves' (2000) study of elite athletes illustrates this, with athletes making the following comments:

I play a lot of golf. When we went to La Manga the camp was actually situated on a golf course. We also take part in activities such as water skiing and swimming. It is like a half holiday, so we try and do as many activities as possible. We have to be careful of injury, but we must make sure that we are able to relax as well. The best way for me to do that is through playing sport.

(Emma Merry, 21, GB & England Intermediate International,
Discus and Shot Put)

We play anything to take the monotony out of athletics training all the time. We might go cycling or swimming, just to get out of the complex. When you are away training you tend to eat, breathe and talk athletics. So for example when I was in Lanzarote in January, we went swimming, played badminton and basketball and joined in with the aerobics.

(Jackie Agyepong, 26, GB & England Senior International,
100 m Hurdles)

We have bicycles and we tend to play a lot of basketball. We do a lot of go-karting in Benidorm as they have brilliant facilities out there. Anything at all to stop the boredom while you are out there training hard twice a day.

(Paul Hibbert, 30, England Senior International,
400 m Hurdles)

The extent to which this recreational participation is likely to translate into subsequent sports tourism behaviours on other trips during which sports training tourism is less important is debatable because such activities are undertaken largely as merely a diversion from elite training. There may, however, be opportunities to encourage athletes to return with their families, or to develop broader sports tourism interests once their elite athletic career has come to an end.

The previous section described Manchester's strategy of exposing sports tourists at the Commonwealth Games to other aspects of the city's tourism offering in order to generate repeat visits. At the city level, specific policy has been developed aimed at using a profile of event sports tourism products as the hook on which city visits can be generated. Consequently, the place experience of Manchester is similar, but the central activity – a test match, European football tie, athletics meet, or other event – is different. This is a strategy that Sheffield has also used to good effect (see Chapter 11).

Perhaps the most obvious areas in which participation profiles might be expanded are in sports participation tourism and luxury sports tourism.

This is because, in most cases, providers of these sports tourism products offer a range of activities. Some visitors to outdoor activity and adventure centres will be committed sports tourists across a range of activities and for such multi-activity participants the expansion of the participation profile is unlikely to be a fruitful provision strategy. However, for those whose sports tourism behaviours on such trips are focused on a single activity, at whatever level, opportunities exist for providers to expand their participation profile through a number of strategies. Several examples of such strategies are related to the use of space. Henderson and Frelke (2000) discuss the close association of space with the activities and practices of those who use it and point out that the provision of social spaces, such as bars and/or restaurants, at multi-activity centres where sports tourists participating in different activities can mix will often be one of the most effective ways of expanding participation profiles. Simply talking to people taking part in different activities may be enough to encourage people to try something new. Similarly, if activities take place in relatively close proximity to each other, then seeing others take part in activities may also encourage new activity take-up. Providers may try to capitalize on this by offering short, supervised 'come and try it' sessions in different activities for those on a single activity trip, or may offer similar taster weekends as might be offered when trying to convert intenders as discussed above. Plas-y-Brenin, the National Mountain Centre in North Wales, does this, offering 'have a go' multi-activity weekends which provide 'a whirlwind tour of canoeing, orienteering, climbing/ abseiling and skiing' (Plas-y-Brenin brochure, 2007). All of the above also applies to the luxury end of the market, although strategies for such providers can often be more focused on capturing spontaneous behaviours, particularly in country house hotels with extensive spa facilities (Weed, 2003e).

For some providers, the provision of opportunities to take in a number of sports tourism activities at a relatively introductory level is the central tenet of their product. Here, the pre-trip decision is to engage in sports tourism behaviours across a wide range of activities, thus the participation profile is expanded at a relatively introductory level. Examples of such providers would be Center Parcs and Club Med, both of which offer a range of recreational sports tourism opportunities in a relaxed environment. The Center Parcs villages are largely sited in Northern Europe in forest locations and are each centred around an indoor simulated subtropical pool environment, with the further provision of, among others, tennis, badminton, cycling, health centre and spa activities. In contrast to Center Parcs, Club Med villages are largely located in warm locations and so there is no need for an indoor pool environment. Club Med also employs 'animators' or activity leaders who tend to the needs of guests, not only in relation to their sports tourism behaviours, but also to virtually any other holiday requirement.

While the strategies discussed under this heading have focused on varying the activity at a particular place, a further strategy may be to vary the place. This may be done by large tour operators who can offer a range of activities at a range of places, but can also occur through arrangements for cooperative marketing of sports tourism opportunities.

COOPERATIVE MARKETING

A variation in activity and/or place experience is perhaps an obvious way to expand sports tourism take-up. In many cases, cooperative marketing is a sensible way forward because the sports tourism behaviours generated by such variations are often supplementary or complementary to current participation, rather than being replacement activities. Even where there may be some displacement of those seeking sports tourism opportunities, the reciprocal benefits of cooperative marketing can far outweigh the disadvantages (Selin, 2000).

Cooperative marketing may take place at a number of levels but, at its most straightforward, it simply involves mutual promotion of activities and facilities at a particular destination (Briggs, 2001). This is often led or supported by local or regional policy-makers who may develop 'destination' marketing strategies and promotional materials. The cases of Manchester and Sheffield in relation to event sports tourism are one example, but there are many others in relation to other sports tourism products. The 'Melbourne Now' campaign by the Victoria Tourism Commission in Australia was seen as effective in collectively marketing parks and recreational facilities as tourism attractions (D'Abaco, 1991), while cooperation among tourism firms on the Waterfront of Wellington in New Zealand (Doorne, 1998) has seen that area emerge as a destination for recreational sports tourism participation.

An example of national level cooperative marketing of a luxury sports tourism product can be found in the promotion of golfing breaks in Scotland. As discussed in Chapter 8, policy partnerships between the Scottish Tourist Board and sportsscotland have promoted Scotland's golf tourism product as the 'Home of Golf', while the commercial consortium 'Connoisseurs Scotland' specifically targets the 'discerning traveller' demanding the highest standards of both accommodation and facilities. A similar national level example, although not from the luxury end of the market, is provided by Vrondou's (1999) work on sports tourism policy and promotion in Greece, where there has been a deliberate policy of marketing a range of areas in Crete as destinations for 'soft' sports tourism as a strategy to diversify away from the traditional mass tourism product.

Cooperative marketing is a strategy usually aimed at sports tourists from the centre of the Sports Tourism Participation Model, more regular participants who may be seeking to expand their portfolio of experiences. This may be related to 'collecting places' (Urry, 2001) as discussed in Chapter 3, or to expanding the participation portfolio, as discussed above. For active participants in event sports tourism, providers of other events see each event as a prime marketing opportunity to promote travel to their event (Green, 2001). The trade exhibitions that accompany large mass participation events, such as the London and Chicago marathons, will always contain a considerable number of stalls promoting other events such as running races, triathlons and endurance cycling, all of which might be seen as appealing to the type of sports tourist who would take part in a marathon. On a smaller scale, cars parked at local 10-kilometre running races, to which people may have travelled as a day trip (McGehee et al., 2003), taking in lunch with family and friends after the event, will always attract a number of flyers for other events under the car windscreen wipers.

There is a great deal of cooperative marketing that takes place between outdoor activity providers. Centres that specialize in some activities may contain material for other centres that provide related and complementary activities. In other cases, instructional centres will provide information on where sports tourists can continue their activity once they have developed the required competences. Skiing providers may also organize some cross-promotion of facilities and destinations. For example, 'Top Ski Austria' is a marketing alliance of the country's top eighteen ski resorts (Hudson, 2000) which, in addition to the mutual promotion of facilities, also aims to organize the type of joint marketing activity described above. While in some of these cases, the cross-promotion may appear to be of competing resorts, this may still be an efficient business strategy given the motivations of many sports tourists. Notwithstanding the importance of generating repeat visits discussed in a previous section, many sports tourists are motivated, as described above, to 'collect places' (Urry, 2001) and, as such, will demand new place experiences. If resorts accept that certain sports tourists will not return year after year, then it makes sense to promote other destinations in return for reciprocal promotion of their resort (McDonald and Milne, 1999).

CAPTURING SPONTANEOUS BEHAVIOURS

One type of cooperative marketing described in the previous section – that of cross-promotion at the destination level – can aid considerably in capturing spontaneous sports tourism behaviours that have not been planned prior to the trip. The capturing of spontaneous behaviours will often be by providers of supplementary sports tourism, but can also be a productive strategy for luxury sports tourism and event sports tourism providers.

While some forms of supplementary sports tourism are provided because the availability of sports tourism activities plays a part in destination choice, for other forms, sports tourism behaviours are the result of decisions made once the destination choice has been made. At some destinations there may be some supplementary sports tourism products that might be considered 'must-see' activities, such as a trip to see the Yankees play baseball during a visit to New York or a visit to the Australian Gallery of Sport or a cricket international at the Melbourne Cricket Ground on a visit to Victoria. At other destinations, sports tourism behaviours are the result of opportunistic decisions, often made on the spur of the moment while at a destination. This is where strategies aimed at capturing spontaneous behaviours, particularly cooperative marketing, are important.

The capture of potential spontaneous behaviours is largely about ensuring that information is available to such participants in the right place at the right time (Ortega and Rodriguez, 2007). This may mean leaflets and posters in local accommodation, information in strategic places around the destination and an awareness of the availability of sports tourism products among those working in other areas of tourism within the destination. For example, the Royal Malta Golf Club, part of the Marsa Country Club in Malta, runs an 'affiliate' programme among hotels on the island whereby hotels can become affiliated to the Royal Malta Golf Club and display the club crest in their foyer. This has been shown to be an effective strategy in capturing spontaneous golf tourism behaviours, aided by the ease with which a round of golf can be booked through the hotels (Bull and Weed, 1999).

In many cases, potential spontaneous sports tourism behaviours may simply be the result of 'coming-across', for example, event sports tourism products while 'wandering around' an area, particularly more low-key local events in urban areas (Law, 2002). Alternatively, supplementary sports tourism products, such as indoor events or fixtures like ice hockey or basketball games, may take place because bad weather has precluded participation in activities that might have been pre-planned. Similarly, the day hire of cycles, along with information regarding routes and potential stopping-off points, can also be a spontaneous, unplanned activity, although many hire centres are promoted in local guides (Koorey, 2001). In such cases, the destination level cooperative marketing and information provisions described above are key elements in strategies aimed at capturing such spontaneous behaviours.

Finally, at the luxury end of the market, country house hotels with extensive leisure and spa facilities may often generate repeat visits by capturing spontaneous behaviours on a trip during which participants originally had no intention of utilizing such leisure and spa facilities. A pilot study at one such hotel by Weed (2003e) showed that a significant group of participants in the health/spa activities on offer decided to take up such participation opportunities upon arrival at the hotel, rather than the facilities playing any part in their pre-trip planning or trip decision. A significant minority of this group stated that their experience of the facilities at this hotel would lead them to consider such provision when considering future holiday plans for similar trips to country house hotels.

CREATING COMPETITIVE ADVANTAGE

While strategies aimed at capturing spontaneous behaviours can be productive at destination level, the provision of opportunities in the luxury sports tourism, supplementary sports tourism and event sports tourism product areas can be part of a wider strategy to create competitive advantage over competitor organizations or destinations. Supplementary sports tourism facilities and events are now being used by a considerable number of tour operators, accommodation providers and destinations to 'add value' to their main product offering (Wright, 2007).

Many hotels now have their own health and fitness suites, either through direct provision or through strategic alliances with health club chains. Related to such provision, the health/spa/wellness concept is an area that is seen to offer considerable growth potential in the hotel sector. This is something that has been recognized by the French Accor hotel group, which has invested substantially in a wide range of health and wellness facilities across all its hotel brands in the last decade (Reznik, 2003). Such health, fitness and wellness facilities are also important in creating advantages over competitors in relation to business tourism. As noted in Chapter 1, if a hotel wishes to attract the lucrative conference market, top-class conference, meeting and exhibition facilities must be complemented by similarly luxurious leisure facilities.

The study of sports tourism in Malta (Bull and Weed, 1999) revealed an interesting way in which event sports tourism provision might be used to create competitive advantage. Some mass participation events, such as the Malta Marathon and Masters Open Swimming Meets, were attracting participants who were combining their trip to the island for event sports tourism participation with a family holiday. Malta had been selected as the destination for a package holiday at a time when it was possible for a member of the family to participate in an event. Here, the sports tourism participation was only a small part of the holiday, but had been a key factor in destination choice. Research on both sides of the Atlantic (Dobson et al., 1997; Scott and Turco, 2007) indicates that sports tourism opportunities provided by events and tournaments, for junior or adult participants, can be the excuse for a longer family holiday at the destination in question.

Discussions in Chapter 8 outlined the extent to which supplementary sports tourism provision is used by the big tour operators to add an additional dimension to their traditional product offering, although increasingly at this level, the provision of this type of supplementary sports tourism is necessary to maintain pace with competitors, rather than create an advantage (Wright, 2007). Similarly, the Butlins Holiday Worlds studies (McKoy, 1991; Reeves, 2000) show how Butlins initially used sports tourism opportunities to update and refresh their product and to create an advantage over competitor providers. However, as time has moved on, almost all 'holiday village/camp' providers have some level of supplementary sports tourism provision (Mintel, 2002a). Furthermore, the arrival of the recreation and leisure village concept, exemplified by Center Parcs, has raised the stakes somewhat in this area of provision.

Despite the investment by a number of the large tourism firms in the provision of supplementary sports tourism products, evidence suggests (Keynote, 2001; Mintel, 2002c) that take-up of such provision is relatively low. Why, then, have providers invested so much in the promotion of such opportunities? The answer lies in the final provision strategy to be discussed in this chapter, the exploitation of intenders.

EXPLOITING INTENDERS

Discussions under the converting intenders section of this chapter described a division in the intenders category between those intenders taking a tourist trip during which sports tourism behaviours were planned to take place alongside many other equally important tourism behaviours and those for whom the conversion from intender to participant takes place with the booking of a trip in which opportunities for sports tourism behaviours have played a major role in the trip decision-making process. The latter category was discussed under the converting intenders heading, however, the former category, where intenders and participants are indistinguishable pre-trip, is the focus of this section.

Research at Butlins Holiday Worlds in the UK (McKoy, 1991; Reeves, 2000) provided primary evidence of the existence of intenders for whom potential sports tourism behaviours play a part in the trip decision-making process, but for whom participation never actually materializes. The following quote, from a focus group of Butlins holidaymakers, is representative of this behaviour:

> *I must admit, I had all these great ideas of taking advantage of the facilities both indoors and outdoors, and in ten days all I've managed is a couple of games of snooker with a guy I met on the first day.*

The use of sports tourism facilities and opportunities as a marketing strategy has been discussed under the previous heading, but a comparison of activity take-up with the priority given to sports tourism provision in marketing and promotional material reveals that the intention to engage in sports tourism behaviours on trips where there are multiple motivations towards a range of tourism behaviours is far greater than actual participation. Furthermore, a cursory inspection of the actual facilities offered at some hotels and a comparison of their capacity with expressed participation intentions (c.f. Keynote, 2001; Mintel, 2002c), leads to the conclusion that many providers are banking on take-up being low, because if the level of participation matched intention to participate, then the level of provision would be woefully inadequate. Thus, intenders are exploited by providers whose market research tells them that sports tourism provision sells holidays, but also tells them that activity take-up is comparatively low.

CONCLUSION – PROVISION OVERVIEW

The discussions of provision in this chapter have been intended to be illustrative of the strategies of providers, rather than provide an exhaustive coverage of such providers' behaviours. The chapter is not intended to be a 'how to' guide for sports tourism managers (see Turco et al., 2002, for that type of material), but offers an insight into the behaviours and objectives of those concerned with sports tourism provision.

The conceptualization of sports tourism as being derived from the unique interaction of activity, people and place has, once again, been useful in appreciating aspects of provision behaviour. Some strategies, such as the generation of repeat visits, aim to create a unique experience of activity, people and place that cannot be accessed at home, while others, such as creating competitive advantage and exploiting intenders, use the image associated with such experiences to sell various types of trips involving sports tourism. Variations in the nature of this interaction are also part of provision, with the expansion of provision profiles being related to the variation of activity, while cooperative marketing strategies are largely about varying the place. Finally, strategies aimed at converting intenders and capturing spontaneous behaviours attempt to introduce potential sports tourists to this unique interaction in the hope that they will subsequently return to engage more regularly and extensively in sports tourism behaviours.

As the last substantive chapter before the case studies in Part 5, the material presented does provide a useful overview of the interconnected nature of knowledge about participants, policy-makers and providers. The Revised Sports Tourism Participation Model, developed in Chapter 5, is useful in informing the strategies of providers, while the Model of Sports Tourism Product Types, derived from the discussions in Chapter 8, provides a useful context for understanding provision strategies. In addition, the chapter has highlighted key areas where the work of policy-makers, in both supporting and making provision, can be important. The final part of the book now examines the behaviours, motivations and strategies of sports tourism participants, policy-makers and providers in relation to five very different sports tourism products.

PART 5

Case Studies

PREFACE

The final part of this volume has been included to provide practical illustrations of the issues discussed in the earlier parts of the text. The cases have been selected to cover a range of sports tourism behaviours and products, but also to illustrate a range of issues. As such, they each relate to varying extents to different parts of the earlier discussions.

However, these chapters are also intended to 'stand alone' and to be full discussions of the cases in question. Consequently, the chapters each locate the cases within their broader context and highlight the nature of the impacts of the particular sports tourism development under discussion, in addition to providing an illustration of various issues associated with participants, policy-makers and providers.

The five case study chapters relate to sports tourism as a diversification strategy, urban sports tourism, rural sports participation tourism, winter skiing and cycling, in relation to Malta, Sheffield, Wales and the European Alps respectively, with the cycling discussion being more generic. This range of areas and products is intended to cover various aspects of sports tourism and specifically to illustrate its nature as derived from the unique interaction of activity, people and place. The discussions of Malta and Sheffield both highlight how specific strategies are being pursued to develop the destination as a sports tourism place, although the nature of the activities and the types of people attracted are very different. The Welsh, Alpine and cycling cases perhaps focus more on the nature of the people involved and how particular activities can interact with places in a way that provides an experience that cannot be replicated through the provision of artificial facilities in the sports tourist's home area. In terms of illustrating the material discussed earlier in the text, the Malta case relates largely to the provision chapters (8 and 9), while the Sheffield case highlights some of the issues discussed in the policy chapters (6 and 7). Both the Wales and European Alps cases are illustrative of the behaviours, motivations and decisions of participants discussed in Chapters 3–5. Finally, the cycling case illustrates both the range of products that a particular activity can straddle (Chapter 8) and the range of behaviours that it provides for (Chapter 5). However, each of the cases is intended to allow some level of reflection on the range of issues discussed throughout the book.

The cycling case (Chapter 14) is an addition to the cases presented in the first edition, while the Sheffield, Welsh and Alpine cases have all been updated to reflect changes in participation, policy and provision in these areas. The Sheffield case demonstrates the continued legacy effect that a major event (the World Student Games of 1991) can have even 18 years later, while the Welsh and Alpine examples show that these established sports tourism products continue to evolve and remain popular among participants. The only chapter not to have been updated is that on Malta. This is because this chapter is included to provide an example of the way in which destinations that have relied on traditional mass tourism have used sports tourism as part of a strategy to diversify. As such, although the Malta case itself is no longer current, it provides a useful illustration of the potential role of sports tourism in product development strategies in destinations that are at a similar stage to that in which Malta found itself at the turn of the Millennium.

CHAPTER 10

Sports Tourism as a Diversification Strategy in Malta

The earlier chapters of this book have documented the increasing recognition, by participants, policy-makers and providers, of sports tourism as an important sector of the tourism industry and Chapter 2 described the range of areas in which sport and tourism might be linked for mutual benefit. Furthermore, Chapters 5 and 8 highlight the nature of sports tourism as a heterogeneous area, with a range of different markets offering potential to a destination seeking to diversify in this area. It would appear that the Mediterranean island of Malta possesses a number of advantages that would enable it to exploit some of these markets, perhaps particularly those relating to sports training, sports participation tourism, tourism with sports content and sports events identified in the Model of Sports Tourism Product Types in Chapter 8. This case study examines the development and potential of sports tourism as an important niche market in Malta, together with various problems which may constrain such development. It is based on an analysis of key documents, correspondence and interviews with Ministry officials, interviews with key personnel at a number of important sports facilities, as well as personal observations gained through several visits to the island.

THE TOURISM PRODUCT ON MALTA

One of the key problems relating to tourism development is that, despite its undoubted economic benefits, over reliance on this one industry area can be problematic (King, 1982; Buswell, 1996; Bull, 1997; Lockhart 1997a). Small islands such as Malta are often regarded as particularly vulnerable because tourism can totally dominate the overall economic structure, in some cases accounting for well over 50 per cent of export earnings (Shaw and Williams, 1994; Hutchings, 1996; Lockhart and Drakakis-Smith, 1997). Apart from the general problems of market fluctuations linked to a range of external factors, there are often problems associated with the precise nature of the tourism involved. Many small islands have allowed mass tourism to develop with scant regard to planning and long-term sustainable development. Apart from the usual vulnerability of such destinations to changes in fashion and the possible desire of tourists to extend their 'gaze' to new places, mass tourism development also brings additional problems which may ultimately lead to decline, such as poor quality accommodation, inadequate infrastructure and degradation of the environment. In addition, many places which embraced rapid tourist development often concentrated on limited markets and may have provided few alternative attractions beyond the basic sun, sand, sea and hotel facilities. While there may be little scope for significant development of other economic sectors, which is why tourism has been encouraged to such an extent in the first place, there is growing recognition that the tourist industry itself might be less vulnerable in such places if it were able to diversify (Lockhart, 1997a).

Malta has experienced many of these problems and has recently sought to establish new markets and attractions. Tourism began to develop in Malta from the mid-1960s and experienced spectacular growth in the 1970s with tourist arrivals increasing from 170 800 in 1970 to 705 500 in 1981; numbers then dropped back to approximately 500 000 for several years but built up again in the late 1980s, reaching nearly 1.2 million in the mid-1990s (Lockhart and Ashton, 1987, 1991; ITR, 1996; Lockhart, 1997b). One of the key factors in the rapid growth of tourism in Malta has been its dependence on a single market. In 1972, British visitors accounted for 50 per cent of all arrivals and, by 1980, this had risen to over 76 per cent. The British legacy on Malta, the use of English, a readiness to respond to a demand for low cost, self-catering accommodation, a favourable exchange rate boosted by exchange rate subsidies and successive schemes to support British tour operators have all helped to encourage British visitors (International Tourism Reports, 1996). The British market has thus not only been welcomed in the past but positively encouraged. But such dependence is double edged; it has seen Malta through some difficult times but it has also made Malta's tourism industry particularly vulnerable. While the UK share of the market has now dropped to just over 40 per cent, it is still high and the problem of such an unhealthy dependence has been demonstrated at various times in the past. For example, in the early 1980s it was the large numbers of British holidaymakers transferring to Spain which was responsible for the substantial decline in overall tourist arrivals and, more recently, in 1995 a new decline was attributable to British tourists going to Turkey.

The problem of relying on a single country for a major proportion of visitors is further aggravated by the fact that much of Malta's tourism has also catered for the cheaper end of the market, a market which is likely to be much more sensitive to price competition. In fact, this was the reason for British tourists transferring to Spain and Turkey. In addition, a high reliance on such a market has meant that greater numbers of tourists are needed than would otherwise be necessary to maintain a given level of income and these large numbers have at times led to tourist facilities being overstrained. Inadequate water supply, traffic congestion, waste disposal and general environmental degradation are all problems which have resulted from the rapid development of low cost, mass tourism, problems which further reduce the island's attractiveness and threaten tourism's long-term sustainability. As the Structure Plan for the Maltese Islands (Government of Malta, 1990) states, 'Malta has now reached the point at which tourist infrastructure is destroying the very features which attract tourists in the first place'.

As a result of these problems, Malta has been seeking to counter its reputation for providing a low quality product by upgrading facilities and has also been attempting to reduce its reliance on its traditional mass tourism (Inskeep, 1994; International Tourism Reports, 1996). As part of this process it has been encouraging diversification and the development of niche markets (Lockhart, 1997b). A number of alternative forms of tourism development have been suggested, one obvious example being that of cultural tourism, which the National Tourist Organization (NTO) has been promoting explicitly in the 1990s. According to Boissevan (1993) this policy has been responsible for the growth of tourism in the off-peak period; whereas in the mid-1980s 70 per cent of tourist arrivals were between June and September, by 1992, although overall arrivals had nearly doubled, only 40 per cent were visiting during this period. A further example of diversification is the growing conference market which, in addition to being less seasonal, is also linked to a policy of upgrading hotel accommodation and only allowing the building of new hotels if they have a 4 or 5 star rating. However, a key area which has been identified by the Maltese authorities as an important market is that of sports tourism (UNDP & WTO, 1989; Inskeep, 1994; Brincat, 1995; Lockhart, 1997b). Currently, the Maltese National Tourist Organization is promoting a wide range of sports events and activities – both for participation and spectating – to foreign tourists (National Tourist Organization – Malta, 1997). Diving, yachting, power boating, golf, football and swimming are just a few examples from a wide range of sports which are seen as having a great deal of potential in this respect.

THE POTENTIAL MARKET AND THE EXTENT OF SPORTS TOURISM AT THE TURN OF THE MILLENNIUM

Opportunities to be gained from the development of sports tourism in Malta relate to the growing importance of sport within society and increasing participation rates in a range of European countries for which Malta provides a convenient location and relatively short flying distances. An analysis of sports participation in such countries – for example Britain, France, Germany, Spain and Poland – shows that general participation in sport has been steadily increasing. While these countries use different definitions of sport and a range of survey methods to measure participation – see Cushman et al. (1996) for a discussion of this – it is possible to identify general increases in participation in cycling, football, golf, tennis and a range of water sports over the last two decades (sources: see note 1). Such increases are highly significant for Malta's development as a sports tourism destination because it already possesses the resources to provide these sports to foreign tourists and has long identified much of Europe as a major target market and, indeed, has existing links with many of these countries, especially the UK. Furthermore, the sports identified have been shown, both in Chapters 3, 4 and 5 and in studies elsewhere, to be mainstays of the sports tourism product (Jackson and Glyptis, 1992; Standeven and Tomlinson, 1994). In addition, Malta's Mediterranean location provides a climate which is suitable for much of this sporting activity throughout the year but especially during the winter months when climatic conditions make the pursuit of sport difficult in many parts of Europe. Consequently, not only has Malta demonstrated the ability to attract the people element of the sports tourism experience, but it is also very well placed to provide for both the activity and place elements.

As the Model of Sports Tourism Product Types in Chapter 8 shows, the market for sports tourism is not homogeneous and a wide range of differentiated areas can be identified. At its simplest 'supplementary sports tourism' involves the provision of sports tourism opportunities as a supplement to providers' main product offer and this type of provision has been made on Malta for many years, just as it has been elsewhere. However, there is growing evidence to show that the provision of these types of opportunities are becoming more important in the trip decision-making process (see Chapter 4), with travel brochures and hotels specifically promoting sports tourism opportunities. Certainly, the better quality hotels are highlighting sports tourism facilities. For example, several hotels advertise gymnasia and opportunities for water sports with the Mellieha Bay Hotel listing, among other things, an 'independently run water-sports centre' offering a range of opportunities including windsurfing, dinghy sailing and water skiing together with a 'PADI Five Star Dive Centre offering professional instruction in scuba diving for beginners to experts'. Similarly, the 5 star Hotel Bay Point in St George's lists 'watersports including canoes and scuba-diving… golf at the Marsa Sports Club 8 km away… and supervised gym (in fitness centre)' (Thomson Summer Sun, 2000). A number of hotels on Malta are 'affiliated' to the Royal Malta Golf Club, which is part of the Marsa Sports and Country Club and, as a result, are allowed to use the Club logo on their notepaper and display a plaque on the wall in their reception areas. In addition to golf being arranged for guests through the hotels, a 'pay-as-you-play' facility is also available for those travellers for whom such sports tourism participation is one among a number of other equally or more important behaviours on their trip. As an official of the Marsa Club commented: 'no-one will leave Malta having been unable to have a game of golf', a situation in stark contrast to that experienced at many other golf courses in Europe.

While golfing opportunities clearly exist for those who wish to participate only once or twice on a trip, Malta also caters for those for whom golf sports tourism participation has been an important trip decision factor and for whom participation will be high, just as it provides for other types of 'sports participation tourism'. However, unlike golf sports tourism provision in many other destinations, the market in Malta does not primarily fall within the 'luxury sports tourism' category. Malta's tradition of catering for 'cloth cap' tourism has helped to bring a golfing holiday within the reach of the 64 per cent of golf players in the UK who are skilled working class and there is every likelihood that this market will continue. However, the policy of promoting higher quality hotels and the possibility of providing additional golf courses may well lead to a shift in the social balance in future. In contrast to golf, it is perhaps the case that much of Malta's provision and potential for water sports does fall more clearly into the 'luxury sports tourism' type. Malta's situation as a small island with a great deal of interesting coast line means that such water sports as scuba-diving, windsurfing and windsailing are an important part of its sports holiday market. Further to this, the development of the marina at Msida has meant that yachting, both competitive and recreational, has become a significant contributor to the Maltese tourism industry. In fact, yachting and scuba-diving, along with golf, have been the subject of specific development plans that aim to develop their potential as niche tourism markets.

'Sports training tourism' in Malta is already provided for in a number of different activities. Once again, golf provides a good example in this respect. Golf raises 40 per cent of the Marsa Sports Club's income, around half of which is from tourists, with golf schools being the major contributor. These schools usually involve a week's stay, with Scandinavia, especially Sweden and Norway, being a particularly important market. Not only does Malta provide physical opportunities to play golf which do not exist in these countries during the winter months, it also provides an opportunity to learn how to play, something that is not always easy to achieve as a result of 'the snobbery of many golf clubs at home' (Marsa Club official). The Marsa Club employs a full-time resident professional who is primarily responsible for holding classes for visiting tourists (Golfing in Malta, undated). As a result, Malta enables such tourists to acquire the skills necessary to allow them to play golf on their return – thus providing the important 'foundation' stage of the sports development continuum and providing sports tourists with an additional leisure opportunity that they would not have possessed prior to such a holiday. In this respect, the provision of golf in Malta is a good example of the sports development potential of sports tourism highlighted in Chapter 1.

Another important area of sports training tourism is that of football. Indeed, the Malta Football Association has a German firm that advertises Malta in northern Europe as a place for training camps (Brincat, 1995). Teams from Scandinavia, Switzerland and Germany regularly use Malta for their pre-season training, taking advantage of the mild winters. In 1994, a team also came from South Korea to train (Brincat, 1995). The training camps are usually held at the Malta Football Association Technical Complex which, in addition to incorporating the National Stadium and possessing training grounds with the lushest and greenest grass on the island, also contains on-site accommodation for up to 24 people, a restaurant catering for up to 50 people per sitting, a food technologist available for special menus, a gymnasium, sauna, sports injuries clinic (including fitness testing), lecture theatre, conference room, games room, TV lounge and bar. These facilities have recently been expanded as part of the ongoing Ta'Qali Action Plan (Maltese Planning Authority), which is developing the area surrounding the Technical Complex as a National Recreation Centre including an indoor and outdoor sports complex, a basketball stadium, a cross-country/jogging track and further opportunities for informal recreation together with some additional accommodation. These developments increase the potential to develop this area of Malta as a major focus, not only for sports training tourism, but also for less formal sports tourism products in the 'sports participation tourism' and 'supplementary sports tourism' areas. Swimming provides a further example of sports training tourism, with the Tal-Qroqq Swimming Pool and University Sports Complex providing an Olympic size pool and a range of associated facilities for visiting groups including sports injuries clinic, underwater viewing facility, conference hall and seminar rooms. This facility is currently very popular with swimming clubs in the UK, with specialist sports tourism operators such as Toucan Tours and Track and Field liaising with the pool, the university and local hotels to provide a complete package to these clubs.

Despite its strengths in relation to golf and in other areas that fall into the 'luxury sports tourism' product category, 'sports participation tourism' is currently perhaps the weakest area of the Maltese sports tourism product. However, Malta does have potential to develop this market. The landscape to the west of the island, away from the main urban areas surrounding the capital, Valletta, provides opportunities for walking and hiking and particularly mountain biking. This, combined with the proposed developments in the Ta'Qali area, particularly those for more informal recreation, enhances Malta's potential to develop sports participation tourism.

Finally, Malta has demonstrated an ability, despite its size, to make some provision for event sports tourism. In recent years, Malta has hosted a number of international events including the World Offshore power boat racing grand prix, a senior APT tennis tournament, the Malta Marathon, the World Paralympics, the Small Nations Games and several editions of Tour Sans Frontières. Participation in the qualifying rounds of the Football World Cup has also brought visiting teams to Malta together with their supporters, the Malta–Ireland match in 1994 having attracted 3000 visiting spectators to the island (Brincat, 1995). But, as Chapters 4, 8 and 9 demonstrate, it is not just the more prestigious events that are important in this respect. The Tal-Qroqq pool, for example, is an important venue for Open Meets and Masters Events and this has a wider tourist impact as competitors will often bring their families with them and combine an event with a holiday. In fact, Malta hosts a number of events where visits by competitors' extended families can have a significant effect on tourist numbers. In order to capitalize on this, the National Tourism Organization produces a comprehensive calendar of such events each year. The commercial potential of such events is further evidenced by the existence of such companies as Sportsmans Travel Malta, a UK-based firm which arranges visits for competitors and their families to them.

Thus it is possible to see that Malta has already begun to exploit the undoubted demand for sports tourism but, while the potential market would appear to be growing inexorably, the extent to which Malta can take full advantage of these opportunities is dependent upon overcoming a number of resource constraints. And, part of the solution to this rests with tourism planners and their ability to recognize the opportunities and their willingness to provide positive commitment to ensuring that development will occur. However, as discussions in Chapters 6 and 7 have shown, such recognition and commitment among policy-makers and planners is not often easy to develop.

RESOURCE CONSTRAINTS ON SPORTS TOURISM DEVELOPMENT IN MALTA

Despite the attractions of its accessible location and mild climate, a number of resource factors combine to constrain the development of sports tourism on Malta. Apart from the general problems of water supply, degraded landscape and poor transport infrastructure, there is also the problem of limited land resources which have to cater for a wide range of demands. Malta involves a relatively small area of only 316 square kilometres and, as outlined earlier, has already experienced substantial tourist development. In addition, its own domestic population of approximately 350 000 is also making increasing demands on the land resource as living standards increase and the need for more housing and other facilities grows. Not only does this mean that land for additional sports facilities is becoming increasingly scarce, but any new development has to be able to overcome strict planning controls which now operate. Golf provides a useful illustration of these problems as, at present, the Marsa golf course is the only course on the island. In the late 1990s, the membership of the club was reaching saturation point with members often antagonistic towards large groups of visitors. However, the club needs the tourist income, without which it would either have to double its membership (which would not solve the saturation problem) or double membership fees. In any case, because the land on which the club is situated belongs to the government and because the government recognizes the importance of golf sports tourism, there is little prospect of a change in the status quo. Consequently, in order that both domestic and tourist participation can flourish in Malta, an additional course is clearly required. However, two potential sites have already been refused planning permission partly because of landscape/environmental considerations but also because they would have impinged on high quality agricultural land, something else that is becoming increasingly scarce. The large land requirements of golf, together with the need for substantial amounts of water on an island where water supply is problematic to begin with, mean that finding an additional course will not be easy[2].

A further issue which complicates the facilities problem is the development of domestic sport. At present, sport is not particularly well developed on the island, something that is due in large measure to what the former Maltese National Football Coach referred to as 'a gross lack of culture for sport' (Pippo Psaila, *Malta Football Association Quarterly Review*, December 1996). The Ministry of Education and National Culture is attempting to remedy this with discussions currently underway to establish '...how sports, culture and the arts may be promoted further both in the school curriculum, as well as extra curricular activities' and has talked about 'a concerted effort (being) made to see that sports' amenities in schools are upgraded together with their general maintenance …. ' (discussion with Ministry official). In some ways, a general lack of participation in certain sports may have provided more opportunities for visitors. This would certainly appear to have been the case with golf in the past and also at the Tal-Qroqq Swimming Pool where there would appear to be spare capacity with no problems in programming the various user groups. In fact, the operations manager claimed that he could programme time for all user groups (when required) throughout the day, all year round. However, as sport becomes more popular on the island, the demands of the domestic population for access to sports facilities could have two very different consequences for sports tourism. On the one hand, the development of a sports culture could well lead to increasing demands for more and better facilities which could enhance opportunities for sports tourists. Alternatively, it could place substantial pressure on existing sports resources and ultimately reduce availability to sports tourists. This would certainly seem to be happening in golf as well as other activities at the Marsa Country Club. For example, the club has 1000 tennis playing members which certainly reduces the market for sports tourists who are only allowed to play on weekdays before 3.30 pm.

In addition to providing new facilities, there is also the problem of accommodation. In order to attract the higher spending sports tourist, improvements in hotel accommodation are required, with possible investment needed in the development of more 5 star hotels. More hotel development, however, will inevitably involve further loss of land as well as landscape impacts and thus developers may find planning permission difficult to obtain, especially given the background of an apparent surplus stock of accommodation. The whole question of increasing the stock of 5 star hotel accommodation has been the subject of considerable debate, with the issue often arising in the *Maltese Times* and including contributions from both the Minister of Tourism and the Shadow Minister. While the overall consensus appears to be supportive, there is still a hint that planning policies could impose constraints.

THE ROLE OF GOVERNMENT IN SPORTS TOURISM DEVELOPMENT

Chapters 6 and 7 show that the future direction and success of sports tourism can, in part, be determined by the policies and commitment of the relevant government departments. Malta is no different to any other country in this respect and the government has an important role to play in a number of areas. First, it is responsible in large measure for some of the key infrastructural requirements of sports tourism, such as the quality of transport facilities and provision of an adequate water supply. Secondly, through its environmental planning policies it can influence both the quality of the physical environment and thus the attractiveness of the places in which sports tourism operates and also through its development control mechanisms the extent to which sports facilities are permitted to develop. Thirdly, through both its sports and tourism policies it can specifically encourage sports tourism development and, finally, through its relevant agencies it can promote its attractions abroad.

For several decades, successive Maltese governments have attempted to promote tourism but, while espousing the principles of effective tourism planning, policy goals have not always been realized. Since the late 1980s, a clearer recognition of the problems has emerged and, according to Lockhart (1997b), evidence of recent progress has been made regarding diversification, niche markets and an improvement in the seasonal spread of arrivals. However, as Chapters 6 and 7 highlight, the development and implementation of policies involving the integration of sport and tourism may be more difficult to achieve. Work in a range of countries has shown that, despite the undoubted advantages of linking the two, the respective sport and tourist bodies have often pursued independent policies with little attempt at integration. A useful comparison is with the situation in Britain where evidence (Weed, 2003c, 2006a) suggests that the lack of integrated policies may be due to the specific organizational arrangements that operate there. In particular, it appears that such problems may be associated with the historically separate development of the two sectors. Unfortunately, in Malta, the sport and tourism sectors have also developed separately.

The administrative arrangements in Malta are similar to those that existed in Britain prior to the creation in 1992 of the Department of National Heritage (renamed the Department for Culture, Media and Sport in 1997). Tourism responsibility rests with the Ministry of Tourism while responsibility for sport is located in the Secretariat for Youth, Sport, Art and Culture within the Education Ministry. Although in Britain the Department for Culture, Media and Sport (DCMS) notionally brings sport and tourism within the same Ministry, the various policies that the DCMS has pursued (with the exception of those relating to major events) appear to have actually weakened the potential for integration rather than strengthened it. Weed (2005a), identifies the reduction of funding to the national and regional tourism agencies allocated to core functions, the adoption of increasingly narrow definitions of sport and the cutting of the only statutory link between sport and tourism agencies in the abolition of the Regional Councils for Sport and Recreation as DCMS policies that have limited the extent to which integration is likely to occur. A paradox is revealed between a government department structure that would appear to encourage sport–tourism relations and a set of policies that seems to do the opposite. The situation in Malta, of course, is slightly different and there may be opportunities to learn from the British experience.

Perhaps the most obvious difference is Malta's position as a small island state, something which Chapter 7 suggests may facilitate the development of strategy at a national level. As such, it has no regional structure of sport or tourism agencies nor does it need the large-scale bureaucracy that exists in Britain to coordinate matters at a national level. In this respect, the historically separate development of the two spheres may not be as problematic as in Britain, as large-scale readjustment would not be required for greater integration. Furthermore, the small-scale nature of the Maltese administration should make it easier and simpler to coordinate things on an informal level between the individuals involved. However, during discussions with officials of the Maltese government in the course of preparing this case study, it became apparent that, in a number of cases, such informal coordination did not appear to be occurring. Informal lines of communication between the planning department (responsible for the Ta'Qali Development Plan) and officials in the government responsible for sport had not even reached the point where the officials concerned knew the names of their colleagues in the other department. This example appears to be indicative of the situation across the Maltese government. In Britain, as elsewhere (see Chapter 7), the inclinations of key staff to develop links across sectors has been identified as one of a number of important factors affecting sport–tourism liaison (Weed, 2006a). It would appear that this is also the case in Malta. It further appears that the attitudes of key staff may be of greater importance in the Maltese situation where there is greater latitude to develop links through informal coordination as a result of its smaller scale (Weed, 2008b). In view of Malta's previously identified potential further to develop its sports tourism market, the obstacles that its government faces in assisting such development would not appear to be insurmountable.

CONCLUSION

While the inexorable growth of tourism means that, on a world scale, it is likely to remain the single most important industry well into the foreseeable future, the prospects for tourism within individual countries may not be so secure. Not only do countries need to ensure that the product they provide is not forsaken for a new product somewhere else, as tourists become increasingly fickle in their desires and requirements, they may also have to improve and rethink their product as a result of the legacy that initial, unplanned tourist development may have caused. These problems are particularly acute in many countries whose economies are especially reliant on mass tourism and one response to this has been the attempt to develop niche markets in order to diversify the tourism sector and possibly also attract visitors with a propensity to spend more.

While Malta is characterized by a number of unique circumstances, it also encounters many of the problems that beset other countries and, like many of them, it too is attempting to diversify through the establishment of niche markets such as sports tourism. This case study chapter shows that not only does Malta possess considerable scope for the development of a wide variety of different types but that some of this potential is already being realized. There are, however, considerable opportunities still to be realized and it is also clear that, despite possessing a number of distinct advantages, various constraints could seriously hinder future progress. The resource constraints of land and water shortages, inadequate transport infrastructure and large areas of unattractive landscape may pose substantial limits on future growth, while the lack of high quality accommodation and the related image problem are also significant hurdles to be overcome.

In addition to resource and environmental problems, the future success of sports tourism development will also depend to a large extent on the attitude and commitment of the Maltese government. Government's involvement in improved infrastructure and environmental planning is obviously an important factor but so too is its commitment and ability to develop and implement specific sport–tourism policies. While successive Maltese governments have embraced the principle of tourism planning, related policy goals have not always been realized and, in the area of sports tourism, additional obstacles may hinder progress towards effective policy development and implementation. Both Chapters 6 and 7 and studies elsewhere have shown that this may be far more problematic than might be imagined, especially where the two sectors of sport and tourism involve separate departments and agencies. While sports tourism is highlighted in a number of policy documents, it would appear that the policy process has not involved the integrated involvement of both the sport and tourism sectors which, as in Britain and many other countries, operate independently. However, despite this, Malta also possesses an important advantage in overcoming such lack of integration, namely its small size. The interest and enthusiasm of key staff is often a crucial factor in joint policy initiatives and the opportunities for joint action, if only on an informal basis in the first instance, must be greatly increased given Malta's situation as a small city state. The growth of sports tourism and its increasing role in travellers' trip decisions provides substantial opportunities for places like Malta but, in overcoming the various constraining problems, such development needs to be planned, resourced and promoted by means of a clear policy.

NOTES

1. The way data are collected across different countries varies significantly (see Cushman, et al., 1996). The dates and methods of collection also vary. The estimates of trends quoted in the text were based on the following sources:

   Office of Population Censuses and Surveys (1985–1992). *The General Household Survey*. London, HMSO.

   Institut National de Statistique et d'Etudes Economiques (INSEE) – see Garrigues (1988).

   National Institute for Sport and Physical Education (INSEP) – see Erlinger et al. (1985).

   Prime Minister's Office (1983–1991). *Public Opinion Poll on Leisure and Travel/Public Census on Lifestyle*.

   Israel Institute of Applied Social Research (IIASR) – see Katz et al. (1992).

   Uczestnictwo w kulturze (1992). Cultural Participation Surveys. Warsaw, GUS.

   Foundation for the Development of Social Studies and Applied Sociology (1976–1994). *Informe Sociologico Sobre la Situacion Social en Espana*. Madrid: Euroamerica.

2. The Marsa golf course occupies a unique site in the Wied il-Kbir valley which means that it is only a metre above the water table. Consequently, it does not experience problems of watering greens and fairways that might be expected of a golf course in Malta, an island with no surface water, where water is obtained from underground aquifers and expensive desalination plants.

CHAPTER 11

Urban Sports Tourism – The Case of Sheffield

Like Alpine skiing, which will be examined in Chapter 13, another well-established example of sports tourism is that associated with large urban areas. However, unlike skiing where the principal involvement is active participation, in urban areas the main emphasis is with vicarious or passive spectating behaviours through event sports tourism. Cities exhibit a number of attractions for the development of this sports tourism product. Given their size and market influence, they inevitably possess high quality facilities and stadiums, established initially for their own residents and teams. However, domestic and subsequent international competitions have encouraged substantial numbers of people to travel to cities either to support their teams or to experience the sporting spectacle. In addition, cities are increasingly hosting mega-events, utilizing their existing facilities as well as creating new ones specifically for such purposes. While perhaps not as obvious as Alpine regions, cities are, nevertheless, important sports tourism places, possessing distinctive sports tourism landscapes (Bull, 2005).

As outlined in Chapter 1, many sports teams have attracted a substantial following of supporters who are prepared to travel to watch their team play away from home, in both domestic and international competitions. Those teams with the greatest level of success are invariably associated with larger cities. For example, in the English Premier soccer league during the 2008/2009 season, all but one of the teams were located in urban centres with populations over 100 000 and 75 per cent were from cities with populations over 200 000 including five from London, two from the West Midlands, two from Manchester, two from Liverpool and one each from Hull, Newcastle and Stoke. Similarly, the two most successful Scottish teams – Rangers and Celtic – are located in Glasgow, Scotland's largest city while, in European football, the teams that dominate European competitions are usually those associated with large cities (e.g. Real Madrid, Barcelona, Ajax of Amsterdam, Inter Milan and AC Milan, Roma and Lazio, Bayern Munich, Paris St Germain). This success is clearly attributable to their larger potential support and subsequent income which itself attracts financial investment from both local and external business, thus helping to maintain future success and support. This clear advantage of larger cities is further reinforced through the infrastructural and other peripheral facilities that such urban centres provide. Transport media, for example, are focused primarily on the major cities (e.g. motorway networks, inter-city train services and international and regional airports) and thus sports tourists can travel more easily to such destinations. In addition, given that cities are major locations for other forms of tourism means that they can also provide accommodation, restaurants, bars, clubs and various forms of entertainment for the visitor beyond the immediate attractions of sports tourism products. Not only are cities able to accommodate spectating sports tourists but, as outlined in Chapter 2, part of the attraction of travelling for event sports tourism is the broader trip experience which may also include experiencing the nightlife and other facilities available.

The large local catchments, transport foci and general tourist infrastructure also mean that large cities, and especially capital cities, are the logical locations for national stadiums. Various sports have their respective national stadiums in London with Wembley, Twickenham, Lords and Wimbledon being obvious examples, although other UK cities are also capable of hosting national and international events (e.g. the Millennium Stadium in Cardiff, Meadowbank in Edinburgh, and the Don Valley Stadium in Sheffield).

While the sports tourism associated with intercity competition is well established, sports tourism in cities has become much more important in recent times as a result of two overlapping influences. The first involves a recognition of the importance of mega-events (including major events sports tourism products) in shaping and supplementing both the national tourism product and the long-term city product (Ritchie, 1984; Getz, 1991; Hall, 1992b; Tyler et al., 1998) and the second is the way that sports tourism development has been used in urban regeneration. Each of these areas is recognized within the Policy Wheel for Sport and Tourism (see Figure 7.1) discussed in Chapter 7. Aside from the identification of 'event sports tourism' within the 'sports tourism products' category, issues surrounding provision for events are a feature of the 'facility issues' category, while 'economic and social regeneration' is a specific subcategory under 'resources and funding'.

According to Law (1993: p. 97) the term mega-event, in an urban context, describes 'large events of world importance and high profile which have a major impact on the image of the host city'. They are 'usually viewed as a highly significant tourist asset…with the event directly attracting participants and the resulting raised profile of the area also indirectly encouraging increased general visitation' (Bramwell, 1997b: p. 168). Roche (2001) distinguishes between 'mega', 'special' and 'hallmark' events on the basis of the target attendance/market and the type of media interest involved (Table 11.1), although other writers use the terms interchangeably which is the approach adopted here.

Event sports tourism provision has emerged as a major policy instrument for governments keen to market their cities and boost local business as a result of visitor spending (Mules, 1998; Green et al., 2003; Gratton et al., 2005; Preuss, 2005). The economic benefits from mega-events are substantial. The total economic impact of the Montreal games in 1976 was reckoned to have generated between US$77 million and $135 million (or between US$124 million and $216 million if multiplier effects are included) while the estimated total impact of the Los Angeles games was US$417 million in value-added terms (Collins and Jackson, 1999). The 1996 Atlanta Olympics generated £645 million. Such figures may be exaggerated and, of course, do not reveal the extent of municipal debt and written off capital involved. The Atlanta games cost £557.9 million and more recent Games have involved substantially more, with Athens costing more than €12 billion, the London 2012 games projected to cost £9.2 billion and

Table 11.1	Types of mega-event		
Type of event	**Example of event**	**Target attendance/ market**	**Type of media interest**
Mega-event	Olympic Games World Cup (soccer)	Global	Global TV
Special event	Grand Prix (F1) World Regional sport (e.g. Pan-Am Games)	World Regional/national	International/ national TV
Hallmark event	National sport event (e.g. Australian Games)	National	National TV
	Big city sport/festivals	Regional	Local TV

Source: Based on Roche (2001)

the 2008 Beijing games costing a staggering £22 billion. However, there are other reasons why such events have become increasingly attractive to both local and national governments. They are seen as a means of changing the image of both the city and the state as a whole (Robertson and Guerrier, 1998). In fact, Weiler and Hall (1992: p. 1) argue that 'Hallmark events are the image builders of modern tourism', while Waitt (1999) suggests that the Olympic Games as spectacle is the ultimate tourist attraction. Such events can enhance the status of smaller states as in the Seoul Summer Olympic Games and also non-capital cities as in the Barcelona and Los Angeles Olympics, the Adelaide Grand Prix, the Calgary Winter Olympic Games or the Victoria, British Columbia, Commonwealth Games (Collins and Jackson, 1999). The Barcelona Olympic Games also helped Spain demonstrate an alternative tourism product to the mass tourism of the 'costas' (Robertson and Guerrier, 1998) and the city has subsequently become one of the top European tourism destinations, being ranked fifth in terms of visitor numbers in the late 1990s after London, Paris, Rome and Dublin (Wöber, 1997). More recent work by Waitt (2003: p. 112), who examined the social impacts of the Sydney Olympic Games, has also suggested that such impacts are positive and can 'generate patriotism and a sense of community or belonging, particularly among the young and ethnic minorities'. He believes that such 'global sporting events provide the opportunity for government and city authorities to (re)establish or increase the attachment and identification of people to place'. Furthermore, such events are also perceived as offering the potential for sporting legacy benefits (Gratton et al., 2005; Weed, 2008a), both in terms of encouraging the development of elite athletes and encouraging more people to take up sport and physical activity as part of health and fitness agendas (Department of Culture, Media and Sport/Strategy Unit, 2002; Weed et al., 2008b). Whatever the overall benefits, there is intense competition among nations to host such prestigious events and governments are willing to help finance bids and fund the building of stadiums and related infrastructure as well as send delegations on 'charm offensives' in order to help secure them. Sport England invested £3.4 million in the bid for the 2006 FIFA World Cup, a decision which the Government fully endorsed (Department of Culture, Media and Sport, 2001) and, as part of the attempt to obtain the 2012 Olympics, both the French President Jacques Chirac and the British Prime Minister Tony Blair were part of their respective country's presenting teams at the IOC meeting in Singapore in July 2005.

As highlighted in the Policy Wheel for Sport and Tourism (see Figure 7.1) discussed in Chapter 7, hallmark events are also part of sports tourism's wider role in helping urban regeneration (Gratton and Henry, 2001; Carlsen and Taylor, 2003). The idea of using tourism in general as a spur to urban economic and environmental regeneration originally came from North America but has now been adopted in many towns and cities throughout the developed world (Law, 1992, 1996, 2000; Swarbrooke, 2000). Various dockland areas such as Liverpool and London are classic examples of this, influenced to a large extent by the success of similar developments in the city of Baltimore (Shaw and Williams, 2002) and sports tourism has often played a prominent role. London Docklands developed the Docklands Sailing Centre, Surrey Docks Water Sports Centre and the London Wetbike Club and has become an important destination (see also Hall and Page, 2006). The 1992 Barcelona Olympic Games led to US$8300 million of public and private sector investment in the area, including a new airport, a ringroad and clearance of a derelict waterfront area for the construction of an Olympic village (Chalkley et al., 1992; Stevens, 1992). Some cities have specifically marketed sports tourism as a central feature of their tourism-led regeneration. Manchester's failed bid for the 2000 Olympic Games acted as a catalyst for a 'vision' for change and expansion (Shaw and Williams, 2002), creating investment and development opportunities and allowing linkages and partnerships to flourish while also providing a basis for the subsequent successful bid for the 2002 Commonwealth Games. Sports tourism opportunities have subsequently become a crucial part of a central marketing initiative involving its football teams, cricket, the new swimming and diving complex at the University, the Velodrome and the Commonwealth Stadium which hosted the Commonwealth Games in 2002. Birmingham also failed in bids for previous Olympics but, like Manchester, gained in civic reputation and event sports tourism facilities which included an indoor arena with 20 000 seats, a 50 metre pool and a refurbished stadium (Collins and Jackson, 1999). Likewise Glasgow and Sheffield have used sports tourism as part of their regeneration attempts (see below).

It is not just in Europe, North America and Australia, however, that sport tourism, especially the use of event sports tourism products, has been used as a specific instrument to develop city economies. The Beijing Olympic Games has already been mentioned and Singapore is a further example of an Asian city adopting such a policy. The Singaporean authorities have promoted ambitious tourism strategies that aim to double visitor arrivals to 15 million a year and tourism receipts to S$20 billion a year by 2012 through, among other things, the development of a 'vibrant events scene' and the establishment of a sports tourism infrastructure is seen as one of the ways by which this might be achieved (Foley et al., 2006). As part of this strategy various high profile international events have been attracted to Singapore including the Formula 1 Grand Prix on September

28, 2008, the Asian Youth Games in 2009, the inaugural Youth Olympic Games in 2010 and the World Netball Championships in 2011.

SPORTS TOURISM IN SHEFFIELD – A CASE STUDY

The city of Sheffield provides an interesting case study for the issues discussed above. While not a capital city, it is, nevertheless, a large urban centre with a population of 530 000. As such, it possesses a variety of sports facilities consistent with its size and boasts a number of stadiums linked to domestic sports teams. It contains a range of world class spectator venues including Bramall Lane and Hillsborough, the respective homes of the city's two football teams, Sheffield United and Sheffield Wednesday, the Sheffield Arena (for ice hockey and basketball), the Don Valley Stadium (athletics and rugby league), Ponds Forge International Sports Centre (ice hockey, basketball, swimming and aquatic sports) and Owlerton Stadium (speedway, stock cars, greyhound racing). In addition to spectator sports tourism, the city also possesses various facilities that can offer opportunities for active sports tourism participation, including various leisure and sports centres, climbing centres, an ice centre with facilities for ice skating and speed skating, ski village (Europe's largest artificial ski resort), golf courses, tenpin bowling venues and a laserzone. In addition, the new English Institute of Sport facility, built with the help of a Lottery award, includes a six lane indoor 200 metre oval banked athletics track plus specialist facilities for seven Olympic sports, including boxing, judo, table tennis, volleyball, badminton, netball and athletics, together with sports science and medicine services. Therefore, event sports tourism products not only attract substantial numbers of spectators to the city but a range of 'supplementary sports tourism' provision for active, vicarious and passive sports tourism participation are also available.

But it is the way sports tourism products have been developed as part of Sheffield's regeneration process that is the major interest of this chapter. As such, it is illustrative of many of the potential linkages identified in the Policy Wheel for Sport and Tourism (see Figure 7.1) in Chapter 7 and also of the importance of specific 'regional contexts' (see, again, Chapter 7), in this case Sheffield's decaying manufacturing industry and employment base, in overcoming many of the barriers to policy liaison. Sheffield built its reputation on its steel and cutlery industries but, like many cities in the developed world, it has seen its traditional industries decline in recent years such that steel now employs less than 10 per cent of its former workforce. In 1971, almost half of the workforce was engaged in manufacturing industry, but this had fallen to 24 per cent by 1984, with job losses in the metal-based manufacturing sector between 1981 and 1984 being double the rate for the UK generally and the city also suffered from a relatively poorly developed service sector (Dulac and Henry, 2001). By 2006, largely as a result of a deliberate policy to regenerate Sheffield as the 'City of Sport', sport and sports tourism was economically more important than large-scale manufacturing and worth £680 million, representing about a fifth of South Yorkshire's economy (*The Times*, 2008).

The Development of Sports Tourism in Sheffield and its Political Context

The development of sports tourism in Sheffield did not simply develop by accident or as a result of market forces but rather as the direct result of specific decisions by local politicians to invest in event sports tourism products. Up to the mid-1980s, investment in sport in Sheffield had been very low, much lower than in the majority of other cities in the UK, with the city council placing far more emphasis on cultural aspects rather than sport. However, as Dulac and Henry (2001) explain, a change in the political make up of the ruling Labour group on the Council and a worsening unemployment situation led to an acknowledgement that finance and other resources had to come from sources other than local taxation (which had been effectively capped by central government legislation) or financial transfers from central government. Partnership with local capital provided one of the few ways forward and, as a result, Sheffield adopted a series of partnership projects with local capital from the late 1980s.

In 1986, the Sheffield Economic Regeneration Committee in the City Council's Department of Employment and Economic Development was established (Strange, 1993, quoted in Dulac and Henry, 2001) which brought together representatives of the City Council, the business community, trades unions, higher-education institutions, central government agencies and local organizations. As Dulac and Henry (2001: p. 66) explain:

> *The aim of the group, as stated in the principal planning document it produced,* Sheffield 2000 *(Sheffield Economic Regeneration Committee, n.d.), was to develop a long-term economic regeneration strategy for the city, with a particular focus on the Lower Don Valley in which most of the old steel plants had existed and which was now largely derelict. As part of the regeneration process and following the recommendation of commercial consultants that a flagship project was required to spearhead the drive for regeneration, the city developed a successful bid over the period 1986–8 to stage the 1991 World Student Games.*

According to Dulac and Henry (2001) the staging of the Games had several objectives: to reorient the image of Sheffield from 'City of Steel' to 'City of Sport'; to promote tourism and sports tourism in the city; to erode central government antagonism to the city and thus improve the city's financial standing with central government; to generate a range of new and exciting facilities for local people to use after the Games, and which would allow, in the post-Games era, the staging of international events; and, finally, to enhance the derelict environment of the Don Valley.

The city invested £147 million in venues for the 1991 World Student Games and these were designed for a range of uses to attract visitors to the city following the Games event (Bramwell, 1998a). These venues included the £34 million Sheffield Arena (now called the Hallam FM Arena) 11 000-seat indoor facility which now hosts sport, concerts, exhibitions and shows; the Ponds Forge complex of Olympic standard swimming and diving pools, leisure pool, sports hall and night club; and the £28 million, 25 000-seat Don Valley Athletics Stadium, the Hillsborough Leisure Centre and the Lyceum Theatre (which was refurbished).

The strategy to host the 1991 Games has attracted much criticism. Sheffield's initial decision to bid for the games did not involve much formal strategic planning but, instead, relied in its early decision-making on 'muddling through' (Bramwell, 1997b: p. 174). This lack of a final plan and insufficient research was probably a factor contributing to the games being depicted as crisis ridden, incompetent and financially highly questionable (Roche, 1994). Bramwell (1997b: p. 174) also believes that the city missed some city development opportunities by being slow to have a clear and adequately funded strategy linking the Games investment with tourism and city development. He cites the example of the city's Visitor and Conference Bureau and Events Unit being quite slow to assemble a range of accommodation packages with events in order to promote staying visits, although they have collaborated successfully later in the 1990s on subsequent major events. As outlined in Chapters 6 and 7, there are very few significant examples of partnerships between agencies in the area of sports tourism and certainly no longer-term strategic collaborations. It is perhaps not surprising, therefore, that collaboration was lacking in the early stages; the fact that it occurred at all is unusual.

Another criticism has been the lack of public consultation, with the consequence that the local public did not feel that it 'owned' the project (Roche, 2001), a problem with added emphasis given the amounts of public funding involved, the related opportunity costs and the fact that the Games made an actual financial loss of £10.4 million. Critcher (1991), for example, has criticized the lack of consideration of alternatives, while Dulac and

Henry (2001: p. 68) are sceptical of the Games' value in terms of meeting the social needs of the local population. For instance, in 1987, at the same time that the project was being planned, the City Council argued it needed £650 million to modernize its public housing and over £70 million to refurbish educational facilities (Bramwell, 1997a). As Collins and Jackson (1999: p. 191) comment, 'the aftermath of debts and recrimination left a sour taste in the electorate's mouths and impoverished the image of the city's managers rather than enhancing it'.

Longer-Term Benefits

While there have clearly been many criticisms in relation to what some would describe as short-term failure (Collins and Jackson, 1999; Roche, 2001), it could be argued that in the medium and longer term the commitment to use sports tourism as a vehicle for urban regeneration in Sheffield has brought various benefits. The World Student Games was the largest multisport event in the UK since the 1948 Olympic Games and the facilities originally developed for the Games helped attract 250 events providing for sports tourism to the city between 1990 and 1996, including ten world and six European championships (Bramwell, 1998a). While no substantial research on the actual economic and social impacts was conducted after the Games, another key criticism, there has been some limited monitoring of the economic effects of events held in the new venues based on event attendances and simple estimates of spectator expenditure (Bramwell, 1997b). For example, numbers in 1994 totalled 900 000 at Sheffield Arena (indoor arena), 880 000 at Ponds Forge and 239 726 at the Don Valley Stadium. By the mid-1990s, the city's sport programme was estimated to have added £31 million to the local economy and gained TV coverage worth £85 million (Bramwell, 1997a, 1997b) and, as mentioned in the previous section, the overall economic value of sport and sports tourism was estimated at £680 million in 2006 (*The Times*, 2008). Individual events like the European Swimming Championships and the UK Special Olympics in 1993 are calculated to have generated £1.7 million of expenditure in the city and more detailed work has shown that the three Euro '96 football matches held in Sheffield produced a substantial economic impact, boosting the city's economy by £5.83 million and generating 157 full-time employment (FTE) jobs (Dobson et al., 1997). This event attracted 61 323 visiting supporters and 5400 accredited visitors (mainly media). Hotels, guest houses, pubs, restaurants and shops all benefited economically. The event was also an organizational success and brought media attention to the city from across the world and, according to Dobson et al. (1997), Destination Sheffield, the city and tourism promotion arm of the City Council, utilized the success of the tournament to market its short-break city trips to the Danes, the major group of visiting supporters. During June/July 1996, four other major events providing for sports tourism injected an additional £4.1 million into Sheffield's local economy, economic impact figures which, as Dobson, et al. (1997) suggest, appear to justify the policy of urban regeneration that utilizes major sporting events as an economic catalyst. Another key international event sports tourism product is the Embassy World Snooker championships which, up to 2003, had been held 27 times in the city. While the event and its famous venue, the Crucible Theatre, existed well before the 1991 Games, it is nevertheless now part of the overall sports tourism strategy. The championship attracts many thousands of visitors to Sheffield every year, including many from abroad, and it is estimated that it generates £1.2 million for the local economy. It is therefore perhaps not unreasonable to believe city officials who reckon that the benefits of the Games now outweigh their costs sevenfold (Collins and Jackson, 1999: p. 191). In fact, in an enquiry into the future of major sporting events in Britain, a central government, all-party National Heritage Select Committee concluded that, despite the resulting burden of debt for the city, the Games investment did appear to be successful (quoted in Bramwell, 1998a).

It is not just the specific economic benefits from event sports tourism products that are important, however, but also the re-imaging involved and its impact on the wider economy. As mentioned in the previous section, one of the key objectives of the initial project was to create a new image for Sheffield based on sport and leisure. Although at first little was done to develop specific strategies aimed at utilizing sport explicitly in this way, this changed substantially in the mid-1990s. Following a report by Friel, a consultant employed to advise on Sheffield's marketing, strategies were formulated specifically linking the Games investment with the development of tourism as a means of promoting city development (Bramwell, 1997b). Friel's report also led to greater cooperation between sport event organizers and tourism staff in the Visitor and Conference Bureau, with the Events Unit moving into the same building as the Bureau. The formal strategic plan of 1995 (Destination Sheffield, *An Event-Led City and Tourism Marketing Strategy for Sheffield*) involved the use of 'profile' events utilizing the venues built for the 1991 Games (Bramwell, 1997b). Such venues are not only used for prestigious event sports tourism products but also high profile concerts. The Arena has been successful as a venue on the circuit of major European and world pop concert tours, while in 1995 100 000 people attended two outdoor concerts by Bon Jovi and the Rolling Stones at the Don Valley Stadium (Bramwell, 1997a).

The 1995 Destination Sheffield strategy was also developed in the context of a strategic plan for Sheffield's wider economic regeneration, *The Way Ahead*, published in 1994, which also contained elements of sport, tourism and city marketing. The conventional wisdom of the urban regeneration process (see Law, 1992) suggests that a city with high profile sport and leisure facilities marketed as key elements of a vibrant and exciting place in which to live is one means of attracting new businesses and Sheffield has clearly adopted this thinking. As Steve Brailey, chief executive of Sheffield International Venues and a member of Sheffield First Partnership commented in a press release issued in 1999:

> ... *important as the cash into our economy is, there is an even more important factor for Sheffield in the provision of sports and leisure facilities. The key issues identified by Sheffield First Partnership when we consulted the people of Sheffield included attracting and keeping business in the city and updating the city's image. The presence of quality sports teams and leisure facilities will do that, along with regular staging of prestigious events — from Euro '96 to the world snooker finals, from the world masters swimming to the speed skating championships heading to the Arena early next year. The range and diversity of what Sheffield offers will also help persuade people this is a location to be considered for their expansion plans. There are many factors a business will take into account when deciding on location. Naturally, great weight will be given to the skills of the labour force and the cost of premises. But research has shown that the standard, range and variety of sporting and leisure facilities is a significant factor. Sheffield needs new investment, new jobs and new businesses. It needs improved education results and improved health. But it also needs a high quality of life – and on the sport and leisure front the city has every right to be extremely proud of what it provides.*

Another key part of the urban regeneration process is that of environmental improvement and its effect on improving a city's image. The facilities developed for the Games certainly had a very positive effect in this respect as they created a sport and leisure 'corridor' through the Don Valley, the area of the city most affected by de-industrialization (Dulac and Henry, 2001).

An examination of current marketing initiatives clearly illustrates the continuing importance of sport and sports tourism being used as a key vehicle to market the city. The Sheffield City Council website, Welcome to Sheffield, highlights the fact that Sheffield was Britain's first National

City of Sport, designated as such by the then Sports Council in 1995. The Destination Sheffield website also lists 'City of Sport' as one of its eight principal web links and the subsequent web page further promotes its sporting excellence in terms of being 'chosen as one of the main regional centres for the UK Sports Institute', having 'Britain's best array of international sports venues' and possessing Sheffield Ski Village, 'Europe's largest artificial ski resort'. In 2003, the Welcome to Sheffield website had the World Snooker Championships as its initial item and was also highlighting the 'wealth of fun events happening in the city centre as part of the "Sheffield on Cue" festival 2003' which the city had organized to celebrate the hosting of the championship. Furthermore, the sheffieldscene2 website was also highlighting the British Open Show Jumping Championships being held at the Hallam FM Arena (formerly known as the Sheffield Arena) in late April, and promoted as 'the biggest international show jumping event in England for over 30 years'.

Another objective of the Games was to provide sport and leisure facilities for the city's population, reflecting a continued concern for social welfare issues (Bramwell, 1997b). The city has certainly gained many high quality sports facilities and more people now see these as assets. However, according to Dobson and Gratton (1995, quoted in Collins and Jackson, 1999: p. 191) 'the degree to which (the) commitment to sport has benefited the community's quality of life, patterns of sporting participation and social regeneration remains unanswered'. Dulac and Henry (2001: p. 68) also suggest that the Games' legacy in terms of meeting the social needs of the local population has been problematic. They believe that this is due to the management of the new facilities being placed in the hands of a City Trust, contracted by the local authority to meet certain standards of financial performance with no significant social goals specified by contract. As a result, social goals have been de-prioritized. They argue, for example, that the policy of centralizing swimming provision in a large city centre facility of international competition standard has radically affected those neighbourhoods which lost their swimming pool to permit this centralization, and quote Taylor (1998) who has shown that participation in swimming in the city has actually declined since the introduction of the new facility, against the national trend. As Dulac and Henry (2001: p. 69) conclude:

> *The overall outcome in terms of sport policy might be characterized therefore as a two tier policy, with an increase in consumer rights for those who can afford to pay private sector or near private sector rates, with some lower level welfare rights (subsidized sports development) for others who do not have the financial resources to benefit from consumer choice.*

Nevertheless, despite such criticisms, there is some evidence that local people are pleased with the new sports and event facilities and see them positively, at least as sports tourism assets. A small survey of residents' satisfaction with Sheffield's sports tourism products undertaken in 1996 (Bramwell, 1998a) showed that, while people still had doubts about the merit of the original decision, many in the sample agreed that the city's new sport and event facilities were 'a great benefit to the city as they attract tourists' (74.8 per cent 'agreed' or 'strongly agreed'), that they 'improved the image of Sheffield' (85.6 per cent) and they are 'something to be proud of' (81.9 per cent).

CONCLUSION

This chapter has outlined the importance of sports tourism in cities and utilized a case study of Sheffield to illustrate some of the salient issues. Like most urban centres, Sheffield possesses a range of sports teams and associated venues which provide the basis for a sizable number of visitors who travel to the city to support their teams in domestic, and occasionally international, competitions. As such, it has been a sports tourism place for many years. In more recent years, however, Sheffield has also developed a substantial array of venues linked to mega-events as part of a regeneration process involving a conscious effort to promote itself on the basis of a new image linked to sport, leisure and tourism. As the history of this development has shown, this was not an automatic process and involved key decisions being made by city councillors and other prominent players, considerable risks being taken, both economically and politically, specific organizations, and especially partnerships, established to facilitate the process, and a considerable amount of marketing and promotion. As such, it provides a useful illustration of many of the key issues and linkages suggested in the Policy Wheel for Sport and Tourism (see Figure 7.1) in Chapter 7. However, it also shows that many of the tensions in the sport–tourism policy process identified in Part 3 of this volume can be overcome, particularly if there is a specific focus for liaison. In the Sheffield case, this was provided by the 'regional context' (see Chapter 7 for a discussion of this and other influences on collaborative sport–tourism policy) of urban decay and unemployment and became strategically focused in the mid-1990s following the hosting of the World Student Games in 1991. While these policy directions did not attract universal support and clearly involved some problems, not least the £147 million cost of hosting the World Student Games and the lack of an initial strategy to capitalize on this event, there are many who would now admit the overall idea has been a success. As a result, Sheffield has become a much more prominent sports tourism location than it was hitherto. Rather than simply being a city possessing some sports tourism, it is clearly a specific sports tourism place which is marketed as such. Not only is sports tourism a key part of the overall tourism product, but sports tourism has also been an instrumental element in the city acquiring so many prestigious sports facilities. Given the recognition of the clear benefits to be gained from the integration of sport and tourism, a claim discussed in earlier parts of this text, it is likely that Sheffield's position as a distinctive sports tourism location is assured.

CHAPTER 12

Rural Sports Participation Tourism in Wales

The countryside has a long history of receiving tourists but its significance has become increasingly important in recent times (Butler et al., 1997; Page and Getz, 1997; Sharpley and Sharpley, 1997). According to Natural England, in 2005, 700 million day visits were made to the English countryside, representing 20 per cent of all leisure trips with National Parks accounting for 35 million trips (Natural England, 2006). It is estimated that rural tourism contributes about £12 billion to local rural economies in the UK, its overall economic importance being especially highlighted, ironically, by the 2001 foot and mouth crisis (English Tourism Council, 2001; Sharpley and Craven, 2001). Furthermore, its significance for local employment has been illustrated by Leslie (2001) who estimated that half the Lake District National Park's population (approximately 42 000) is directly supported by tourism.

Much of the tourism associated with the countryside has been largely of a benign nature involving such activities as walking, pleasure motoring, sightseeing, picnicking, nature study and fishing (Glyptis, 1991b, 1992; Harrison, 1991; Butler, 1998). However, in the last couple of decades there has been a discernable growth in participation in active outdoor pursuits, a trend acknowledged by the Sports Council (1992) in its policy document *A Countryside for Sport*. Clark et al. (1994) also highlighted the growth of countryside sport as part of the increasing specialization and diversity of leisure and cited the evidence of the growing range of related niche/specialist magazines as testimony to this. They also identified further specialization in the holiday market, especially in relation to short breaks, and list, among others, specialized and general rural sports participation tourism products (e.g. skiing, walking and canoeing). More recent evidence of growth in outdoor pursuits can be seen in the 2005 Mintel Report on Sports Participation in the UK (Mintel, 2005b), which highlights the 'growth in popularity of sports in which free play is the norm' such as 'cycling, hiking and rambling …' suggesting that their popularity could be due to a 'major sea change' in British consumers' attitudes to health and exercise and the fact that they cost nothing to pursue (at least insofar as there are no costs for such aspects as facility use, or club membership, etc.). In addition, further evidence of growth can be seen in what commercial analysts tend to refer to as the 'activity holidays' sector which showed an overall increase of 8.2 per cent between 2001 and 2005 (Keynote, 2006). However it should be stressed that this was entirely due to the growth in the overseas market, the domestic market having witnessed a slight decline over this period. Finally, these sports tourism products are also encouraged for certain rural localities for, as various authors have highlighted, sports participation tourism products involving outdoor pursuits can make an important contribution to the overall rural tourism product, especially in those upland areas where the local economy is limited and marginalized (Roberts and Hall, 2001; Costa and Chalip, 2005).

Apart from the more traditional forms of outdoor pursuit involving hiking, climbing, caving and various water sports such as sailing and canoeing, some totally new forms have emerged such as snow skiing, snowmobiling, mountain biking, orienteering, survival, windsurfing, endurance sports and paragliding (Butler, 1998). Some are developments of existing activities, while others have been influenced by new technology, such as lower priced and more friendly equipment, allowing easier, safer, and more comfortable operation than in the past and many of these new activities have become accessible and popular with a vast new market (ibid). In addition, a further development in recent years has been the growth of what is now sometimes referred to as 'adventure tourism', which Chapter 2 suggests can be a significant part of the sports participation tourism product. Buckley (2007a: p. 1428) defines adventure tourism as meaning 'guided commercial tours, where the principal attraction is an outdoor activity that relies on features of the natural terrain, generally requires specialized equipment and is exciting for the tour clients' and which includes activities such as 'climbing, caving, abseiling, sea kayaking, whitewater kayaking, rafting, diving, snorkelling, skiing, snow boarding, surfing, sail boarding, sailing, ballooning, skydiving, parapenting, horse riding, mountain biking, snowmobiling and off-road driving' (ibid) (see also Hudson, 2003a; Swarbrooke et al., 2003; Buckley, 2007b).

In the context of the particular concerns of this volume, these rural sports participation tourism products are characterized by a number of key issues including the nature of the market and the particular profile of the participants, the nature of the places that are utilized and associated environmental impacts and, finally, the organization of the activities and the businesses involved. It is the intention of this chapter to consider these issues and illustrate them in the context of the UK and, more specifically in the later part of the chapter, in relation to rural Wales.

THE MARKET FOR RURAL SPORTS PARTICIPATION TOURISM AND ITS SOCIOECONOMIC PROFILE

As outlined above, these rural sports participation tourism products include a wide range of outdoor pursuits undertaken for physical pleasure. The activities include highly popular pursuits such as cycling, hiking and hill walking together with those requiring special skills and equipment involving very few participants. They may be organized as a specific trip where both the importance of, and the participation in, sports tourism activities are high, or participation may be pursued more informally. All activities, however, are linked together by the enjoyment of natural landscape features and simply being out in the 'open air' (Mintel, 1998). In addition, given that the majority of resources are located at some distance from where people reside, travel and possibly a stay of one or more nights is often involved. In 2001, rural sports participation tourism products featured in over 11 per cent of all UK holidays involving 16.1 million trips (the domestic market accounting for 10.7 million) (Keynote, 2006). By 2005, trips featuring these products accounted for almost 14 per cent (17.9 million trips) with an overall value of £8.3 billion (and £2.2 billion for the domestic market, the much smaller amount being due to far less being spent on a domestic holiday than a foreign one) (ibid).

In terms of outdoor pursuits generally, both cycling and hiking/rambling involve 22 per cent of the population taking part at least occasionally with half doing so at least once a month (Mintel, 2005b). One of the key changes between 2000 and 2005, according to Mintel (2005b), has been the 'elevation' of hiking/rambling from sixth to fourth place in the top six 'fitness sports' with the proportion of adults enjoying hiking or rambling increasing by 3 per cent. Most outdoor pursuits exist as rural sports participation tourism products as well as day-to-day leisure activities. In terms of trips featuring sports participation tourism products, the most popular pursuit is walking (in its various forms) followed by water sports (Table 12.1), although a significant number of people's participation is multi-activity. According to Keynote (2006), 14 per cent of trips taken in the UK by the

Table 12.1	Trips featuring rural sports participation tourism products taken by residents of Great Britain in a five-year period (2001–2005) (% and million)	
Type	**Millions (estimate)**	**%**
Skiing	0.5	1.0
Boating	2.4	5.1
Walking or trekking	6.7	14.3
Cycling	1.5	3.2
Fishing	1.3	2.8
Multi-activity holiday	4.2	8.9
Other type of activity holiday	5.1	10.9
Any type of activity holiday	12.7	27.1
Total adult population of Great Britain	**47.0**	**100**

Source: Based on Keynote/NEMS Market Research November 2005

British involve walking (or trekking), although, as can be seen in Table 12.1, other forms involve much lower participation rates. Overall, 27 per cent of the adult UK population had taken some form of trip featuring rural sports tourism products in the UK during the 5-year period 2001–2005.

It is difficult to identify a particular socioeconomic profile for outdoor pursuits as the different activities display different characteristics. While 54 per cent of all regular cyclists are male and 45 per cent are aged under 35, the demography for hiking/rambling is somewhat different (Mintel, 2005b). Here, the gender balance is reversed (47 per cent male compared with 53 per cent female) and hiking and rambling are one of the few groups of sporting activities in which regular participation is biased towards those aged over 35 (73 per cent, with 34 per cent aged 55 and over). In terms of trips involving participation in these activities as sports tourism behaviours, these demographic patterns are similar. Men are more interested in such trips than women (45 per cent compared with 27 per cent respectively) with youth especially important (Table 12.2). One key difference is that there is not quite the same bias in favour of older age groups in relation to trips focused on walking as there is in relation to walking as a whole and, in terms of all trips featuring rural sports participation tourism products, the dominance of youth is particularly high, with 57 per cent of all 16–19 year olds participating, substantially higher than the next highest participating

Table 12.2	All trips featuring rural sports participation tourism products taken during the five years to 2005

	% of Population
All adults	36.1
Sex	
Male	44.7
Female	27.4
Age	
16–19	57.4
20–24	38.2
25–34	42.2
35–44	33.8
45–54	39.4
55–64	31.2
65+	22.7
Social Grade	
A	58.8
B	43.1
C1	37.6
C2	34.1
D	24.6
E	11.6

Source: Based on Keynote/NEMS Market Research November 2005

group (42 per cent for the 25–34-year group) and contrasting markedly with the 23 per cent for the over 65-year-old group (Keynote, 2006).

Outdoor pursuits tend to be pursued primarily by those in the top three socioeconomic groups. The Mintel (2005b) Sports Participation report shows that with both cycling and hiking/rambling there is a clear bias in terms of A, B and C1 (67 per cent and 73 per cent respectively) with 44 per cent of hikers/ramblers coming from the A and B groups. In relation to trips featuring rural sports participation products, once again ABs show the greatest involvement, with those in the A group being five times more likely to participate than those in group E (Keynote, 2006).

Those who regularly take part in outdoor pursuits do not just participate in one particular activity but tend to engage in several. Overall, they are more likely to participate in multiple activities than other sports persons. According to Mintel (2000), nearly 10 per cent of those who regularly went hiking or rambling also climbed on a regular basis (compared with only 2 per cent of all sports participants) and 7 per cent regularly went skiing or snowboarding. Similarly, 60 per cent of watersports participants swam on a regular basis, while a third cycled regularly. Trips involving significant participation in outdoor pursuits as a sports tourism behaviour would thus tend to be part of a particular lifestyle which emphasizes the active, usually linked to fitness and health, although such lifestyles are not uniform and may embrace different values (see Chapter 4 for a discussion of the role of 'lifestyle' and 'subculture' in trip decision-making). The degree to which fitness is pursued varies between different pursuits, with some activities having far higher proportions of what Mintel (2000) referred to as 'fitness fanatics'. The Revised Sports Tourism Participation Model is adaptable for different sports tourism products as illustrated in Figure 5.5. However, while these sports tourists consume a number of different activities within the rural sports tourism product range, the nature of their behaviours as high importance and high participation suggests a similar participation profile across a range of activities.

'For most people, a holiday offers the chance to unwind, to relax and "do nothing". A typical holiday is usually an "in-active" one' (Mintel, 1999). Trips featuring rural sports participation tourism products thus appeal to a specific niche within the overall tourism market where the motivations of participants would appear to be different to those more normally associated with holidaymaking. However, as Chapter 3 pointed out, motivations are far from simple and relaxation is not necessarily synonymous with inactivity. In fact, as will be pointed out in the Wales case study later in this chapter, those taking trips featuring rural sports participation tourism products also see their sports tourism behaviours as relaxing. Thus, while it may not be possible to identify particular socioeconomic and demographic profiles among these sports tourists, it is possible that they may be distinguished by certain behavioural and motivational characteristics associated with activity and place. In addition, many individual outdoor activities are associated with specific subcultures, as discussed in Chapter 4.

Outdoor pursuits have also become fashionable, especially among the young, with the new and better quality clothing and footwear becoming fashionable items in their own right. Butler (1998) also identifies some different values in relation to the newer forms of rural activities that were mentioned earlier in this chapter and these are illustrated in Table 12.3. Whereas he is comparing all forms of countryside recreation, it is still possible to see how the more traditional outdoor pursuits such as rambling and walking, which tend to be non-competitive, non-mechanized, basically sympathetic to rural land uses and the landscape and can be group oriented, are very different from many of the newer forms. Butler (1998: p. 215) suggests that the development of these new activities is linked more

Table 12.3 Characteristics of rural leisure activities

Traditional activities	New activities
Relaxing	Individualistic
Family/group oriented	Competitive
Non-competitive	Active
Passive	High cost
Non-mechanized	Relatively high per capita impact
Rural landscape complementary	Mechanized
Rural land use complementary	High technology
Low cost	Prestigious
Low per capita impact	Fast paced
Low technology	Rural landscape irrelevant
Non-urban	Rural land uses competitive
Minimum skill or training required	Urban related
	Skill demanding

Source: Butler (1998: p. 216)

readily to urban lifestyles and that many of them have 'no specific rationale for being located in rural areas except that they require considerable expanses of land and water'. The fact that they tend to be competitive with rural land uses and that the rural landscape may be irrelevant can thus lead to negative environmental impacts, an issue which will be considered in the following section.

Environmental Impacts

Although many rural sites offer opportunities for outdoor pursuits, the areas offering the greatest potential are those associated with the more remote parts of the countryside, often areas of upland or less developed coasts. These are the places that have the specific resources that different pursuits require, such as cliff faces for climbing or rugged terrain for mountain biking, or they are areas of wild, open landscape providing at least a semblance of the great outdoors, if not actual wilderness. In Britain, such areas relate most closely to the National Park areas in England and Wales and the upland areas of Scotland. But the remoteness and physical attributes that provide the distinctive attractions for outdoor pursuits also provide the potential for conflict. Many of these areas are the least able to sustain the impacts of sporting activity and sports tourism because they contain relatively fragile ecosystems which are both easily damaged and slow to recover. In addition, such areas often possess rare wildlife species and communities. The growth of outdoor pursuits clearly puts pressure on such resources but, in addition, such pressure is more acute due to the growing concern in society generally for the environment. As Standeven and De Knop (1999: p. 236) point out, 'sport tourism is nowadays putting intense pressure on the natural environment, endangering it, and because of that sport tourism is also in danger'.

The various impacts that countryside recreation, including outdoor pursuits, can have on the environment have been discussed by many authorities over the years (Patmore, 1983; Mathieson and Wall, 1989; Glyptis, 1991b; Selman, 1992; Croall, 1995; Standeven and De Knop, 1999). A few studies have looked specifically at the impacts of outdoor pursuits, one such being that of Sidaway (1988) on the impacts on wildlife. His work involved a detailed analysis of various pursuits including caving, climbing, hiking/rambling (upland access), orienteering, sub-aqua diving and watersports. His overall conclusions were that 'problems of conflict are localized and should be put into the wider perspective of more widespread habitat losses and damage from pollution and agriculture, and increasing numbers of examples of creative conservation'. He also acknowledges, however, that there are 'some sites of such value to both sport and nature conservation that each interest is unwilling to concede priority to the other' and here planning and management will be necessary.

The importance of using the countryside for sport was spelt out in the Sports Council's policy document *A Countryside for Sport* published in 1992. The document stated the Council's belief that it had 'a significant role to play in encouraging the coordinated development of countryside activities' (p. 3) and, as part of its 'sport for all' policy, its belief 'that everyone should have the opportunity to take part in countryside and water activities and to improve their level of skills and confidence' (p. 5). Nevertheless, while on the one hand encouraging growth, it was also conscious of the need to balance such growth with the need to protect natural resources and thus it argued that such promotion must be sustainable. However, Clark et al. (1994: p. 103) criticize the policy for, among other things, failing to 'acknowledge the variety of countryside activities and their widely different impacts on the environment, through identifying the term "countryside activity" as a singular category ...'

Subsequent joint efforts by the Sports Council and Countryside Commission produced the publication *Good Practice in the Planning and*

Management of Sport and Active Recreation in the Countryside (Elson et al., 1995). This involved a study of the impacts of sport and recreation on sensitive environmental sites with attempts to demonstrate good practice in accordance with the principles of sustainable development. Six principles of good practice were identified including systematic knowledge on the state of the environment; clarity of purpose (establishing goals and objectives); participatory management (involving voluntary agreements, multiple use agreements, partnerships, negotiation and liaison); the voluntary approach involving the governing bodies of sports organizations; local involvement and consultation; and monitoring and review. While the need for good management is clearly an essential issue and there is no doubt that serious impacts do occur at certain sites, some writers have suggested that the over-all level of impact can be overstated (Sidaway and O'Connor, 1978; Sidaway, 1988, 1997; Countryside Recreation Network, 1995). It can be severe in specific localities and along certain paths and bridleways but is not extensive.

In some respects, the impacts are as much the result of perceptions of the role of the countryside and conflicts between different recreational groups wanting to use the same space as they are about actual physical damage. The countryside is a contested space with many different groups and individuals, often with different values and perceptions, claiming it as their own (Harrison, 1991; Urry, 2001). Even among those seeking to use the countryside for recreation, sport and sports tourism, there exist different views as to the nature of the countryside and what activities it should support – for example, between those seeking peace and tranquillity and those wanting to practise noisy pursuits (Butler, 1998). Outdoor pursuits and sports tourism are clearly involved in this contest, especially where some of the newer forms are felt to be somewhat alien to a broader consensus of what constitutes appropriate activity. Consequently, 'rural, environmental, and water issues' was one of the six main areas for joint policy attention highlighted in the Policy Wheel for Sport and Tourism (see Figure 7.1) discussed in Chapter 7.

Organization and Facilities

As outlined at the outset of this chapter, the rural economy has become highly dependent on tourism and in many upland areas and remoter parts of the countryside it offers one of the few alternative economic enterprises to agriculture, itself a rather marginal activity. Outdoor pursuits and rural sports participation tourism form an important part of this economy and a number of different forms of facility and accommodation are involved in its operation. These range from specialized centres run by local authorities, schools and voluntary organizations as well as the private sector, to small private concerns involving guest houses, farm-based accommodation and caravan and camping sites. Nevertheless, despite this variety, there are some distinctive elements.

In addition to the specific forms of accommodation, there also exist a number of specific tour operators that have emerged to cater for such trips, ranging from small specialist tour operators serving niche markets to subsidiaries of large integrated travel companies, such as First Choice. In many cases, such subsidiaries began as independent specialist operators, but were subsequently taken over by one of the larger players (Keynote, 2006). The limited scale of demand for most activity holidays means that specialists come to the fore ahead of major travel groups (Mintel, 1999). At the turn of the century, it was estimated that around 120 members of the Association of Independent Tour Operators offered some type of activity-themed holiday, although many of these also offered conventional holidays (Mintel, 1999).

One particular characteristic of rural sports participation tourism is that trips involving outdoor pursuits have been promoted as appropriate forms of leisure for young people for well over half a century. Such activity was encouraged by the establishment of the Outward Bound Trust in 1946 and later by the Duke of Edinburgh Award Scheme and has also been a key feature of the Scout movement. The same ideals have been echoed more recently by The Hunt Report (1989), in particular the recommendation that, '…every young person in the United Kingdom (should have) the opportunity to take part in adventurous activities'. This report led to the immediate establishment of the Foundation for Outdoor Adventure committed to the promotion of the values of outdoor and adventurous experiences for young people. And, in 1990, the Countryside Recreation Research and Advisory Group (CRRAG) devoted its annual conference to the theme 'Young People, Adventure and the Countryside' (CRRAG, 1991).

As part of the above tradition, although of slightly longer origin, the Youth Hostels Association (YHA) has, for over seventy years, encouraged the use of the outdoors and helped young people, and others, of limited means by providing suitably priced accommodation. The YHA has 300 000 members and 228 hostels throughout England and Wales (YHA website, May 2003) and, in addition to providing accommodation, it also advertises activity holidays at some of its hostels. Such holidays embrace family breaks, training, special interest, caving, climbing, horse riding, multi-activity, hill and mountain walking, watersports and cycling. Its hostels at Edale and Okehampton are particularly important in this respect but other activity holidays are also advertised at hostels in Wales, Cornwall and the Lake District.

The unique characteristic of rural sports participation tourism is the specialist activity centre which exists to facilitate these forms of sports tourism behaviours. According to Clark et al. (1994) multi-activity centres provide a wide range of activities, the average number being 11, with the four most common being rock climbing, orienteering, skiing and canoeing. Examples of such centres in Wales are described below.

RURAL SPORTS PARTICIPATION TOURISM IN WALES

Wales contains a wealth of resources for rural sports participation tourism. It possesses three National Parks (Snowdonia, Brecon Beacons and Pembrokeshire Coast), five Areas of Outstanding Natural Beauty and a varied coastline, including 300 miles of Heritage Coast. In the Wales Tourist Board's (WTB) (2000: p. 39) tourism strategy such areas are highlighted as one of the principality's strengths, along with its ability to cater for 'activity holidays'. As a result, the Board has engaged in the proactive marketing and development of campaigns specifically promoting a number of activities including walking, adventure activities, cycling, fishing and riding and, in 2002, produced tourism strategies on each of these five activity products.

The Welsh Rural Sports Participation Tourism Product

According to the walking strategy (WTB, 2002a), sports tourism involving walking is clearly very popular in Wales, either on day trips or trips involving an overnight stay, with research showing that almost three quarters of UK holiday visitors, and two thirds of overseas holiday visitors to Wales go walking at some point during their stay, and over half of all day visits in Wales include walking. Walking as a sports tourism product offers considerable economic benefits to Wales with spending by walking visitors estimated to bring over £550 million into its rural and coastal economies. While walking is by far the most significant, other activities are also important. An estimated 800 000 horse riding occasions are taken by visitors in Wales each year with an estimated direct expenditure of £18.55 million. Riders comprise three broad groups:

- Holidaymakers taking a horse ride as one activity during their stay – c.55 per cent of riding occasions

- Between 30 000–40 000 people take a riding holiday – accounting for 15–20 per cent of Wales' tourism riding occasions

- Day visitors (excluding local riders regularly exercising their horse close to stabling) – c.25 per cent of riding occasions (WTB, 2002b).

Cycle sports tourism also offers considerable economic benefits and, like horse riding, this involves cycling holidays as well as those participating in cycling as a day visit activity (see also Chapter 14). This represents a growing and valuable market for Wales with estimates suggesting that cycle sports tourism is currently worth as much as £18 million and that it could be worth over £34 million by 2007 (WTB, 2002c).

A wide range of other pursuits, grouped together as 'adventure tourism' by the Wales Tourist Board (WTB) also take place in rural and coastal Wales. In their adventure tourism strategy (WTB, 2002d: p. 1), adventure tourism is defined as 'holiday and day visits that involve participation in active or adventurous outdoor activities, either as a primary or secondary purpose of visit' and the following varied activities are identified:

- Climbing – mountaineering, rock climbing, abseiling, bouldering, sea level traversing, coasteering

- Caving and pot-holing

- Non-motorized watersports – sailing, windsurfing, kitesurfing, canoeing, kayaking, white water rafting, surfing

- Motorized watersports – jet-skiing, water-skiing, ribbing, wakeboarding

- Diving

- Motorized land sports – 4 × 4 driving, trail biking, quad biking

- Airsports – hang gliding, paragliding, microlighting, gliding

- Mountain biking – trail riding, downhill riding

- Hill walking/trekking

- Other land based activities – orienteering, gorge walking, skiing, snowboarding, land yachting, parakarting, bungee jumping, paintballing, archery, clay pigeon shooting, rope courses.

According to the strategy:

Adventure tourist visits involving these activities either as their main or a secondary purpose of visit, currently account for at least 1.25 million visits to Wales per year, and in the order of £180 million of direct visitor spending. They make up approximately 13 per cent of domestic trips, nights and spend in Wales. Adventure holidays (where participation in adventure activities is the main holiday purpose) account for about 4 per cent of the domestic holiday market for Wales – a figure almost comparable to walking holidays (which account for around 5 per cent of domestic holidays in Wales).

The most popular adventure activities are non-motorized watersports and climbing, with hill walking and, to a lesser extent, mountain biking, also being popular. Most of the other activities appeal to particular niche markets which, by comparison, tend to be minority pursuits.

The detail that has been described above refers to Wales in general, but one of the key aspects of rural sports participation tourism is that it can make substantial economic contributions to the more marginal, local rural areas, such as the uplands, where most forms of economic activity are severely limited. Without the advent of such sports tourism, the economies of areas such as Snowdonia and the Brecon Beacons would be extremely weak and rural sports participation tourism products are clearly making a substantial contribution to the overall tourism market in these National Parks. One recent study has shown 'adventure tourism' to be worth £140 million per annum to the North West Wales economy, with £60 million of this relating to the Snowdonia National Park economy. This creates (directly and indirectly) over 8400 jobs (FTEs) across the area, almost 6 per cent of all employment across North West Wales and, for every pound spent on outdoor activities and accommodation, a further £0.76 is generated for the local economy (Snowdonia Green Key Initiative, 2005).

As with other forms of sports tourism considered in this volume, people with a wide range of experience levels, motivations and interests participate in such adventure activities. They range from the very experienced and highly skilled adventure sports tourism enthusiast, to the beginner learning an adventure activity with a view to future independent participation, or somebody on holiday who decides to try out an adventure activity during their stay. They thus range from the spontaneous participant at the bottom left of the Revised Sports Tourism Participation Model discussed in Chapter 5 (see Figure 5.5), to those for whom this form of sports tourism has played an important role in the trip decision and for whom participation is high. Given that the 1999 Mintel Report also records that there are many people who have not participated that express a desire to do so, there are also significant numbers of 'intenders'.

Reeves (2000) examined the profiles of travellers visiting the Twr-y-Felin outdoor activity centre and St David's area of Pembrokeshire in Wales to engage in sports tourism behaviours and identified various types of participants. There was a varied age and sex distribution as well as significant variation in socioeconomic status, with a relatively high number of respondents in the lowest income category, no doubt reflected by the not insignificant numbers of retired people, students and those in part-time employment. A wide range of different activities were undertaken, with swimming followed by walking and canoeing being the most popular, although such activities were influenced by the particular coastal location. While 31 per cent of those surveyed engaged in activities by themselves, the vast majority were involved with others, either with partners or with larger groups, including some involving club, school or college groups. This is related to the reasons for undertaking a trip involving this type of sports tourism, as that of companionship was ranked second in importance (Table 12.4). What is interesting in these results is the fact that this social dimension along with that of relaxation were the two most highly ranked motives for holiday choice, rather than the physical and mental challenge posed by the activity and the adventure inherent in such participation (Reeves, 2000: p. 181). Motives more readily associated with mainstream tourism would appear to be more important here than those more normally associated with mainstream sport. This not only emphasizes the complexity of motivation in sports tourism but also lends support to the ideas discussed in Chapter 3 that sports tourists are distinctly different from those who pursue sport *per se*.

Resources and Organization of Rural Sports Participation Tourism in Wales

According to the adventure tourism strategy, Wales has some of the finest natural resources for adventure sports tourism of anywhere in the UK and, coupled with its ease of access from English markets, these make Wales one of the leading UK destinations for many adventure activities (WTB,

Table 12.4	Ranked importance of factors in trip decision – Twr-y-Felin Activity Centre	
Factor		**Ranking**
Relaxation		1
Companionship/social dimension		2
Physical fitness/well-being		3
Novelty of experience		4
Challenge (physical and mental)		5
Adventure		6

Source: Reeves (2000: p. 181)

2002d: p. 2). Snowdonia, for example, is one of the best and most accessible climbing and mountaineering destinations in the UK; half of all UK caving trips are taken in Wales; the Gower is one of the best places in the UK to learn to surf; Wales is one of the best locations in the UK for scenic diving; Wales boasts three or four of the top 10 UK sites for paragliding; and the National White Water Centre at Tryweryn near Bala provides international standard white waters for canoeing and rafting (ibid). The Wales Tourist Board's promotional guide, *Cycling Wales* lists 34 traffic-free rides, 26 lane network areas/rides (roads where traffic is minimal) and 27 mountain bike areas/rides.

In addition to the natural resources, there is also a well-developed supply of activity centres, operators and freelance instructors, including three national centres of excellence – Plas-y-Brenin (climbing), Plas Menai (watersports) and the National White Water Centre at Tryweryn (WTB, 2002d). According to the strategy:

183 adventure activity operators are currently licensed by the Adventure Activities Licensing Authority (AALA), or accredited under WTB's Activity Holiday Accreditation Scheme. In addition, there are many other operators and training schools that are accredited through appropriate national governing body inspection schemes. The activity operators sector is highly independent, fragmented and weakly organized, with no tradition of joint working, Activity operator networks have, however, recently been set up in Snowdonia, the Brecon Beacons, Pembrokeshire, the Gower and the Llangollen area. Waterfront Wales also exists as a national private sector led organization to promote Wales as a sailing and watersports destination (ibid: p. 3).

Although certain centres specialize in particular activities, they also offer opportunities for a much greater range. Plas-y-Brenin, for example, which is run by the Mountain Training Trust on behalf of the Sports Council, boasts a training wall, an artificial ski slope and a canoe pool and offers courses in rock climbing, summer mountaineering and hillwalking, winter climbing and mountaineering, alpine skiing and mountaineering, mountaineering qualifications and awards, kayaking and canoeing, paddle-sport qualifications, alpine paddling as well as various courses relating to personal and professional development. In addition to providing courses, it also offers accommodation for those who wish to visit the area and make their own activity arrangements. In addition to activity centres, there are also more specialist centres – for example, the WTB guide *Riding in Wales* lists 22 accredited equestrian centres.

As outlined earlier in the chapter, the YHA also provides opportunities for trips involving those types of sports tourism behaviours which extend beyond simply that of accommodation and, in Wales, these are promoted at four of its hostels – hill and mountain award and assessment weekends at Llywyn-y-Celyn in the Brecon Beacons; trail riding in the Brecon Beacons and riding courses in the Black Mountains at Capel-y-Ffin; navigation and walking courses at Poppit Sands, Cardigan Bay; and cycling in Snowdonia at Conwy.

Twr-y-Felin outdoor activity centre, the subject of Reeves' (2000) study, is one of the largest centres of its kind in West Wales in terms of volume and diversity of courses offered. The company organizes management development courses, trips for children involving activities, and courses for groups and individuals of all standards who wish to participate and/or gain the relevant coaching/leadership qualifications. Another such centre is Black Mountain Activities, established in 1992, which organizes a wide variety of outdoor pursuits and activity courses for individuals, families, social groups, businesses, schools, colleges and youth groups (Table 12.5). Situated on the edge of the Brecon Beacons National Park and very near the banks of the River Wye, the centre utilizes adjacent resources rather than having significant facilities of its own. It does not provide accommodation, although it does advertise a variety of accommodation in the vicinity on its website and is prepared to organize accommodation for its clients. As a non-residential centre it has no significant overheads and no fixed programmes and its principal activity is thus bringing visitors and training staff together. It offers two-, three- or five-day packages and emphasizes weekend breaks in its promotions. This sort of trip is a good example of the tourism product highlighted by the Wales Tourist Board (2000: p. 25) 'which closely matches the needs of the short break market, offering diversity in a naturally inspiring landscape that is within easy reach of large centres of population'.

Environmental Impacts on the Welsh Coast and Countryside

The general issues associated with the environmental impacts of rural sports participation tourism have already been addressed in an earlier section of this chapter and apply equally to the various resources found in Wales. It is worth noting that, in the study by Sidaway (1988), a number of the case studies examined involved activities at locations in Wales. One involved caving, a popular activity in outdoor pursuits centres which frequently include a day's caving in their courses. Given the large number of such centres in Wales, the pressures on popular, accessible caves from this source are considerable. Damage from cavers included litter, physical damage, such as the

Table 12.5 Activities available at Black Mountain Activities

Land-based activities	Water-based activities	Activities available on multiactivity breaks	Team-building events	Activities available to schools, youth groups and colleges
Climbing and abseiling	Kayaking	Hill walking	Development training	Kayaking
Caving and pot holing	Open canoeing	Gorge walking	Black Mountain challenge day	Canoeing
Mountain biking	Wye expeditions	Caving		Rafting
Clay pigeon shooting	Raft building	Pot holing		Raft building
Archery		Mountain biking		Hot dogging
Orienteering		Clay pigeon shooting		White water rafting
Land carting		Kayaking		Caving
High level ropes course		Canoeing		Mountain biking
		White water rafting		Archery
		Mountain biking		Orienteering
		Orienteering		Land carting
		Gorge walking		High level ropes
		High level ropes		Climbing
		Climbing tower		Abseiling
		Archery		Hill walking
		Raft building		Mountain expeditions

removal of stalactites and the removal of mud deposits, disturbance to wild-life, such as hibernating bats, and graffiti. Other Welsh case studies in the Sidaway report included the impacts of climbing on cliff-nesting birds such as peregrine falcons and various seabirds, and the impacts of sub-aqua diving on marine wildlife. Specialist sports tourism activities involve a greater range of environmental impacts than simply the erosion of surface vegetation and damage to routeways.

Apart from the more direct impacts arising from such activities, the other impact is that of the car. As mentioned above, one key characteristic of rural sports participation tourism in Wales is its appeal to the short breaks market and much of this activity is based on car travel. Much of rural Wales is within easy travelling distance from key population centres, such as the West Midlands conurbation, Merseyside and Greater Manchester, the Bristol area as well as the urban areas of South Wales and the car is the obvious mode of travel given its speed and convenience, the need to transport equipment and the extensive system of minor roads enabling cars to reach relatively inaccessible locations. Cars cause a variety of problems including congestion, air pollution, visual impact, danger to vulnerable users and wildlife on narrow roads caused by speeding traffic, noise and loss of tranquillity and loss of countryside character (Speakman and Speakman, 1999). The impact of the car is highlighted in a study by Owen et al. (1999) who report that 90 per cent of Snowdonia's 6.6 million visitors a year arrive by this form of transport with their vehicles polluting the environment and producing substantial congestion along the roadsides, given that roadside parking is freely available. Although much of this car use involved passive recreationists, rural sports participation tourism, which is expected to expand in the coming years, still makes a significant contribution to the problem. In fact, it is worth noting that the problem was also cited at several of the sites examined by Sidaway (1988) in the 1980s.

While the impacts can be overstated, as mentioned earlier, there is no doubt that at certain popular locations they can be severe and the need for management linked to sustainable tourism policies is required. The Northern Snowdonia study (Owen et al., 1999) is one such attempt to suggest more sustainable solutions to the car problem involving increasing transport options and greater use of public transport. Some of the options involve improving walking and cycling opportunities and thus such sports participation tourism can actually play a role in helping to develop sustainable tourism. The question of improved access arrangements for many adventure sports tourism products has also been cited as a key development requirement by the WTB adventure tourism strategy (2002d).

CONCLUSIONS

This chapter has examined rural sports participation tourism, a further form of sports tourism that involves a distinctive interaction of activity, people and place. The places and environments are characterized by areas of scenic landscape and often rugged terrain, in Britain, areas most typified by the National Parks and Heritage Coasts. The activities themselves are highly dependent on such resources as well as specific facilities such as activity/

adventure centres and various types of accommodation. As with the Alpine skiing environments examined in the following chapter, such places produce distinctive sports tourism places and, although the demographic and socio-economic profiles of participants may vary, due to the very different activities involved, they all nevertheless seek enjoyment of natural landscape features and, with the exception of cavers, being in the 'open air'. In addition, the chapter has demonstrated how a particular form of sports tourism accords with the Revised Sports Tourism Participation Model discussed in Chapter 5. Sports tourism behaviours associated with these rural areas are, to a large extent, multi-activity, in which opportunities often play an important part in the trip decision with participation being high. However, for some participants, the behaviours have a less important role in the trip decision or trip planning and, for some, participation will be spontaneous. In addition, within the general population, there are also many non-participants who express an interest to participate and who can be clearly seen as 'intenders'.

As a specific case study for rural sports participation tourism, Wales possesses a wealth of suitable resources and has established a substantial collection of varied facilities to aid its development. Its importance to the overall tourism product has been highlighted in various strategies at both the national and regional level (WTB, 2000, 2002d; Snowdonia Green Key Initiative, 2005), where it is regarded as having significant future potential and is being marketed quite vigorously through specific guides and websites. As the *Time for Action – adventure tourism strategy* (WTB, 2002d: p. 4) makes clear, the vision is to see 'Wales as a world class Adventure Tourism destination offering the widest choice, the highest quality and the best managed and promoted adventure activity experiences of anywhere in the world'.

CHAPTER 13

Winter Skiing in the European Alps

Skiing is perhaps the best known and most developed form of sports tourism. As outlined in Chapter 1, Alpine skiing dates back to the late nineteenth century and, by the early decades of the twentieth, a significant skiing sports tourism industry was in place with Switzerland possessing several clusters of ski resorts serviced by a well established infrastructure. Today, the ski market is extremely large and accounts for a substantial segment of all tourism. The snowsports market in Britain, for example, breaks down into three categories: inclusive tours or skiing packages (accounting for around 703 000 holidays), independently organized skiing sports tourism (384 000) and school trips (140 000) (Crystal, 2008). Skiing accounts for about 20 per cent of the total European holiday market with the European Alps attracting 40–50 million visitors to the 40 000 ski runs (Standeven and De Knop, 1999) while, in America, the 490 ski resorts attracted 57.3 million skier/snowboarder visits in 2000/2001 (Hudson, 2003b).

Skiing provides the classic form of sports tourism. It is a physical activity and physical skill and it can be pursued at various levels of competence, competitively or otherwise. At one level, it features in Olympic competition, at the other, it involves families with young children pursuing it for fun. Like many other sports tourism activities, it involves goals, challenge and stimulation and, in some cases, risk. Apart from a few artificial ski slopes and more recently developed snow domes (such as the facility at Milton Keynes), it is a sports tourism product that is dependent on specific natural resources found only in certain locations. Thus, the vast majority of participants have to travel significant distances to particular types of places (resorts) and stay at the destination for several days or longer. No matter what definition is adopted, skiing is clearly a sports tourism behaviour.

Attempts to conceptualize sports tourism in the first part of this text suggested that it might be defined as a social, economic and cultural phenomenon arising from the unique interaction of activity, people and place and, while Chapter 3 considered the uniqueness of sports tourism places, the nature of activities and the motives of people, Chapter 5 developed a Revised Sports Tourism Participation Model (see Figure 5.5) as a means of understanding the phenomenon. How then does Alpine skiing relate to these aspects?

THE SKIING ENVIRONMENT

As mentioned above, skiing requires a particular type of upland environment with appropriate physical conditions, namely snow cover and slopes. Snow cover is the main determinant of the length of season, and related aspects such as duration, earliness of first snow, quality of snow cover and reliability of snow cover from year to year are all key factors in establishing the quality, and hence success, of a particular location. Slopes are also important, as a range of slopes is needed to provide for a variety of skiers, from novices who need gentle slopes, to advanced skiers who need exhilarating runs. But the unique environment that is the modern ski resort is much more than simply a natural phenomenon – it involves a combination of both natural and human attributes. In addition to there being sufficient natural environment, ski resorts also require a collection of built features such as ski lifts, ski schools, equipment shops, hotel accommodation, restaurants, car parking and possibly other leisure facilities to provide for après ski entertainment. Thus, there is a need for flat land as well as slopes to enable such facilities to be provided.

Apart from the basic requirements of slopes and snow, there are also several other factors that influence the quality and viability of ski resorts. Avalanche risk may restrict skiing to a limited number of slopes, wind can affect the functioning of ski lifts and produce significant wind chill, and natural features may provide opportunities for cross-country ski trails. The quality of accommodation and après ski facilities are also important as well as the extent to which resorts are fashionable (see discussion on motives below).

Despite the need for specific requirements, skiing is well established in many mountainous areas and, in the European Alps alone, for example, there are an estimated 40 000 ski runs with 14 000 ski lifts that are capable of handling 1.5 million skiers an hour (Ward et al., 1994). Alpine ski resorts have clearly been socially constructed as mass tourist destinations – as recognizable places for the tourist gaze through various markers and signposts (Urry, 2001). In the latter half of the twentieth century, the tourist image creators have promoted ski resorts along with seaside resorts and, to a lesser extent, rural idylls such as National Parks, as the rightful objects of the tourist gaze (Shaw and Williams, 2002: p. 218). Although the Alps had originally been an area of summer tourism, related to the romantic tourist gaze and including some sports tourism products among them through the attractions of climbing, walking and viewing the scenery (see Chapter 1), writers and other image creators subsequently re-imaged the Alps as a highly desirable winter destination.

Although there is a tendency for uniformity in terms of the production of mass winter sports tourism, it is possible to discern a degree of differentiation among resorts. Barker (1982, cited in Shaw and Williams, 2002), for example, identified differences between the eastern and western Alps. The former have been developed at lower altitudes and are more integrated with the economic and cultural lives of the indigenous communities than are the high altitude resorts of the western Alps, where more external capital and labour are involved. Some resorts have also developed a significant summer season based on warm-weather pursuits or developing means to transport tourists to high altitude skiing areas (Shaw and Williams, 2002). Table 13.1 describes a continuum of skiing resorts based on these differences and, whereas those at the low altitude end of the continuum have a varied function, it is clear that those at high altitudes are distinct sports tourism places.

The French resorts, in particular, have been developed for the mass market. As a Mintel (2002b) report points out they are:

mostly purpose built and provide a high level of convenience for the skier. They are designed for the maximum number of skiers

Table 13.1   The continuum of characteristics in Alpine resorts

Low altitude	High altitude
Integrated settlement	New settlement
Local capital	External capital
Local labour	External labour
Cultural exchanges	Cultural islands
Environmental pressures	Environmental pressures
Temporal polarization	Temporal polarization

Source: Shaw and Williams (2002: p. 236).

to be able to ski to and from their accommodation to the ski lift system. Overall convenience has been provided at the expense of ambience and the French resorts tend to lack the Alpine charm of the more traditional resorts found in Austria and Switzerland. The extensive lift systems in French resorts have opened up glacier skiing; attracting tourists throughout the year and investment in snowmaking equipment and snow management has enabled resorts to remain open despite unpredictable snow conditions.

Another feature characteristic of mass tourism generally is that of accommodation. While France offers a wide range of accommodation, much of it is provided in apartments rather than hotels. The apartment blocks, built during the early development of the mass-market ski industry were cramped and now fall short of the expectations of today's sports tourists (Mintel, 2002b), a feature reminiscent of much apartment development in many coastal Mediterranean resorts.

Another key aspect of quality is the extent to which resorts can cope with environmental impacts. Alpine environments are fragile and, in the last few decades, there have been increasing concerns from a growing environmental lobby about the impacts that skiing sports tourism products produce. According to Ryan (1991: p. 95), 'previously unvisited areas are continually being made accessible' and this is producing a range of different problems. The alteration of traditional Alpine land for construction of dams, skiing facilities and hotels has led to both widespread deforestation, soil erosion and alteration of drainage patterns with the resulting increased risk of both avalanches and landslides as well as the disappearance of rare habitats (Ryan, 1991; Standeven and De Knop, 1999; Hudson, 2000). It is estimated that, in the early 1990s, some $100 \, km^2$ of forest had been removed throughout the Alps for skiing sports tourism development (Shaw and Williams, 2002) and deforestation also releases destructive geomorphological processes that have impacts on local communities. For example, in the Austrian Alps it is believed that the creation of $0.7 \, km^2$ ski runs for the Winter Olympics contributed to a major mud slide in 1983 (Jenner and Smith, 1992). There is also some evidence that, in the French Alps, the impact of skiing sports tourism has affected the black grouse population (Jenner and Smith, 1992). While the exact causes are still uncertain, they may well include the growth of extensive off-piste skiing, an increase in predators attracted by litter and waste produced by tourists and the displacements of the grouse by ski activities. Furthermore, skiing in sparse snow conditions contributes to the significant damage of sensitive vegetation (Selman, 1992; Shaw and Williams, 2002). To many, the new built environment appears unsightly and there are also problems of pollution from car exhausts, from chemicals used to manufacture snow and noise pollution from snow guns, the latter two stemming from attempts to extend the season (Standeven and De Knop, 1999).

THE SKIING MARKET AND ECONOMIC IMPACT

The ski market was estimated to be 65–70 million skiers worldwide in the mid-1990s, with Europe accounting for approximately 30 million, 20 million from North America and 14 million from Japan (Cockerell, 1994). According to figures published in the UK Ski Industry Report (Crystal, 2008), the UK market involved 1 227 000 overseas trips involving skiing and snowboarding made by UK residents in the 2007/08 season. This compares with 720 000 trips made in 1980/81 and, despite a decline in the 1980s, the market had recovered by the mid-1990s and continued to grow thereafter, with eight consecutive annual increases since 1999/2000 (Table 13.2).

As outlined in the introduction, the market can be segmented into the tour operator market, independently organized holidays and the school trip sector. UK statistics for each of these categories are also provided in Table 13.2 and show that while the overall market has grown since the early

Table 13.2   The UK ski market size, by tour operators, independent travel and schools, 1980/81–2007/08

	Tour operator (000s)	Independent travel (000s)	School trips (000s)	Total (000s)
1980/81	150	20	550	720
1990/91	278	90	110	478
2000/01	560	231	130	921
2001/02	588	243	123	954
2002/03	594	294	123	1011
2003/04	602	314	125	1041
2004/05	626	330	125	1081
2005/06	670	356	130	1156
2006/07	682	376	133	1191
2007/08	703	384	140	1227

Source: UK Ski Industry Reports 2006 and 2008 (Crystal 2006, 2008).

1980s, there has been a marked change in the type of consumers. The most dramatic change has involved the number of school trips, which have declined by over 500 000 during this period. Whereas in 1980/81, school trips accounted for over 76 per cent of all trips, in 2007/08 they accounted for only 11.4 per cent (Table 13.3). The decline has resulted in part from a change in UK local authority funding for extra-curricular activities that has shifted the burden of payments to parents and also the necessity for risk assessments and increasing risks of litigation which has reduced the willingness of teachers to lead such trips (Mintel, 2002b). In addition, however, the growth of tour operators, the rise of real incomes, the role of skiing sports tourism as part of a fashionable, healthy lifestyle and a growing belief that trips involving skiing are great for families have also contributed to this decline. As can be seen in Table 13.3, as the proportion of school trips has declined so the proportion accounted for by tour operators and independent travel has increased, although, since the early 1990s, it has been the independent sector that has witnessed the greatest amount of relative growth and these figures could be even higher, as according to some, Crystal significantly downplays the size and growth of the independent sector (j2ski, 2008).

A further factor influencing the skiing market is accessibility. One of the key attractions of the European Alps is its location in relation to substantial population centres. It is no surprise, therefore, to find that the

Table 13.3 The UK ski market share, by tour operators, independent travel and schools, 1980/81–2007/08

	Tour operator (%)	Independent travel (%)	School trips (%)
1980/81	20.8	2.8	76.3
1990/91	58.1	18.8	23.0
2000/01	60.8	25.1	14.1
2001/02	61.6	25.5	12.9
2002/03	58.8	29.1	12.2
2003/04	57.8	30.2	12.0
2004/05	57.9	30.5	11.6
2005/06	58.0	30.7	11.2
2006/07	57.3	31.6	11.2
2007/08	57.3	31.3	11.4

Source: UK Ski Industry Reports 2006 and 2008 (Crystal 2006, 2008)

European Alps is the most developed area for skiing sports tourism in the world. Concentrated primarily in France, Italy, Austria, Switzerland and Germany, countries which themselves possess substantial affluent populations, the region is also within easy travelling distance from other densely populated countries of the European Union and beyond. This proximity has meant that a variety of travel options – road, rail and air – are available and also the short travel times provide opportunities for weekend trips as well as longer stays. The influence of accessibility is illustrated in relation to the travel characteristics of UK skiers with France, the most accessible location, dominating the market. France accounts for 37 per cent of all UK trips involving skiing sports tourism, followed by Austria (22 per cent), Italy (12 per cent) and Switzerland (5 per cent) (Crystal, 2008). While other factors have played a key role, such as purpose built resorts with substantial accommodation geared to the mass market and the establishment of a large number of tour operators specializing in these resorts, the ease of access to the French resorts does attract independent holiday makers who can travel by train or car or fly cheaply with the low-cost carriers (Minnol, 2002b).

Another key feature of the skiing sports tourism product is the way tourism developers and tour operators have promoted participation among mass markets (see previous section). As Shaw and Williams (2002: p. 234) point out, 'mass winter sports tourism shares many features in common with mass beach tourism'. While the origins of the winter sports tourism market lie in the nineteenth and early twentieth centuries, mass international winter sports tourism only developed in the 1950s and 1960s (Barker, 1982). The necessary conditions were similar to international mass coastal tourism, involving the reconstruction of the tourist gaze, rising real disposable incomes and car ownership levels, and falling real costs allied to increased tour company activity (Shaw and Williams, 2002). As with coastal tourism, the industry is characterized by a high degree of external control and its promotion has, of course, been encouraged for two important economic reasons. One is the fact that skiers tend to be reasonably affluent and are more likely to spend more than most other types of tourists. In addition, given that most mass tourism involves sun seeking and takes place primarily during the summer months, the fact that skiing takes place in the winter months is a useful counter to the problems of seasonality.

THE NATURE OF PROVIDERS

As outlined in Chapter 8, the provision of sports tourism products is made by a wide range of providers, from large multinational organizations to small independent businesses. Chapter 8 also notes that skiing sports tourism is an industry in its own right. However, it is distinctly different from more general forms of tourism, in that as a specific niche or, more accurately, a collection of niches, it has particular requirements that can only be provided through particular organizations. This would be partially true of skiing in relation to what Hudson (2000) refers to as 'channels of distribution'. Trips involving skiing sports tourism are organized primarily through a very limited number of operators. While around 200 operators trade in the snowsports market, six operators – Crystal, Inghams, Thomson, Neilson, First Choice and My Travel – account for 73 per cent of packages sold, with the majority of small specialist companies serving the needs of particular niche groups (Crystal, 2008). Crystal Holidays, owned by TUI UK (formerly Thomson Travel Group), retains a quarter of the market (24.2 per cent) which, when added to Thomson's own market share of 10 per cent gives TUI UK a total market share of 34.2 per cent. While some of these companies are clearly major players in the overall tourism industry, they have developed specialist sections of their companies to cater for skiing sports tourism, acquiring specialist ski operators as part of the process. In addition to Crystal Holidays, TUI UK promotes its skiing operations through Thomson Ski & Snowboarding Holidays as well as owning the more specialist snowsports company Simply Ski which runs catered chalets in the Alps. The Thomson Ski and Snowboarding programme for 2002/2003 aimed:

> *to have appeal to skiers from all sectors and offers group discounts, free pre-season skiing trips for group leaders, special party holidays, family holidays with children's clubs, a nanny service and ski and board guides/rangers. Accommodation options include hotels, apartments, chalets, chalet hotels, club hotels and the transport options are for flights, ski train or self-drive. Increasing flexibility is being built into the programme and special packages allow the consumer to book ski weekends and short breaks, ski weddings, twin-centre holidays or tailormake a holiday with accommodation only, scheduled flights or car hire (Mintel, 2002b).*

Although the four major UK travel companies dominate the general snowsports market in terms of volume, there are many other independent companies that play an important role in supplying the market with niche products and several of these have a large and loyal consumer base, usually specializing in a particular region. For example, independent companies are particularly numerous in France where in one case 'more than 20 independent operators are dedicated to a single French resort' (Mintel, 2002b).

THE PROFILE OF THE ALPINE SKIER

Despite the large number of participants, skiing tends to be associated with a more restricted profile of sports tourist. For example, according to Mintel (2002b) 85 per cent of UK residents have never skied and those who do so are concentrated in the ABC1 socioeconomic groups with over one quarter of the ABC1 15–54 groups being skiers. In fact 98 per cent of the C2DEs aged over 55 years have never skied.

The Mintel Report on Snowsports (2002b) identified both those who had skied at some time in their lives (15 per cent) and potential skiers (18 per cent) who were those who had stated that, while they had never been on a trip involving skiing sports tourism, they were either planning one or would consider going on one (the intenders group illustrated in the Revised Sports Tourism Participation Model in Chapter 5). The demographic details for these two groups are listed in Table 13.4. Skiing sports tourism is clearly a product consumed primarily by relatively young, affluent consumers and is also more attractive to males, with 18 per cent of male respondents being recorded as skiers compared to only 10 per cent of women. With the potential skiers, however, the gap between the two is considerably smaller.

The concentration of skiers among the more affluent socioeconomic groups is not surprising given the various constraints of cost, perception of danger and the degree of difficulty involved (Williams and Basford, 1992). Cost is clearly a major factor deterring those with limited incomes who might consider skiing. In fact, almost a quarter of consumers think that skiing holidays are too expensive. Unlike most other forms of tourism and even various forms of sports tourism, participation in skiing sports tourism involves additional costs of equipment, special clothing, entry charges to the slopes and, for the beginner, the costs of acquiring the necessary skills, in addition to the normal costs of travel and accommodation. It is likely that the lower proportion of skiers in the 25–34 age group in Table 13.4 is constrained by costs, as this is the age group where young families produce additional expenditures and possibly reduced incomes. In addition to cost, various risks and perceived dangers such as speed, steepness of the slopes, fear of being out of control, chances of injury and fear of ski-lifts, together with the physical demands and necessary skill acquisition, also pose significant constraints for many people and especially those with family commitments and older age groups. It is probably these constraints which account for the substantial number of potential skiers listed in various categories in Table 13.4 (for a more detailed discussion of the socioeconomic and demographic characteristics of skiers and the various constraining factors for

Table 13.4	Skiers and potential skiers by demographic subgroup, 2002	
Base: 976 adults aged 15+	**Skiers (%)**	**Potentials (%)**
Men	18	19
Women	10	16
15–24	25	29
25–34	16	27
35–44	23	19
45–54	11	12
55–64	4	12
65+	4	5
AB	21	18
C1	22	20
C2	9	18
D	6	12
E	4	15
Socio-economic age groups:		
ABC1 15–34	28	35
ABC1 35–54	25	14
ABC1 55+	7	6
C2DE 15–34	11	21
C2DE 35–54	9	18
C2DE 55+	2	9

Source: BMRB/Mintel

non-skiers see the work of Williams and Basford, 1992; Carmichael, 1996; Hudson, 1998, 2000).

Despite a more restricted profile, however, Alpine skiers do not constitute an entirely homogeneous group. Hudson (2000: p. 65), for example, highlights a number of differences between skiers in the USA and those visiting European ski resorts based on data from the National Sporting Goods Association (in relation to American skiers) and a Mountain International Opinion Survey (MINOS) conducted in European ski resorts in the mid-1990s. In the USA, skiing sports tourists are predominantly male (60 per cent), 35 years old and have a median household income of $56 614 a year. They are college educated and tend to have managerial and professional jobs. Besides skiing, they participate in tennis, cycling and racquetball, and are twice as likely to buy wine, invest in real estate and travel overseas as the average person. Among European skiing sports tourists, incomes tend to be lower, age is younger and self-ranked skiing ability levels are lower. In addition, European ski resorts attract a more cosmopolitan clientele from around the world than do the United States resorts. Another key difference, according to Hudson (2000), concerns the different requirements of the respective groups. Those at European resorts are far more interested in snow and sun whereas Americans are more interested in the terrain. These differences are clearly linked to motivations (see section below) and the fact that most of those at European resorts are intermediate skiers with many northerners tending 'to balance their downhill participation with a keen interest in basking in the sun, having a good lunch with a bottle of wine, and enjoying the conviviality of friends' (Hudson, 2000: p. 65).

MOTIVATIONS

As suggested in the previous paragraph, the type of sports tourist who participates in skiing must in part be identified on the basis of motives. However, motivation is a particularly complex issue, as outlined in Chapter 3. Pearce (1987: pp. 24–25) reports the findings of a survey of Grenoble skiers by Keogh (1980) who found the 'physical sporting experience' (57.6 per cent) and the 'aesthetic outdoor experience' (33.6 per cent) were the prime motivations in influencing the decision to take a trip involving skiing sports tourism, with the opportunity to participate in an activity with family or friends coming a distant third (7.7 per cent). On the basis of these motivations, Keogh then identified three groups of skiers – the 'sporting', 'contemplative' and 'social' – and found that statistically significant differences occurred between the groups in terms of the resorts they frequented. As Pearce (p. 25) points out, however, 'while this study provides some original insights into skiers' motivations, it does not tell us why those interviewed were seeking either a "physical sporting" or "aesthetic outdoor experience" in the first place'.

Keogh's study is now somewhat dated and more recent studies have suggested that a more complex set of motivations is likely to be involved, with social motives in particular being more important. According to Hudson (2000), who reviewed various studies of North American skiers, several basic motivations have been identified over the years including personal achievement, social reasons, enjoyment of nature, escape and thrill. In the context of the discussion in Chapter 3, while skiing clearly embraces some of the motives associated in the literature with sport, all of these motivations can also be found embedded within the classic tourism literature. For example, Boon (1984, quoted in Hudson, 2000) in a study of the benefits sought by skiing sports tourists at Ski Beech in North Carolina identified various 'push' factors as being important, such as 'getting away from the usual demands of life', 'having a change from your daily routine', 'giving your mind a rest' and 'experiencing new and different things'. The sociability factor was also found to be important in Boon's study; in fact the benefits of 'being with friends' and 'being with others who enjoy similar things' obtained the highest rankings. Such benefits have also been identified among European skiing sports tourists. The Mintel (2002b) study found that the second most popular statement chosen from a group of attitudinal statements regarding snowsports was that 'it would be fun to go skiing with a group of friends' followed by the perception that 'skiing holidays are great for families'. An earlier Mintel report (1996, quoted in Hudson, 2000) also suggested the importance of social benefits together with that of skiing offering 'pleasant and attractive surroundings'. As with the findings for those taking trips involving rural sports participation tourism products, reported in the previous chapter, these motives are not those that are most readily associated with sport in isolation and, thus, this provides yet further support for the contention proposed in Chapter 3 that sports tourism is *related to 'but more than the sum of'* the single activities of sport and tourism. Such motivations are clearly consistent with the guiding theme of this volume that sports tourism experiences arise from the unique interaction of activity, people and place. Not only is the place essential for the activity, but some of the principal motives of participants would seem to involve social interactions that are only possible through such activities at these locations.

A study of UK skiers by Lewis and Wild (1995, quoted in Hudson, 2000) identified four specific types of skier – expert, sports skier, recreational skier and novice – based upon level of skill and experience combined with behavioural and attitudinal aspects of skiing. As Hudson (2000: p. 76) points out, both the recreational skier and sports skier may be capable of skiing the most difficult runs but the reason why they ski such runs will be totally different. This typology can be linked to the Revised Sports Tourism Participation Model outlined in Figure 5.5 in Chapter 5. Given the nature of skiing sports tourism discussed earlier as requiring significant investments of time and money, each of the groups are likely to fall towards the top of the model, with skiing sports tourism behaviours being of fundamental importance in trip decisions. This is illustrated in the specific shape of the Revised Sports Participation Model for skiing sports tourism products illustrated in Figure 5.6 in Chapter 5. This shows that trips involving skiing sports tourism, by necessity, involve a consideration of skiing sports tourism behaviours in the trip decision and destination choice. For 'expert' and 'sport skier' alike, both participation levels and importance are likely to be high and they will thus fall towards the top right of the model, while recreational skiers could, in theory, fall anywhere within the participation shape for skiing sports tourism illustrated in Figure 5.6, depending on their motives and levels of participation.

THE FUTURE OF THE INDUSTRY

According to Tuppen (1998), the ski market in Europe had reached a mature phase at the turn of the Millennium, with increasing problems of saturation and oversupply of facilities. 'Resorts have been forced to invest and innovate to remain competitive; new ski lifts, snow making machines, cultural, sports and entertainments facilities and refurbished buildings are all part of the armoury of measures employed to render resorts more attractive' (Tuppen, 1998: p. 260) with the large, internationally renowned, often high altitude locations with resources to invest, more likely to retain their competitiveness. Global warming and the uncertainty of snow cover have also contributed to a slow down, especially for those resorts at lower altitudes, while the growth of other areas, such as in Eastern Europe, has also been a factor. European skiers have also been attracted increasingly to North America, as have Japanese skiers (Hudson, 2000). While the European Alps may have experienced some decline in skiing, the UK market has continued to grow and the 2008 Ski Industry Report (Crystal, 2008) predicts that this will continue, despite the various challenges of rising fuel costs and general economic uncertainty. It does, however, suggest that skiing sports tourists may 'trade down' and become more value conscious.

According to Hudson (2003b), today 'visitors to winter resorts are seeking a variety of niche options' with 'the trend back towards the early days of winter sports, with a diversification of activities'. As with the rural sports participation tourism products discussed in Chapter 12, there is also a range of new winter sports tourism products which are gaining popularity and competing with traditional ones (Table 13.5).

This diversification has been partly encouraged by the resorts as a response to the declining skiing sports tourism market, especially as an increasing proportion of those who take trips involving winter sports tourism in both North America and Europe do not ski at all (Hudson, 2000). In addition, 'even avid skiers are typically skiing less' as the average skier

Table 13.5	The diversification of winter sports tourism products
Traditional winter sports tourism products	**Contemporary winter sports tourism products**
Skiing	Snowboarding
Cross-country skiing	Snowmobiling
Telemarking	Snowshoeing
Cat-skiing	Heli-skiing
Winter sports events	Para gliding/hang gliding
Ice-skating	Tubing
Horse-drawn sleigh	Dog sledging
Curling	Snowcycling
Tobogganing	Thrill-sleds/extreme sledding
Ice-climbing	
Ice-driving	
Ice-sculpting	
Snowskating	

Source: Hudson (2003b)

tends to be getting older and is thus switching to more gentle winter sports tourism activities. As Hudson (2003b) points out, 'the more progressive resorts are now treating skiing as a form of entertainment by establishing more off slope diversions' and, although he is referring primarily to resorts in North America, such developments can also be seen in Europe.

The other key development affecting the skiing market has been the massive growth of snowboarding. According to Hudson (2000), it is probably the biggest winter sports tourism activity in the USA and its popularity in Europe is also growing. It has the advantage over skiing in that it is easier to master the technical skills and thus may be far more appealing to the recreational winter sports tourist who can confidently take to the slopes far more quickly than with skiing. It is particularly popular among young people and thus has substantial potential for growth in the future, with some projections suggesting that it may overtake skiing as the most popular winter sports tourism activity in the next ten to twenty years (Scott, 1995, cited in Hudson, 2000).

CONCLUSION

This chapter has sought to provide a further example of sports tourism to illustrate the various themes and concepts that are the central concerns of this volume. Skiing represents not only one of the largest segments of sports tourism but, in many ways, provides the classic form of sports tourism, given its precise environmental requirements, its distinct organization of tour operators and its unique interaction of activity, people and place. Like the vast majority of people who consume sports participation tourism products, the overwhelming majority of skiers have to travel to particular places and thus, by definition, become sports tourists. But, unlike the typical tourist who seeks an 'in-active' holiday, the skier is involved in an active pursuit. Nevertheless, as has been illustrated above, some of the key motives that drive such activity are not necessarily those immediately associated with sport and active pursuits alone but include various sociability motives, enjoyment of the natural environment and those of escape. Thus, skiers are neither tourists specifically nor sportspersons but clearly participants in a phenomenon, sports tourism, that is *related to but more than the sum of* sport and tourism. As with many other forms of sports tourism, skiers do not constitute a homogeneous group but differ to some extent in terms of their socioeconomic and demographic characteristics and their levels of skill and commitment. However, they do tend to have more in common than other groups, being dominated by relatively young, affluent consumers and characterized by regular levels of participation. Thus, as a distinct form of sports tourism, skiing provides a further illustration of the utility of the Revised Sports Tourism Participation Model illustrated in Figures 5.5 and 5.6 in Chapter 5, with different levels of participation and importance, a growing diversification involving multi-activities and a clearly identifiable group of potential participants who might be seen as 'intenders'.

CHAPTER 14

Cycling Sports Tourism

While skiing is often regarded as a classic example of a sports tourism activity, given the well defined winter sports tourism industry that has developed to accommodate it (see Chapter 13), cycling, for different reasons, might also compete for such a claim. Although some cycling takes place within a rather restricted spatial context, such as a velodrome, most involves travel through and between places and, thus, a link with tourism is immediately established. In fact, for many cyclists, the idea of touring is an explicit part of the cycling activity, with trips involving recreational cycling, either as a mode of travel or a day activity, being the most obvious example. However, even at the most elite/excellence end of the cycling activity spectrum, the 'tour' idea can be central as evidenced by events such as the Tour de France and Tour of Britain, and Bull (2006) has shown that racing cyclists demonstrate many characteristics typical of tourist behaviour. Not surprisingly, therefore, cycling sports tourism exemplifies many of the core ideas of this text. It clearly involves the interaction of people, activity and place, and its various forms, from day-trip cycling, through various types of longer trips involving cycling sports tourism, to elite racing, involving both active participants and spectators, provide both a useful illustration of participation issues and validation of the Revised Sports Tourism Participation Model. Furthermore, it also has important policy implications, partly through its association with 'greener', more sustainable forms of tourism but, also, in a very different way, as a result of the major cycling events and the eagerness of various local governments to leverage various benefits from these. It is thus a sports tourism product that constitutes an extremely useful, illustrative case study.

To date there has been scant coverage of cycling sports tourism in academic literature. Richie's (1998) study of cycling sports tourists on the South Island of New Zealand, Simonsen and Jorgenson's (1996) study of cycling sports tourists on the Danish tourist islands of Fyn and Bornholm and that by Lumsdon et al. (2004) of the cycling sports tourism on the North Sea cycle route are rare examples of academic studies of the broader aspects. A few other works have focused on specific types of cycling sports tourism (such as Bull's 2006 study of racing cyclists), policy aspects such as sustainability (Lumsdon, 2000; Downward and Lumsdon, 2001; Lumsdon et al., 2004) or major cycling events such as the Tour de France (Bull and Lovell, 2007; Desbordes, 2007). Beyond this, the principal coverage tends to be found in either more popular publications (e.g. Lumsdon, 1996; Breakwell, 2006), publications linked to a particular interest group (Sustrans, 1999a) or various reports that focus on economic impacts and tourism growth in particular regions or destinations (e.g. Maine Department of Transportation, 2001; EcoGIS, 2002; Wales Tourist Board, 2002c; Picton and Bull, 2003; Fraietta, 2004; Lumsdon et al., 2004; Greenwood and Yeoman, 2006; Mintel 2007). These latter reports are thus ostensibly about tourism rather than sports tourism.

Unlike the other case studies included in this section of the book, a slightly different approach is adopted in this chapter as a result of the role of place. Whereas the other sports tourism examples involve activities that relate to particular places and facilities, cycling sports tourism, except in the case of spectators attending a major event, involves places that the cyclist travels through and between. Thus, whereas the other chapters are organized around various distinct places (Malta, Sheffield, upland Wales and the European Alps), this chapter is more focused on the activity itself and how it interacts with a variety of places. The purpose of the chapter will be to concentrate on three key themes. First, it will attempt to identify the variety and extent of cycling sports tourism and see how this variety relates to some of the core ideas of this text. Secondly, it will consider cycling sports tourism in a policy context linked to sustainable sports tourism. Thirdly, it will look at cycling sports tourism from the perspective of event sports tourism, embracing further policy issues and the involvement of spectators; in this regard, the particular the case of the *Tour de France* will be utilized.

THE VARIETY AND EXTENT OF CYCLING SPORTS TOURISM

Unlike many other sports tourism products covered in this book, cycling sports tourism encompasses a number of different forms involving relatively low levels of participation on trips incorporating many other equally or more important tourist behaviours, various forms of trips where cycling sports tourism is a fundamental part of the trip decision and participation is extensive (often being the mode of transport) during the trip, sponsored cycle rides, and elite cyclists participating in various races, including major events like the *Tour de France*. Furthermore, the actual form may be influenced by the environment or route involved and, whereas most cycling sports tourism involves active participants, on occasions, where major racing events are involved, it may also involve spectators. Given these varied options, it is difficult to provide a clear definition of cycling sports tourism and it is certainly not the intention of this chapter to dwell on such things. Discussion of definitions has already taken place in Chapter 3 and one purpose of the case study chapters is to examine various forms of sports tourism insofar as they relate to the conceptualization of sports tourism as articulated in that chapter. In the limited literature that exists on cycling sports tourism, there is some variation as to what is included and what is not. Some include participation on day and part-day trips (Lumsdon, 1996; Sustrans, 1999a; Munda Biddi Trail Foundation, 2005) as opposed to being restricted to being away from the normal place of residence for more than 24 hours (Ritchie, 1998). Most only include activities in which cycling sports tourism is a fundamental and significant part of the trip and thus exclude spontaneous participation in cycling sports tourism, or participation that has been planned post-trip decision, such as an occasional cycle ride on trips including many other equally or more important tourist behaviours; most also exclude those who travel to race competitions either explicitly (Simonsen and Jorgenson, 1996) or by relegating it to an 'other' category (Sustrans, 1999a) and most exclude any reference to major cycling events such as the *Tour de France* or sponsored cycle events and the inclusion of spectators. Of course, where most definitions are concerned, they are part of a specific purpose, for example, as part of the context of a particular study or as part of a broader policy agenda such as growing tourism or developing sustainable tourism. Given that the specific purpose of this book is to explore and understand sports tourism in its broadest sense, as wide a definition as possible is adopted here and that suggested by the South Australian Tourism Commission (2005: p. 3) in its Cycle Tourism Strategy 2005–2009 would seem particularly appropriate:

> *cycle tourism visits are considered to be for the purpose of holidays, recreation, pleasure or sport; and to include either overnight stays, or day trips to other tourism regions during which the visitor either engages in active cycling, or is a spectator at a cycling event.*

Such a broad and inclusive definition can encompass a wide range of different cycling sports tourism products based on a variety of criteria. The

Sustrans typology (1999a) probably represents the most comprehensive attempt to date to identify the various different forms and involves three 'main types' with their individual sub-categories and an 'other' group (Table 14.1). However, while at first sight it appears an obvious and apparently useful framework for examining cycling sports tourism, it is not without its problems. Putting to one side the problems of regarding sports tourism as a trip purpose rather than a trip behaviour as discussed at various points in this text, but most extensively in Chapter 3, four specific issues can be identified. First is an implication that the typology is hierarchical with 'cycle

---

Table 14.1   Types of cycling sports tourism

a. Cycling Holidays

Where cycling is the main purpose of the holiday (participants sometimes referred to as 'dedicated cyclists')

The holidays may be *Long Cycling Holidays* of four or more nights or, more commonly, *Cycling Short Breaks* of one to three nights.

There is also a distinction to be made between *Centre-based Cycling Holidays* based at one overnight place and *Cycle Touring Holidays* where the overnight stay changes. Cycling holidays can be either self-organized or organized by a cycling holiday operator as a *Packaged Cycling Holiday*. The majority of UK cycling holidays are self-organized in both the UK and Europe.

b. Holiday Cycling

Cycling while on holiday, away from home, where cycling is one of a number of activities undertaken during the holiday.

c. Cycling Day Visits

Trips from home to places outside a person's usual place of residence. These trips may involve setting out from home by bike, or taking the bike by car or train, for a day or half-day cycle ride.

d. Other

The following types of cycling can also be seen as part of cycling sports tourism:

- Offroad cycling/mountain biking
- Club cycling
- Organized cycle rides
- Sponsored charity rides
- Schools/youth group cycling
- Cycle racing

Source: Sustrans (1999a)

holidays', involving 'dedicated' cyclists, being more important than cycling day visits. Secondly, this hierarchical categorization is clearly orientated towards a tourism and economic perspective, with little or no accommodation for the sport and health benefits or the impact of cycling ability. Thirdly, it does not accommodate activity at the elite end of the spectrum in its main categories, with club cycling and cycle racing being relegated to the 'other' category alongside mountain biking, with the implication that such forms are less important. Furthermore, there is no explicit mention of major cycling events and the involvement of spectators. Fourthly, there is no facility for identifying the level of participation or the importance that the cyclists attribute to their sports tourism activity, the key elements in the Revised Sports Tourism Participation Model outlined in Chapter 5. The 'cycling day visits' category, for example, makes no distinction between people who might go out for a one-off Sunday afternoon ride, possibly as an alternative to what they might usually do, and those who do this every week, possibly as part of a training regime for racing competitions or sponsored cycle events. Also, while the 'cycling holiday' category implies that such cyclists are 'dedicated', this is probably more to do with their level of interest and the importance they may place on such activities and says little about their skills and abilities as cyclists. Some people who take trips involving cycling sports tourism as a mode of transport may simply want a holiday using a gentler and slower form of transport that might also afford a different perspective on the landscape through which they will travel – they are tourists using cycles. Others, however, may well be involved in what Stebbins (1992) has referred to as 'serious leisure' and be committed sports tourists (Green and Jones, 2005). Thus, the Sustrans typology not only fails to include all the different forms of cycling sports tourism but has little value as an analytical tool. Its contribution to furthering an understanding of the sports tourist *per se* is clearly limited but, even as a tool for analysing tourism potential and likely economic impacts, its use must be questionable because it is clearly limited in its ability to identify the variation in market segments.

The Sustrans and other cycling sports tourism typologies are essentially based on the type of activity, but Faulks et al. (2007: p. 14) argue that the 'wide variety of individuals and potential market segments' that constitute the range of cycling sports tourism should perhaps be differentiated on the basis of 'motivations' as well as 'activity'. Based on the work of Simonsen and Jorgenson (1996), they suggest that a continuum ranging from cycling enthusiast, or hard core cyclist, to occasional cyclist could be considered and cite the South Australian Tourism Commission (2002) who suggest that cycling sports tourists can be categorized as being dedicated, interested, or incidental/opportunistic. This report also noted that individuals are not necessarily confined to one group, as cycling might take on different levels of importance for different trips. This thinking has much in common with ideas underpinning the Revised Sports Tourism Participation Model outlined earlier in this book (see Chapter 5) and it is suggested here that, rather than attempting to identify specific types, a better approach to understanding this variety would be to view it in terms of this model both in its generic form (see Figure 5.5) and its variants for particular sports tourism products (see Figure 5.6). This would allow for the profiling of the full range of characteristics to be included as well as the meanings and values of the cycling sports tourism experience and, in particular, the level of importance attached to it together with the amount of participation involved. So, for example, elite racing cyclists are towards the top right hand corner of the triangle as their participation rates and the importance they attach to the activity are both high, whereas recreational cycling sports tourists are towards the bottom left as they participate very occasionally and, partly as a result of this, they also do not view cycling sports tourism as very important, either in trip decisions or in trip planning. In fact, some who fall into this category may even see such activity in a negative light, being persuaded to cycle with others when they really do not wish to. The various other forms of cycling sports tourist, such as those listed in the Sustrans typology, are located at various points between these extremes. The 'holiday cycling group', for example, are likely to be in the lower left hand area, although not exclusively so depending on the role of cycling sports tourism in the trip decision. Those on various types of 'cycling holidays', however, are distributed at various points in the top half of the model and to the right, where cycling sports tourism has been a fundamental part of the trip decision. There are also likely to be various potential cycling sports tourists who fall into the 'intenders' part of the model. It is likely that in the current climate of rising fuel costs, increasing delays in travelling through airports, calls for more sustainable lifestyles and the growing emphasis on health and fitness, many people could be considering cycling sports tourism as a serious alternative to their previous tourism behaviours.

Given its many different forms and its spatially diverse nature, the extent of cycling sports tourism is difficult to determine. However, there have been some attempts to estimate the numbers involved together with the associated impact and there are also a number of specific localized impact studies. According to a recent Mintel (2007) Report, 450 000 British people spent £120 million on 'cycling holidays' in 2005 with an additional 2.25 million holidays involving some kind of 'incidental' cycling sports tourism such as a day's bike hire or a mounted bike sightseeing tour. Furthermore, the market is likely to grow, with the report suggesting that 16 per cent of adults (8 million) have already been on some kind of 'cycling holiday' with a further 12 per cent (6 million) having not had one but wanting to do so in the future, a clear example of 'intenders'. Another study, this time looking specifically at Scotland, has suggested that, in 2003, trips involving cycling sports tourism in Scotland by UK residents was worth £219 million and represented 1 million trips. These figures focus on 'trip purpose' and involved 'cycling as a main purpose of trip', accounting for £20 million and 100 000 trips, and 'cycling as part of a holiday trip' with £199 million expenditure and 900 000 trips (Greenwood and Yeoman, 2006). In the UK, 2 per cent of all leisure/day trips and 1 per cent of all holiday trips involve cycling sports tourism in the trip decision-making process. The 2005 English Leisure Visits Report (Natural England, 2006) estimated that there were 1.36 million trips involving cycling sports tourism to the English countryside, producing an overall revenue of approximately £40 million and 110 000 trips involving cycling sports tourism to National Parks worth £22 million. At a more local level, Regeneris Consulting (2005: p. 23) has estimated that there were 116 000 holiday makers in North East England in 2003 who participated in cycling sports tourism, producing between £1 million and £7 million income and supporting between 400 and 600 full-time jobs. Furthermore, the Report suggests that the cycling sports tourism product in the North East region could be worth as much as £32.8 million by 2010.

In other countries, cycling sports tourism is no less important. For example, 25 per cent of the German population participates in cycling sports tourism on holiday and, in Ireland, 9 per cent of all overseas visitors are considered 'cycle tourists', spending on average £538 each (Sustrans, 1999a). Austria's Danube Trail attracts over 1.5 million visitors a year while Germany's Bodensee Cycle attracts an estimated 380 000 riders, producing an economic contribution of €75 million to the region. Furthermore, it has been estimated that the whole of Europe is expected to generate £14 billion in 'cycle tourism', revenue per year by 2020 (Sustrans, 1999a). In 1999, direct spending in Maine by over 2 million 'bicycle tourists' is estimated to have totalled $36.3 million USD, and in New Zealand it has been estimated that 3 per cent of overseas tourists and 1.6 per cent of domestic holiday makers cycle between destinations in the South Island, which is worth $72 million per annum to the economy (Faulks et al., 2007). In Australia, data on the extent of cycling sports tourism are lacking, although it is estimated that 10.5 per cent of Australians participate in cycling (Australian Sports Commission, 2005 quoted in Faulks et al., 2007) and that the vast majority (86 per cent) cycle for fun/leisure (Faulks et al., 2007).

The other area of the cycling sports tourism product range for which data are available involves cycling events. As outlined in the final section of this chapter, 15 million spectators watch the Tour de France race along its 20 stage route with expenditure in each of the places involved usually totalling many millions and similar findings can be shown throughout the world. For example, in Australia, it is estimated that cycling sports tourism expenditure for each big bike race is between $1.2 million and $4.5 million. In fact, the Jacob's Creek Tour Down Under annual road race in 2005 attracted 495 000 people altogether and, across all its six stages, provided an economic benefit of $13.2 million to South Australia (Faulks et al., 2007) and the 2003 Road World Cycling Championships held in Hamilton, Ontario generated a total estimated economic activity of $48.3 million CDN in the province (Fraietta, 2004).

It is clear, therefore, that cycling sports tourism, in its many different forms, constitutes a widespread and substantial activity and, as Greenwood and Yeoman (2006: p. 2) suggest, 'almost every country in the world has a developed recreational cycle culture, from the Netherlands to Vietnam'. Not only is it of considerable extent and value but evidence would suggest that it is also growing (Sustrans, 1999a; Fraietta, 2004; Greenwood and Yeoman, 2006; Faulks et al., 2007) and is being encouraged to do so, not only because it offers valuable tourism revenue but also because of its potential to provide a green tourism alternative. It therefore involves important policy agendas and the following two sections are intended to explore such issues.

CYCLING SPORTS TOURISM AS SUSTAINABLE TOURISM DEVELOPMENT

One particular aspect that has figured prominently in the limited literature on cycling sports tourism is its contribution to the sustainable tourism agenda (Simonsen and Jorgenson, 1996; Sustrans, 1999a; Lumsdon, 2000; Downward and Lumsdon, 2001; Faulks et al., 2007). Sustainability has become one of the principal policy goals of the last two decades following the publication of the Brundtland Report in the late 1980s (World Commission on Environment and Development, 1987) and, while initial applications of sustainability were focused on development impacts in the developing world, the concept has subsequently been applied with equal vigour to the developed world. Tourism presents a classic target for sustainable policies, given its environmental impacts, its consumption of scarce resources and its rapid, unplanned development in certain destinations and, perhaps not surprisingly, there is now a substantial literature on the subject including a specific journal, the *Journal of Sustainable Tourism*. What is perhaps surprising, however, is that within this literature, other than the few references cited above, there is little on cycling sports tourism, despite its potential to offset one of the most environmentally damaging impacts of tourism activity, namely travel between or through tourism places.

As various authors have highlighted, transport lies at the heart of the tourism system given that travel facilitates the sense of movement of visit derived from the experience of unusual tourism places (Leiper, 1990; Lumsdon and Page, 2004; Page, 2005). But, as Lumsdon (2000: p. 361) highlights, it is a system that is 'heavily dependent on the world's two most energy consuming and polluting forms of transport – air transport and the motorized vehicle'. Cycling as a mode of transport, however, does not involve such problems and its only environmental impact is minimal, restricted to erosion in a few limited places as a result of mountain bike activity. Thus, it provides a benign form of transport where the transport is 'a contextual component of the tourism offering' rather than simply a means to an end (Lumsdon, 2000: p. 361). Cycling sports tourism as a means of transport is thus an activity that many policy-makers would encourage as making a contribution towards creating more sustainable forms of tourism. Of course, it is not an overall panacea but it may be important in certain circumstances, especially in rural areas where persuading people to swap cars for bicycles could reduce both pollution and congestion.

The world's most cycle friendly country, due to its low, flat physical landscape, is probably the Netherlands where cycle paths are provided throughout the country from the smallest village to the largest town (Standeven and De Knop, 1999). Elsewhere in Europe, cycle friendly countries are growing in number and in the UK, France and Denmark, for example, cycling trails and route development have helped stimulate the demand for trips involving various levels of cycling sports tourism participation. Furthermore, cycling routes and cycling sports tourism developments in Europe have been integrated into sustainable development and transport policies leading to the development of well planned regional, national and pan-European networks (Faulks et al., 2007). One such route system that forms part of the European network is the National Cycle Network (NCN) in the UK, which is often cited as a prime example of sustainable transport (Lumsdon, 2000). The network comprises a series of traffic-free paths, traffic-calmed and minor roads, connecting urban centres and the countryside throughout the UK and was pioneered by Sustrans which describes itself as the 'UK's leading sustainable transport charity' (Sustrans, 2008). In 1995, it received a grant of £43.5 million from the Millennium Commission Lottery Fund to create an initial 6500 miles of cycle routes, but the project has been an ongoing one and, working in partnership with hundreds of local authorities and many other organizations and funders, over 12 000 miles of routes and links had been completed by December 2007. By this date, the network passed within one mile of half the UK's population and over 354 million walking and cycling trips were estimated to have been made on the Network in 2007 alone (Sustrans, 2008).

The principal reasons for establishing the NCN are essentially concerned with increasing cycle use in line with sustainable transport and health agendas. However, as Page (2005: p. 357) points out, there are also 'implications for tourism, which can utilize any infrastructure put in place for residents and leisure users in local areas'. In fact, Sustrans and partner organizations have recognized that the network could become a major tourist attraction in its own right, either in its entirety or on sections that have tourism appeal (Sustrans, 1999b cited in Lumsdon, 2000) and Cope et al. (1999) have already demonstrated this potential in their study of the C2C route across the Northern Pennines which, in the mid-1990s, was generating over 10 000 holiday trips per annum. In 2007, Sustrans published a report revealing that the National Cycle Network offers 'huge potential for sustainable tourism' (cited in Sustrans, 2008). The report revealed that, during 2006, four long distance routes of the Network directly contributed £9.6 million to the North East economy and £13.4 million to the wider economy. In commenting on the report, the 2007 Review suggested that, 'as demand for domestic holidays is predicted to rise in response to climate change and increasing oil prices, this report represents a case for further investment in walking and cycling routes as a way of creating much more sustainable tourism, significantly reducing greenhouse gas emissions by encouraging people to holiday nearer to home'.

The extent to which the NCN and other networks can make a significant contribution to sustainable tourism is still a matter of debate as evidence is somewhat limited. While it is clear that large numbers of people are utilizing the routes, as shown by the figures above, it is the extent to which they are making a significant sustainability impact that is questionable. Lumsdon (2000), for example, has raised the following reservations about the wider benefits:

- Some cycle routes can stimulate day visitation which is predominantly car based, especially where they have been developed in isolation from a wider network (although it must be stressed that a key purpose of the NCN is to try to reduce such isolation)

- When such routes are located in attractive countryside such as national parks, it is likely that the destination will remain the prime attraction, with the activity of cycling serving only to enhance the experience, in a similar way to walking or horse riding. Therefore, it could be argued that visitors would have made the journey by car, regardless of whether a cycle route exists or not

■ In many instances, sections of the NCN have been developed in order to secure or take advantage of funding opportunities, with the consequence that the line of the route might by-pass visitor attractions or historic villages and therefore be less appealing to the cycle tourist. There are also limitations in terms of inter-modality, although a project was established to investigate links from railway stations to the NCN.

Nevertheless, despite these potential limitations which, in any case, have weakened as the NCN has expanded, evidence is gradually emerging to suggest that such a network is making a noticeable contribution, at least in certain areas. For example, the C2C study did demonstrate that the route provided a considerable stimulus to the local economy with minimal social and environmental impact and Lumsdon (2000: p. 368) cites the example of the Bath to Bristol cycle path where empirical data indicated that 'routes offer a sustainable alternative to car based recreation'. In addition, more recent data (which, like the Sustrans (1999a) typology, focuses on trip purpose) from a study of the North Sea Cycle Route (NSCR) (Lumsdon et al., 2004; Cope et al., 2004) showed that over 91 per cent of trips were for recreational or tourism purposes, with 58 per cent of trips being day or part day trips and 33 per cent of journeys involving what the authors define as tourism purposes, either for short break stays (up to 3 nights) or for cycle sports tourism touring (more than 3 nights) and 85 per cent of journeys were by cycle only, i.e. involving no other forms of transport to access the route, with only 10 per cent of the trips involving access by car.

One of the key issues relating to the NCN is that it has developed as a result of a clear policy objective 'to provide leisure opportunities, as well as more utilitarian transport links between towns and within towns for schools and work' and its development has involved both sports tourism policy-makers and providers (Downward, 2005). While there is no denying that the various groups and individuals involved are motivated by very different objectives, the NCN is a good example of an initiative that has brought different policy communities together to achieve outcomes that are of mutual benefit. At first sight, this might suggest a situation that is very different to that usually associated with sports tourism for, as explained in Chapter 6 of this text, examples of integrated sports tourism policy initiatives have been rare as the structures of both sport and of tourism policy communities have the potential to cause problems for such development. However, although tourism and sport policy communities have been involved in the development of the NCN (both the Sports Council/ Sport England and various tourism agencies are sponsors of Sustrans), they have not been at the heart of the policy-making. As explained above, this has been pioneered by Sustrans whose main concerns involve sustainable transport and thus the sport and tourism policy communities have not been dealing with each other but with, in this instance, a more influential third party.

Nevertheless, whether the sports tourism policy aspects are fortuitous or not, it is clear that the NCN has clear implications for the development of cycling sports tourism and accords with broader policies aimed at developing greener forms of tourism as well as the emerging health agenda and policies to encourage more active forms of leisure. Furthermore, in line with these broader agendas, it also accords with the various provision strategies outlined earlier in this text, especially in relation to persuading people with limited or no experience of cycling to take it up (see Chapter 9). There is clear evidence that the NCN has been instrumental in converting 'intenders' and capturing 'incidentals' (for example, over 12 per cent of cyclists in the NSCR study identified themselves as 'new' or 'occasional' cyclists – Lumsdon et al., 2004: p. 19). Thus, cycling sports tourism is not only making an important contribution to broader green transport and tourism development but is also enabling people to engage in more active forms of tourism that may well have additional health benefits.

CYCLING EVENT SPORTS TOURISM: THE EXAMPLE OF THE TOUR DE FRANCE

Another key policy area associated with cycling sports tourism is that linked to cycling events. The hosting of major events is usually associated with urban areas and, as explained in Chapter 11, this is one of the key reasons why such areas can be identified as sports tourism places. Major cycle racing events also visit towns and cities, the *Tour de France* (TdF), for example, usually starting in a major city and, of course, culminating in Paris. However, given the travel element involved in the activity, such races also pass through many other places en route and thus enable sports tourism activity for both active participants and spectators to be spatially distributed over a wide area; in the case of the Tour of Britain and the TdF, for example, most of the respective countries and more besides, with the TdF also visiting parts of adjacent countries. In 2007, for example, it began in London and also visited Belgium and Spain. In fact, the TdF crosses all the French regions every four years with 350 000 kilometres having been traversed in France since 1903 and 500 different towns and cities having already organized a stage's start or finish (Desbordes, 2007).

The TdF is now the largest annual sporting event in the world (although the Olympic Games/Paralympics and the Soccer World Cup are undoubtedly larger events, they only take place every four years). Also, unlike most other event sports tourism products, the TdF is free to view and comprises 20 separate stages covering approximately 4000 kilometres on closed public roads from start to finish. The race involves 21 teams and 189 riders (figures for 2007), most of whom tend to stay together in a single group, the *peloton*, which means that at any one point along the route spectators glimpse the cyclists for only a few seconds. However, the race is also accompanied by a publicity *'caravanne'* of approximately 200 supporting vehicles and floats which adds to the spectacle. An estimated 4500 people are involved in organizing the event, which is followed by 2000 journalists and the estimated number of spectators along the entire 20 stage route is 15 million, with the event being televised to 84 countries, 43 of them relaying the race live. More than 2960 hours of TV programmes about the Tour are broad cast and thousands of pictures and information are also available on the Internet. It is the most broadcast sport event in France, ahead of the tennis French Open and the Champions League (in 2005, each French TV viewer consumed 5.5 hours of live TdF coverage, compared with 3.1 hours for the French Open, 2.8 for the F1 Championship, 1.9 for the Six Nations rugby tournament and 1.3 for the football Champions League) (Desbordes, 2007).

As outlined in Chapter 11, the permission to host major event sports tourism products is keenly sought by city authorities as a result of the economic and social benefits that are perceived to accrue from such activities. This phenomenon is well documented in the literature, which tends to highlight the generally held belief within policy-making circles that hosting such important events and even those that are less globally recognized, is hugely beneficial (Burns et al., 1986; Mules, 1998; Collins and Jackson, 1999; Gratton et al., 2005; Desbordes, 2007). According to Gratton et al. (2005) many governments around the world have adopted national sports policies that specify the hosting of major events as a key objective, with perceived benefits involving urban regeneration legacy, sporting legacy, tourism and enhanced image, social and cultural benefits as well as economic ones. However, while all these benefits are generally cited, it is the wider economic related aspects that have tended to drive policy and which have attracted most attention from academics (Ritchie, 1984; Mules and Falkner, 1996) with economic impact studies being an almost obligatory part of the proceedings. Governments are usually keen to finance such studies in the strongly held belief that results will justify the use of taxpayers' money in hosting such events.

The desire to host major cycling events is no different. In France, there is intense competition among towns to host the various stages (*étapes*) for the prestige and perceived beneficial impacts that the race produces, including the massive press coverage, and such perceptions have also influenced towns and cities in neighbouring countries to lobby to host a stage of the race. Other types of major event sports tourism products usually involve extremely large costs and other negative externalities, with the Athens Olympic Games, for example, costing more than €12 billion, leaving Greece with a hefty budget deficit of 6.1 per cent of gross domestic product in 2004 (Scotsman, 2005). However, the costs associated with major cycling events are relatively small because, as Desbordes (2007) highlights, there is no necessity to build stadiums, there are no ticketing expenses and there is no cost for taking care of the infrastructure. And, while the legacy benefits may be limited, they are probably no less important than for other major event sports tourism products. Kirkup and Major (2006: p. 293), in their analysis of the reliability of economic impact studies of the Olympic Games, conclude that 'the main economic impacts of the Games are primarily tourism related and remain the sole legacy once the Games are over'. With the TdF, also, it tends to be the potential tourism legacy that is the key element in the rationale of those who wish to host it, involving not only the temporary boost to tourism expenditure during the event itself but also the 'free' promotion and advertising involved.

These benefits are clearly illustrated in Box 14.1 and Table 14.2a, b which highlight the economic impact for the TdF for two different places during two separate races, the first involving the small town of Digne in France in 2005 and the second relating to London and Kent in 2007. Digne, a town with a population of only 16 064, located in the Department of Alpes-de-Haute-Provence, hosted the twelfth stage of the TdF in 2005 and the importance of the event to the town, especially in relation to promoting its image and developing awareness, is evidenced by the fact that this was the eleventh time it had hosted the event since 1933 (Desbordes, 2007). The estimated economic benefits reported in Desbordes' (2007) paper and listed in Box 14.1, show that the direct tourist expenditure was €476 000 and, after allowing for the expenses of hosting the event, the net amount of money that was estimated to have been injected into the local economy was €326 000, a not inconsiderable sum for such a small town. But this direct tourist expenditure is only part of the benefit for, as Box 14.1 also shows, there are other, less tangible, promotional benefits arising from the substantial media coverage. As Desbordes (2007: p. 538) concludes, the TdF 'has an undeniable impact on the local economy and cities can be very happy with the event'.

Box 14.1 Economic impact data and related methodology for the Tour de France 2005 event in Digne

Spectators:

25000 people in the city, 64% non-living in Digne, and 77% were French

4500 other people (organization, media, cycling teams, sponsors)

On an average of six overnights, 91% of the hotels were full on July 14

Average expense for spectators non-living in Digne = 23 euros (food, drinks, souvenirs)

23 × 16000 spectators (non-living in Digne) = 368000 euros that were injected in the local business

Average expense for the local population = 12 €

12 × 9000 = 108000 euros

Global impact = 368000 + 108000 = 476000 €

The City of Digne had to pay 75000 euros to the organizer ASO to host the event and had to spend 75000 euros for technical services (security, access, signage, communication, etc.), which in total amounted to 150000 €

Total amount injected into the local economy is thus calculated as:

476000 − 150000 = 326000 euros.

This amount, however, largely underestimated the overall impact because it did not take into account the qualitative improvement of Digne's image through various media

About 350 articles in the French press (78 journals or magazines)

Average audience on French TV = 5.72 million people and 6.88 million for the arrival (58.1% market share when it focuses on Digne). Length of the diffusion = 3h38

About 70 channels broadcast the stage in 180 countries (2 billion potential persons)

About 14763 people visited the city's website on July 14

The tourism office received many emails (+113% compared to a usual month of July)

Source: Desbordes (2007)

Similar findings can also be seen in Table 14.2a, b for London and Kent for the first stage of the 2007 race, which began with *Le Grande Depart* in the capital and involved travelling through Kent and finishing in Canterbury. The data are taken from an impact study report for Transport for London (Social Research Associates, 2007). While the actual amounts are very different, reflecting not only the different sizes of the respective places but also the different methodologies that were employed to produce them (that for London/Kent does not attempt to estimate costs), it is clear, nevertheless, that both were generating considerable economic impact.

But the lobbying by the Greater London Authority, Kent County Council and Canterbury City Council, in concert with other agencies, to 'win' the

Table 14.2a	Analysis of Tour de France 2007 spectator expenditure – London total spectator expenditure		
Spectators	**%**	**Expenditure per day**	**Total**
Commercial accommodation	25	£116.33	£40.8 million
Staying with family/friends	9	£45.48	£ 5.9 million
Day visitors	20	£26.15	£ 7.2 million
London residents	45	£19.71	£ 12.4 million
Total spectator expenditure (rounded)			**£65.6 million (adjusted)**

Expenditure from other groups, including cyclists, media, officials and other sponsors, amounted to more than £2.6 million. The organizational spend of £5 million brought the total up to more than **£73 million** in London.

Source: Social Research Associates (2007).

Table 14.2b	Analysis of Tour de France 2007 spectator expenditure – Kent total spectator expenditure		
Spectators	**%**	**Expenditure per day**	**Total**
Commercial accommodation	13	£61.84	£5.9 million
Staying with family/friends	7	£20.99	£1 million
Day visitors	20	£18.82	£2.9 million
London residents	61	£9.42	£4.3 million
Total spectator expenditure (rounded)			**£14.1 million plus adjustment £14.8 million**

The overall expenditure in Kent was estimated at around £15 million averaging £20 per person. Kent expenditure has a rather different profile as fewer spectators were from outside Kent.

Source: Social Research Associates (2007).

opportunity to host this stage was, as with Digne, based on much wider objectives than simply generating tourist revenue from the event itself. Marketing London on a world stage and encouraging tourism, demonstrating that London could bid for and win major events and promoting cycling in the capital were also key objectives (Social Research Associates, 2007). The London Development Agency (LDA) was concerned that this event should be part of the marketing and promotion of London 'as a vibrant place to live, study, visit and do business' and the Mayor's objectives included 'making London a city where people of all ages and abilities have the incentive, confidence and facilities to cycle whenever it suits them'.

Although it tends to be the economic benefits, either direct or longer term, that are promoted and highlighted and, more latterly, as outlined in the previous section, some environmental ones, cycling sports tourism events also generate various social benefits as well. Events management literature considers social impacts, focusing on community involvement, integration and interaction (Shone and Parry, 2004; Yeoman et al., 2004; Bowdin et al., 2006) and building in these impacts as a component in the process of event planning. Shone and Parry (2004: p. 54), for example, list such benefits as creating better social interaction, helping to develop community cohesion, increasing cultural and social understanding and improving the community's identity and confidence in itself. Practitioners can perceive events as a means to achieve strategic social leverage (Chalip, 2006) and promote inclusion and wider cohesiveness, confronting the isolation of computer and television and the breakdown of the traditional family and wider community scaffolding (Shone and Parry, 2004). Such ideas also relate to what Shaw and Williams (2004: p. 22) refer to as the 'experience economy' whereby those who are planning the event, in order to leverage a range of benefits, attempt to create a particular atmosphere which, in the case of mega events, often involves spectacle (Chalip, 2006). Chalip, borrowing from Turner and Turner (1978), also refers to the concepts of 'liminality' and 'communitas'. The former refers to a state 'in which the structure and order of normal life dissolves, everyday obligations cease to exist and new forms of relationship are founded, based upon a levelling of structures' (Holden, 2005: p. 148). The other concept, 'communitas', involves the sense of community, albeit on a temporary basis, that is engendered through community cohesion, unity and participation where the sense of 'unity' refers both to the celebratory 'feel-good factor' and physical mass gathering.

Whereas the social benefits associated with major event sports tourism products are usually confined to large cities, major cycle touring events, such as the TdF, enable these social benefits to be brought to a range of places, sometimes small towns. Furthermore, the creation of 'communitas' can be enhanced where an event, such as the TdF, is free because the capacity of a free and free-range spectacle is more open than a restricted, ticketed event. Desbordes (2007) lists the promotion of social cohesion as one of the objectives of the Digne event and the TfL study shows that the event in London and Kent was a social occasion – 'overall...a family and social event with people arriving with family and friends' (Social Research

Associates, 2007). A pre-event survey of Canterbury residents showed substantial interest and support for the event and suggested that about 60 per cent of the population (about 2000) had plans to participate (Bull and Lovell, 2007). Both in London and in Canterbury organizers attempted to create a carnival atmosphere with a programme of additional events. In London, this included a People's Village and Cycling Festival (a free celebration in Hyde Park of cycling in London) while, in Canterbury, there was a programme of free music, sport, health and cultural events during the week prior to the race and during the race weekend, together with parades and street markets (Bull and Lovell, 2007).

Cycling event sports tourism, involving both elite cyclists and their entourages as well as spectators of various types, can thus be seen as an important part of the cycling sports tourism product range and are clearly illustrative of a number of themes encountered in this text. They provide further evidence of the importance of major urban centres as sports tourism places but also show that the activities and associated benefits of this form of sports tourism can be distributed to a wide range of settlements both large and small. In addition, such events also provide further illustration of the importance that key decision-makers attach to such events and the fact that sports tourism is being seen as part of broader strategies for developing and regenerating local economies.

CONCLUSION

This chapter has provided an additional case study of sports tourism, namely cycling sports tourism. Cycling sports tourism itself, however, is a multifaceted phenomenon and the first section of the chapter was concerned to offer some insights into this complexity and the difficulties associated with identifying and defining cycling sports tourism's many different forms. It also provided a useful illustration of how one of the principal conceptual ideas of the book, the Revised Sports Tourism Participation Model, could be utilized to provide a better understanding of such complexity. In addition to examining the nature and extent of cycling sports tourism, other sections of the chapter engaged key policy issues, another key theme of this text, and provided useful insights into the ways in which cycling sports tourism is making substantial environmental, economic and social impacts in a variety of different places through its potential as a green, more sustainable, form of tourism and, in the case of major cycle races, as a vehicle for providing spectator events and the generation of income. In some places, such as certain rural areas, its development can generate both badly needed revenue and jobs as well as a sustainable form of tourism that avoids the congestion and pollution more often associated with car-borne tourists, thus helping to preserve those environments that attract tourists in the first place. Thus, it is not surprising that policy-makers are encouraging its expansion but, elsewhere in non-rural areas, as has been seen in the context of major cycle races, it is an activity that is encouraged for its social and economic benefits with substantial revenue being generated by those towns and cities which host key stages in such events. In relation to these various policy initiatives, however, what this chapter has also shown is that, once again, there is no clear integrated sport–tourism policy network at work and that the sports tourism benefits are fortuitous. In the main, the policy-makers are located primarily within the tourism policy community, seeing cycling sports tourism as a means of generating more tourism development, while, in the case of sustainable cycling sports tourism, the agenda has been driven by those interested in sustainable transport.

Epilogue – Progress in Sports Tourism?

In the epilogue to the first edition of this text, we cast our eyes back over twenty years to Sue Glyptis' (1982) study of sport and tourism in five European countries because we felt that her work marked the beginning of a growth of interest and research in the area. In doing so, we examined the three 'needs' for the field that Glyptis (1982) identified. It is perhaps a useful exercise, five years on from the first edition of this text, and now over a quarter of a century on from Glyptis' (1982) work, to re-examine these 'needs':

1. A recognition of the tourist potential of sport and the sports development potential of tourism

2. The establishment of working partnerships between sport and tourism policy-makers and providers at national, regional and local level to develop facilities and services for active holidays

3. Undertaking more detailed market research to establish consumer profiles and satisfaction, and potential market sectors (p. 70).

In 2004, we noted that much of the literature in the field since Glyptis' (1982) paper had focused on the first 'need' and fell into the category of 'advocacy' work that argues and makes the case for the links between sport and tourism. We emphasized our belief that the days of such advocacy work had passed and that the second and third of Glyptis' (1982) needs had become the most pressing. In the five years since 2004, there has been little or no evidence of such advocacy work and, as such, it would appear that researchers are now focusing on more substantive concerns.

However, we also noted in 2004 that sports tourism research was becoming dominated by research into impacts and, furthermore, that often such impacts research was in the shape of 'unconnected small-scale case studies' (Weed and Bull, 2004: p. 205) that made little or no contribution to the body of knowledge in sports tourism. This is a theme that one of us has continued to address (Weed, 2005c, 2006b), demonstrating through an extensive systematic review and meta-evaluation of sports tourism knowledge development that, 'sports tourism as an area of study lacks methodological diversity [and] rarely tends to answer "why" questions' (Weed, 2005c: p. 231) with more than a third of studies failing to 'embed discussions within a clear theoretical framework' (Weed, 2006b: p. 22). Therefore, although advocacy work has fortunately become obsolete, there have still been issues relating to the quality of sports tourism research that have concerned the field in recent years. These can perhaps be summarized as: a preponderance of poor quality impacts research; a lack of a clear body of theory; and a lack of methodological diversity.

It is interesting that impacts research was not one of the 'needs' identified by Glyptis in 1982, as this is certainly the area that has most concerned researchers in sports tourism. Weed's (2006b) systematic review showed that event impact research was the single largest body of work in the five years from 2000. However, as the discussions in Chapter 2 implied, there is an increasing trend to replace impacts research with an approach based on leveraging. Chalip (2004) explains the difference:

> *Unlike impact assessments, the study of leverage has a* strategic and tactical focus. *The objective is to identify strategies and tactics that can be implemented prior to and during an event in order to generate particular outcomes. Consequently, leveraging implies a much more* pro-active approach *to* capitalizing on opportunities, *rather than impacts research which simply measures outcomes.*

Laurence Chalip and his colleagues have been at the forefront of developing a leveraging approach to developing strategies to maximize the economic benefits of event sports tourism (e.g. Chalip and Leyns, 2002; Chalip 2004; O'Brien and Chalip, 2007). We feel that this is an important 'paradigm shift' and, although not extensively addressed in this text due to its focus on sports tourism stakeholders, the need for leveraging strategies features strongly in our examinations of the way in which the economic benefits of event sports tourism can be developed (Bull and Lovell, 2007; Weed, 2008a). Chalip and colleagues have also more recently turned their attention to wider aspects of leverage (e.g. Costa and Chalip, 2005; Chalip, 2006; O'Brien and Chalip, 2007) beyond both economic impacts and events, and a recent systematic review into the potential physical activity and sports participation legacies of the London 2012 Olympic Games further demonstrates the utility of a leveraging approach beyond economic impacts (Weed et al., 2008; Weed, 2008a). As such, we suggest that the way forward in developing positive impacts and minimizing negative impacts from sports tourism across its full product range is to employ a leveraging approach. Not least because, as Chapter 2 notes, the concept of leveraging helps bridge knowledge of participation, policy and provision, something that both this and the previous edition of this text have striven to do.

Several authors have embarked on projects to address the lack of a clear body of theory in sports tourism research. Examples include the special issues of *Sport in Society* and *European Sport Management Quarterly*, edited in 2005 by Heather Gibson and Mike Weed respectively, and their subsequent book projects, *Sport Tourism Concepts and Theories* (Gibson, 2006) and *Sport & Tourism: A Reader* (Weed, 2008c). However, these examples represent collections of theoretically robust but disparate papers each addressing separate issues in sports tourism. Taking a more integrated approach, Tom Hinch and James Higham have suggested a framework for research (Hinch and Higham, 2001) and a geographic approach (Higham and Hinch, 2006) respectively. Yet, while their approaches have been integrated, they have been, by their own admission, limited to largely geographical perspectives.

In this text, therefore, we have attempted to present an approach that is both integrated and multidisciplinary. We have drawn on perspectives from psychology, geography, sociology, policy studies, marketing and management to present an integrated analysis of the relationships between the behaviours, motivations and strategies of stakeholders in sports tourism. In doing so we have noted that the 'working partnerships' between policy-makers for sport and for tourism called for by Glyptis (1982) have not been widely established (see Chapters 6 and 7), with agencies responsible for sport and for tourism still being generally reluctant to work together or showing a lack of appreciation of the nature and extent of the relationship between sport and tourism. Gibson noted in 1998 that such lack of appreciation and reluctance to work together was mirrored in some areas of academia, where some doubted the legitimacy of sports tourism as an area for academic attention. Ten years on, the issue appears to have progressed from being one of academic legitimacy to being one of the most appropriate subject perspectives from which to examine sports tourism. Even within sports tourism, some academics feel that research should be underpinned by either perspectives from tourism or by perspectives from sport, with few recognizing the potential of an integrated approach. However, to insist on examining sports tourism from the perspective of only either sport or tourism fails to understand the unique experience of sports tourism as an interaction of activity, people and place that cannot be reduced to a mere tourism market niche or sports activity away from home. Furthermore, examining sports tourism as a part of the tourism or the sports industry focuses attention on providers and neglects the development of understanding of the motivations and behaviours of the sports tourists themselves. This area has been addressed in Chapters 3, 4 and 5 of this book, which attempt to make a theoretically informed contribution to the third 'need' identified by Glyptis (1982) in an area which, although expanding, has been plagued by descriptive research that rarely offers conceptual insight.

The lack of methodological diversity in sports tourism has been commented upon by Weed (2005b, 2006c) and Higham and Hinch (2006). Specifically, that sports tourism is dominated by postivist research approaches to the collection of largely quantitative data. In discussing the reasons for this, Weed (2006c) notes that research in any area is shaped by the way in which research in that area is currently conducted and suggests corollaries with Kuhn's (1962) concept of 'normal science', where research in an area (Kuhn was talking at the much broader level of science as a whole) is conducted according to the conventions of what is considered to be 'normal science'. Kuhn's (1962) seminal text was called *The Structure of Scientific Revolutions* and remains a much quoted, and still hotly contested, text in the philosophy of research today. The title of the text represents Kuhn's (1962) view that 'normal science' will remain the norm until a critical mass of alternative research conducted according to a more insightful approach is achieved. Until this point, any 'dissenting voices' from the practice of 'normal science' will be seen as anomalous, or small adaptations will be made – Kuhn (1962) calls this 'stretching normal science' – to accommodate such dissenting voices.

McFee (2007) claims that there is no such thing as 'normal science' in the social sciences because there are a multiplicity of competing and complementary paradigms, none of which are dominant or hegemonic. McFee (2007) sees this as being a healthy state of affairs which brings a range of alternative perspectives to bear on the issues that the social sciences face. Drawing on McFee's (2007) view, the intention is not to suggest that a 'scientific revolution' replacing the dominant positivist approach in sports tourism research with a different dominant approach is required. Rather, the recommendation is that the sports tourism research enterprise makes an effort to become epistemologically and methodologically heterogeneous and diverse, as befits a multidisciplinary research area that draws on a range of subject areas for synergistic insights.

In drawing this text to a close, therefore, the question (reflecting the question-marked title of this epilogue) is what progress is being made in research into sports tourism? First, as the authors, we of course claim that this text contributes considerably to progress. Specifically, that the conceptualization of sports tourism experiences as deriving from the interaction of activity, people and place provides an important foundation and that considering sports tourism as a set of trip behaviours rather than a trip purpose represents important progress. Similarly, we see the analysis of the role of sports tourism in the trip decision-making process as an important progression. We also suggest that the Revised Sports Tourism Participation Model developed in Chapter 5 provides a framework to progress towards a more theoretically robust *understanding* (rather than description) of sports tourism behaviours. In relation to policy, it appears that progress is required in practice rather than research, although the analysis in this text does suggest that liaison might be most effectively developed on a smaller geographical scale (be it on a regional basis, or nationally in small countries) or in relation to single products. It also suggests that liaison might be stimulated by an exogenous shock to the policy system, such as that provided by the hosting of an Olympic Games. The Policy Wheel for Sport and Tourism presented in Chapter 7 represents an evolution of the areas in which it might reasonably be expected that sports and tourism agencies should collaborate and we feel that this is a useful tool to inform both future policy development and future policy research. Finally, the text has made progress in understanding provision, particularly in developing an updated Model of Sports Tourism Product Types (Chapter 8) that incorporates new perspectives on a 'Supplementary Sports Tourism' product type and on the vicarious consumption of sports tourism products.

Of course, it would be an exercise in supreme arrogance to claim that we alone were contributing to progress in sports tourism and, as such, Chapter 2 provided an overview of what we consider to be the most significant sports tourism research conducted since the turn of the Millennium. In particular, we feel that the perspectives provided by Laurence Chalip on leveraging, Heather Gibson on Role Theory and Tom Hinch and James Higham on Authenticity represent important aspects of progress. However, in concluding this epilogue we wish to encourage all researchers working in sports tourism to ask three key questions of their research:

1. What theoretical perspectives underpin my research?

2. Are my methods appropriate to answer my research questions?

3. How do the answers to my research questions contribute to knowledge?

We feel that the ability to provide full and adequate answers to these three questions for all sports tourism research will represent the most significant progress in sports tourism.

References

Agne-Traub, (1989). Volkssporting and tourism: something for the working class. *Leisure Information Quarterly*, 15(4), 6–8.

Bailey, P. (1987). *Leisure and class in Victorian England: rational recreation and the contest for control*, 1830–1885. London: Methuen.

Baker, M.J. and Gordon, A.W. (1976). *Market for winter sports facilities in Scotland*. Edinburgh: Scottish Tourist Board.

Baker, W.J. (1982). *Sports in the western world*. Totowa, NJ: Rowman and Littlefield.

Bale, J. (1989). *Sports geography*. London: E & FN Spon.

Bale, J. (1994). *Landscapes of modern sport*. Leicester: Leicester University Press.

Bale, J. (2003). *Sports geography*, 2nd edn. London: Spon.

Barker, M.L. (1982). Traditional landscape and mass tourism in the Alps. *Geographical Review*, 72, 395–415.

Bartram, S.A. (2001). Serious leisure careers among whitewater kayakers: a feminist perspective. *World Leisure Journal*, 43(2), 4–11.

Bayeux, P. and Chazaud, P. (1997). Les Collectivités Locales face au Tourisme Sportif. *Cahiers Espaces*, 52, 76–94.

Beedie, P. (2003a). Mountain guiding and adventure tourism: reflections on the choreography of the experience. *Leisure Studies*, 22(2), 146–167.

Beedie, P. (2003b). Adventure tourism. In *Sport and adventure tourism* (Hudson, S., ed.). New York: Haworth Hospitality Press.

Beedie, P. and Hudson, S. (2003). Emergence of mountain-based adventure tourism. *Annals of Tourism Research*, 30(3), 625–643.

Benson, J.K. (1982). Networks and policy sectors: a framework for extending intergovermental analysis. In *Inter-Organisational Co-ordination* (Roger, D. and Whitten, D., eds). Iowa: Iowa State University.

Biddle, S.J.H. (2006). Research synthesis in sport and exercise psychology: chaos in the brickyard revisited. *European Journal of Sport Science*, 6(2), 97–102.

Boissevan, J. (1993). Some problems with cultural tourism in Malta, Paper presented at the *International Conference on Sustainable Tourism in Islands and Small States*. Foundation for International Studies, Malta (unpublished).

Boon, M.A. (1984). Understanding skiing behaviour. *Society and Leisure*, 7(2), 397–406.

Bourdieu, P. (1978). Sport and social class. *Social Science Information*, 18(6), 820–833.

Bowdin, G., Allen, J., O'Toole, W. and Harris, R. (2006). *Events management*, 2nd edn. Oxford: Elsevier.

Bramwell, B. (1997a). A sport mega-event as a sustainable tourism development strategy. *Tourism Recreation Research*, 22(2), 13–19.

Bramwell, B. (1997b). User satisfaction and product development in urban tourism. *Tourism Management*, 19(1), 35–47.

Bramwell, B. (1998a). Strategic planning before and after a mega-event. *Tourism Management*, 18(3), 167–176.

Bramwell, B. (1998b). Event tourism in Sheffield: a sustainable approach to urban development. In *Sustainable tourism management: principles and practice*, (Bramwell, B., Goytia Prat, I., Henry, I.P., Jackson, G.A.M., Richards, G. and van der Straaten, J., eds), 2nd edn. Tilburg: Tilburg University Press.

Braun-LaTour, K., Grinley, M.J. and Loftus, E.F. (2006). Tourist memory distortion. *Journal of Travel Research*, 44(4), 360–367.

Breakell, B. (2006). Activity tourism – developing cycle tourism in the North York moors and coast. *Countryside Recreation*, 14(2), 14–16.

Briggs, S. (2001). *Successful tourism marketing: a practical handbook*, 2nd edn. London: Kogan Page.

Brincat, I. (1995). Sport tourism', *Cobweb, Business Journal*, Special Issue on Sustainable Tourism in Malta, AIESEC.

British Tourist Authority (1981). *Tourism, the UK – the broad perspective*. London: BTA.

British Tourist Authority/ English Tourist Board (1990). *The UK tourist statistics*. London: BTA/ETB.

Brown, G. (2007). Sponsor hospitality at the Olympic Games: an analysis of the implications for tourism. *International Journal of Tourism Research*, 9(5), 315–327.

Buckley, R. (2007a). Adventure tourism products: price, duration, size, skill, remoteness. *Tourism Management*, 28(6), 1428–1433.

Buckley, R. (ed.) (2007b). *Adventure tourism*. Wallingford: CABI.

Buckworth, J. and Dishman, R.K. (2002). *Exercise psychology*. Champaign, IL: Human Kinetics.

Bull, C.J. (2005). Sport tourism destination resource analysis. In *Sport tourism destinations* (Higham, J., ed.). Oxford: Elsevier.

Bull, C.J. (2006). Racing cyclists as sports tourists: the experiences and behaviours of a case study group of cyclists in East Kent, England. *Journal of Sport & Tourism*, 11(3/4), 259–274.

Bull, C.J. and Lovell, J. (2007). The impact of hosting major sporting events on local residents: an analysis of the views and perceptions of Canterbury residents in relation to the *Tour de France* 2007. *Journal of Sport & Tourism*, 12(3/4), 229–248.

Bull, C.J. and Weed, M.E. (1999). Niche markets and small island tourism: the development of sports tourism in Malta. *Managing Leisure*, 4(2), 142–155.

Bull, C.J., Hoose, J. and Weed, M.E. (2003). *An introduction to leisure studies*. Harlow: Financial Times Prentice Hall.

Bull, P. (1997). Mass tourism in the Balearic Islands: an example of concentrated dependence. In *Island tourism: trends and prospects* (Lockwood, D.G. and Drakakis-Smith, D., eds). London: Pinter.

Burbank, M., Andranovich, G. and Heying, C.H. (2001). *Olympic dreams: the impact of mega events on local politics*. Colorado: Lynne Rienner Publishers.

Burke, V. and Collins, D. (2002). Outdoor management development: the provider's perspective on optimising the process of skills transfer. In *Proceedings of the 10th European Congress on Sport Management* (Laaksonen, K., Lopponen, P., Nykanen, E. and Puronaho, K., eds). Jyvaskyla: EASM.

Burns, J.P.A., Hatch, J.H. and Mules, T.J. (1986). *The Adelaide Grand Prix: the impact of a special event*. Adelaide: Centre for South Australian Economic Studies, University of Adelaide.

Burton, R. (1995). *Travel geography*. London: Pitman Publishing.

Busby, G. and Rendle, S. (2000). The transition from tourism on farms to farm tourism. *Tourism Management*, 21(6), 635–642.

Buswell, R.J. (1996). Tourism in the Balearic Islands. In *Tourism in Spain: critical perspectives* (Towner, M. and Newton, M., eds). Wallingford: CAB International.

Butler, R.W. (1998). Rural recreation and tourism. In *The geography of rural change* (Ilbery, B., ed.). London: Longman.

Butler, R.W. (2005). The influence of sport on destination development: the case of golf at St Andrews. In *Sport tourism destinations* (Higham, J., ed.). Oxford: Elsevier.

Butler, R.W., Hall, C.M. and Jenkins, J.M. (eds) (1997). *Tourism and recreation in rural areas*. Chichester: John Wiley & Sons.

Butts, S.L. (2001). Good to the last drop: understanding surfers' motivations. *Sociology of Sport on Line*, 4(1). http://physed.otago.ac.nz/sosol/v4i1/v4i1butt.htm

Carlsen, J. and Taylor, A. (2003). Mega-events and urban renewal: the case of the Manchester 2002 Commonwealth Games. *Event Managament*, 8, 15–22.

Carmichael, B. (1996). Conjoint analysis of downhill skiers used to improve data collection for market segmentation. *Journal of Travel and Tourism Marketing*, 5(3), 187–206.

Carnibella, G., Fox, A., Fox, K., McCann, J., Marsh, J. and Marsh, P. (1996). *Football violence in Europe*. Oxford: Social Issues Research Centre.

Carron, A.V. and Hausenblaus, H.L. (1998). *Group dynamics in sport*. Morgantown, Virginia: Fitness Information Technology.

Chalip, L. (2004). Beyond impact: a general model for sport event leverage. In *Sport tourism: interrelationships, impacts and issues* (Ritchie, B. and Adair, D., eds). Clevedon: Channel View.

Chalip, L. (2006). Towards social leverage of sport events. *Journal of Sport & Tourism*, 11(2), 109–127.

Chalip, L. and Leyns, A. (2002). Local business leveraging of a sport event: managing an event for economic benefit. *Journal of Sport Management*, 16(2), 132–158.

Chalkley, B., Jones, A., Kent, M. and Sims, P. (1992). Barcelona: Olympic City. *Geography Review*, 6(1), 2–4.

Chapin, T.S. (1996). A new era of professional sports in the northwest: facility location as an economic development strategy in Seattle, Portland and Vancouver. Paper presented to the *Sport in the City* Conference, Sheffield, UK.

Chubb, M. and Chubb, H. (1981). *One third of our time? An introduction to recreation behavior and resource*. New York: Wiley.

Church, N.J., Laroche, M. and Rosenblatt, J.A. (1985). Consumer brand categorisation for durables with limited problem solving: an empirical test and proposed extension of the Brisoux-Laroche model. *Journal of Economic Psychology*, 6, 231–253.

Clark, G., Darrall, J., Grove-White, R., Macnaghten, P. and Urry, J. (1994). *Leisure landscapes, leisure culture and the English countryside: challenges and conflicts*. Lancaster: Centre for Environmental Change, Lancaster University/CPRE.

Clark, J. and Critcher, C. (1985). *The devil makes work: leisure in capitalist Britain*. London: Methuen.

Clawson, M., Held, R. and Stoddard, C. (1960). *Land for the future*. Baltimore: Johns Hopkins Press.

Clowes, J. and Tapp, A. (1998). From the 4 Ps to the 3 Rs of marketing: using relationship marketing to retain football club supporters and improve income. *Managing Leisure*, 3(1), 18–25.

Cockerell, N. (1994). Market segments: the international ski market in Europe. *EIU Travel and Tourism Analyst*, 3, 34–55.

Cohen, E. (1983). The social psychology of tourist behaviour. *Annals of Tourism Research*, 15(1), 29–46.

Collins, M.F. (1995). Sights on sport. *Leisure Management*, 15(9), 26–28.

Collins, M.F. and Jackson, G.A.M. (2001). Evidence for a sports tourism continuum. Paper to *Journeys in Leisure*, Leisure Studies Association Conference, Luton, July.

Collins, M.F. and Jackson, G.A.M. (1999). The economic impact of sport and tourism. In *Sport tourism* (Standeven, J. and De Knop, P., eds). London: Human Kinetics.

Cooper, C.P., Fletcher, J., Wanhill, S., Gilbert, D. and Shepherd, R. (1998). *Tourism: principles and practice*, 2nd edn. Harlow: Pitman.

Cope, A., Doxford, D. and Millar, G. (1999). Counting users of informal recreational facilities. *Managing Leisure*, 4, 229–244.

Cope, A., Downward, P. and Lumsdon, L. (2004). The North Sea cycle route: economic impacts of linear trails. *Countryside Recreation*, 12(1), 2–5.

Costa, C. and Chalip, L. (2005). Adventure sport tourism in rural revitalisation: an ethnographic evaluation. *European Sport Management Quarterly*, 5(3), 259–281.

Countryside Recreation Network (1995). *Sport in the countryside: planning and management for sport and active recreation*. Proceedings from a workshop held at Aston Business School, Birmingham, 27 April, 1995.

Countryside Recreation Research and Advisory Group (1991). *Young people, adventure and the countryside*. Bristol: CRRAG.

Critcher, C. (1991). Sporting civic pride: Sheffield and the World Student Games of 1991. In *Leisure in the 1990s: rolling back the welfare state*. Brighton: Leisure Studies Association.

Croall, J. (1995). *Preserve or destroy: tourism and the environment*. London: Calouste Gulbenkian Foundation.

Crompton, J.L. (2006). Economic impact studies: instruments for political shenanigans. *Journal of Travel Research*, 45(1), 67–82.

Cross, G. (1990). *A Social history of leisure since 1600*. State College, PA: Venture Publishing.

Crosset, T. and Beal, B. (1997). The use of 'subculture' and 'subworld' in ethnographic works on sport. *Sociology of Sport Journal*, 14(1), 73–85.

Crouch, G.I. and Ritchie, J.R.B. (1999). Tourism, competitiveness, and societal prosperity. *Journal of Business Research*, 44(3), 137–152.

Crozier, M. (1964). *The bureaucratic phenomenon*. Chicago: University of Chicago Press.

Crystal (2006). *The Ski Industry Report 2006*. Luton: Crystal Holidays.

Crystal (2008). *The Ski Industry Report 2008*. Luton: Crystal Holidays.

Cunningham, H. (1975). *Leisure in the industrial revolution*, c. 1780–1880. London: Croom Helm.

Cushman, G., Veal, A.J. and Zuzaneck, J. (eds) (1996). Cross-national leisure participation research: a future. In *World leisure participation: free time in the global village*. London: CAB International.

D'Abaco, G. (1991). Marketing parks and recreational facilities as tourism attractions – experiences from the Victoria Tourism Commission's 'Melbourne Now' campaign. In *Who dares wins – parks, recreation and tourism*, Conference Proceedings, Vol. 2. Canberra: Royal Institute of Parks and Recreation.

Dahl, R.A. (1956). *A preface to democratic theory*. Chicago: University of Chicago Press.

Dalton, M. (1959). *Men who manage*. New York: Wiley.

Davidson, T.L. (1985). Strategic planning: a competitive necessity. Paper to the *16th TTRA Conference, the battle for market share: strategies in research and marketing*, Salt Lake City, June.

Davies, N. (1997). *Europe: a history*. London: Pimlico.

Decrop, A. (2006). *Vacation decision making*. Wallingford: CABI.

Decrop, A. and Snelders, D. (2005). A grounded typology of vacation decision-making. *Tourism Management*, 26, 121–132.

De Knop, P. (1987). Some thoughts on the influence of sport on tourism. In *Proceedings of the International Seminar and Workshop on Outdoor Education, Recreation and Sport Tourism*. Netanya, Israel: Wingate Institute for Physical Education and Sport.

De Knop, P. (1990). Sport for all and active tourism. *Journal of the World Leisure and Recreation Association*, Fall, 30–36.

Delpy, L. (1999). Disney's approach to sports tourism: developing sports facilities to increase tourism. In *Sport tourism* (Standeven, J. and De Knop, P., eds). Champaign: Human Kinetics.

Department of Culture, Media and Sport (2001). *Staging international sporting events*. Government response to the Third Report from the Culture, Media and Sport Committee Session 2000–2001, Presented to Parliament by the Secretary of Culture, Media and Sport By Command of Her Majesty, October 2001.

Department of Culture, Media and Sport/Strategy Unit (2002). *Game plan: a strategy for delivering government's sport and physical activity objectives*. London: Cabinet Office.

Department of National Heritage (1995). *Sport: raising the game*. London: DNH.

Desbordes, M. (2007). A review of the economic impact studies done on the Tour de France: methodological aspects and first results. *International Journal of Sport Management and Marketing*, 2(5/6), 526–540.

Destination Sheffield (1995). *An event-led city and tourism marketing strategy for Sheffield*. Sheffield: Destination Sheffield.

Dimanche, F. and Havitz, M.E. (1994). Consumer behaviour in tourism: review and extension of four study areas. *Journal of Travel and Tourism Marketing*, 3(3), 37–57.

Dobson, N. and Gratton, C. (1995). From 'city of steel' to 'city of sport': an evaluation of Sheffield's attempts to use sport as a vehicle for urban regeneration. Paper presented at the *Recreation in the City* conference, Staffordshire University, Stoke on Trent.

Dobson, N. and Gratton, C. (1997). *The economic impact of sports events: Euro '96 and VI Fina World Masters Swimming Championship in Sheffield*. Sheffield: Leisure Industries Research Centre.

Dobson, N., Gratton, C. and Holliday, S. (1997). The economic impact of sports events: Euro '96 and the VI FINA World Masters Swimming Championships in Sheffield. *The Regional Review*, 16–19.

Donnelly, M.P., Vaske, J.J., DeRuiter, D.S. and Loomis, J.B. (1998). Economic impacts of state parks: effects of park visitation, park facilities, and county economic diversification. *Journal of Park and Recreation Administration*, 16(4), 52–72.

Donnelly, P. (1993). Subcultures in sport: resilience and transformation. In *Sport in social development* (Ingham, A.G. and Loy, J.W., eds). Illinois: Human Kinetics.

Doorne, S. (1998). Power, participation and perception: an insider's perspective on the politics of the Wellington Waterfront redevelopment. *Current Issues in Tourism*, 1(2), 129–166.

Dowding, K. (1995). Model or metaphor? A critical review of the policy network approach. *Political Studies*, 43(1), 136–158.

Downs, A. (1967). *Inside bureaucracy*. Boston: Little Brown.

Downward, P. (2005). Critical (realist) reflection on policy and management research in sport, tourism and sports tourism. *European Sport Management Quarterly*, 5(3), 302–322.

Downward, P. and Lumsdon, L. (2001). The development of recreational cycle routes: an evaluation of user needs. *Managing Leisure*, 6(1), 50–60.

Duda, J. (2001). Achievement goal research in sport: pushing the boundaries and clarifying some misunderstandings. In *Advances in motivation in sport and exercise* (Roberts, C.G., ed.). Champaign, IL: Human Kinetics.

Dulac, C. and Henry, I. (2001). Sport and social regulation in the city: the cases of Grenoble and Sheffield. *Society and Leisure*, 24(1), 47–78.

Dunning, E., Murphy, P. and Williams, J. (1988). *The roots of football hooliganism: an historical and sociological study*. London: Routledge and Kegan Paul.

Dwyer, L. and Forsyth, P. (eds) (2006). *International handbook on the economics of tourism*. Cheltenham: Edward Elgar.

EcoGIS (2002). *Submission on cycle tourism to the tourism strategy group*. Paper prepared by EcoGIS on behalf of the Cycling Promotion Fund of Australia and Bicycle Federation of Australia.

Elson, M.J., Heaney, D. and Reynolds, G. (1995). *Good practice in the planning and management of sport and active recreation in the countryside*. London: The Sports Council and Countryside Commission.

English Tourism Council (2001). *Foot and mouth disease and tourism*. www. englsihtourism.org.uk

Erlinger, P., la Louveau, C. and Metoudi, M. (1985). *Practiques sportives des francais*. Paris: Ministere de Jeunesse et Sports.

European Commission (1995). *Tourism and the European Union: a practical guide*. Luxembourg: Office for Official Publications of the European Communities.

Everden, N. (1992). *The social creation of nature*. Baltimore: Johns Hopkins Press.

Fairley, S. (2003). In search of relived social experience: group-based nostalgia sport tourism. *Journal of Sport Management*, 17(3), 284–304.

Fairley, S. and Gammon, S. (2005). Something lived, something learned: nostalgia's expanding role in sport tourism. *Sport in Society*, 8(2), 182–197.

Farmer, R.J. (1992). Surfing: motivations, values and culture. *Journal of Sport Behaviour*, 15(3), 241–257.

Faulks, P., Richie, B. and Fluker, M. (2007). *Cycle tourism in Australia: an investigation into its size and scope*. Queensland, Australia: Sustainable Tourism Cooperative Research Centre.

Feldman, F. (2004). *Pleasure and the good life*. Buckingham: Oxford University Press.

Ferras, R., Picheral, H. and Vielzeuf, B. (1979). *Languedoc Roussillon*. Paris: Flammarion et Editions Famot.

Finley, M.I. and Pleket, H.W. (1976). *The Olympic Games*. Edinburgh: R and R Clark.

Fredline, E. (2005). Host and guest relations and sport tourism. *Sport in Society*, 8(2), 263–279.

Foley, M., McPherson, G. and Matheson, C. (2006). Globalisation and Singaporean festivals. *International Journal of Event Management Research*, 1(2), 1–15.

Fox, K. (1999). *The racing tribe: watching the horsewatchers*. London: Metro Books.

Fraietta, J. (2004). *Cycle tourism research summary*, Paper prepared for Alberta Economic Development, Canada.

Freeman, J.L. (1955). *The political process*. New York: Doubleday.

Gammon, S. (2002). Fantasy, nostalgia and the pursuit of what never was. In *Sport tourism principles and practice* (Gammon, S. and Kurtzman, J., eds) Eastbourne: LSA.

Gammon, S. (2004). Secular pilgrimage and sport tourism. In *Sport tourism: interrelationships, impacts and issues* (Ritchie, B. and Adair, D., eds). Clevedon: Channel View.

Gammon, S. and Kurtzman, J. (eds) (2002). Editors' introduction. In *Sport tourism: principles and practice*. Eastbourne: LSA.

Gammon, S. and Ramshaw, G. (eds) (2007). *Heritage, sport and tourism*. London: Routledge.

Gammon, S. and Robinson, T. (1997/2003). Sport and tourism: a conceptual framework. *Journal of Sport Tourism*, 8(1), 21–26.

Garrigues, P. (1988). *Evolution de la practique sportive des francais*, Coll. De l'INSEE, 134 M., October. Paris: Institut National de Statistique et d'Etudes Economiques.

Gartner, W. (1996). *Tourism development: principles, processes and policies*. New York: Van Nostrand Reinhold.

Getz, D. (1991). *Festivals, special events and tourism*. New York: Van Nostrand Reinhold.

Getz, D. (2003). Sport event tourism: planning, development and marketing. In *Sport and adventure tourism* (Hudson, S., ed.). New York: Haworth Hospitality Press.

Getz, D. (2005). *Event management and event tourism*, 2nd edn. New York: Cognizant Communication Corporation.

Gibson, H.J. (1994). *Some predictors of tourist role preference for men and women over the adult life course*, (PhD Thesis). Storrs: The University of Conneticut.

Gibson, H.J. (1996). Thrill seeking vacations: a lifespan perspective. *Loisir et Societe/Society and Leisure*, 19(2), 439–458.

Gibson, H.J. (1998). Sport tourism: a critical analysis of research. *Sport Management Review*, 1(1), 45–76.

Gibson, H. (2001). Sport tourism at a crossroad? Considerations for the future. Keynote Address to the Leisure Studies Association Annual Conference, *Journeys in Leisure*, Luton, July.

Gibson, H.J. (2002). Sport tourism at a crossroad? Considerations for the future. In *Sport tourism: principles and practice* (Gammon, S. and Kurtzman, J., eds). Eastbourne: LSA.

Gibson, H.J. (2004). Moving beyond the 'what is and who' of sport tourism to understanding 'why'. *Journal of Sport Tourism*, 9(3), 247–265.

Gibson, H.J. (2005a). Sport tourism concepts and theories: an introduction. *Sport in Society*, 8(2), 133–141.

Gibson, H.J. (2005b). Understanding sport tourism experiences. In *Sport tourism destinations* (Higham, J., ed.). Oxford: Elsevier.

Gibson, H.J. (2005c). Towards an understanding of why sport tourists do what they do. *Sport in Society*, 8(2), 198–217.

Gibson, H.J. (ed.) (2006). *Sport tourism concepts and theories*. London: Routledge.

Gibson, H.J. and Pennington-Gray, L. (2005). Insights from role theory: understanding golf tourism. *Europen Sport Management Quarterly*, 5(4), 443–468.

Gibson, H.J. and Yiannakis, A. (2002). Tourist roles: needs and the adult life course. *Annals of Tourism Research*, 29, 358–383.

Gibson, H., Willming, C. and Holdnak, A. (2003). Small-scale event sport tourism: fans as tourists. *Tourism Management*, 24(2), 181–190.

Gillett, P. and Kelly, S. (2007). Non-local masters games participants: an investigation of competitive active sport tourist motives. *Journal of Sport & Tourism*, 11(3/4), 239–257.

Giulianotti, R. (2002). Supporters, followers, fans and flaneurs: a taxonomy of spectator identities in football. *Journal of Sport and Social Issues*, 26(1), 25–46.

Glyptis, S.A. (1982). *Sport and tourism in Western Europe*. London: British Travel Education Trust.

Glyptis, S.A. (1991a). Sport and tourism. In *Progress in tourism, recreation and hospitality management* (Cooper, C.P., ed.), Vol. 3. London: Belhaven Press.

Glyptis, S. (1991b). *Countryside recreation*. Harlow: Longman.

Glyptis, S. (1992). The changing demand for countryside recreation. In *Contemporary rural systems in transition* (Bowler, I.R., Bryant, C.R. and Nellis, M.D., eds), Vol. 2. Wallingford: CAB International.

Goldsmith, M.J. and Rhodes, R.A.W. (1986). *Register of research and research digest on central-local government relations in Britain*. London: ESRC.

Gottdiener, M. (2000). *New forms of consumption: consumers, culture and commodification*. Maryland: Rowman & Littlefield.

Gouldner, A.W. (1954). *Patterns of industrial bureaucracy*. Illinois: Free Press.

Government of Malta (1990). *Structure plan for the Maltese islands*. Valletta: Government of Malta.

Grabler, K. and Zins, A.H. (2002). Vacation decision styles as basis for an automated recommendation system: lessons from observational studies. In *Information and communication technologies in tourism 2002: proceedings of the international conference* (Wober, K.W., Frew, A.J. and Hitz, M., eds). New York: Springer.

Graburn, N.H.H. (1983). The anthropology of tourism. *Annals of Tourism Research*, 10(1), 9–33.

Graburn, N.H.H. (1989). Tourism: the sacred journey. In *Hosts and guests: the anthropology of tourism* (Smith, V., ed.), 2nd edn. Philadephia: University of Pennsylvania.

Grant, W., Patterson, W. and Whitson, C. (1989). *Government and the chemical industry: a comparative study of Britain and West Germany*. Oxford: Clarendon Press.

Gratton, C. and Henry, I.P. (eds) (2001). *Sport in the city: the role of sport in economic and social regeneration*. London: Routledge.

Gratton, C. and Taylor, P. (1985). *Sport and recreation: an economic analysis*. London: E and FN Spon.

Gratton, C., Dobson, N. and Shibli, S. (2000). The economic impacts of major sports events: a case-study of six events. *Managing Leisure*, 5(1), 17–28.

Gratton, C., Shibli, S. and Coleman, R. (2005). The economics of sport tourism at major sports events. In *Sport tourism destinations* (Higham, J., ed.). Oxford: Elsevier.

Grcic-Zubcevic, N. (2001). Swimming and other water activities in tourist centres. In *Sport for all and health tourism* (Bartoluci, M., ed.). Zagreb: CESS.

Green, B.C. (2001). Leveraging subculture and identity to promote sport events. *Sport Management Review*, 4(1), 1–19.

Green, B.C. and Chalip, L. (1998). Sport tourism as the celebration of subculture. *Annals of Tourism Research*, 25(20), 275–291.

Green, B.C. and Jones, I. (2005). Serious leisure, social identity and sport tourism. *Sport in Society*, 8(2), 164–181.

Green, B.C., Costa, C. and Fitzgerald, M. (2003). Marketing the host city: analysing exposure generated by a sport event. *International Journal of Sport Marketing & Sponsorship*, (Dec/Jan), pp. 335–353.

Green, M. (2002). *Western approaches to sport policy*, Loughborough University: *Unpublished Review Paper*.

Green, M. and Houlihan, B. (2005). *Elite sport development: policy learning and political priorities*. London: Routledge.

Green, S. (1982). *Cricketing bygones*. Princes Risborough: Shire Publications.

Greenwood, C. and Yeoman, I. (2006). *Forecast for cycle tourism in Scotland to 2015*. Edinburgh: VisitScotland.

Gregory, A. (1991). *The golden age of travel, 1880–1939*. London: Cassell.

Gunn, C.A. (1990). The new recreation-tourism alliance. *Journal of Park and Recreation Administration*, 8(1), 1–8.

Guttmann, A. (1992). Chariot races, tournaments and the civilizing process. In *Sport and leisure in the civilizing process* (Dunning, E. and Rojek, C., eds). Basingstoke: Macmillan.

Hagger, M.S. and Chatzisarantis, N.L.D. (2005). *The social psychlogy of exercise and sport*. Buckingham: Open University Press.

Hagger, M.S., Chatzisarantis, N.L.D. and Biddle, S.J.H. (2002). A meta-analytic review of the theories of reasoned action and planned behavior in physical activity. *Journal of Sport & Exercise Psychology*, 24(1), 3–32.

Hall, C.M. (1992a). Adventure, sport and health. In *Special interest tourism* (Hall, C.M. and Weiler, B., eds). London: Belhaven Press.

Hall, C.M. (1992b). *Hallmark tourist events: impacts, management and planning*. London: Belhaven.

Hall, C.M. (2000). *Tourism Planning*. Harlow: Prentice Hall.

Hall, C.M. (2001). Imaging, tourism and sports event fever. In *Sport in the city: the role of sport in economic and social regeneration* (Gratton, C. and Henry, I.P., eds). London: Routledge.

Hall, C.M. (2003). *Tourism: rethinking the social science of mobility*. Harlow: Prentice Hall.

Hall, C.M. and Jenkins, J.M. (2003). *Tourism and public policy*. London: Thomson.

Hall, C.M. and Muller, D.K. (2004). *Tourism, mobility and second homes*. Clevedon: Channel View.

Hall, C.M. and Page, S.J. (2006). *The geography of tourism and recreation: environment, place and space*, 3rd edn. London: Routledge.

Hamilton-Smith, E. (1993). In the Australian bush: some reflections on serious leisure. *World Recreation and Leisure*, 35, 10–13.

Harris, J. (2006). The science of research in sport and tourism: some reflections upon the promise of the sociological imagination. *Journal of Sport & Tourism*, 11(2), 152–171.

Harrison, C. (1991). *Countryside recreation in a changing society*. London: TMS Partnership.

Harwood, C.G. (2002). Assessing achievement goals in sport: caveats for consultants and a case for contextualisation. *Journal of Applied Sport Psychology*, 14, 106–119.

Hay, B. (1989). Leisure day trips: the new tourism. In *Tourism and leisure (part two): markets, users and sites* (Botterill, D., ed.). Eastbourne: Leisure Studies Association.

Haywood, L. (1994). Community sports and physical recreation. In *Community leisure and recreation* (Haywood, L., ed.). Oxford: Butterworth Heinemann.

Haywood, L., Kew, F.C., Bramham, P., Spink, J., Capenerhurst, J. and Henry, I.P. (1995). *Understanding leisure*, 2nd edn. Cheltenham: Stanley Thornes.

Hearne, J. (2003). A stakeholder analysis of Nottingham Forest Football Club, *Unpublished BSc Dissertation*. Loughborough: Loughborough University.

Heclo, H. and Wildavski, A. (1974). *The private government of public money*. London: Macmillan.

Henderson, K.A. and Frelke, C.E. (2000). Space as a vital dimension of leisure: the creation of place. *World Leisure Journal*, 42(3), 18–24.

Hennessey, S.M., MacDonald, R. and Maceachern, M. (2008). A framework for understanding golfing visitors to a destination. *Journal of Sport & Tourism*, 13(1), 5–35.

Henry, I.P. (2001). *The politics of leisure policy*, 2nd edn. London: Palgrave.

Henry, I.P. (1993). *The politics of leisure policy*. London: Macmillan.

Henry, I.P. and Matthews, N. (1998). Sport policy and the European Union: the post-Maastricht agenda. *Managing Leisure*, 4(1), 1–17.

Higham, J. (ed.) (2005). *Sport tourism destinations*. Oxford: Elsevier.

Higham, J. and Hinch, T. (2002). Tourism, sport and seasons: the challenges and potential of overcoming seasonality in the sport and tourism sectors. *Tourism Management*, 23(2), 175–185.

Higham, J. and Hinch, T. (2006). Sport and tourism research: a geographic approach. *Journal of Sport & Tourism*, 11(1), 31–50.

Hill, E., O'Sullivan, T. and O'Sullivan, C. (1995). *Creative arts marketing*. Oxford: Butterworth Heinemann.

Hinch, T.D. and Higham, J.E.S. (2001). Sport tourism: a framework for research. *International Journal of Tourism Research*, 3(1), 45–58.

Hinch, T.D. and Higham, J.E.S. (2004). *Sport tourism development*. Clevedon: Channel View Publications.

Hinch, T.D. and Higham, J.E.S. (2005). Sport, tourism and authenticity. *European Sport Management Quarterly*, 5(3), 245–258.

Hinch, T.D. and Higham, J.E.S. (2009). *Sport & tourism: globalisation, mobility & authenticity*. Oxford: Elsevier.

Holden, A. (2005). *Tourism studies and the social sciences*. London: Routledge.

Holloway, J.C. (2003). *The business of tourism*, 6th edn. Harlow: Financial Times Prentice Hall.

Holloway, J.C. and Taylor, N. (2006). *The business of tourism*, 7th edn. Harlow: Pearson.

Holt, R. (1989). *Sport and the British: a modern history*. Oxford: Oxford University Press.

Horne, J., Tomlinson, A. and Whannel, G. (1999). *Understanding sport: an introduction to the sociological and cultural analysis of sport*. London: E & FN Spon.

Houlihan, B. (1991). *The Government and the politics of sport*. London: Routledge.

Houlihan, B. (1994). *Sport and international politics*. London: Harvester Wheatsheaf.

Houlihan, B. (1997). *Sport, policy and politics: a comparative analysis*. New York: Harvester Wheatsheaf.

Houlihan, B. (2002) Personal communication to the author.

Houlihan, B. (ed.) (2003). *Sport and Society*. London: Sage.

Houlihan, B. (ed.) (2008). Sport and globalisation. In *Sport and society*. London: Sage.

Houlihan, B. and Green, M. (eds) (2007). *Comparative elite sport development systems*. Oxford: Butterworth Heinemann.

Houlihan, B. and White, A. (2002). *The politics of sports development: development of sport or development through sport?* London: Routledge.

Hautbois, C. and Durand, C. (2004). Public strategies for local development: the effectiveness of an outdoor activities model. *Managing Leisure*, 9(4), 212–226.

Howard, J.A. (1963). *Marketing management, analysis and planning*. Homewood, IL: Irwin.

Howard, J.A. (1977). *Consumer behavior: application of theory*. New York: McGraw-Hill.

Howard, J.A. and Sheth, J.N. (1969). *The theory of buyer behavior*. New York: John Wiley.

Hudson, S. (1998). There's no business like snow business! Marketing skiing into the 21st century. *Journal of Vacation Marketing*, 4(4), 393–407.

Hudson, S. (2000). *Snow business*. London: Cassell.

Hudson, I. (2001). The use and misusue of economic impact analysis. *Journal of Sport & Social Issues*, 25(1), 20–39.

Hudson, S. (ed.) (2003a). *Sport and adventure tourism*. New York: Haworth Hospitality Press.

Hudson, S. (2003b). Winter sport tourism. In *Sport and adventure tourism*. New York: Haworth Hospitality Press.

Hudson, S., Ritchie, B. and Timur, S. (2004). Measuring destination competitiveness: an empirical study of Canadian ski resorts. *Tourism and Hospitality Planning and Development*, 1(1), 79–94.

Hunt Report (1989). *In search of adventure: a study of the opportunities for adventure and challenge for young people*. Guildford: Talbot Adair Press.

Hutchings, C. (1996). Trouble in paradise. *The Geographical Magazine*, January, 20–22.

Inglis, F. (2000). *The delicious history of the holiday*. London: Routledge.

Inskeep, E. (1994). Tourism planning approach of Malta, Ch. 11 in *National and regional tourism planning*. London: Routledge.

International Tourism Reports (1996). *Malta report no. 4*. Travel and Tourism Intelligence.

IPK International (2001). *Sport activities during the outbound holidays of Germans, the Dutch and the French*. Madrid: WTO.

Iso-Ahola, S.E. (1980). *The social psychology of leisure and recreation*. Iowa: William Brown.

Iso-Ahola, S.E. (1982). Toward a social psychological theory of tourism motivation: a rejoinder. *Annals of Tourism Research*, 9(2), 256–262.

Iso-Ahola, S.E. (1989). Motivation for leisure. In *Understanding leisure and recreation: shaping the past, charting the future* (Jackson, E.L. and Burton, T.L., eds). State College, PA: Venture Publishing.

Iso-Ahola, S.E. and Wissingberger, E. (1990). Perceptions of boredom in leisure: conceptualisation, reliability and validity of the leisure boredom scale. *Journal of Leisure Research*, 22(1), 1–17.

j2ski (2008) www.j2ski.com/ski_news/index.php/industry/uk-ski (accessed 22/8/08)

Jackson, C. (1999). Pedalling in the parks. *National Parks*, March/April, 34–36.

Jackson, G.A.M. and Glyptis, S.A. (1992). Sport and tourism: a review of the literature. *Report to the Sports Council, Recreation Management Group, Loughborough University*. Loughborough: Unpublished.

Jackson, G.A.M. and Reeves, M.R. (1996). Conceptualising the sport-tourism interrelationship: a case study approach. *Paper to the LSA/VVA Conference*, Wageningen, September.

Jackson, G.A.M. and Reeves, M.R. (1998). Evidencing the sport-tourism interrelationship: a case study of elite British athletes. In *Leisure management: issues and applications* (Collins, M.F. and Cooper, I., eds). London: CABI.

Jackson, G.A.M. and Morpeth, N. (1999). Local Agenda 21 and community participation in tourism policy and planning : future or fallacy. *Current Issues in Tourism*, 2(1), 1–38.

Jackson, G.A.M. and Weed, M.E. (2003). The sport-tourism interrelationship. In *Sport and society* (Houlihan, B., ed.). London: Sage.

Jeffries, D. (2001). *Governments and tourism*. Oxford: Butterworth Heinemann.

Jenner, P. and Smith, C. (1992). *The tourism industry and the environment*. London: EIU, cited in Shaw, G. and Williams, A. (2002). *Critical issues in tourism: a geographical perspective*. Oxford: Blackwell.

Jennings, G. (2003). Marine tourism. In *Sport and adventure tourism* (Hudson, S., ed.). New York: Haworth Hospitality Press.

Johansson, S. (2000). Selecting the team: how to get the best value when planning and developing rural sports facilities. In *Planning and developing rural sports facilities*, Official Forum Proceedings. New South Wales: Department of Sport and Recreation.

Johnson, B.R. and Edwards, T. (1994). The commodification of mountaineering. *Annals of Tourism Research*, 21(3), 459–478.

Jones, I. (2000). A model of serious leisure identification: the case of football fandom. *Leisure Studies*, 19(4), 283–298.

Jordan, A.G. (1990). Sub-governments, policy communities and networks: refilling old bottles? *Journal of Theoretical Politics*, 2(3), 319–338.

Jordan, A.G. and Richardson, J.J. (1987). *British politics and the policy process*. London: Allen and Unwin.

Judd, D.R. (ed.) (2002). *The infrastructure of play: building the tourist city*. New York: M.E. Sharpe.

Kane, M. and Zink, R. (2004). Package adventure tours: markers in serious leisure careers. *Leisure Studies*, 23(4), 329–345.

Kasimati, E. (2003). Economic aspects and the summer Olympics: a review of related research. *International Journal of Tourism Research*, 5(6), 433–444.

Katz, E. et al (1992). *The culture of leisure in Israel: changes in patterns of cultural activity, 1970–1990*. Jerusalem: Israel Institute of Applied Social Research.

Kaufman, J.K. (2005). *Consuming visions: mass culture and the Lourdes shrine*. New York: Cornell University Press.

Kavaratzis, M. (2004). From city marketing to city branding: towards a theoretical framework for developing city brands. *Place Branding*, 1(1), 58–73.

Keogh, B. (1980). Motivations and the choice decisions of skiers. *Tourist Review*, 35(1), 18–22.

Kerr, J.H. (1994). *Understanding soccer hooliganism*. Buckingham: Open University Press.

Kerr, W.R. (2003). *Tourism public policy and the strategic management of failure*. Oxford: Elsevier.

Keynote (2001). *Market review: UK travel and tourism*. London: Keynote Market Information.

Keynote (2002). *Market report – health clubs and leisure centres*. London: Keynote Market Information.

Keynote (2006). *Market assessment – activity holidays*. London: Keynote Market Information.

Kim, S.S. and Petrick, J.F. (2004). Segmenting horse-racing gamblers using the concept of involvment. *Tourism Analysis*, 9(1/2), 103–116.

King, L., Crabtree, R. and Alexander, E. (2002). A critical appraisal of relationship marketing: the effectiveness of a professional UK football club at retaining and developing loyalty of customers. In *Proceedings of the 10th European congress on sport management* (Laaksonen, K., Lopponen, P., Nykanen, E. and Puronoho, K., eds). Jyvaskyla: EASM.

King, R.L. (1982). Southern Europe: dependency or development. *Geography*, 67, 221–234.

Kirkup, N. and Major, B. (2006). The reliability of economic impact studies of the Olympic Games: a post games study of Sydney 2000 and considerations for London 2012. *Journal of Sport & Tourism*, 11(3–4), 275–296.

Koorey, G. (2001). National cycle touring routes: some thoughts on where to go from here. Paper to the *New Zealand cycling conference: transport for living*. Christchurch, New Zealand, September.

Kretchmarr, A.S. (1994). *Practical philosophy of sport*. Illinois: Human Kinetics.

Kreutzwiser, R. (1989). Supply (outdoor recreation). In *Outdoor recreation in Canada* (Wall, G., ed.). Toronto: J. Wiley and Sons.

Kuhn, T.S. (1962). *The structure of scientific revolutions*. Chicago: University of Chicago Press.

Kurtzman, J. and Zauher, J. (1997). A wave in time – the sports tourism phenomena. *Journal of Sport Tourism*, 4(2), 10–17.

Laffin, M. (1986). Professional communities and policy communities in central-local relations. In *New research in central-local relations* (Goldsmith, M., ed.). Aldershot: Gower.

Lambton, D. (2001). Changing times on the top table. *Sports Business International*, 61, 54–56.

Laumann, E.O. and Knoke, D. (1987). *The organizational state*. Madison: The University of Wisconsin Press.

Law, C.M. (1992). Urban tourism and its contribution to economic regeneration. *Urban Studies*, 29(3–4), 599–618.

Law, C.M. (1993). *Urban tourism, attracting visitors to large cities*. London: Mansell.

Law, C.M. (ed.) (1996). *Tourism in Major Cities*. London: International Thomson Business Publishing.

Law, C.M. (2000). Regenerating the city center through leisure and tourism. *Built Environment*, (26), 117–129.

Law, C.M. (2002). *Urban tourism: the visitor economy and the growth or large cities*. London: Continuum.

Law, S. (1967). Planning for outdoor recreation. *Journal of the Town Planning Institute*, 53, 383–386.

Lawson, R. and Thyne, M. (2001). Destination avoidance and inept destination sets. *Journal of Vacation Marketing*, 7(3), 199–208.

Lefebvre, H. (1991). *The production of space* (trans: Nicholson-Smith, D.). Oxford: Blackwell Publishers.

Leiper, N. (1990). *Tourism systems: an interdisciplinary perspective*, Occasional Paper 2. Auckland, New Zealand: Department of Management Systems, Massey University.

Leitner, M.J. and Leitner, S.F. (2004). *Leisure enhancement*. New York: Haworth Press.

Leslie, D. (2001). *An environmental audit of the tourism industry in the Lake District National Park*. Report Commissioned by Friends of the Lake District.

Lewis, R. and Wild, M. (1995). *French ski resorts and UK ski tour operators*, The Centre for Occasional Papers: Sheffield Hallam University.

Lilley, W. and DeFranco, L.J. (1999). The economic impact of the European Grands Prix. Paper presented to the *FIA European Union and Sport Workshop*, Brussels, Belgium, February.

Lockhart, D.G. (1997a). Islands and tourism: an overview. In *Island tourism: trends and prospects* (Lockhart, D. and Drakakis-Smith, D., eds). London: Cassell.

Lockhart, D.G. (1997b). Tourism to Malta and Cyprus. In *Island tourism: trends and prospects* (Lockhart, D. and Drakakis-Smith, D., eds). London: Cassell.

Lockhart, D.G. and Ashton, S.E. (1987). Recent trends in Maltese tourism. *Geography*, 72, 255–258.

Lockhart, D.G. and Ashton, S.E. (1991). Tourism in Malta. *Scottish Geographical Magazine*, 107(1), 22–32.

Lockhart, D. and Drakakis-Smith, D. (eds) (1997). *Island tourism: trends and prospects*. London: Cassell.

Long, J. (ed.) (1990). Leisure, health and wellbeing: editor's introduction. In *Leisure, health and wellbeing*. Conference papers, No 44, Eastbourne: Leisure Studies Association.

Longhurst, B. (1995). *Popular music and society*. Oxford: Polity Press.

London Marathon Ltd (2008). Marathon Info. *www.london-marathon.co.uk/marathoninfo/racehistory.shtml*, Accessed 15/4/2008.

Lowerson, J. and Myerscough, J. (1977). *Time to spare in Victorian England*. Hassocks: Harvester Press.

Lumsdon, L. (1996). Cycle tourism in Britain. *Insights* March, 27–32. London: English Tourist Board.

Lumsdon, L. (2000). Transport and tourism: cycle tourism – a model for sustainable development? *Journal of Sustainable Tourism*, 8(5), 361–377.

Lumsdon, L. and Page, S.J. (eds) (2004). *Tourism and transport: issues and agenda for the new millennium*. Oxford: Elsevier.

Lumsdon, L., Downward, P.M. and Cope, A. (2004). Monitoring of cycle tourism on long distance trails: the North Sea Cycle Route. *Journal of Transport Geography*, 12, 13–22.

MacCannell, D. (1996). *Tourist or traveller?* London: BBC Education.

MacCannell, D. (1999). *The tourist: a new theory of the leisure class*. California: University of California Press.

MacCannell, D. (2002). The ego factor in tourism. *Journal of Consumer Research*, 29, 146–151.

Maine Department of Transportation (2001). *Bicycle tourism in Maine: economic impacts and marketing recommendations*. Maine: Maine Department of Transportation.

Mannell, R. and Iso-Ahola, S.E. (1987). Psychological nature of leisure and tourism experience. *Annals of Tourism Research*, 14(3), 314–331.

Mannel, R.C. and Kleiber, D.A. (1997). *A social psychology of leisure*. State College, PA: Venture Publishing.

Mansfield, Y. (1994). The 'value-stretch' model and its implementation in detecting tourists' class-differentiated destination choice. In *Spoilt for choice: decision making processes and preference change of tourists – intertemporal and intercountry perspectives* (Gasser, R.V. and Weiermair, K., eds). Thaur: Kulturverlag.

March, R. and Woodside, A.G. (2005). Testing theory of planned versus realised tourism behaviour. *Annals of Tourism Research*, 32(4), 905–924.

Marsh, D. (ed.) (1983). Interest group activity and structural power: Lindblom's politics and markets. In *Capital and politics in Western Europe*. London: Frank Cass.

Marsh, D. and Rhodes, R.A.W. (eds) (1992). Policy communities and issue networks: beyond typology. In *Policy networks in British government*. Oxford: Oxford University Press.

Marsh, P., Rosser, E. and Harre, R. (1978). *The rules of disorder*. London: Routledge and Kegan Paul.

Mason, T. (1980). *Association football and English society, 1863–1915*. Brighton: Harvester.

Mason, T. (ed.) (1989). *Sport in Britain: a social history*. Cambridge: Cambridge University Press.

Mathieson, A. and Wall, G. (1989). *Tourism: economic, physical and social impacts*. Harlow: Longman.

McDonald, M.A. and Milne, G.R. (1999). *Cases in sport marketing*. Sudbury, Massachusetts: Jones and Bartlett.

McFee, G. (2007). Paradigms and possibilities: or, some concerns for the study of sport from the philosophy of science. *Sport, Ethics and Philosophy*, 1(1), 58–77.

McGehee, N.G., Yoon, Y. and Cardenas, D. (2003). Involvement and travel for recreational runners in North Carolina. *Journal of Sport Management*, 17(3), 305–324.

McGibbon, J. (2007). Teppich-swingers and skibums: differential experiences of ski tourism in the Tirolean Alps. In *Tourism consumption and representation: narratives of place and self* (Meethan, K., Anderson, A. and Miles, S., eds). Wallingford: CABI.

McIntosh, R.W. and Goeldner, C.R. (1986). *Tourism principles, practices, philosophies*, 5th edn. Columbus, Ohio: Grid Publishing.

McIntyre, S. (1981). Bath: the rise of a resort town, 1600–1800. In *Country Towns in Pre-Industrial England* (Clark, P., eds). Leicester: Leicester University Press.

McKercher, B. (1998). The effect of market access on destination choice. *Journal of Travel Research*, 37(1), 39–47.

McKoy, C.M. (1991). *The role of sport at Butlins*, Unpublished MSc Thesis, Loughborough University.

Millward, P. (2006). We've all got the bug for Euro-aways: what fans say about European football club competition. *International Review for the Sociology of Sport*, 41(3–4), 375–393.

Mintel (1996). *Leisure intelligence – snowsports*. London: Mintel.

Mintel (1998). *The sports market*. London: Mintel.

Mintel (1999). *Leisure intelligence: activity holidays*. London: Mintel.

Mintel (2000). *The sports market*. London: Mintel.

Mintel (2002a). *Leisure intelligence: holiday centres*. London: Mintel.

Mintel (2002b). *Leisure intelligence: snowsports*. London: Mintel.

Mintel (2002c). *Leisure intelligence – hotels in the UK*. London: Mintel.

Mintel (2003a). *Leisure intelligence: golf*. London: Mintel.

Mintel (2003b). *Leisure intelligence: health and beauty treatments*. London: Mintel.

Mintel (2005a). *Leisure intelligence: activity holidays*. London: Mintel.

Mintel (2005b). *Sports participation UK*. London: Mintel.

Mintel (2007). *Leisure intelligence: cycling holidays*. London: Mintel.

Mitchie, D.A. (1986). Family travel behaviour and its implications for tourism management. *Tourism Management*, 13(1), 8–20.

Morgan, D. (1998). Up the wall: the impact of the development of climbing walls on British rock climbing. In *Leisure management: issues and applications* (Collins, M.F. and Cooper, I., eds). London: CABI.

Morgan, G. (1986). *Images of organisation*. London: Sage.

Morgan, G. (1997). *Images of organization*, 2nd edn. London: Sage.

Morgan, N. and Pritchard, A. (2000). *Advertising in tourism and leisure*. Oxford: Butterworth Heinemann.

Morse, J. (2001). The Sydney 2000 Olympic Games: how the Australian Tourist Commission leveraged the Games for tourism. *Journal of Vacation Marketing*, 7(2), 101–107.

Mortlock, C. (1984). *The adventure alternative*. Cumbria, UK: Cicerone Press.

Moutinho, L. (1987). Consumer behaviour in tourism. *European Journal of Marketing*, 21(10), 3–44.

Mules, T. (1998). Events tourism and economic development in Australia. In *Managing tourism in cities: policy, process and practice* (Tyler, D., Guerrier, Y. and Robertson, M., eds). Chichester: John Wiley & Sons.

Mules, T. and Dwyer, L. (2005). Public sector support for sport tourism events: the role of cost-benefit analysis. *Sport in Society*, 8(2), 338–355.

Mules, T. and Falkner, B. (1996). An economic perspective on special events. *Tourism Economics*, 2, 314–329.

Munda Trail Biddi Foundation (2005). *Cycle tourism: a new tourism market emerges in Western Australia*, http://www.mundabiddi.org.au/cycling sports tourism/images/ctlowres.pdf (Accessed 18/8/2008).

Myerscough, J. (1974). The recent history of the use of leisure time. In *Leisure research and policy* (Appleton, I., ed.). Edinburgh: Scottish Academic Press.

Narayana, C.L. and Markin, R.J. (1975). Consumer behaviour and product performance: an alternative conceptualisation. *Journal of Marketing*, 39, 81–89.

National Ski Areas Association (2000). *1998/99 Economic analysis of United States ski areas*. Colorado: NSAA.

National Tourist Organisation – Malta (1997). *Malta sports calendar*. Valletta: NTO – Malta.

Natural England (2006). *England leisure visits, 2005*. Cheltenham: Natural England.

Nauright, J. (1996). 'A besieged tribe'?: nostalgia, white cultural identity and the role of rugby in a changing South Africa. *International Review for the Sociology of Sport*, 31(1), 69–89.

Neulinger, J. (1991). *The psychology of leisure*, 2nd edn. Springfield, Ill: Charles C Thomas Publishing.

Niininen, O., Szivas, E. and Riley, M. (2004). Destination loyalty and repeat behaviour: an application of optimum stimulation measurement. *International Journal of Tourism Research*, 6, 439–447.

Nixon, H.L. and Frey, J.H. (1995). *A sociology of sport*. London: Wadsworth Publishing.

O'Brien, D. (2006). Event business leveraging of the Sydney 2000 Olympic Games. *Annals of Tourism Research*, 33(1), 240–261.

O'Brien, D. and Chalip, L. (2007). Executive training exercise in sport event leverage. *International Journal of Culture, Tourism and Hospitality Research*, 1(4), 296–304.

Oh, H. (2008). *Handbook of hospitality marketing management*. Oxford: Butterworth-Heinemann.

OPCS (1999). *Family expenditure survey*. London: OPCS.

Ortega, E. and Rodriguez, B. (2007). Information at tourism destinations. Importance and cross-cultural differences between international and domestic tourists. *Journal of Business Research*, 60(2), 146–152.

Ousby, I. (1990). *The Englishman's England: taste, travel and the rise of tourism*. Cambridge: Cambridge University Press.

Owen, E., Bishop, K. and Speakman, C. (1999). The northern Snowdonia study – an innovative approach to sustainable development. *Countryside Recreation*, 7(2). Cardiff: Countryside Recreation Network.

Page, S.J. (1990). The role of sport tourism: arena development and urban regeneration in the London Docklands. *The Geographer*, 8(4), 18–25.

Page, S.J. (1999). *Transport and tourism*. Harlow: Longman.

Page, S.J. (2003). *Tourism management: managing for change*. Oxford: Butterworth-Heinemann.

Page, S.J. (2005). *Transport and tourism: global perspectives*, 2nd edn. Harlow: Pearson Education.

Page, S.J. and Getz, D. (1997). *The business of rural tourism: international perspectives*. London: Thompson Business Press.

Parrish, R. (2003). *Sports Law and Policy in the European Union*. Manchester: Manchester University Press.

Parry, M. and Malcolm, D. (2004). England's Barmy Army: commercialisation, masculinity and nationalism. *International Review for the Sociology of Sport*, 39(1), 75–94.

Patmore, J.A. (1983). *Recreation and resources*. Oxford: Blackwell.

Pearce, D.G. (1987). *Tourism today: a geographical analysis*. Harlow: Longman.

Pearce, D.G. (1993). Comparative studies in tourism research. In *Tourism research: critiques and challenges* (Pearce, D.G. and Butler, R.W., eds). London: Routledge.

Pearce, P.L. and Lee, U-I. (2005). Developing the travel career approach to tourist motivation. *Journal of Travel Research*, 43(3), 226–237.

Petrick, J.F. (2002). An examination of golf vacationers' novelty. *Annals of Tourism Research*, 29(2), 382–400.

Petrick, J.F. and Backman, S. (2002a). An examination of the determinants of golf travellers' satisfaction. *Journal of Travel Research*, 40(3), 252–258.

Petrick, J.F. and Backman, S. (2002b). An examination of the construct of perceived value for the prediction of golf travelers' intentions to revisit. *Journal of Travel Research*, 41(1), 38–45.

Petrick, J.F. and Backman, S. (2002c). An examination of golf travelers' satisfaction, perceived value, loyalty, and intentions to revisit. *Tourism Analysis*, 6(3/4), 223–238.

PGL (2002). www.pgl.co.uk/online/moreinformation/corporate/profile.asp (Accessed 6/11/2002).

Picton, K. and Bull, C.J. (2003). *Economic impact of cycle tourism in relation to the Viking cycle trail in Thanet*. Unpublished Report for Kent Highways.

Pigeassou, C. (2002). Contribution to the analysis of sport tourism. Oral presentation to the *10th European Sport Management Congress*, Jyvaskyla, Finland, September.

Pigeassou, C., Bui-Xuan, G. and Gleyse, J. (1998/2003). Epistemological issues on sport tourism: challenges for a new scientific field. *Journal of Sport Tourism*, 8(1), 27–34.

Pigram, J. (1983). *Outdoor recreation and resource management*. Beckenham: Croom Helm.

Pimlott, J.A.R. (1947). *The Englishman's holiday*. London: Faber & Faber.

Preuss, H. (2004). *The economics of staging the Olympics – a comparison of the games, 1972–2008*. Cheltenham: Edward Elgar.

Preuss, H. (2005). The economic impact of vistors at major multi-sport events. *European Sport Management Quarterly*, 5(3), 283–303.

Preuss, H. (2007). The conceptualisation and measurement of mega sport event legacies. *Journal of Sport & Tourism*, 12(3/4), 207–228.

Priest, S. (1992). Factor exploration and confirmation of the dimensions of an adventure experience. *Journal of Leisure Research*, 24(2), 127–139.

Ramshaw, G. and Gammon, G. (2005). More than just nostalgia? Exploring the heritage/sport tourism nexus. *Journal of Sport Tourism*, 10(4), 229–241.

Readman, M. (2003). Golf tourism. In *Sport and adventure tourism* (Hudson, S., ed.). New York: Haworth Hospitality Press.

Reasons, C. (1984). Real estate: the land grab. In *Stampede and city: power and politics in the West* (Reasons, C., ed.). Toronto: Between the Lines.

Redmond, G. (1988). Points of increasing contact: sport and tourism in the modern world. Paper presented at the Second International Conference, *Leisure, Labour, and Lifestyles: International Comparisons*, Brighton, UK.

Reeves, M.R. (2000). *Evidencing the sport–tourism interrelationship*, Unpublished PhD Thesis, Loughborough University.

Regan, M. (1999). Commonwealth gains. *The Leisure Manager*, 17(12), 20–22.

Regeneris Consulting. (2005). *Economic and Social Benefits of Countryside Access in the North East*. Altrincham: Regeneris Consulting.

Reznick, J.R. (2003). Health tourism in action – a best practice case study from France. Paper presented to the English Tourism Council Insights Seminar, *Health Tourism – The Future*, at the British Travel Trade Fair, Birmingham, UK, March.

Rhodes, R.A.W. (1981). *Control and power in centre-local government relations*. Farnborough: Gower/SSRC.

Rhodes, R.A.W. (1986). *The national world of local government*. London: Macmillan.

Rhodes, R.A.W. (1988). *Beyond Westminster and Whitehall*. Unwin Hyman, London.

Rhodes, R.A.W. and Marsh, D. (1992). Policy networks in British politics: a critique of existing approaches. In *Policy networks in British government* (Marsh, D. and Rhodes, R.A.W., eds). Oxford: Oxford University Press.

Richardson, J.J. and Jordan, A.G. (1979). *Governing under pressure*. Oxford: Martin Robertson.

Ripley, R. and Franklin, G. (1980). *Congress, the bureaucracy and public policy*. Illinois: Dorsey Press.

Ritchie, B. (1998). Bicycle tourism in the South Island of New Zealand: planning and management issues. *Tourism Management*, 19(6), 567–582.

Ritchie, B. and Adair, D. (eds) (2004). *Sport tourism: interrelationships, impacts and issues*. Clevedon: Channel View.

Ritchie, B. and Hall, C.M. (1999). Cycle tourism and regional development: a New Zealand case study. *Anatolia: an International Journal of Tourism and Hospitality Research*, 10(2), 89–112.

Ritchie, J.R.B. (1984). Assessing the impact of hallmark events: conceptual and research issues. *Journal of Travel Research*, 23(1), 2–11.

Roberts, L. and Hall, D. (2001). *Rural tourism and recreation: principles to practice*. Oxford: CABI.

Robertson, M. and Guerrier, Y. (1998). Events as entrepreneurial displays: Seville, Barcelona and Madrid. In *Managing tourism in cities: policy, process and practice* (Tyler, D., Guerrier, Y. and Robertson, M., eds). Chichester: John Wiley & Sons.

Robinson, H. (1976). *A geography of tourism*. Plymouth: Macdonald and Evans.

Robinson, T. and Gammon, S. (2004). A question of primary and secondary motives: revisiting and applying the sport–tourism framework. *Journal of Sport Tourism*, 9(3), 221–233.

Roche, M. (1992). Mega events and micro modernisation: on the sociology of the new urban tourism. *British Journal of Sociology*, 43(4), 22–29.

Roche, M. (1994). Mega-events and urban policy. *Annals of Tourism Research*, 21(1), 1–19.

Roche, M. (2001). Mega-events, Olympic Games and the World Student Games 1991 – understanding the impacts and information needs of major sports events. Paper presented at the SPRIG Conference, UMIST Manchester, 1 May 2001.

Rosentraub, M.S. (2000). Sports facilities, redevelopment and the centrality of downtown areas: observations and lessons from experiences in the Rustbelt and Sunbelt City. *Marquette Sports Law Journal*, 10(2), 219–235.

Rosh-White, N. and White, P.B. (2007). Home and away: tourists in a connected world. *Annals of Tourism Research*, 34(1), 88–104.

Rotter, J.B. (1966). Generalised expectancies for internal versus external control of reinforcement. *Psychological Monographs: General and Applied*, 80(1), 1–28.

Ryan, C. (1991). *Recreational tourism: a social science perspective*. London: Routledge.

Ryan, C. (2002). *The tourist experience: a new introduction*. London: Continuum.

Ryan, C. (2003). *Recreational tourism: demand and impacts*. Clevedon: Channel View.

Ryan, C. and Trauer, B. (2005). Sport tourist behaviour: the example of the Masters Games. In *Sport tourism destinations* (Higham, J., ed.). Oxford: Elsevier.

Sanahuja, R. (2002). Olympic city – the city strategy ten years after the Olympic Games in 1992. Paper to the *Sports Events and Economic Import Conference*, Copenhagen, April.

Sandiford, K.A.P. (1994). *Cricket and the Victorians*. Aldershot: Scholar Press.

Schreiber, R. (1976). Sports interest: a travel definition. *The Travel Research Association 7th Annual Conference Proceedings*. Boca Raton, Florida: TRA.

Scotsman (2005). Athens counting cost of the Olympics. *The Scotsman*, 4 August.

Scott, A. (1995). Gearing up. *Sunday Times*, 19 November, cited in Hudson, S. (2000).

Scott, A.K.S. and Turco, D.M. (2007). VFRs as a segment of the sport event tourism market. *Journal of Sport & Tourism*, 12(1), 41–52.

Selin, S. (2000). Developing a typology of sustainable tourism partnerships. In *Tourism collaboration and partnerships: politics, practice and sustainability* (Bramwell, B. and Lane, B., eds). Clevedon: Channel View.

Selman, P. (1992). *Environmental planning*. London: PCP.

Shakespear, W. (2002). Developing sustained high performance services and systems that have quality outcomes. In *Proceedings of the 12th Commonwealth International Sport Conference*. London: Association of Commonwealth Universities.

Sharpley, R. and Craven, B. (2001). The 2001 foot and mouth crisis – rural economy and tourism implications: a comment. *Current Issues in Tourism*, 4(6), 527–537.

Sharpley, R. and Sharpley, J. (1997). *Rural tourism: an introduction*. London: Thomson Business Press.

Shaw, G. and Williams, A.M. (1994). *Critical issues in tourism: a geographical perspective*. Oxford: Blackwell.

Shaw, G. and Williams, A. (2002). *Critical issues in tourism: a geographical perspective*, 2nd edn. Oxford: Blackwell.

Shaw, G. and Williams, A.M. (2004). *Tourism and tourism spaces*. London: Sage.

Sheffield Children's Festival (SCF) (1994). *Sheffield's youth festival – a five year plan*. Sheffield: SCF.

Sheffield City Council Sports Development and Event Unit (SCCSDEU) (1995). *Major sports events strategy*. Sheffield: SCCSDEU.

Sheffield City Liaison Group (SCLG) (1994). *The way ahead – plans for the economic regeneration of Sheffield*. Sheffield: SCLG.

Shibli, S. and Gratton, C. (2001). The economic impact of two major sports events in two of the UK's national cities of sport. In *Sport in the city: the role of sport in economic and social regeneration* (Gratton, C. and Henry, I.P., eds). London: Routledge.

Shipway, R. and Jones, I. (2008). The great suburban Everest: an 'insiders' perspective on experiences at the 2007 Flora London marathon. *Journal of Sport & Tourism*, 13(1), 61–77.

Shone, A. and Parry, B. (2004). *Successful events management a practical handbook*, 2nd edn. London: Thomson.

Short, J.R. (1991). *Imagined country: society, culture and environment*. London: Routledge.

Sidaway, R. (1988). *Sport, recreation and nature conservation*. London: Sports Council/Countryside Commission.

Sidaway, R.M. (1997). Recreation pressure on the countryside: real concerns or crises of the imagination?. In *Leisure management: issues and applications* (Collins, M.F. and Cooper, I.S., eds). Wallingford: CAB International.

Sidaway, R.M. and O'Connor, F.B. (1978). Recreation pressures in the countryside *Countryside for all? Proceedings of Countryside Recreation Research Advisory Group conference*. Cheltenham: CRRAG.

Silk, M. and Amis, J. (2005). Sport tourism, cityscapes and cultural politics. *Sport in Society*, 8(2), 280–301.

Simmons, I.G. (1994). *Interpreting nature: cultural constructions of the environment*. London: Routledge.

Simonsen, P. and Jorgenson, B. (1996). *Cycling tourism: environmental and economical sustainability?* Unpublished Report. Bornholm, Denmark: Bornholm Research Centre.

Skinner, Q. (1978). *The foundations of modern political thought* (volumes I–II). Cambridge: Cambridge University Press.

Slusher, H.S. (1967). *Men, sport and existence: a critical analysis*. Philadelphia: Lea & Febiger.

Smith, B.M. and Weed, M.E. (2007). The potential of narrative research in sports tourism. *Journal of Sport & Tourism*, 11(3/4), 249–269.

Smith, M.J. (1993). *Pressure, power and policy*. Hemel Hempstead: Harvester Wheatsheaf.

Smith, S. (1989). *Tourism analysis: a handbook*. Harlow: Longman.

Smith, S.L.J. (1983). *Recreation geography*. Harlow: Longman.

Smith, S.L. (1998). Athletes, runners and joggers: participant-group dynamics in a sport of 'individuals'. *Sociology of Sport Journal*, 15, 174–192.

Smith, V.L. (ed.) (1977). *Hosts and guests: an anthropology of tourism*. Philadelphia: University of Pennsylvania Press.

Snepenger, D., King, J., Marshall, E. and Uysal, M. (2006). Modelling Iso-Ahola's motivation theory in the tourism context. *Journal of Travel Research*, 45(2), 140–149.

Snowdonia Green Key Initiative (2005). *Strategy and working plan 2005/2006*.

Snyder, E. (1991). Sociology of nostalgia: halls of fame and Museums in America. *Sociology of Sport Journal*, 8, 228–238.

Social Research Associates (2007). *The Tour de France Grand Depart 2007, research summary*. Leicester: Social Research Associates.

Sofield, T.H.B. (2003). Sports tourism: from binary division to quadripartite construct. *Journal of Sport Tourism*, 8(3), 144–165.

Sonstroem, R.J. and Morgan, W.P. (1989). Exercise and self esteem: rationale and model. *Medicine and Science in Sports and Exercise*, 21, 329–337.

South Australian Tourism Commission (2002). *Fast facts: cycling tourism fact sheet*.

South Australian Tourism Commission (2005). *Cycling sports tourism strategy 2005–2009*. www.tourism.sa.gov.au/tourism/plan/cycley_tourism_strategy.pdf (Accessed 18/8/2008).

Speakman, L. and Speakman, C. (1999). Car-dependency and countryside recreation – the need for an alternative culture. In *Countryside Recreation*, 7(2), Cardiff: Countryside Recreation Network.

Spiggle, S. and Sewall, M.A. (1987). A choice sets model of retail selection. *Journal of Marketing*, 51(2), 97–111.

Sport Business (2005). *The business of sports tourism*. London: Sport Business Group.

Sports Council (1988a). *Sport in the community: into the nineties*. London: Sports Council.

Sports Council (1988b). *Sharing does work*. London: Sports Council.

Sports Council (1990). *Sport and urban regeneration*. London: Sports Council.

Sports Council (1992). *A countryside for sport*. London: Sports Council.

Sports Council (1994). *Community use of sports facilities on school sites – a review of the 1992/93 management awards*. London: Sports Council.

Spreng, R.A., Mackenzie, S.B. and Olshavsky, R.W. (1996). A re-examination of the determinants of consumer satisfaction. *Journal of Marketing*, , (60), 15–32.

Standeven, J. and De Knop, P. (1999). *Sport tourism*. Champaign: Human Kinetics.

Standeven, J. and Tomlinson, A. (1994). *Sport and tourism in South East England: a preliminary assessment*. London: SECSR.

Stebbins, R. (1992). *Amateurs, professionals and serious leisure*. London: McGill.

Stebbins, R. (1999). Serious leisure. In *Leisure studies: prospects of the 21st century* (Jackson, E.L. and Burton, T.L., eds). State College, PA: Venture Publishing.

Stebbins, R. (2002). *The organisational basis of leisure participation*. State College, PA: Venture Publishing.

Stevens, T. (1987). Dallas. *Leisure Management*, 7, 35.

Stevens, T. (1992). Barcelona: the Olympic city. *Leisure Management*, 12(6), 26–30.

Stevens, T. (2005). Sport and urban tourism destinations: the evolving sport, tourism and leisure functions of the modern stadium. In *Sport tourism destinations* (Higham, J., ed.). Oxford: Elsevier.

Strange, I (1993). *Public-private partnership and the politics of economic regeneration policy in Sheffield, c. 1985–1991*. Unpublished Ph.D. thesis, University of Sheffield.

Sung, H. (2004). Classification of adventure travellers: behaviour, decision making and target markets. *Journal of Travel Research*, 42(4), 343–356.

Sustrans (1999a). *Cycle tourism*. Bristol: Sustrans.

Sustrans (1999b). *Network news*. Bristol: Sustrans.

Sustrans (2008). *Annual review 2007*. Bristol: Sustrans.

Swarbrooke, J. (2000). Tourism, economic development and urban regeneration: a critical evaluation. In *Reflections on international tourism: developments in urban and rural tourism* (Robinson, M., Sharpley, R., Evans, N., Long, P. and Swarbrooke, J., eds). Sunderland: Centre for Travel and Tourism.

Swarbrooke, J. and Horner, S. (1999). *Consumer behaviour in Tourism*. Oxford: Butterworth-Heinemann.

Swarbrooke, J., Beard, C., Leckie, S. and Pomfret, G. (2003). *Adventure tourism: the new frontier*. Oxford: Butterworth-Heinemann.

Tananone, B. (1991). International tourism in Thailand: environment and community development. *Contours* (Bangkok), 5(2), 7–9.

Thapa, B. and Graefe, A.R. (2003). Level of skill and its relationship to recreation conflict and tolerance among adult skiers and snowboarders. *World Leisure Journal*, 1, 13–25.

The Times (2003). How Scottish fans fell out of love with Hampden and their team. *The Times*, 29 March, (Scottish edition).

The Times (2008). London 2012 should follow Sheffield's lead. *The Times*, 24 May.

Tischler, S. (1981). *Footballers & Businessmen – The origins of professional soccer in England*. New York: Holmes & Meier.

Tokarski, W. (1993). Leisure, sports and tourism: the role of sports in and outside holiday clubs. In *Leisure and tourism: social and economic change* (Veal, A.J., Jonson, P. and Cushman, G., eds). Sydney: Sydney University of Technology.

Tomlinson, A. (1996). Olympic spectacles: opening ceremonies, and some paradoxes of globalisation. *Media, Culture & Society*, 18, 583–602.

Tomlinson, A. and Walker, H. (1990). Holidays for all: popular movements, collective leisure and the pleasure industry. In *Consumption, identity and style: marketing, meanings and the packaging of pleasure* (Tomlinson, A., ed.). London: Routledge.

Towner, J. (1985). The Grand Tour: a key phase in the history of tourism. *Annals of Tourism Research*, 12(3), 297–333.

Towner, J. (1996). *An historical geography of recreation and tourism in the western world* 1540–1940. Chichester: Wiley.

Train, P. (1995). *Tourism and economic impacts of staging a special event: the Europa Cup, Birmingham 1994*. Unpublished MSc thesis, Loughborough University.

Truno, E. (1994). Sport for all and the Barcelona Olympic games. Paper to the *2nd European Congress on Sport for all in Cities*, Barcelona, Spain, October.

Tuppen, J. (1998). France. In *Tourism and economic development: European experiences* (Williams, A. and Shaw, G., eds), 3rd edn. Chichester: Wiley.

Turco, D.M., Riley, R.S. and Swart, K. (2002). *Sport tourism*. Morgantown: Fitness Information Technology.

Turner, V. (1974). *Dramas fields and metaphors*. New York: Cornell University Press.

Turner, V. and Turner, E. (1978). *Image and pilgrimage in Christian culture*. New York: Columbia University Press.

Tyler, D., Guerrier, Y. and Robertson, M. (eds) (1998). *Managing tourism in cities: policy, process and practice*. Chichester: John Wiley & Sons.

Um, S. and Crompton, J.L. (1990). Attitude determinants in tourism destination choice. *Annals of Tourism Research*, 17, 432–448.

UNDP & WTO (1989). *The Maltese Islands tourist development plan*. Madrid: WTO.

Urry, J. (1990). *The tourist gaze*. London: Sage.

Urry, J. (2001). *The tourist gaze*, 2nd edn. London: Sage.

Vamplew, W. (1988). Sport and industrialisation: an economic interpretation of the changes in popular sport in nineteenth-century England. In *Pleasure, profit and proselytism: British culture and sport at home and abroad, 1700–1914* (Mangan, J.A., ed.). London: Frank Cass.

Van Dalen, D.B. and Bennett, B. (1971). *A world history of physical education*. Englewood Cliffs, NJ: Prentice Hall.

van Raaij, W.F. (1986). Consumer research on tourism: mental and behavioural constructs. *Annals of Tourism Research*, 13(1), 1–9.

Varley, P. (2006). Confecting adventure and playing with meaning: the adventure commodification continuum. *Journal of Sport & Tourism*, 11(2), 173–194.

Vaske, J.J., Carothers, P., Donnelly, M.P. and Baird, B. (2000). Recreation conflict among skiers and snowboarders. *Leisure Sciences*, 22(4), 297–313.

Vaske, J.J., Dyar, R. and Timmons, N. (2004). Skill level and recreation conflict among skiers and snowboarders. *Leisure Sciences*, 26(2), 215–225.

VisitScotland (2000). A new strategy for golf tourism in Scotland. *VisitScotland*.

Vrondou, O. (1999). *Sports related tourism and the product repositioning of traditional mass tourism destinations: a case study of Greece*. Loughborough University: Unpublished PhD Thesis.

Vrondou, O. and Kriemadis, A. (2006). Sport in the restructuring of tourism policy in Crete: public and private sector roles and perspectives. Paper to the *Annual Congress of the European Association of Sport Management*, Nicosia, Cyprus, September.

Wahlers, R.G. and Etzel, J. (1985). Vacation preference as a manifestation of optimal stimulation and lifestyle experience. *Journal of Leisure Research*, 17(4), 287–295.

Waitt, G. (2003). Social impacts of the Sydney Olympics. *Annals of Tourism Research*, 30(1), 194–215.

Waitt, G. (1999). Playing games with Sydney: marketing Sydney for the 2000 Olympics. *Urban Studies*, 36, 1055–1077.

Wales Tourist Board (2000). *Achieving our potential: a tourism strategy for Wales*. Cardiff: Wales Tourist Board.

Wales Tourist Board (2002a). *Best foot forward: a walking tourism strategy for Wales*. Cardiff: Wales Tourist Board.

Wales Tourist Board (2002b). *Saddling up for success: a riding tourism strategy for Wales*. Cardiff: Wales Tourist Board.

Wales Tourist Board (2002c). *Moving up a gear: a cycle tourism strategy for Wales*. Cardiff: Wales Tourist Board.

Wales Tourist Board (2002d). *Time for action – an adventure tourism strategy for Wales (2002–8)*. Cardiff: Wales Tourist Board.

Walton, J.K. (1981). *The English seaside resort: a social history, 1750–1914*. Leicester: Leicester University Press.

Walton, J.K. (2000). *The British seaside*. Manchester: Manchester University Press.

Walton, J.K. and Walvin, J. (eds) (1983). *Leisure in Britain, 1780–1939*. Manchester: Manchester University Press.

Wang, Y. (2007). Customized authenticity begins at home. *Annals of Tourism Research*, 34(3), 789–804.

Wann, D.L., Melnick, M.J., Rssell, G.W. and Pease, D.G. (2001). *Sports fans: the psychology and social impacts of spectators*. London: Routledge.

Ward, J., Higson, P. and Campbell, W. (1994). *Advanced leisure and tourism* Cheltenham: Stanley Thornes.

Weber, K. (2001). Outdoor adventure tourism: a review of research approaches. *Annals of Tourism Research*, 28(2), 360–377.

Weed, M.E. (1999a). *Consensual Policies for Sport and Tourism in the UK: An Analysis of Organisational Behaviour and Problems*, (PhD Thesis). Canterbury: University of Kent at Canterbury/Canterbury Christ Church College.

Weed, M.E. (1999b). More than sports tourism: an introduction to the sport-tourism link. In Proceedings of the Sport and Recreation Information Group Seminar, *Exploring Sports Tourism* (Scarrot, M., ed.). Sheffield: SPRIG.

Weed, M.E. (2000). The social dynamics of sports groups: arguments for a meso-level analysis. In *Proceedings of the Fifth Annual Congress of the European College of Sport Science* (Avela, J., Komi, P.V. and Komulainen, J., eds). Jyvaskyla: LIKES Research Centre.

Weed, M.E. (2001a). Developing a sports tourism product. Paper to the First International Conference of the Pan Hellenic Association of Sports Economists and Managers, *The Economic Impact of Sport*, February.

Weed, M.E. (2001b). Tourism and sports development: providing the foundation for healthy lifestyles. Paper to the 1st International Congress, *Sport and Quality of Life*, Villa Real, Portugal, December.

Weed, M.E. (2001c). Ing-ger-land at Euro 2000: how 'handbags at 20 paces' was portrayed as a full-scale riot. *International Review for the Sociology of Sport*, 36(4), 407–424.

Weed, M.E. (2001d). Towards a model of cross-sectoral policy development in leisure: the case of sport and tourism. *Leisure Studies*, 20(2), 125–141.

Weed, M.E. (2002a). Understanding cricket crowd behaviour: a note of caution for event managers. Paper to the *12th Commonwealth International Sport Conference*, Manchester, UK, July.

Weed, M.E. (2002b). Football hooligans as undesirable sports tourists: some meta analytical speculations. In *Sport tourism: principles and practice* (Gammon, S. and Kurtzman, J., eds). Eastbourne: LSA.

Weed, M.E. (2002c). Organisational culture and the leisure policy process in Britain: how structure affects strategy in sport-tourism policy development. *Tourism, Culture and Communication*, 3(3), 147–164.

Weed, M.E. (2002d). Sports tourism and identity: developing a sports tourism participation model. In *Proceedings of the 10th European Congress on Sport Management* (Laaksonen, K., Lopponen, P., Nykanen, E. and Puronaho, K., eds). Jyvaskyla: EASM.

Weed, M.E. (2003a). Mediated and inebriated: the pub as a sports spectator venue. Paper to the Leisure Studies Association Conference, *Leisure and Visual Culture*, Roehampton, UK, July.

Weed, M.E. (2003b). Emotion, identity and sports spectator cultures. Paper to the *11th European Congress of Sports Psychology (FEPSAC)*, Copenhagen, July.

Weed, M.E. (2003c). Why the two won't tango: explaining the lack of integrated policies for sport and tourism in the UK. *Journal of Sports Management*. Special Edition on Sports Tourism.

Weed, M.E. (2003d). Sports tourism services: understanding provision strategies. Paper to the 11th European Association of Sport Management Congress, *Sport Management in a Changing World*, Stockholm, Sweden, September.

Weed, M.E. (2003e). Healthy holidays? Motivations, intentions and perceptions of health/spa tourists – a pilot study. Paper to the *17th Annual Conference of the European Health Psychology Society*, Kos, Greece, September.

Weed, M.E. (2005a). A grounded theory of the policy process for sport and tourism. *Sport in Society*, 8(2), 356–377.

Weed, M.E. (2005b). Research synthesis in sport management: dealing with chaos in the brickyard. *European Sport Mangement Quarterly*, 5(1), 77–90.

Weed, M.E. (2005c). Sports tourism theory and method: concepts, issues and epistemologies. *European Sport Management Quarterly*, 5(3), 229–242.

Weed, M.E. (2005d). Sport and tourism policy: the national and regional policy contexts for sports tourism destinations. In *Sport tourism destinations* (Higham, J., ed.). Oxford: Elsevier.

Weed, M.E. (2006a). The influence of policy makers' perceptions on sport-tourism policy development. *Tourism Review International*, 10(4), 227–240.

Weed, M.E. (2006b). Sports tourism research 2000–2004: a systematic review of knowledge and a meta-evaluation of method. *Journal of Sport & Tourism*, 11(1), 5–30.

Weed, M.E. (2006c). Olympic tourism? The tourism potential of London 2012. *eReview of Tourism Research*, 4(2), 51–57.

Weed, M.E. (2006d). The story of an ethnography: the experience of watching the 2002 World Cup in the pub. *Soccer and Society*, 7(1), 76–95.

Weed, M.E. (2006e). Sports spectators and travel: insights from a meta-interpretation of sort spectator behaviours'. Paper to the *Annual Congress of the European Association of Sport Management*, Nicosia, Cyprus, September.

Weed, M.E. (2007). Away sport spectator behaviour: a meta-interpretation. Paper to the *Annual Congress of the European College of Sport Science*, Jyvaskyla, Finland, July

Weed, M.E. (2008a). *Olympic tourism*. Oxford: Elsevier.

Weed, M.E. (2008b). Developing policy for sport and tourism: issues for smaller and developing countries. Keynote paper to the *First Commonwealth Conference on Sport Tourism*. Kata Kinabalu, Sabah, Malaysia, May.

Weed, M.E. (ed.) (2008c). *Sport & tourism: a reader*. London: Routledge.

Weed, M.E. and Bull, C.J. (1997a). Integrating sport and tourism: a review of regional policies in England. *Progress in Tourism and Hospitality Research*, 3(2), 129–148.

Weed, M.E. and Bull, C.J. (1997b). Influences on sport-tourism relations in Britain: the effects of government policy. In *Tourism Recreation Research*, Sport and Tourism Special Edition.

Weed, M.E. and Bull, C.J. (1998). The search for a sport-tourism policy network. In *Leisure management: issues and applications* (Collins, M.F. and Cooper, I.S., eds). Wallingford: CAB International.

Weed, M.E. and Bull, C.J. (2004). *Sports tourism: participants, policy and providers*. Oxford: Elsevier.

Weed, M.E. and Jackson, GA.M. (2008). The relationship between sport and tourism. In *Sport and society* (Houlihan, B., ed.). London: Sage.

Weed, M.E., Coren, E. and Fiore, J. (2008a). Using the Olympic Games to leverage sport and physical activity participation and health-related behaviours – a worldwide systematic review of the evidence base. Paper to the *Annual Congress of the European Association of Sport Management*, Heidelberg, Germany, September.

Weed, M.E., Coren, E., Fiore, J. et al (2008b). *A systematic review of the evidence base for developing a physical activity, sport and health legacy from the London 2012 Olympic and Paralympic Games* (Report to English Regional Physical Activity Leads). Canterbury: Centre for Sport, Physical Education & Activity Research (SPEAR), Canterbury Christ Church University.

Weiler, B. and Hall, C.M. (eds) (1992). *Special interest tourism*. London: Bellhaven.

Weinberg, R.S. and Gould, D. (1995). *Foundations of sport and exercise psychology*. Champaign, Ill: Human Kinetics.

Weiss, O., Norden, G., Hilschers, P. and Vanreusel, B. (1998). Ski tourism and environmental problems. *International Review for the Sociology of Sport*, 33(4), 367–379.

Whannel, G. (1985). Television spectacle and the internationalisation of sport. *Journal of Communication Enquiry*, (2), 54–74.

Wheaton, B. (1998). The changing gender order in sport? The case of windsurfing subcultures. *Journal of Sport and Social Issues*, 22(3), 252–274.

Wheaton, B. (2000). 'Just do it': consumption, commitment and identity in the windsurfing subculture. *Sociology of Sport Journal*, 17(3), 254–274.

Wheaton, B. (2004). *Understanding lifestyle sports: consumption, identity and difference*. London: Routledge.

Wickers, D. (1994). Snow alternative. *Sunday Times*, 27 November, p. 9.

Wilcox, R. and Andrews, D. (2003). Sport in the city: cultural, economic and political portraits. In *Sporting dystopias: the making and meanings of urban sport cultures* (Wilcox, R., Andrews, D., Pitter, R. and Irwin, R., eds). New York: SUNY Press.

Wilks, S. (1989). Government-industry relations. *Public Administration*, 67, 329–339.

Wilks, S. and Wright, M. (1987). *Comparative government-industry relations*. Oxford: Clarendon Press.

Williams, C. (1994). Exercise and well-being. *Unpublished Paper to the Sports Science Research Group*. Loughborough University.

Williams, D.R. (1989). Great expectations and the limits to satisfaction: a review of recreation and consumer satisfaction research. In *Outdoor recreation benchmark 1988: Proceedings of the national outdoor recreation forum* (Watson, A.E., ed.). Tampa, FL: USDA Forest Service.

Williams, P. and Basford, R. (1992). Segmenting downhill skiing's latent demand markets. *American Behavioural Scientist*, 36(2), 222–235.

Williams, P. and Dossa, K. (1990). *British Columbia downhill skier survey 1989–90*. British Columbia: Centre for Tourism Policy and Research, Simon Fraser University and Canada West Ski Areas Association.

Williams, P. and Fidgeon, P. (2000). Addressing participation constraint: a case study of potential skiers. *Tourism Management*, 21(4), 379–393.

Williams, S. (ed.) (2004). *Tourism: critical concepts in the social sciences*. London: Taylor & Francis.

Williams, T. and Donnelly, P. (1985). Subcultural production, reproduction and transformation in climbing. *International Review for the Sociology of Sport*, 20(1/2), 3–16.

Wilson, J.Q. (1973). *Political organizations*. New York: Basic Books.

Wilson, R. (2006). The economic impact of local sport events: significant, limited or otherwise? A case study of four swimming events. *Managing Leisure*, 11(1), 57–70.

Withey, L. (1997). *Grand tours and Cook's tours: a history of leisure travel, 1750 to 1915*. London: Aurum Press Ltd.

Wöber, K. (1997). International city tourism flows. In *International City Tourism* (Mazanec, J.A., ed.). London: Pinter, pp. 39–53.

Woodside, A.G. and Carr, J.A. (1988). Consumer decision making and competitive market strategies: applications for tourism planning. *Journal of Travel Research*, 26(3), 2–7.

Woodside, A.G. and Lysonski, S. (1989). A general model of traveler destination choice. *Journal of Travel Research*, 27(4), 8–14.

Woodward, S. (1990). Lucky dip. *Leisure Management*, 10(6), 36–39.

World Alliance of YMCAs (1998). *YMCA directory*. Geneva: WAYMCA.

World Commission on Environment and Development (1987). *Our common future*. London: Oxford University Press.

World Tourism Organisation (1963). *United Nations Conference on International Travel and Tourism*. Madrid: WTO.

World Tourism Organisation (1988). *Special interest tourism*. Madrid: WTO.

World Tourism Organisation (1991). *Tourism to the year 2000: qualitative aspects affecting global growth*. Madrid: WTO.

World Tourism Organisation (2002). *Sport and tourism*. Madrid: WTO.

Wright, M. (1988). Policy community, policy network and comparative industrial policies. *Political Studies*, 36(4), 593–692.

Wright, R.K. (2007). Planning for the great unknown: the challenge of promoting spectator-driven sports event tourism. *International Journal of Tourism Research*, 9(5), 345–359.

Yeoman, I., Robertson, M., Ali-Knight, J., Drummond, S. and McMahon-Beattie, U. (2004). *Festival and events management, an international arts and culture perspective*. Oxford: Elsevier Butterworth Heinemann.

Yiannakis, A. and Gibson, H.J. (1992). Roles tourists play. *Annals of Tourism Research*, 19, 287–303.

Index

A

A Countryside for Sport, 237, 244
AALA *see* Adventure Activities Licensing
    Authority
Accor hotel group (France), 178, 202
Achievement Goal Theory, 73
Active participation, 39
Active/passive:
    classification, 67
    sports tourism concept, 108–9, 184
Activities in sports tourism, 67–70
Activity holidays, 16, 169, 246
Activity Holidays Advisory Committee, 140
Adirondack North Country Region, New
    York State, 149
Adventure activities:
    arousal levels, 74
    destinations, 98
    risk, 36–7
    travellers, 39
Adventure Activities Licensing Authority
    (AALA), 251
'Adventure education', 37, 39
Adventure, health and tourism model, 108–9
Adventure Kayak, 193
Adventure tourism:
    concept, 52
    products, 37
    rural areas, 238
    Wales, 248–9, 254
Advocacy, sports tourism, 28–9, 294
Affiliation, 72
Air transport, 13
AIS *see* Australian Institute of Sport
Alpine club, 10
Alpine skiing:
    demographics, 266, 271
    economic impact, 261–3
    environment, 258–61, 260
    France, 259–60, 262, 264
    future, 269–70
    Grenoble, 267
    market, 261–3
    motivations, 267–9

    operators, 264
    providers, 263–4
    skier profile, 265–7
    socioeconomic groups, 265, 271
    sports tourism, 223, 257–8
    travel, 263
Alps, cycling, 207–8
Amateur Athletics Association, 10
Amateur Rowing Association, 10
American Constitution, 129
American football trip, 172
American Volkssports Association, 17
Anthony, Don, 27
AOC *see* Australian Olympic Committee
'Après ski' concept, 96–7
Aquitane coast, France, 155
Arousal levels in outdoor activities, 74–6
ASC *see* Australian Sports Commission
Ashes test match, 186
Association of Independent Tour Operators,
    246
Athens:
    Olympic Games (1896), 25
    Olympic Games (2004), 235, 286
Athletics:
    BBC, 192
    Britain, 192
    elite athletes, 99–100
    European Cup, 103
    spectators, 87–9
    World Cup, 87, 103
Athletics World Cup, 121
Atlanta, Olympic Games (1996), 147, 225
Atlanta Braves Baseball team, 147
Attendances, 40
Australia:
    cycling, 279–80
    elite sport focus, 156, 161
    rural communities, 19
    sports bodies, 138–9
Australian Gallery of Sport, 201
Australian Institute of Sport (AIS), 138
Australian Olympic Committee (AOC),
    138
Australian Sports Commission (ASC), 137–8

Austria:
    cycling, 279
    Danube trail, 279
    Winter Olympic Games, 260
Authenticity in sports tourism, 34–5
Avalanche risks in skiing, 258

B

Badminton, 197
Ball games, 4
Baltimore urban economic regeneration, 227
Barcelona, Olympic Games (1992), 16, 21, 23, 101, 226
'Barmy Army' (cricket), 116
Baseball:
    Major league, 121
    New York Yankees, 67, 80, 101
    trip, 172–3
Basketball, 197, 201
Bathing, 4
Bay Point Hotel, Malta, 213
BBC (British Broadcasting Corporation) and athletics, 192
Beach holidays, 111, 171, 195
Behaviour:
    post-decision trip-planning, 103–6
    research, 32–40, 41, 69–70
    spontaneous trip, 105–6
    trip decision-making, 78–81, 81–103
    trip purpose comparison, 55–6
Beijing, Olympic Games (2008), 23, 227
Benidorm, 197
Birmingham Olympic bid, 227
Bisham Abbey, 180, 195
Black Mountain Activities, 252–3
Blackburn Olympic football team, 7
Blair, Tony, 226
Boating, 240
Bodensee Cycle, Germany, 279
Body maintenance, 71
Bramall Lane stadium, Sheffield, 228
Brecon Beacons national park, 247, 252
Britain:
    National parks, 243
    scenic landscapes, 254
    sector links, 219
    televised athletics, 192
    Visit Britain agency, 138
    youth hostels, 13
British Columbia, Ultimate Outdoor Adventures, 177
British tour operators to Malta, 209

British Tourist Authority, 60
British tourists, 83–4
British Treasury, 130
Butlins:
    holiday camps, 83–4
    Holiday World, 113, 172, 194, 203–4

C

C2C national cycle routes, 24–5, 282–3
Calgary, Winter Olympic Games, 226
Camp America, 177
Canada:
    Cross-Sectoral Policy Development, 145
    elite sport focus, 156
    regional focus, 139
    skiing, 48, 97
    sports policy, 140
    state independence, 139–40
    tension between agencies, 152
Canadian Tourism Commission (CTC), 137
Canoeing, 66, 177, 238
Canterbury and Tour de France, 49, 290
'Capital' concept, 37, 40
Cardiff, Millenium stadium, 224
Cars, 13, 253–4
Cascade Bicycle Club, Seattle, 175
Case studies summary, 207–8
Caving, rural areas, 238, 244
Caving/potholing, 169, 177, 248, 251, 252–3
Center Parcs, 13–14, 167, 177, 198, 203
Central Council for Physical Education, 27
Chicago marathon, 186, 200
Children and sports tourism, 177
Chirac, Jacques, 226
Cities:
    breaks, 171
    Event Sport Tourism, 223, 225
    mega-events, 224–5
    Policy Wheel for Sport and Tourism, 224
    urban regeneration, 223–4
    vicarious spectating, 223
'City marketing', 139–40
'City of Sport' concept, Sheffield, 229–30, 234
Climbing:
    multi-activity, 177
    natural resources, 66
    rural sports, 238, 243, 244
    solitary nature, 96
    Switzerland, 9–10
    Wales, 248–9
Club La Santa, Lanzarote, 122, 179, 193, 195

Club Med, 167, 177–8, 198
'Collect places' concept, 115, 175, 200
College fixtures in USA, 45
Colonization, 11
Commercialization, 15
Commodification of sports tourism, 38
Commonwealth Games:
    Event Sports Tourism, 180
    Manchester (2002), 18, 22, 147, 196–7, 227
    non-capital cities, 226
    television, 15
    trip motivation, 89
'Communitas' concept, 289
Communities policy, 136–43
Competitive advantage, 202–3
Conceptualization:
    'sport away from home', 61–4
    sport and tourism as separate entities, 57
    sports tourism, activity, people and place interactivity, 51, 54, 144, 204–5, 258, 296
Conference market in Malta, 210
Connoiseurs Scotland, 183, 199
Converting intenders, 191–4
Cooperative marketing, 199–200
Corporate and Hospitality Event Association, 193
Corporate Outdoor Training, Melbourne, 177
Council of Europe, *sport* definition, 59
Country culture, 173
Country house experience and golf, 98
Country House Hotels, 177, 182–3, 185, 193, 201–2
Countryside Commission, *Good Practice in the Planning of Sport and Recreation...*, 244–5
Countryside Recreation Research and Advisory Group (CRRAG), 246
Countryside tourism, 237
County Cricket Ground, Lancashire, 196
Crete, Greece, 19
Cricket:
    'Barmy Army', 116
    British imperialism, 11
    crowds, 9
    fixtures, 90
    spectators, 59, 93
    television, 15
    The Ashes, 101, 186
Cross-Sectoral Policy Development model, 129, 145, 150, 157

CRRAG *see* Countryside Recreation Research and Advisory Group
Crucible Theatre, Sheffield, 232
CTC *see* Canadian Tourism Commission
Culture:
    country, 173
    motives, 73
Customer loyalty, 195
Cycle Tourism Strategy, South Australian Tourism Commission, 275, 277
Cycling:
    Australia, 279–80
    Austria, 279
    C2C routes, 282–3
    day visits, 276–7
    Denmark, 281
    elite athletes, 197
    endurance, 200
    environmental impact, 281
    extent, 274–80
    France, 281
    Germany, 279
    Greece regions, 19
    hire of cycles, 189–90, 201
    holiday cycling, 276, 278
    holidays, 276, 278
    locations, 274
    Millenium Commission Lottery Fund, 281–2
    National Cycling Network, 281–4
    Netherlands, 281
    New Zealand, 279
    outdoor adventure, 177
    Revised Sports Tourism Participation Model, 277–8, 290
    rural sports, 239, 240
    Scotland, 279
    sports tourism, 207–8, 273–91
    sustainable tourist development, 280–4
    Sustrans, 276–8
    Tour of Britain, 273
    Tour de France, 273–4, 275, 279–80, 284–90
    touring, 175
    UK, 281
    variety, 274–80
    velodromes, 273
    Wales, 248
Cycling Touring Club, UK, 175
Cycling Wales, 251

D

Danube trail, Austria, 279
Day trips in sports tourism, 60

Day visits and cycling, 276–7
Day-dreaming and trip decision-making, 118
DCMS *see* Department of Culture Media and Sport
De Gaulle, General, 141
Decision Making Units (DMUs):
  constituents, 78–80, 86
  destination choice, 81
  destination pre-determined/trip chosen, 87
  elite athletes, 100
  lifestyle, 98
  opportunity planning, 104
  planning, 104
  pre-purchase of tickets, 103
  requirement, 102
  sports fans profiling, 90–1
  subculture, 96
  trip decision, 81
  trip decision-making, 106
  trip/destination choice, 82–3
Decision-making process and trips, 79–80, 117–19
Definitions:
  sport, 57–9
  sports policy community, 157
  sports tourism, 61, 64
  tourism, 59–61
'Demand types' in sports tourism, 108, 169
Democratization, 14
Demographics of skiing, 265–6, 271
Denmark, cycling, 281
Department for Culture, Media and Sport (DCMS), 136, 142, 218–19, 226
Der Internationale Volkssportverbrand (IVV), 17
Destination Sheffield promotion, 231–2
Destinations:
  adventure activities, 98
  awareness, 78
  decisions, 80
  experience, 40
  marketing strategies, 199
  'sets', 79–80
  Sports Tourism Training, 179
  trip decision, 81–7
Digne, Tour de France, 286–7, 289
Directorate Generale for Enterprise (DGE), 141
Diversification:
  Malta strategy, 209–11
  Winter sports, 269–70
Diving, Wales, 248

DMUs *see* Decision Making Units
Docklands Sailing Centre, London, 227
Domestic sport, Malta, 216–17
Don Valley stadium, Sheffield, 224, 228, 230, 231–2
Duke of Edinburgh Award Scheme, 246

E

Economic benefits of Tour de France, 285–8
Economic impacts, 41–3
Economic and Social Research Council, 131
Edinburgh, Meadowbank stadium, 224
Elite athletes:
  Revised Sports Tourism Participation Model, 195
  sports training, 196
  trip decisions, 99–100
Elite sport focus, 156, 161, 185
Endurance cycling, 200
England:
  regional policy, 125–6
  Regional Tourist Boards (RTBs), 151
English Hockey Association, 180
English Institute of Sport, 195
English Leisure Visits Report (2005), 279
English Premier soccer league, 223–4
English Sport Council, 111, 157
Environment:
  Alps, 260
  countryside and water issues, 147, 149
  sports tourism, 66
Environmental impact:
  cycling, 281
  rural sites, 243–5
  Welsh coast/countryside, 252–4
Equestrian activities in France, 47
Escapism motives, 72, 75
Ethnographic study, 36
EU *see* European Union
Euro '96 Football Championships, 16, 231
Europa Cup athletics, 87
European cities, football, 224
European countries, Malta, 212
European Cup, athletics, 103
European Grand Tour, 5, 9
European ski market at turn of the Millennium, 269
European Sport Management Quarterly, 29, 31, 295
European Union (EU):
  Directorate Generale for Enterprise, 141
  recreational sport, 149
  tourism directorate, 141

Event Sports Tourism:
  cities, 223, 225
  description, 180–2
  features, 185–6
  Malta, 215
  models, 119–21
  place element, 147
  products, 68, 169–70
Events:
  attendances, 40
  impact assessment, 41
  small-scale, 44–5
  spectators, 169
  'tailgating', 45
Experience of sports tourism, 33–4, 38, 40, 55, 69

F

FA (Football Association) Cup, 7
Facility issues, 147
Farm tourism, 149
Fashion for out door pursuits, 242
First Choice, 190, 246
Fishing, 240
Focus groups and spectators, 173
Football:
  European cities, 224
  fans, 116
  fixtures, 90
  Glasgow, 224
  history, 7
  hooliganism, 40, 116, 140
  Malta, 214
  spectators, 59, 89–90, 93
  tours, 176
  women's, 93
  World Cup, 68, 81, 101, 180, 186, 215
Forests, 65
Formula One Motor Racing, 181, 227–8
France:
  Aquitane coast, 155
  cycling, 281
  equestrian activities, 47
  'language' for policy issues, 161
  Languedoc Roussillon region, 141, 155
  non-skiers, 97
  public sector involvement, 138–9
  rural communities, 19
  ski resorts, 259–60, 262, 264
  social tourism, 160

G

Geographical perspectives of sports tourism, 53
German tourists, 83–4
Germany:
  Bodensee Cycle, 279
  cycling, 279
  Volkssports concept, 17
Gibson, Heather, 28
GIR *see* government-industry relations
Glasgow:
  football, 224
  sports tourism, 227
Gleneagles Hotel, 183
Glyptis, Sue:
  categorization of products, 169
  'demand types', 108–9
  research study, 27–8, 50–1, 67, 293–5
GM Palace, Vancouver, 24
Go-karting, 197
Gold Coast and leverage, 40
Golf:
  country house experience, 98
  courses, 65
  La Manga, 196
  learning, 86
  Luxury Sports Tourism, 182–3
  Malta, 213–15, 216
  Sports Training Tourism, 179
  tourism, 34, 39, 96–7
  tourism in Scotland, 163
Good Practice in the Planning of Sport and Recreation…, (report), 244–5
Government policy:
  Malta, 217–19, 220
  sports policy community, 157
  tensions, 156
Government-industry relations (GIR):
  models, 132–3, 134–6
  policy community, 131
Grand Tour *see* European Grand Tour
Great Britain Sports Council, 50
Greece:
  Crete, 19
  sports tourism policy, 19, 24, 199
  Thrace region, 190
Grenoble, Alpine skiing, 267

H

Hallam FM Arena, 228, 230, 231–2, 234
'Halls of Fame', 171
Harvard Sports Management Group, 176

Hawaii, 95, 115
'Health spa' concept, 178
Heartland policy, 159–60
Heli-kayaking, 37
Henry Lunn travel agents, 9
'Heritage' concept, 39
Hierarchy of needs, Maslow, 74
Hiking, 10, 19, 169, 175, 177, 238, 239, 241, 244
Hill walking, 239, 248–9
Hillsborough stadium, Sheffield, 228
Hilton Head Island, South Carolina, 179
Hire of cycles, 201
History of sports tourism, 3
Holiday cycling, 276, 278
Holidays:
    activity, 169, 246
    beach, 111, 171, 195
    camps, 13, 82–3, 86
    cycling, 276
    'do nothing' concept, 242
    sports opportunities, 169
    sports tourism, 18, 68, 72, 75
    Thomson's, 165, 167, 170
    UK, 239
    'up-market' sports, 169
Holidays with Pay Act (1938), 12
'Home of Golf' campaign, 199
Hooliganism, football, 40, 116, 140
Horse racing:
    railways, 9
    Royal Ascot, 86, 187
    spectators, 84–6
    tours, 9
Horse riding in Wales, 247
Hostel organizations, 175, 177
Hunting, 58

I

Ice hockey, 201
Ideologies and sports policy community, 157
IGR see inter-governmental relations
Impacts:
    economic, 42–3
    Olympic Games, 42
    research in sports tourism, 294
    social, 44
    sport and tourism, 32
    sports tourism, 40–5
'Incidental' sports tourism, 169
Income generation/strategic direction tension, 151–2

Individuals and sports policy community, 157
Industrial age, 6–7
Informality in sport–tourism networks, 161
Information and promotion, 147
Integrated approach to sports tourism, 28, 145–64, 295
Intenders:
    cycling in Scotland, 279
    model, 116–17, 172
    provision strategies, 203–4
Inter-governmental relations (IGR), 131
Internal foci/external foci, tensions, 151, 154
International Bicycle Fund, 175
International Olympic Committee (IOC), 143
International Sports Tours, 176
IOC see International Olympic Committee
IVV see Der Internationale Volkssportverbrand

J

Jacob's Creek Tour Down Under (cycle race), 280
Jogging, 58
Journal of Sport & Tourism (JS&T), 31
Journal of Sport Management}, 31
Journal of Sport Tourism (JST), 31
Journal of Sustainable Tourism, 280
Journals for sports psychologists, 30
JS&T see *Journal of Sport & Tourism*
JST see *Journal of Sport Tourism*
Judo, 181
'Jumpers for goalposts', 66
Jungfrau mountain, 9

K

Kayaking, 177
Kent and Tour de France, 286–90
Key Arena, Seattle, 24
Key West, Women's Flag Football Tournament, 73
Knights, 4

L

La Manga Club, Spain, 179, 195, 196
Lancashire County Cricket Ground, 196
Land based activities in Wales, 248
Languedoc Roussillon region, France, 141, 155
Lanzarote:
    Club La Santa, 122, 179, 193, 195
    elite athletes, 197

Lawn Tennis Association, 180
LDA *see* London Development Agency
'Leadership development', 177
Learning sport, 86
Leverage:
    benefits, 36
    Canterbury and Tour de France, 49
    Gold Coast, 49
    sports tourism, 43–4, 49, 294
'Liminality' concept, 289
Liverpool docklands, 227
Local communities, 44
London:
    Cycling Festival, 290
    docklands, 227
    Lords cricket ground, 67, 101, 224
    marathon, 92, 200
    mayor, 289
    Olympic Games (1948), 231
    Olympic Games (2012), 158–9, 235,
        294
    Paralympic Games (2012), 158–9
    stadiums, 224
    Tour de France, 286–90
    Wetbike Club, 227
London Development Agency (LDA), 288–9
Lord's cricket ground (London), 67, 101, 224
Los Angeles Olympic Games (1984), 226
Lottery Sports Fund, 136, 142
Loughborough University, 179, 195
Luxury Sports Tourism:
    description, 182–4
    features, 185–6
    Malta, 215
    models, 119–21
    participation, 197–8
    products, 68, 169–70
    repeat visits, 193

M

Madison, James, 129
Major, John, 156–7
Major League Baseball, 103, 121, 181
Malta:
    active events sports tourist, 115
    British tour operators, 209
    conference market, 210
    cycling, 207–8
    diversification strategy, 209–21
    domestic sport, 216–17
    European countries, 212
    Event Sports Tourism, 215
    football, 214

Football Association Technical Complex,
        214
    football World Cup, 215
    golf, 213–15, 216
    government role, 217–19, 220
    Hotel Bay Point, 213
    Luxury Sports Tourism, 215
    marathon, 215
    Marsa golf course, 216
    Marsa Sports and Country Club, 213, 217
    Mediterranean climate, 212
    Mellieha Bay Hotel, 212
    Ministry of Tourism, 218
    National Recreation Centre, 214
    National Tourist Organization, 210–11,
        215
    planning authority, 214
    resource constraints, 216–17
    Scandinavian visitors, 213–14
    small size, 162–3, 220
    spontaneous behaviour, 201
    Sports Participation Tourism, 215
    sports tourism at turn of the millenium,
        212–15
    sports tourism combination, 202
    Sports Tourism Product Types, 209, 212
    Sports Training Tourism, 213–14
    swimming, 214–15
    Tal-Qroqq swimming pool, 214–15, 217
    Ta' quali Action Plan, 214–15, 219
    tourism product, 209–11
    Maltese Times}, 217
Management of sports tourism, 45–9
Manchester:
    Commonwealth Games (2002), 18, 22,
        147, 227
    Olympic Games bid (2000), 227
    provisions, 190
    velodrome, 22
Manchester City football club, 147
Manchester United Old Trafford stadium,
        175, 196
Mandela, Nelson, 23
Marathons:
    Chicago, 186, 200
    city, 181
    London, 92, 200
    Malta, 202, 215
    New York, 193
Marsa golf course, Malta, 216
Marsa Sports and Country Club, Malta, 213,
        217
Marylebone Cricket Club (MCC), 7–8

Maslow, hierarchy of needs, 74
Masters Open Swimming, Malta, 202–3
Mayor of London, 289
MCC *see* Marylebone Cricket Club
Meadowbank stadium, Edinburgh, 224
Mediterranean climate of Malta, 212
Mega events:
    cities, 224–5
    Tour de France, 289
Melbourne:
    Corporate Outdoor Training, 177
    cricket ground, 201
'Melbourne Now' campaign, 199
Mellieha Bay Hotel, Malta, 212
Meta-review, sports tourism, 36, 49–54, 294
Millenium Commission Lottery Fund, 281–2
Millenium stadium, Cardiff, 224
Ministry of Tourism for Malta, 218
MINOS *see* Mountain International Opinion
    Survey
Mintel Reports:
    Snowsports, 265, 268
    Sports Participation (2005), 238, 241, 249
Models:
    adventure, health and tourism, 108–9
    Cross-Sectoral Policy Development, 129,
      145, 150, 157
    government-industry relations, 132–3,
      134–6
    'Intender', 116–17
    participation, 107–23
    policy community, 131–6
    spectators, 115–16
    sports tourism, 108–10, 109–10, 110–17,
      166
    Sports Tourism Product Types, 189–90,
      205, 297
'Moderators' and economic impact, 42
Monaco Grand Prix, 183
Montreal Olympic Games, 225
Motives:
    affiliation, 72
    'collect places', 115
    culture, 73
    destinations, 80
    escapism, 72, 75
    holidays, 72
    Olympic Games, 73
    sport tourism, 68–9
    sports tourism, 70–6
    winning, 73
Motorized land sports in Wales, 248
Mountain biking in rural areas, 238, 248–9

Mountain International Opinion Survey,
    266–7
Mountain Training Trust, 251
Mountaineering:
    adventure tourists, 38
    guides, 37, 39
    Switzerland, 9–10
'Multiple motivational position' concept, 84

N

National Baseball Hall of Fame, 174–5
National Cycle Network (NCN), 24, 281–4
National Hockey League, 171
National Lottery Sports Fund, UK, 179
National Mountain Centre, Wales, 192, 198
National Olympic Committee, 46
National Parks, 65, 247, 251
National Recreation Centre in Malta, 214
National Tourism Organization (NTO), 46,
    210
'National Unity', policy, 140
National Water Sports Centre, Holme Pier-
    repoint, 179
National White Water Centre, 251
NCAA Women's Basketball Tournament, 43
NCN *see* National Cycle Network
Netherlands and cycling, 281
New York:
    marathon, 92, 193
    Yankees baseball, 67, 80, 101, 186, 201
New York state, Adirondack North Country
    Region, 149
New Zealand:
    cycling, 279
    Regional Tourism Organizations, 151
    rugby union, 48
    Wellington, 199
'Nineteenth hole' concept, 96–8
Non-skiers, 48, 97–8
'Normal science' concept, 296
North America:
    rural communities, 19
    skiing, 267–8, 269
    sport definition, 58–9
    urban economic regeneration, 227
North Sea Cycle Route (NSCR), 283–4
North Shore, Hawaii, 95
Northern Europe, 20
Nostalgia and sports tourism, 39
'Not for profit' sector, 170–1
Nottingham Forest Football Club, 195
'Novelty' concept, 97
NSCR *see* North Sea Cycle Route

O

Old Carthusians' football team, 7
Old Trafford stadium, Manchester, 196
Olympia pan-Hellenic games, 3
Olympic Games:
  776BC, 27
  Athens (1896), 25
  Athens (2004), 73, 235, 286
  Atlanta (1996), 147, 225
  Austria (Winter), 260
  Barcelona (1992), 16, 21, 23, 101, 226
  Beijing (2008), 23, 227
  Event Sports Tourism, 180, 185
  hosting, 43, 163
  impact analysis, 42
  leverage, 43–4
  London (1948), 231
  London (2012), 158–9, 235, 294
  Los Angeles (1984), 21, 226
  Manchester bid, 227
  Montreal (1976), 225
  Moscow (1980), 181
  motivation, 73
  multisport events, 186
  Olympia pan-Hellenic, 3
  provisions, 190
  Seoul (1998), 226
  spectacle, 226
  sports tourism activities, 68
  Sydney (2000), 73, 139, 159, 226
  television, 15
  tourism, 159, 163
  tourism model, 41–2, 43
  trip motivation, 89
Opportunity planning, 104–5
Organization/individual and tension, 151,
    153–4
Organizational culture/structure and sports
    policy community, 157
Orienteering, 19, 66, 244
Outdoor pursuits:
  activity, people and place interaction,
    98
  adventure tourism, 52
  arousal levels, 74
  countryside recreation, 244
  cycling, 239
  fashion, 242
  hiking/rambling, 239
  new types, 238
  rural sports participation, 245–6
  sports tourism, 36–7

Outward Bound Trust, 246
Owlerton stadium, Sheffield, 228

P

PADI dive centre, 213
Pan-American Games, 89
Paragliding, 36, 238
Paralympic Games, London (2012), 158–9
Parks, 64–6
Participation:
  model, 107–23
  passive, 39
  profiles, 196–9
  sports tourism, 32–3, 35, 39, 80, 91–2
  trips decision-making, 117–19
Passive participation, 39
Pawleys Plantation Country Club, 193
Pembrokeshire coast national park, 247
Periphery policy, 159–60
PGL Activity Holidays, 177
Physical appearance, 71
'Place collecting' see collect places
Places for sports tourism, 64–7
Plans (general intentions), 103–4
Plas-Y-Brenin Activity Centre, Wales, 251
Pluralism in sports tourism, 130
Policy:
  communities, 136–43
  community, 134
  community concept origins, 129–31
  context, 127–9
  heartland, 159–60
  insulation from other policy areas, 140
  integration, 146–50
  'National Unity', 140
  networks, 131–2, 134
  periphery, 159–60
  sports tourism development, 47–8
  summary, 125–6
  universe, 133
Policy Area Matrix, 108, 126, 146–7, 150
'Policy network', term, 131
Policy and Planning, 147
Policy Wheel for Sport and Tourism:
  agency collaboration, 297
  cities, 224
  hallmark events, 226–7
  policy matrix, 126, 145–6, 190
  Sheffield, 228, 235
Ponds Forge International Sports Centre,
    Sheffield, 22–3, 147, 228, 230, 231
Portland, Oregon, Rose Garden, 24
Portugal, 36

Post-decision trip planning, 102–6
Potholing *see* caving/potholing
Pre-purchase of tickets, 103
Premiership football, UK, 103, 121
Private business in sports–tourism, 15–16
Products:
　categorization, 168–9
　Event Sports Tourism, 180–2
　Luxury Sports Tourism, 182–4
　Sports Participation Tourism, 174–8
　Sports Training Tourism, 178–80
　Supplementary Sports Tourism, 170–4
Progress in sports tourism, 293–7
Project based/ongoing liaison tensions, 151, 154–5
Providers for sports tourism, 165–6
Provision strategies:
　competitive advantage, 202–3
　converting intenders, 191–4
　cooperative marketing, 199–200
　intenders, 203–4
　participation profiles, 196–9
　repeat visits, 194–6
　spontaneous behaviours, 200–2
　summary, 189–90
Psychographics, 78
Psychologists, sports, 30
Psychology of Sport and Exercise, 30

Q

Quebec sports policy, 140

R

'Race-goers', 85–6
Railways, 6, 9–10
Rambling, 58, 239, 241, 244
Real tennis, 5
Recreation, 64–5
Recreational Planning Agency in South Africa, 149
Regional context:
　federal systems of government, 139
　sport and tourism, 146
　and sports policy community, 156–7
Regional Tourism Organizations in New Zealand, 151
Regional Tourist Boards (RTBs):
　England, 151
　UK, 140
Repeat visits, 194–6
Research:
　Agencies/communities in UK, 144
　behaviours studies, 32–40

'critical analysis', 51
　development, 49
　impacts, 42
　management, 46
　meta-review of perspectives, 49–54
　outdoor adventure tourism, 52
　questions, 298
　review, 70
　satisfaction, 35
　social science, 49–50
　Sue Glyptis study, 27–8, 50–1, 67, 293–5
Resource constraints in Malta, 216–17
Resources and Funding, 147, 149
Revised Sports Tourism Participation Model:
　Alpine skiing, 258
　continuum of sports tourism, 112
　cycling, 273, 277–8, 290
　elite athletics, 195
　'Intenders', 172
　participants, 249
　participation profiles, 196
　practical use, 122–3
　products, 119–22
　providers, 168
　provisions, 187, 189–90, 205
　research framework, 49
　rural areas, 242, 255
　skiers classification, 268
　skiing, 49, 265, 269, 271
　sports tourism behaviours, 297
　trip decisions, 56, 107–8, 117–19
Riding in Wales, 251
'Ritual inversion' concept, 75
Rock climbing, 169
Role theory in sports tourism, 40
Romans, 4
Rose Garden, Portland, Oregon, 24
Royal Ascot (horse racing), 86, 187
Royal Malta Golf Club, 201, 213
Royal Yachting Association (RYA), 178
RTBs *see* Regional Tourist Boards
Rugby union:
　New Zealand, 48
　tours, 176
Rugby World Cup, South Africa (1995), 23
Runners World, 193
Rural sports participation:
　activity, people and place interaction, 254–5
　characteristics, 242–3
　environmental impacts, 243–5
　market, 239–43
　organization and facilities, 245–7

socioeconomic profile, 239–43
tourism, 207
trip demographics, 241
trips, 240
Wales, 247–50, 250–5
RYA *see* Royal Yachting Association

S

Sailing, 175–6, 178, 182, 238
St. Andrews, 183
San Diego, California, 179
Satisfaction research, 35
Scandinavian visitors to Malta, 213–14
School holidays, 47
Scotland:
    cycling trips, 279
    golf tourism, 163, 183
    upland areas, 243
Scottish Tourist Board, 60, 199
Scuba diving, 171
Seattle, Key Arena, 24
Seoul Olympic Games, 226
'Sets' and destinations, 79–80
Sheffield:
    City Liaison Group, 23
    'City of Sport' concept, 229–30, 234
    'City of Steel' concept, 230
    cycling, 207–8
    Destination Sheffield promotion, 231–2
    Don Valley stadium, 224, 228, 230, 231–2
    Economic Regeneration Committee, 229
    Euro' 96 football, 231
    Hallam FM Arena, 228, 230
    Policy Wheel for Sport and Tourism, 228
    political context, 229–31
    Ponds Forge International Sports Centre, 22–3
    Ponds Forge International Sports Centre, 228, 230, 231
    Ponds Forge swimming pool, 147
    provisions, 190
    SheffeildScene2 website, 234
    Ski Village, 234
    sport and tourism policy, 163
    Sports Council, 234
    sports tourism, 227, 228–35
    stadiums, 228
    The Way Ahead, 233
    urban sports tourism, 223–38, 228–35, 235–6
    Welcome to Sheffield website, 233–4, 234
    World Snooker Championships, Sheffield, 232

World Student Games (1991), 22–3, 147, 181, 230–1, 235
Sheffield Arena *see* Hallam FM Arena
Sheffield Football Club, 7
SheffieldScene2 website, 234
Shooting, 58
Show jumping, 234
'Simplified Sports Tourism Participation Model', 112–13
Singapore and sports tourism, 227–8
Ski Beech, North Carolina, 268
Ski Industry Report (2008), 269
Skiing:
    Canada, 48
    cross promotion, 200
    demographics, 265–6, 271
    industry, 48
    learning, 86
    Luxury Sports Tourism, 182
    North America, 267–8, 269
    recreation conflict, 35
    rural sports participation, 240, 241
    socio-economic groups, 266–71
    spectators, 223
    sports tourism, 270–1
    Switzerland, 10, 97–8
    tourism, 25, 66, 96–7, 121
    USA, 267
    winter, 207
    see also Alpine skiing
Small-scale events, 44–5
Snow Business, 1
Snow cover for skiing, 258
Snowboarding, 35, 94, 238, 241, 270
Snowdonia national park, 247, 249, 251, 254, 255
Snowsports report (Mintel), 265
Social impacts, 44
Social tourism:
    France, 138, 160
    public provision, 168
    UK, 160
Socio-psychological rationales, 70–1
Solitary nature of climbing, 96
South Africa:
    Recreational Planning Agency, 149
    Rugby World Cup (1995), 23
    sports tourism, 23
South African Tourism Agency, 149
South Australian Tourism Commission Cycle Tourism Strategy, 275, 277
South Carolina, Hilton Head Island, 179
Southwater Watersports, UK, 178–9

Spain, La Manga Club, 106, 179, 195
Spectators:
  athletics, 87–9
  behaviour, 40
  cricket, 59, 93
  deviant behaviour, 87
  events, 169
  focus groups, 173
  football, 89–90, 93
  horse racing, 84–6
  interaction, 68
  models, 115–16
  New York Yankees Baseball Game, 186
  skiing, 223
  television, 192
  Tour de France, 279–80
Spontaneous trip behaviour, 105–6, 200–2
Sport:
  comparison with ' sports', 63
  concept, 72
  definition, 57–9
  features, 61
  social institution, 63
Sport & Tourism: A Reader, 295
Sport Canada, 137
Sport England:
  Department of Culture, Media and Sport, 142
  government agencies, 136
  regional agencies, 128
  Sustrans, 284
  World Cup (2006) bid, 226
'Sport lover' concept, 34
Sport policy communities excluding tourism, 143
Sport, Raising the Game report, 157
Sport in Society, 30–1, 295
Sport and tourism:
  agencies liaison, 150
  policy development, 162–3
  regional policies, 140
  Venn diagram, 134–5
Sport Tourism Concepts and Theories, 295
'Sport tourism' term, 63, 68–9
' Sport tourism'/ 'tourism sport' framework, 68
Sports:
  comparison with 'sport', 63
  psychologists journals, 30
Sports Council:
  A Countryside for Sport, 237, 244
  Good Practice in the Planning of Sport and Recreation..., 244–5

Sheffield, 234
  Sustrans, 284
Sports Councils in UK, 153
'Sports Development Continuum', 111
'Sports fantasy camps', 174
Sports Holidays, 147
Sports Participation Tourism:
  converting intenders, 191–2
  description, 174–8
  features, 185–6
  Malta, 215
  model, 119–21
  participation profiles, 197–8
  products, 68, 170
Sports policy community, 157–8
Sports psychologists, 30
Sports science support in UK, 195
Sports tourism:
  diversification strategy, 207
  leverage, 294
  term, 62–3
  types, 166
Sports Tourism Demand Continuum, 111–12
Sports Tourism International Council (STIC), 30–1
Sports Tourism Participation Model, 117–19, 199
  see also Revised Sports Tourism Participation Model
Sports Tourism Product Types:
  classification, 147
  Malta, 209, 212
  Model, 189–90, 205, 297
'Sports tourists', 61, 69, 70–6
Sports training for elite athletes, 196
Sports Training Tourism:
  description, 178–80
  destinations, 179
  features, 185–6
  Malta, 213–14
  models, 119–21
  products, 68, 169–70
Sportsman Travel Malta, 215
Sport– tourism link, 46–7
Sport– tourism policy:
  higher authority, 161–2
  informality, 161
  networks, 158–62
  tensions, 150–8
  worldwide, 163–4
'Stadium Tours', 171

STIC *see* Sports Tourism International
    Council
Sub-aqua diving, 244
Sub-governments, 130
Subculture concept, 91–3, 93–6, 98
Supplementary Sports Tourism:
    description, 170–4
    features, 184–6
    instruction, 185
    Malta, 212
    models, 119–21
    'not for profit' sector, 170–1
    product type, 297
    products, 68
    spontaneous trips, 105–6
Supply side of sports tourism, 165–6
Surfing, 94, 115, 251
Surrey Cricket Club, 8
Surrey Docks Water Sports Centre, London,
    227
Sustrans (cycling), 276 0
Swimming, 58, 65, 171, 197, 214
Switzerland:
    Alpine Club, 10
    climbing, 9–10
    hiking, 10
    mountaineering, 9–10
    non-skiers, 97–8
    skiing, 97–8, 257
Sydney (2000), Olympic Games, 73, 139,
    159, 226
Synergy in sports tourism, 62, 69

T
'Tailgating' of events, 45
Tal-Qroqq swimming pool, Malta, 214–15,
    217
Ta' quali Action Plan, 214–15, 219
'Team development/building', 177
Television, 15, 116, 192, 285
Tensions:
    government policy, 156
    income generation/strategic direction,
        151–2
    organization/individual, 151, 153–4
    package tour/adventure, 37
    project based/ongoing liaison, 151, 154–5
    sport-tourism policy, 150–8
    top-down/bottom up development, 151–2
'Territory' concept, 129–31
Thailand, 19
Thames and Chiltern Regional Tourist
    Board, 154

The Ashes, 101, 186
The International Federation of Popular
    Sports, 17
'The Racing Tribe', 85–6
The Structure of Scientific Revolution, 296
The Way Ahead, 233
Thomas Cook travel agents, 9
Thomson' s holidays, 165, 167, 170, 190
Thrace region, Greece, 19
Tickets pre-purchase, 103
Time for action - adventure tourism strategy,
    255
'Top Ski Austria' marketing alliance, 200
Tour of Britain (cycling), 273, 284
Tour de France:
    adjacent countries, 284
    Canterbury, 49, 290
    caravanne (publicity), 285
    Digne, 286–7, 289
    economic benefits, 285–8
    elite cyclists, 275
    Kent, 286–90
    Le Grande Depart, 287
    London, 286–90
    mega events, 289
    peloton, 285
    size, 285
    spectators, 279–80
    sports tourism, 273–4, 284–90
    television, 285
Tourism:
    communities excluding sport, 143
    definition, 59–61
    destinations and ' sets', 79
    European Union, 141
    European Union (EU), 141
    features, 61
    Olympic Games, 159
    sport agencies liaison, 150
    UK, 139
'Tourism sport' term, 62, 69
'Tourism tourists', 61
'Touristification', 38
Trade exhibitions, 200
'Travel', 60
Travel Industry Association of America, 138,
    160–1
Travel International Sports, 176
Trekking *see* walking
'Trialectic concept', 110
Triathlete, 193
Triathlons, 200
Trinidad, 163

Trip decisions:
  destination pre-determined/trip chosen,
    87–93
  process, 79–80, 117–19, 297
  trip pre-determined/destination chosen,
    93–8
  trip/destination chosen, 81–7
  trip/destination pre-determined, 98–102
Trip motivation:
  Commonwealth Games, 89
  Olympic Games, 89
  Pan-American Games, 89
Trips:
  behaviours, 55–6, 78–81, 81–103, 297
  importance, 112
  opportunities, 111
  planning, 102–6
  rural sports participation, 240
  'trip purpose', 34, 56
Turn of the Millenium:
  European ski market, 269
  sports tourism, 16–25
Turnberry Hotel, 183
Twentieth century and sports tourism, 11–16
Twickenham (rugby), 224
Twr-Y-Felin Activity Centre, Wales, 95, 102,
    177, 194, 249–50, 252

U

UK:
  Athletics, 192
  cycling, 281
  Cycling Touring Club, 175
  holidays, 239
  hospitality market, 193
  National Cycle Network, 281–2
  National Lottery Sports Fund, 179
  Premiership football, 103, 121
  regional focus, 139
  Regional Tourist Boards, 140
  research, 144
  Royal Yachting Association, 178
  ski market, 261–2
  social tourism, 160
  Sport, 128, 136, 158
  Sports Councils, 153
  sports science support, 195
  Thames and Chiltern Regional Tourist
    Board, 154
  tourism, 139
Ultimate Outdoor Adventures in British
    Columbia, 177
'Unique Selling Position', 171

'Unit of analysis' for sports tourism, 68
United States Olympic Committee (USOC),
    137, 139, 143
United States Travel and Tourism Association
    (USTTA), 137, 139
'Up-market' sports holidays, 169
Urban regeneration in cities, 223–4
Urban sports tourism in Sheffield, 207,
    223–38, 228–35, 235–6
USA:
  Adirondack North Country Region, 149
  American football trip, 172
  Baseball trip, 172–3
  Camp America, 177
  'city marketing', 140
  college fixtures, 45
  Cross-Sectoral Policy Development, 145
  government control, 137
  Major League Baseball, 103, 121, 181
  National Baseball Hall of Fame, 174–5
  professional sports teams, 42
  regional focus, 139
  skiing, 267
  snowboarding, 270
  Travel Industry Association of America,
    160–1
  see also United States
USOC see United States Olympic
    Committee
USTTA see United States Travel and
    Tourism Association

V

Vancouver, GM Palace, 24
Velodrome in Manchester, 22
Venn diagram for sport and tourism, 134–5
VFR see 'Visiting Friends and Relatives'
Vicarious participation, 39, 67–8, 108, 118,
    174, 184
Victoria Tourist Commission, 199
Visit Britain, 128, 136, 158
'Visiting Friends and Relatives' (VFR), 173
'Volcano Triathlon Training Camp', 193
Volkssports concept, 17
Voluntary sector, 168

W

Wales:
  Adventure tourism, 248–9
  Black Mountain Activities, 252
  caving and potholing, 248
  climbing, 248
  cycling, 207, 248

distance to rural locations, 253–4
diving, 248
equestrian centres, 251
hill walking, 248
horse riding, 247
land based activities, 248
motorized land sports, 248
mountain biking, 248
National Mountain Centre, 192
National Parks, 247, 251–5
National White Water Centre, 251
Plas-Y-Brenin Activity Centre, 251
rural sports participation, 247–50, 250–5
surfing, 251
Twr-Y-Felin Activity Centre, 95, 102, 177, 194, 249–50, 252
walking, 247
water sports (non motorized), 248
White Water Centre, Twywryn, 251
Youth Hostel Association, 252
Wales Tourist Board (WTB), 140, 247–8, 251–2, 254, 255
Walking, 169, 240, 247
see also hill walking
'Warm weather training', 115
Water skiing, 111, 171, 197
Water sports:
Wales, (non-motorized), 248
wildlife impact, 244
Weather, 47
Weight control, 71
Welcome to Sheffield website, 233–4
Wellington, New Zealand, 199
Welsh coast environmental impact, 252–4

Welsh countryside environmental impact, 252–4
Wembley stadium, 224
White Water Centre, Twywryn, Wales, 251
White-water kayaking, 37–8
Wilderness areas, 65
Wildlife, 244
Wimbledon (tennis), 224
Wimbledon Tennis Museum, 174
Windsurfing, 94, 238
Winter Olympic Games, Calgary, 226
Winter skiing:
case study, 207, 257–71
see also Alpine skiing; skiing
Winter sports diversification, 269–70
Women's, football, 93
World Cup:
athletics, 87, 103
football, 68, 81, 101, 180, 186, 226
television, 15
World Cycling Championships (2003), 280
World Snooker Championships, Sheffield, 232, 234
World Student Games, Sheffield (1991), 22–3, 181, 230–1, 235
World Tourism Organisation, 19
WTB *see* Wales Tourist Board

Y

Yankee baseball, New York, 67, 101, 201
YHA *see* Youth Hostel Association
YMCA, 175
Youth Hostel Association (YHA), 246, 252
Youth Hostels in Britain, 13

Lightning Source UK Ltd.
Milton Keynes UK
UKOW07f1804190116

266701UK00004B/220/P